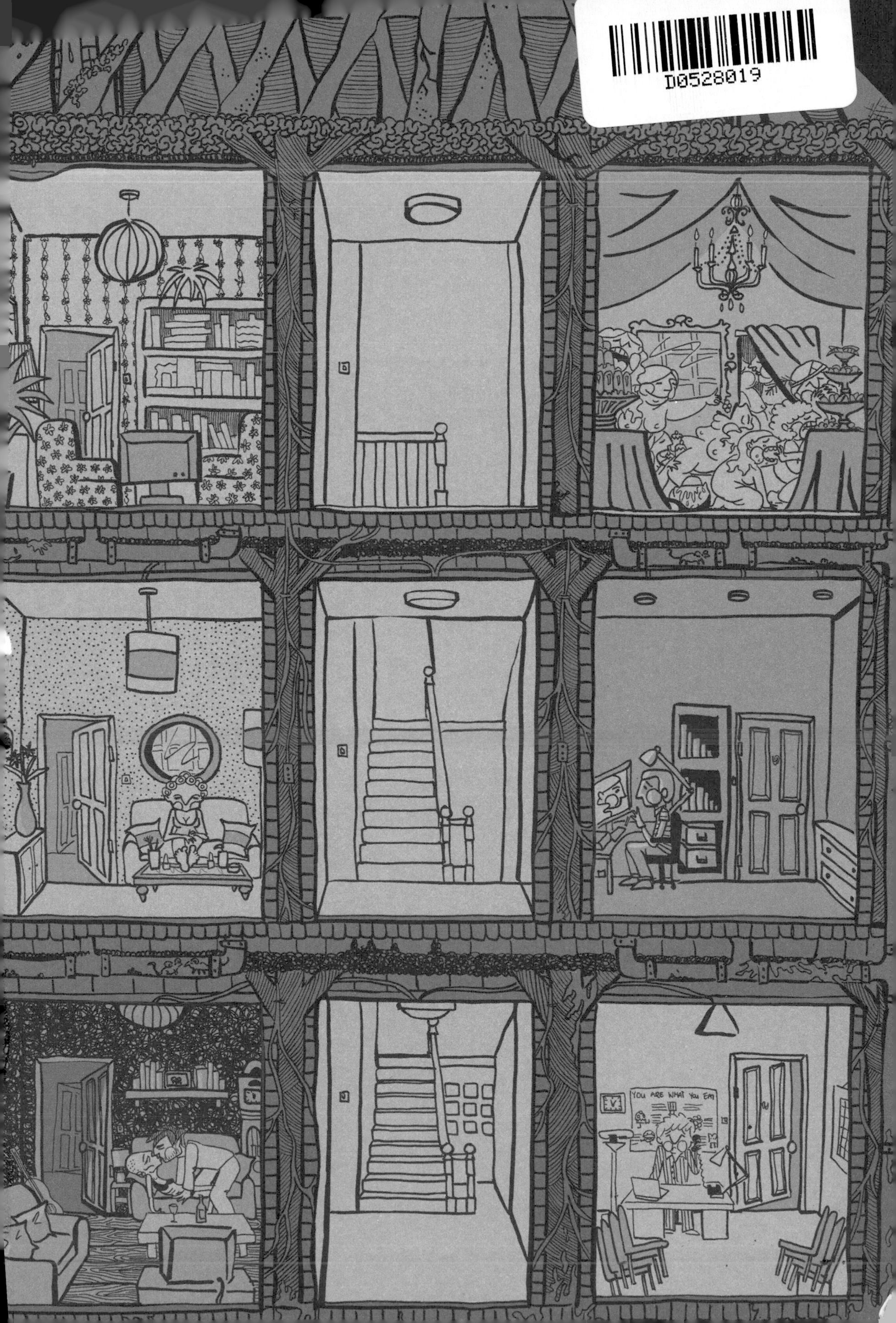
YOU ARE WHAT YOU EAT

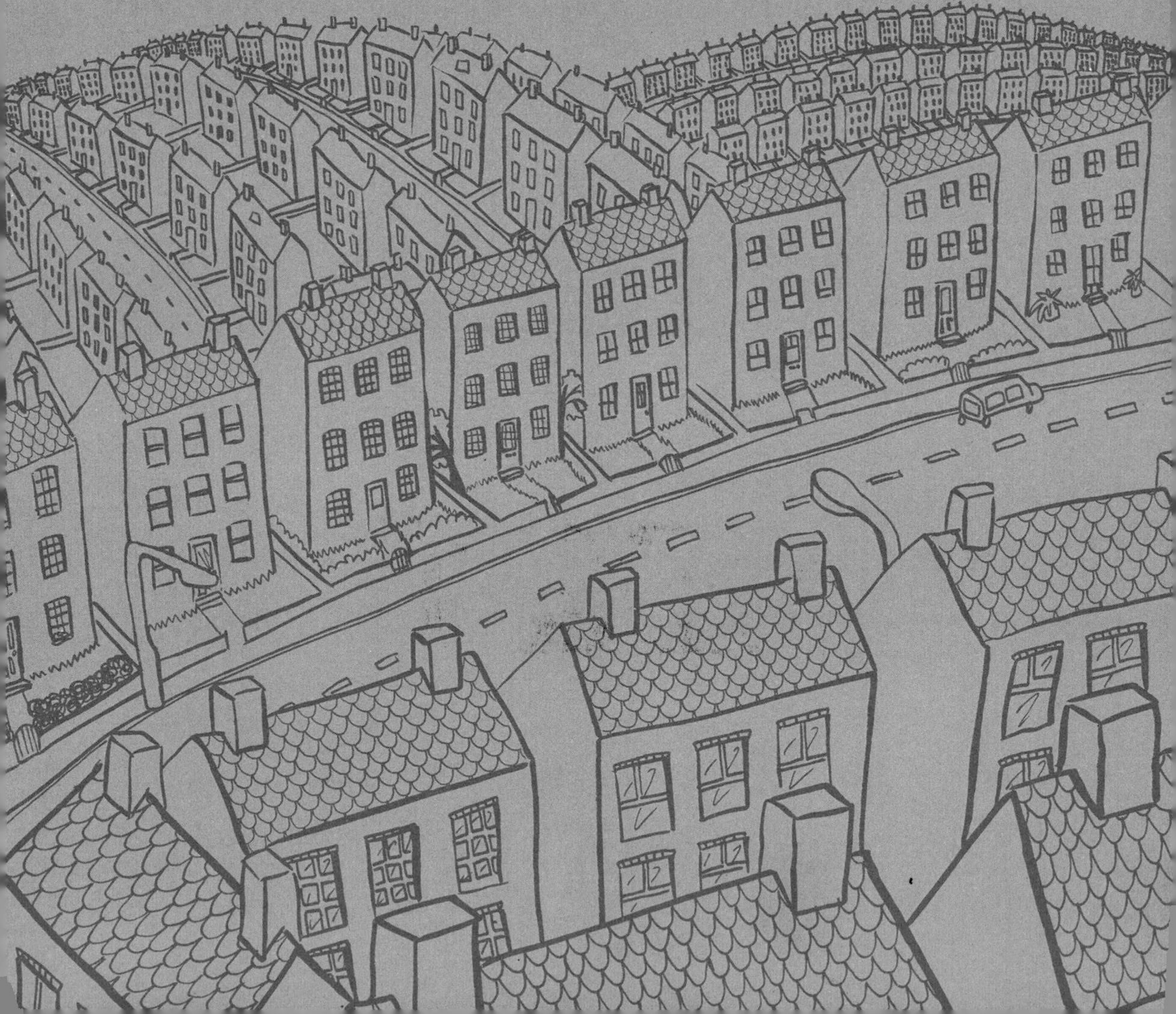

THE HOUSE THAT GROANED

BY KARRIE FRANSMAN

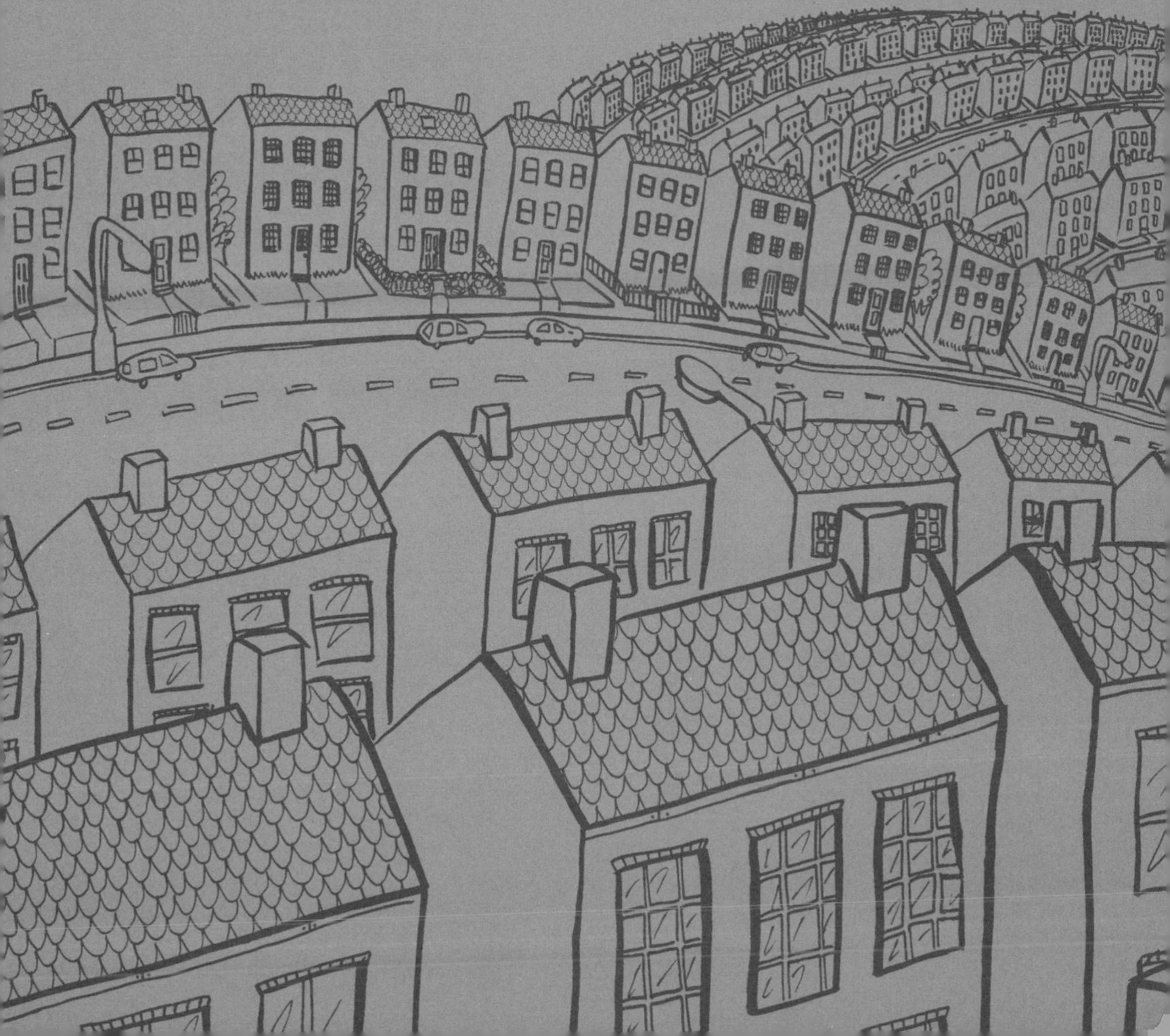

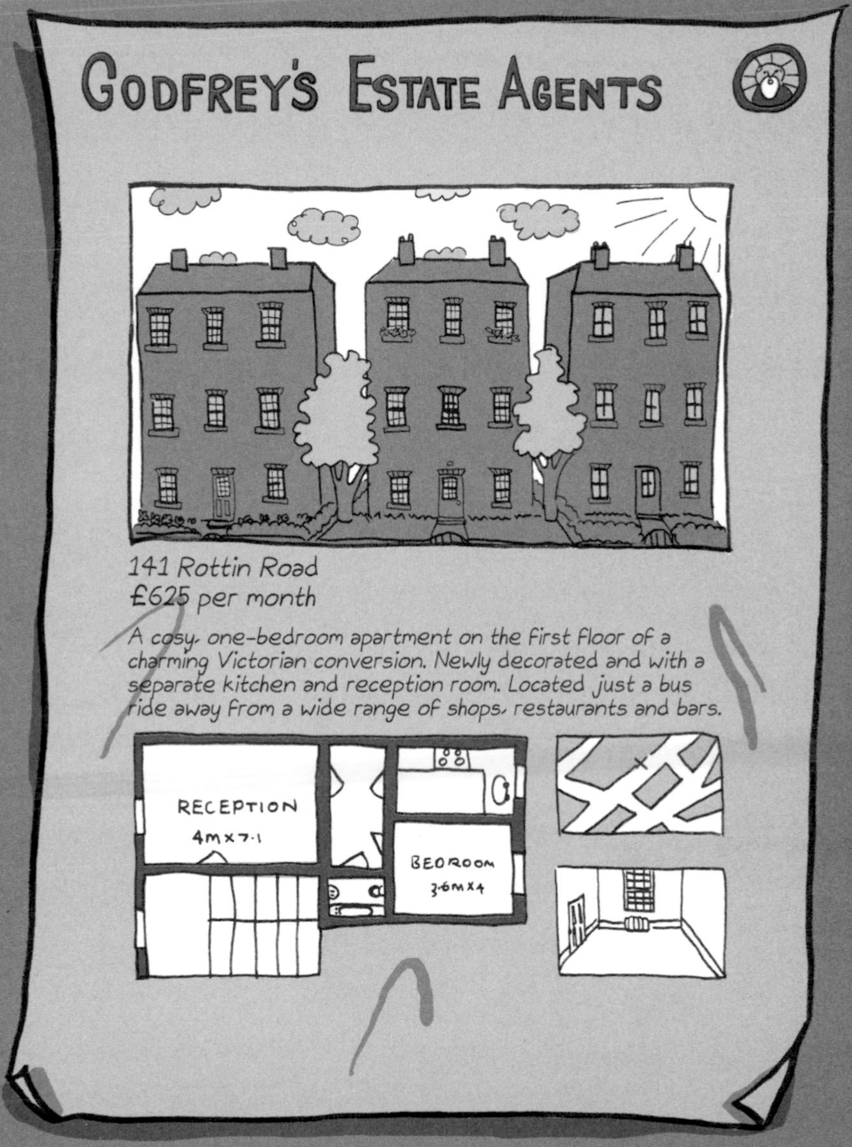
GODFREY'S ESTATE AGENTS
141 Rottin Road
£625 per month
A cosy, one-bedroom apartment on the first floor of a charming Victorian conversion. Newly decorated and with a separate kitchen and reception room. Located just a bus ride away from a wide range of shops, restaurants and bars.
RECEPTION
4M X 7·1
BEDROOM
3·6M X 4

Chapter One

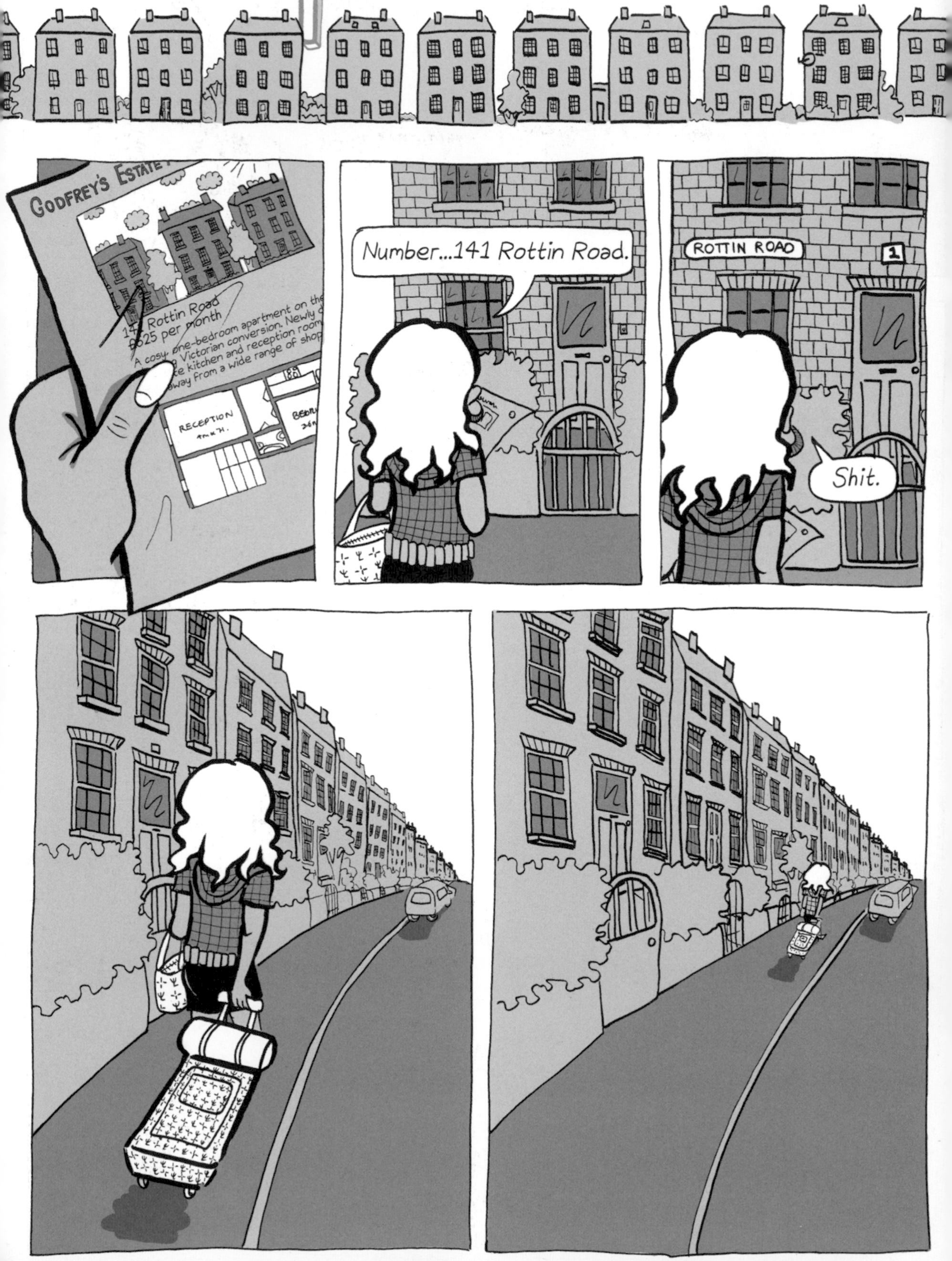
GODFREY'S ESTATE
Rottin Road
per month
RECEPTION
Number...141 Rottin Road.
ROTTIN ROAD
1
Shit.

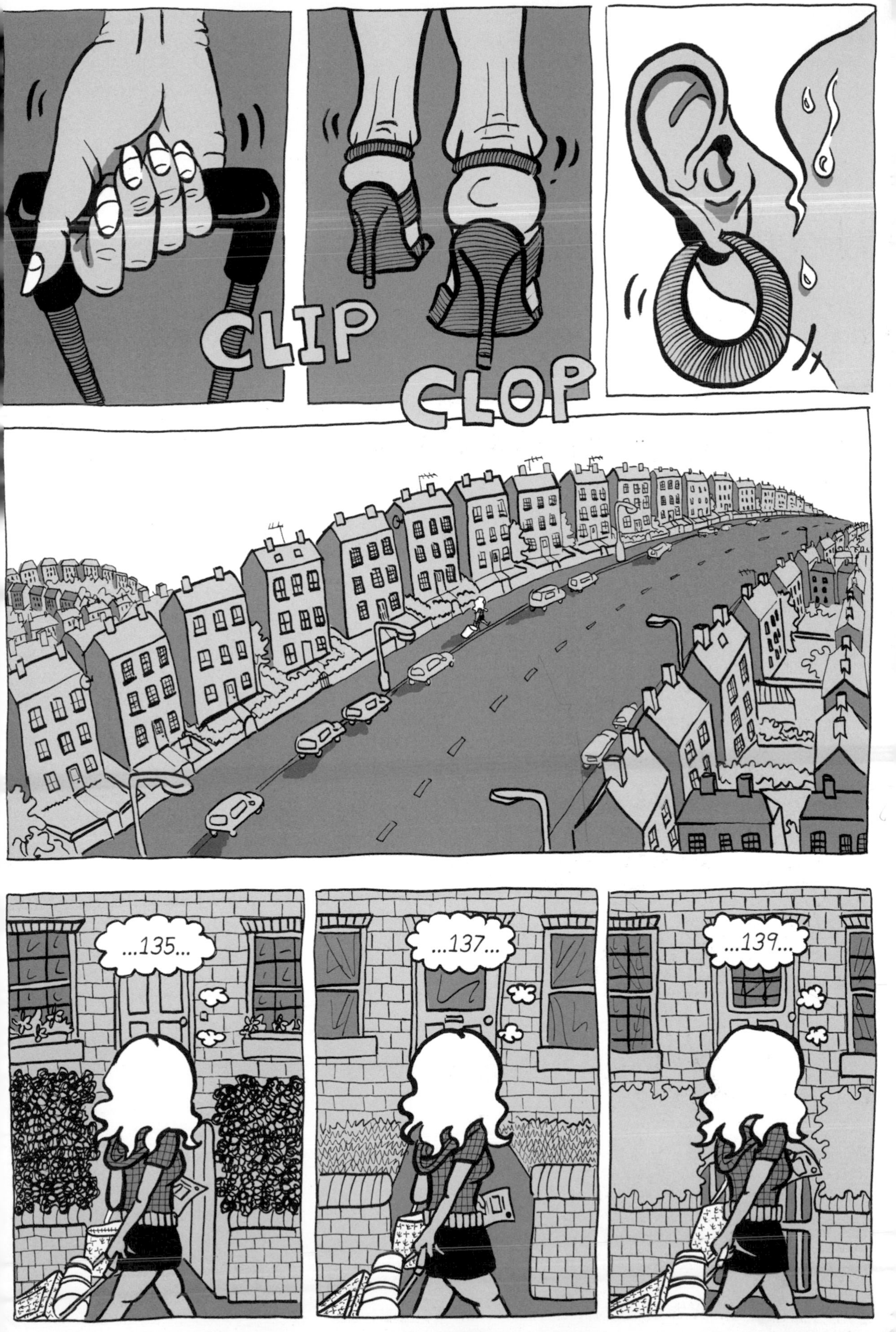
CLIP
CLOP
...135...
...137...
...139...

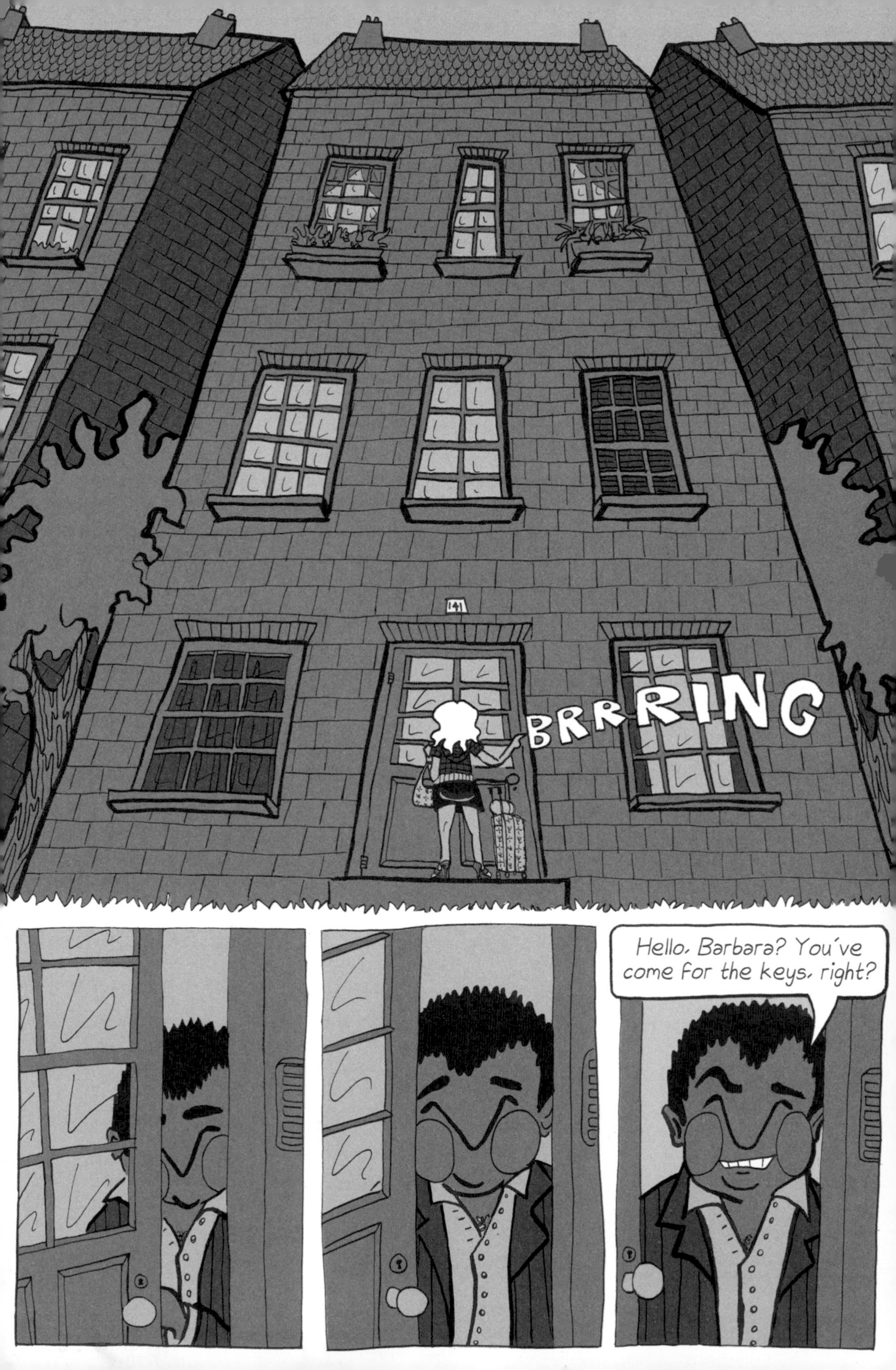

141
BRRRING
Hello, Barbara? You've come for the keys, right?

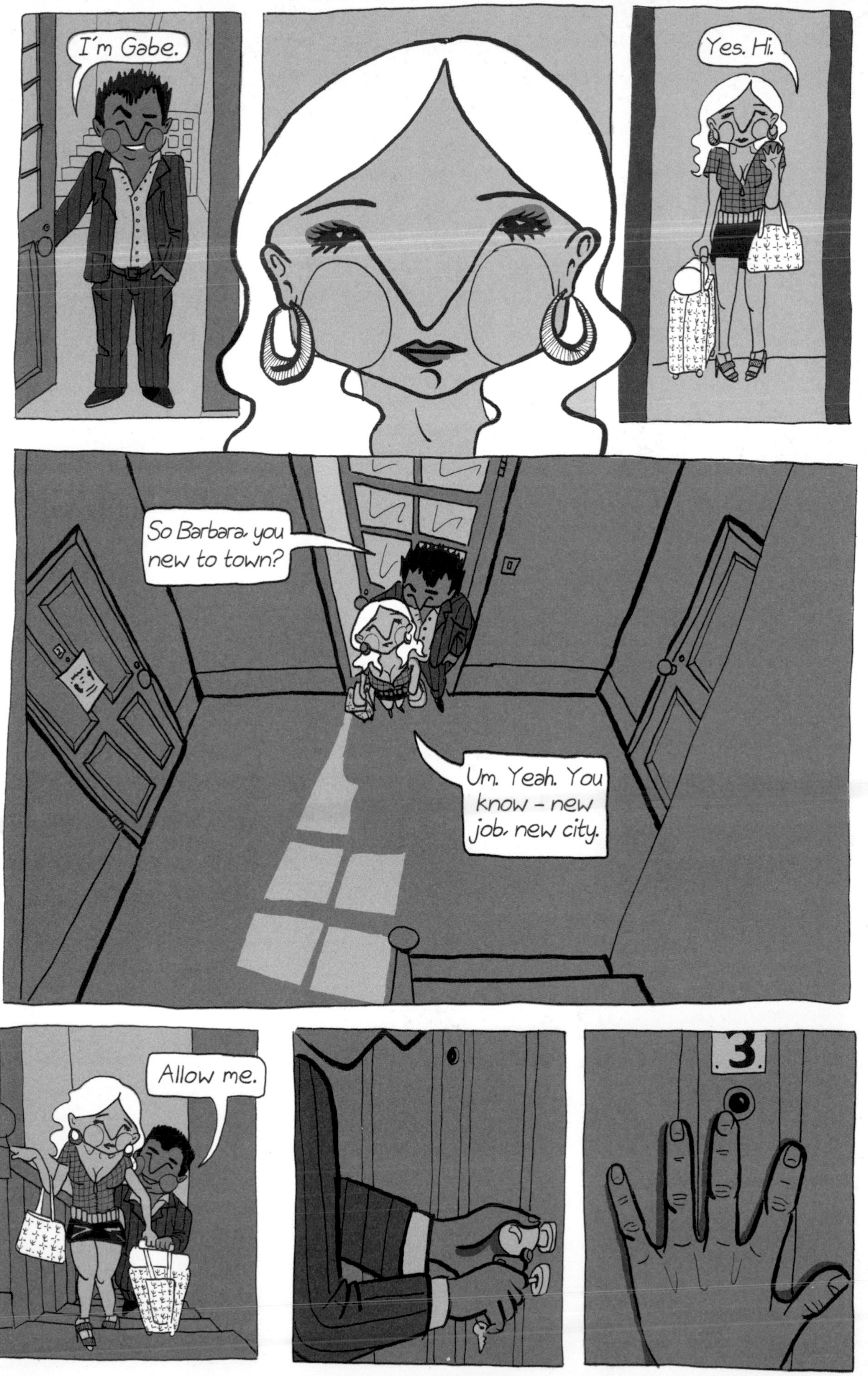
I´m Gabe.
Yes. Hi.
So Barbara, you new to town?
Um. Yeah. You know – new job, new city.
Allow me.
3

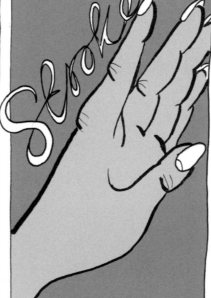

These are good, thick walls which means good insulation. It's a sturdy house this.

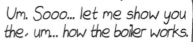

Knock Knock

CREEEK

CLUNK

CRASH

Um. Sooo... let me show you the, um... how the boiler works.

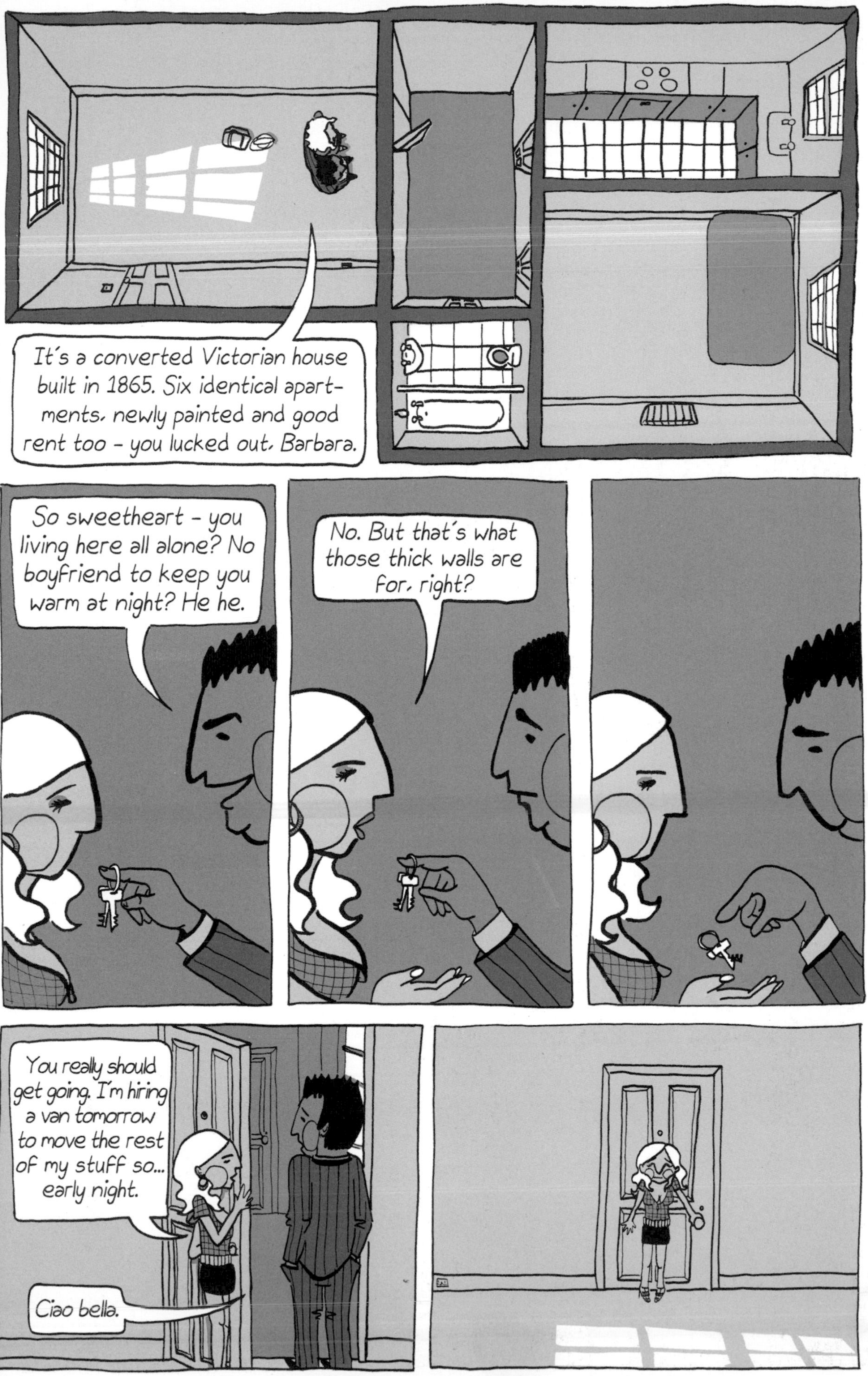
It's a converted Victorian house built in 1865. Six identical apartments, newly painted and good rent too - you lucked out, Barbara.
So sweetheart - you living here all alone? No boyfriend to keep you warm at night? He he.
No. But that's what those thick walls are for, right?
You really should get going. I'm hiring a van tomorrow to move the rest of my stuff so... early night.
Ciao bella.

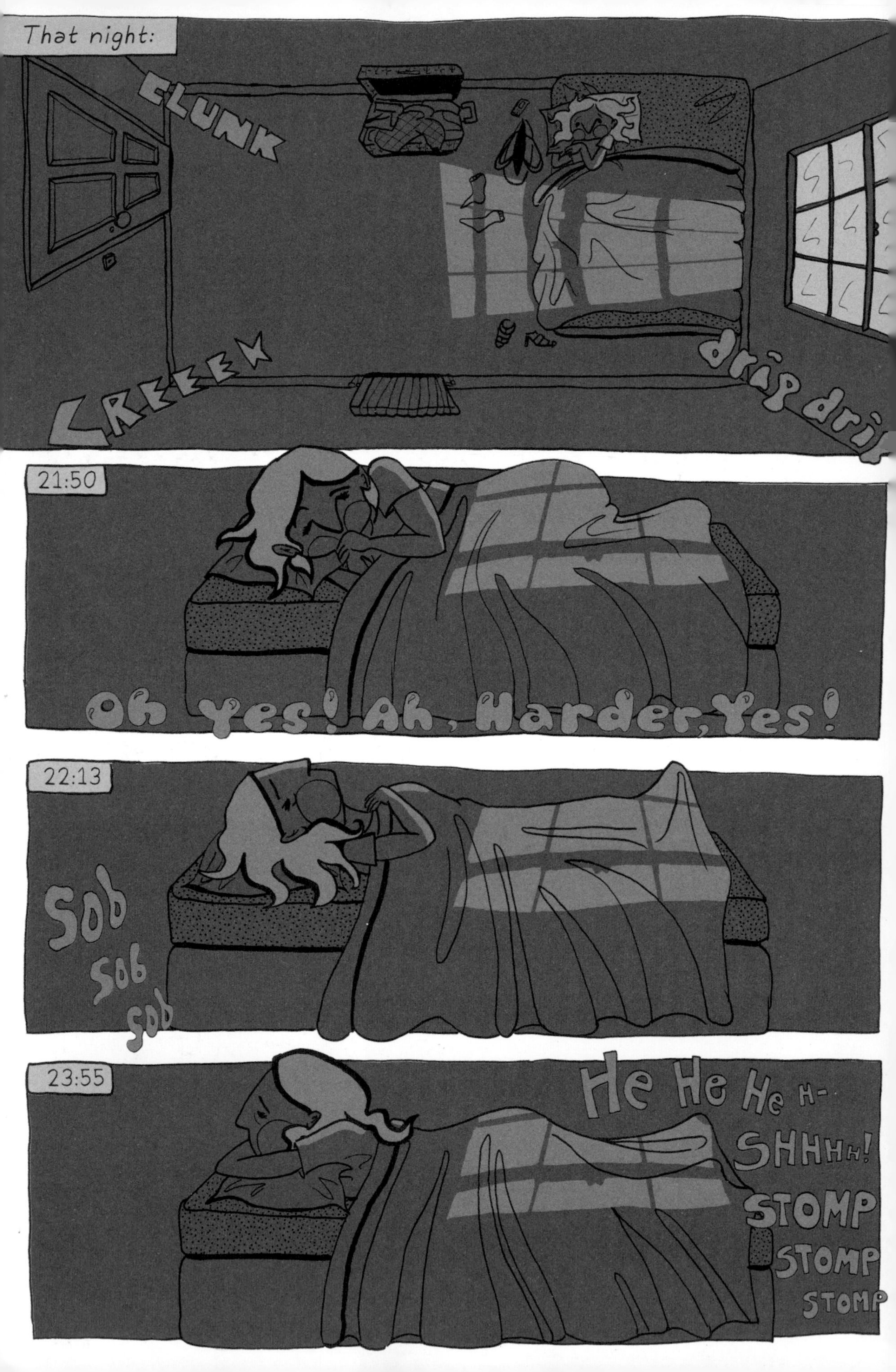
That night:
CLUNK
CREEEK
drip drip
21:50
Oh yes! Ah, Harder, Yes!
22:13
Sob
Sob
Sob
23:55
He He He H-
SHHHH!
STOMP
STOMP
STOMP

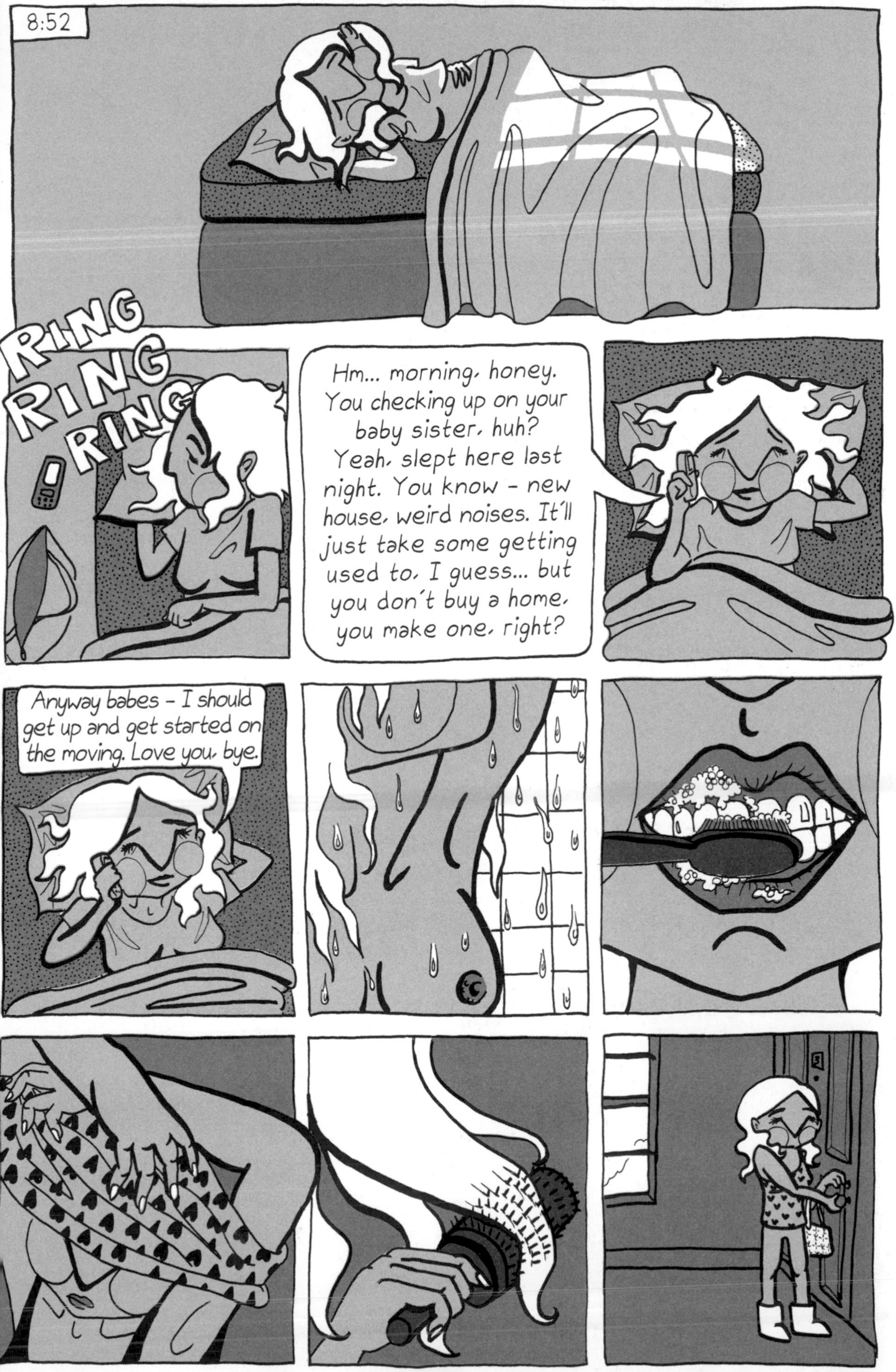
8:52
RING RING RING
Hm... morning, honey. You checking up on your baby sister, huh? Yeah, slept here last night. You know - new house, weird noises. It'll just take some getting used to, I guess... but you don't buy a home, you make one, right?
Anyway babes - I should get up and get started on the moving. Love you, bye.

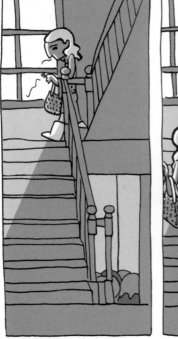

Pardon.

Excuse me.

Sorry...

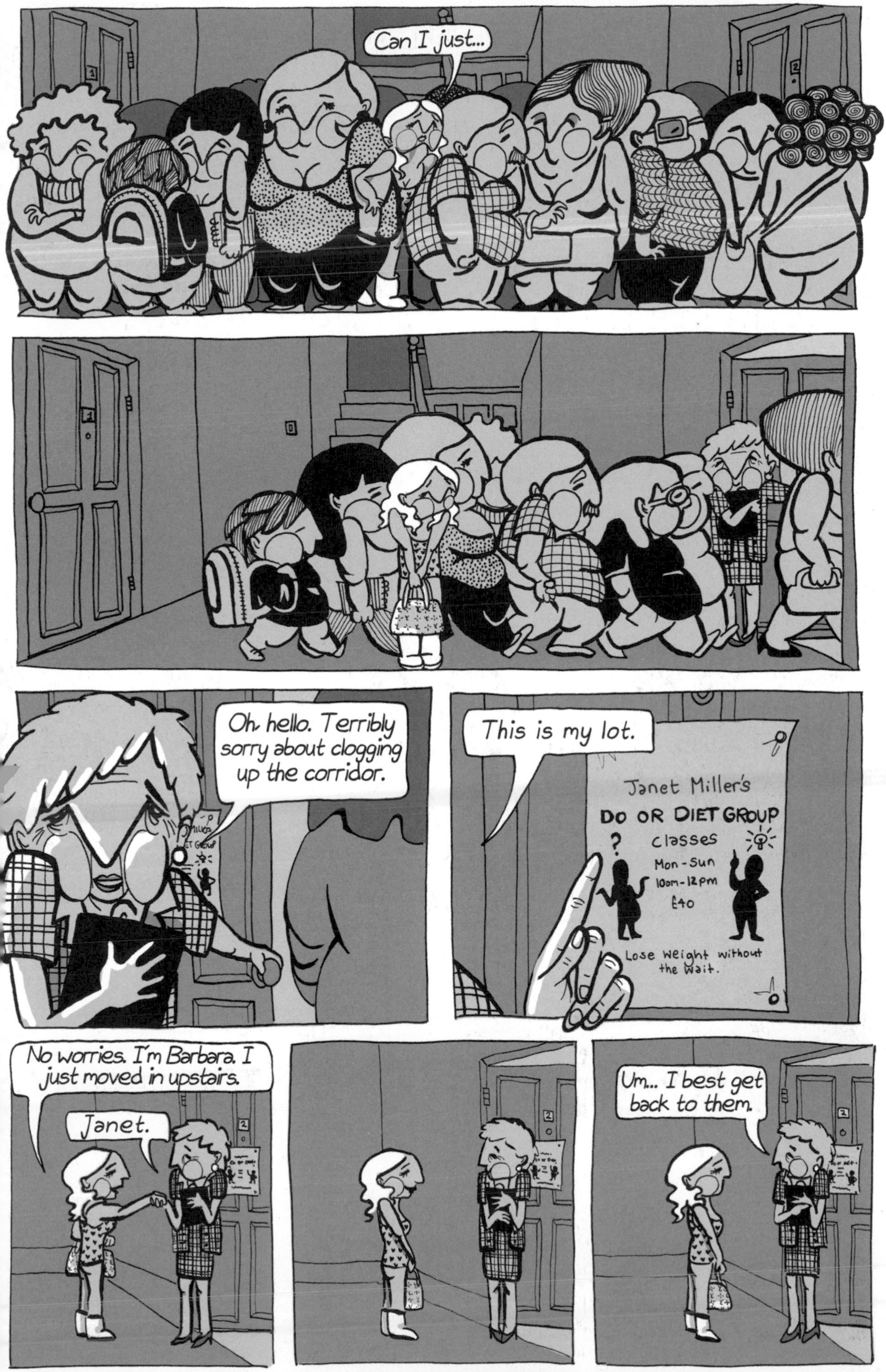
Can I just...
Oh, hello. Terribly sorry about clogging up the corridor.
This is my lot.
Janet Miller's
DO OR DIET GROUP
classes
Mon-Sun
10am-12pm
£40
Lose weight without the wait.
No worries. I'm Barbara. I just moved in upstairs.
Janet.
Um... I best get back to them.

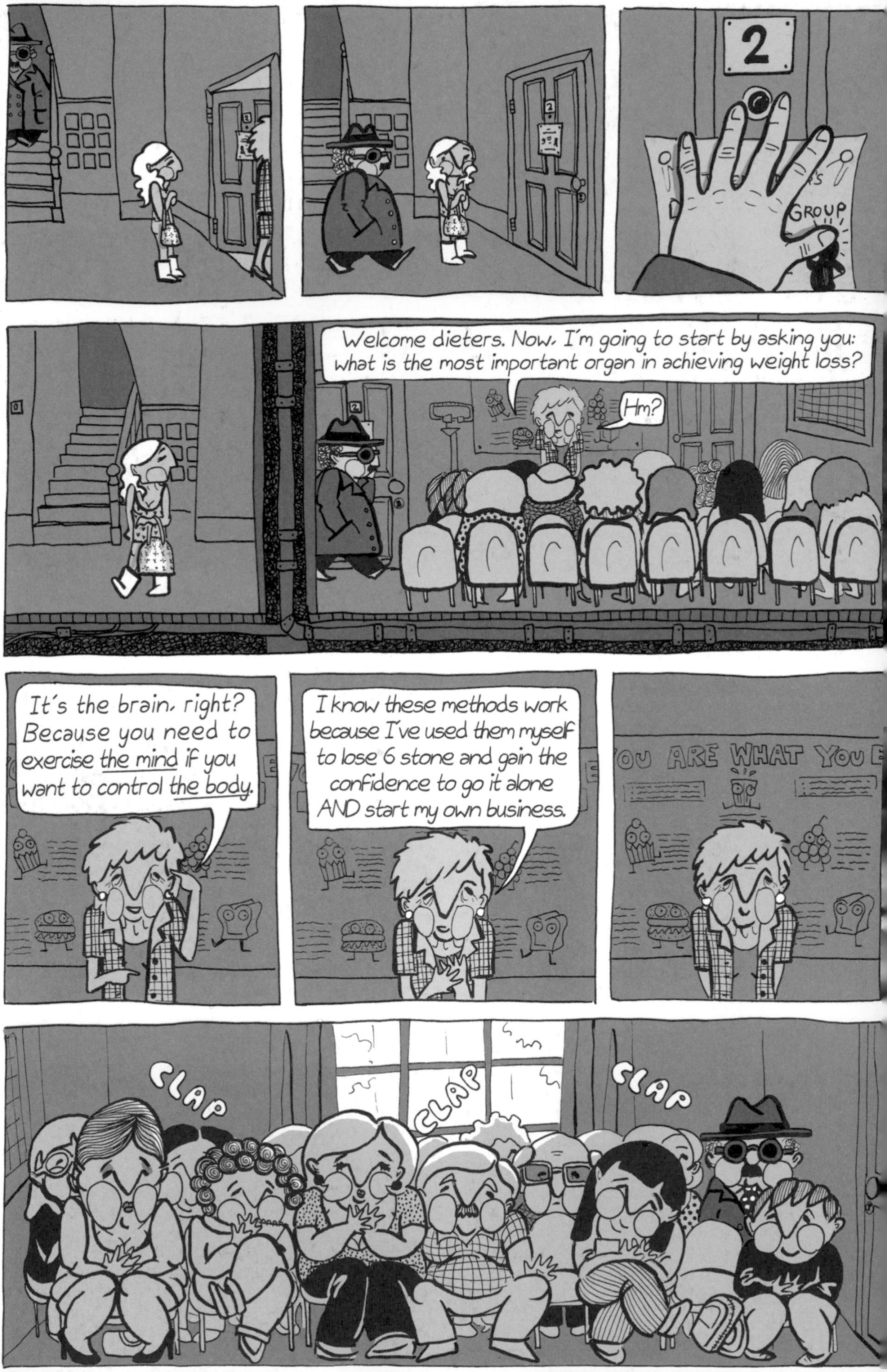
2
GROUP
Welcome dieters. Now, I'm going to start by asking you: what is the most important organ in achieving weight loss?
Hm?
It's the brain, right? Because you need to exercise the mind if you want to control the body.
I know these methods work because I've used them myself to lose 6 stone and gain the confidence to go it alone AND start my own business.
YOU ARE WHAT YOU
CLAP
CLAP
CLAP

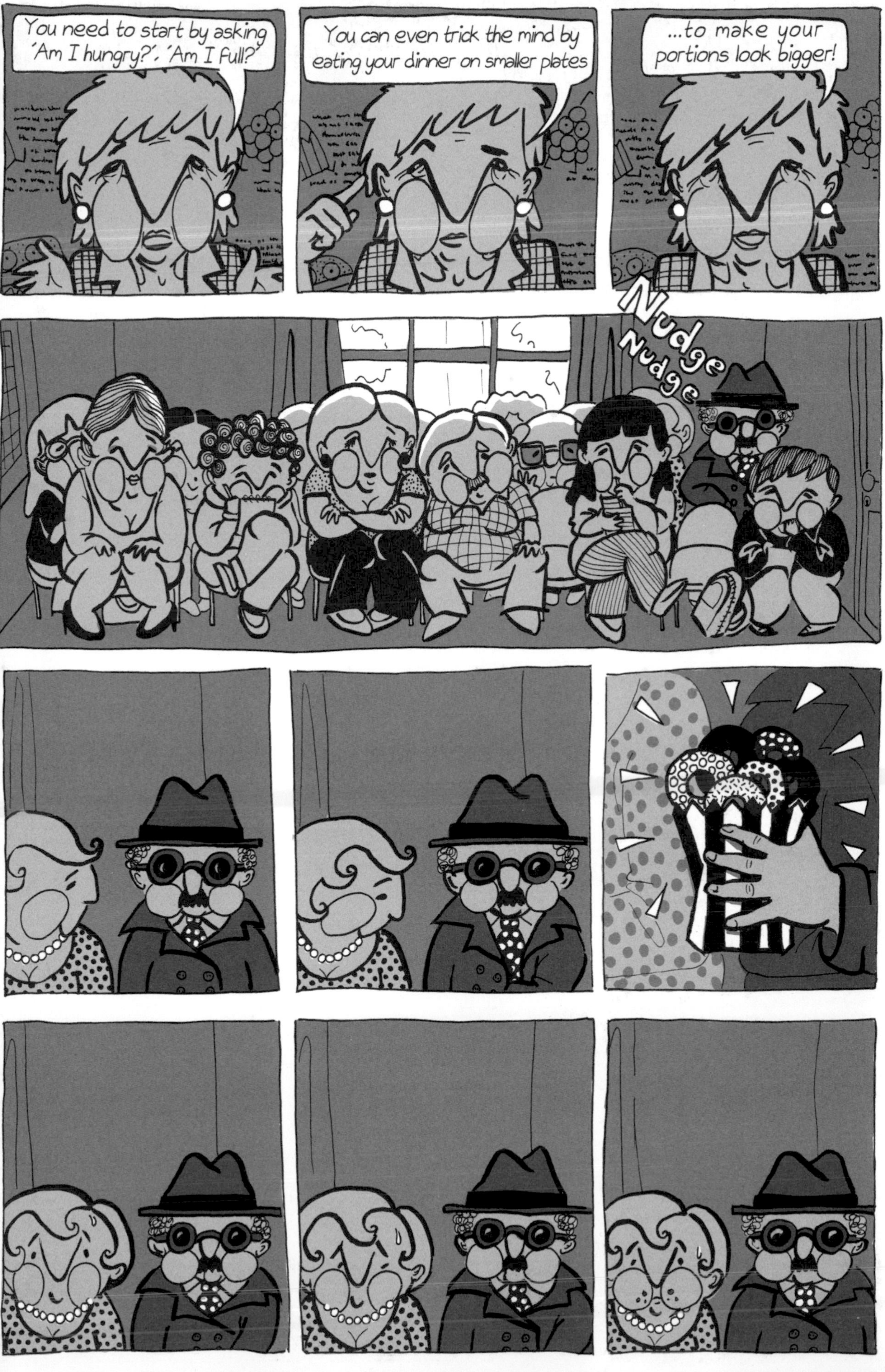
You need to start by asking 'Am I hungry?', 'Am I full?'
You can even trick the mind by eating your dinner on smaller plates
...to make your portions look bigger!
Nudge
Nudge

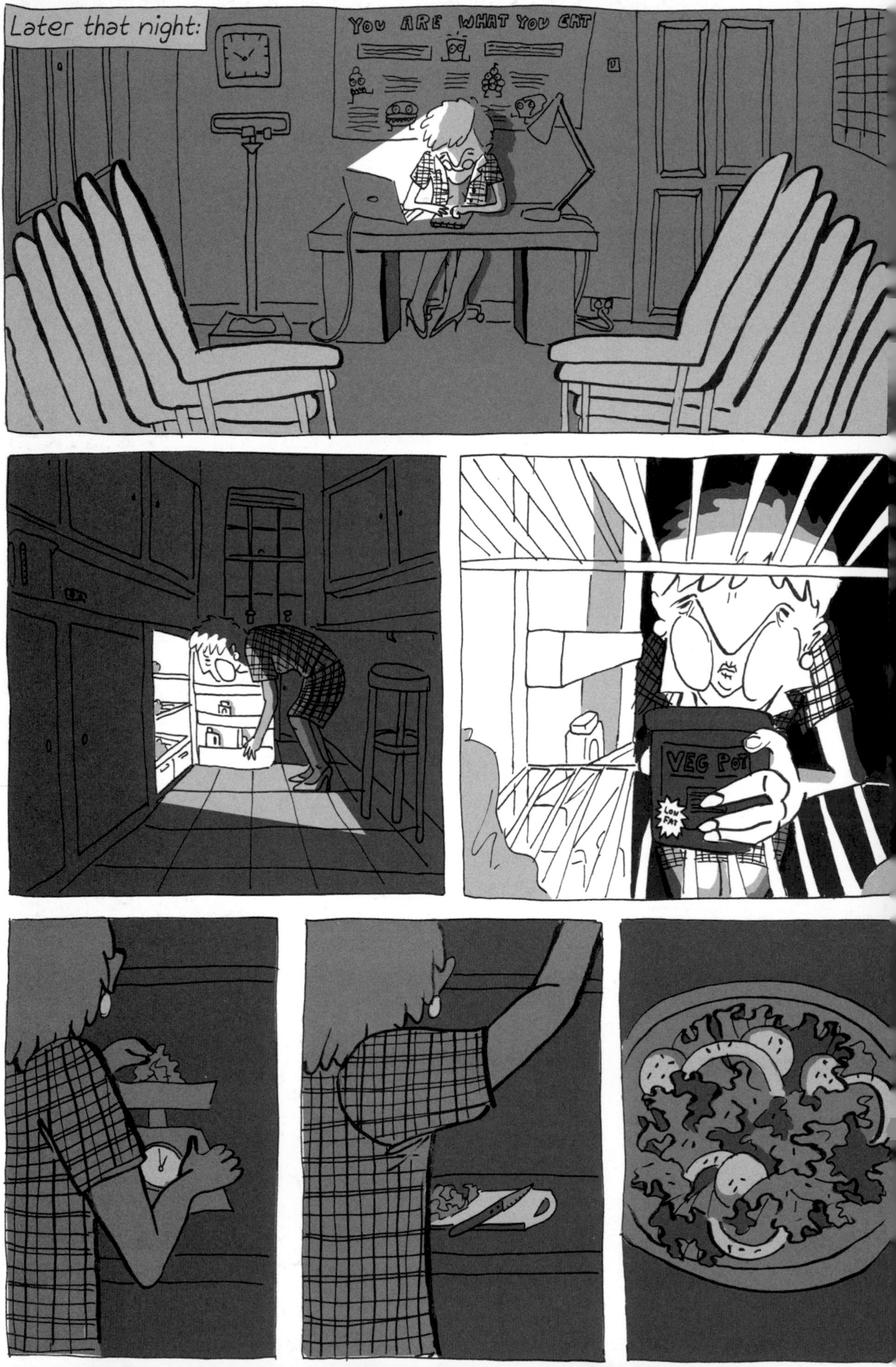

Later that night:
YOU ARE WHAT YOU EAT
VEG POT
LOW FAT

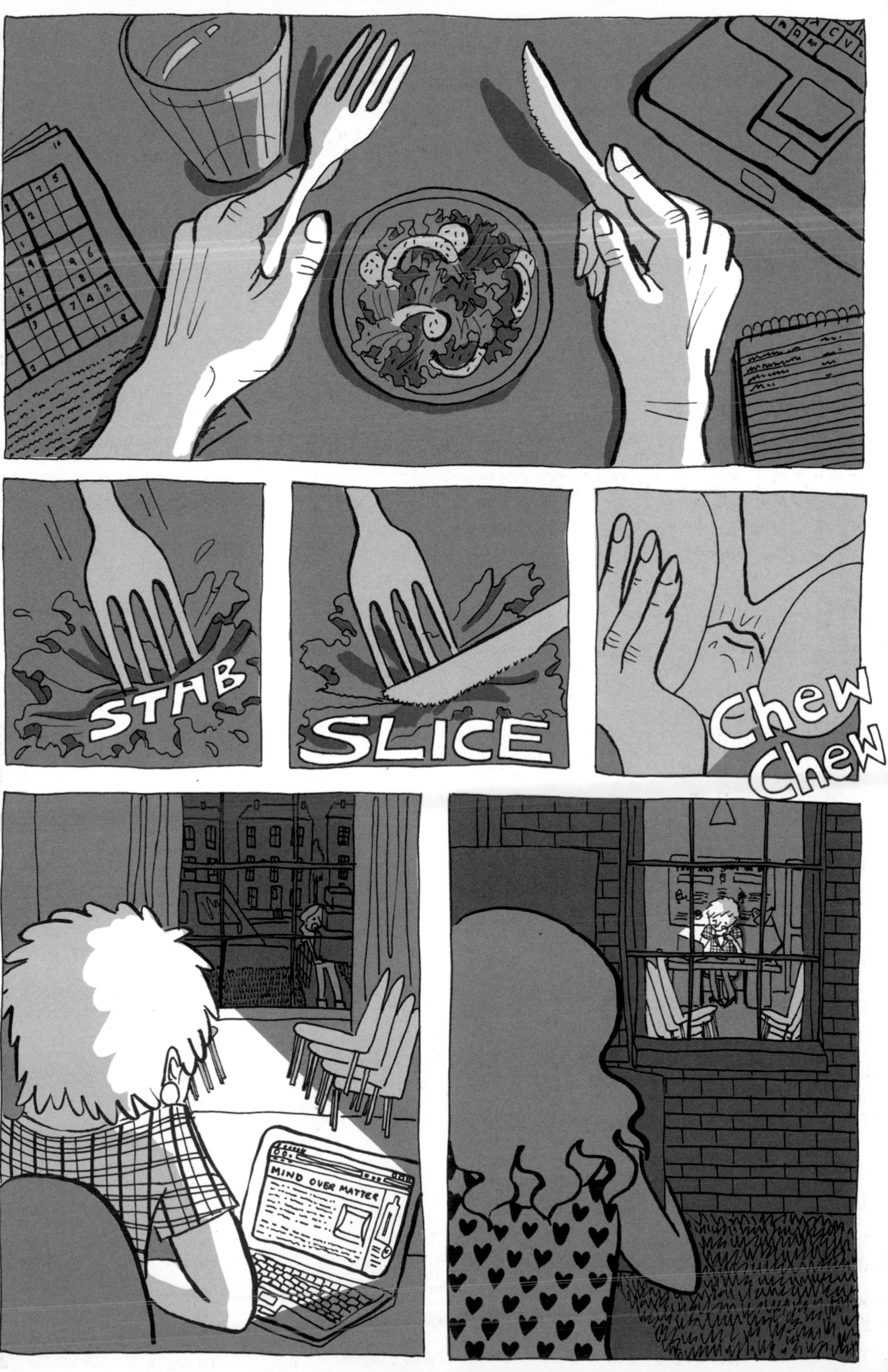
STAB
SLICE
Chew
Chew
MIND OVER MATTER

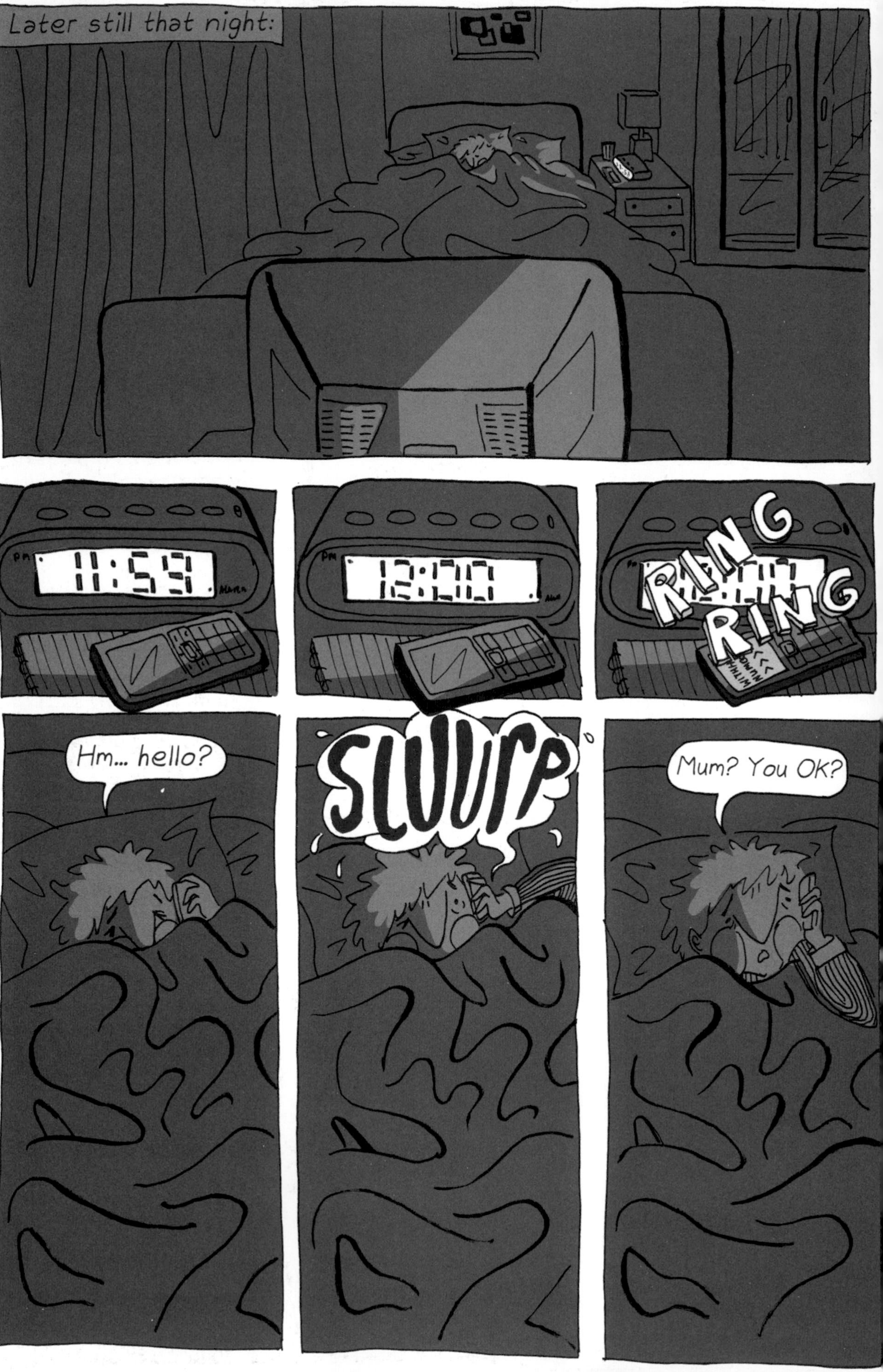
Later still that night:
11:59
12:00
RING
RING
Hm... hello?
SLUURP
Mum? You OK?

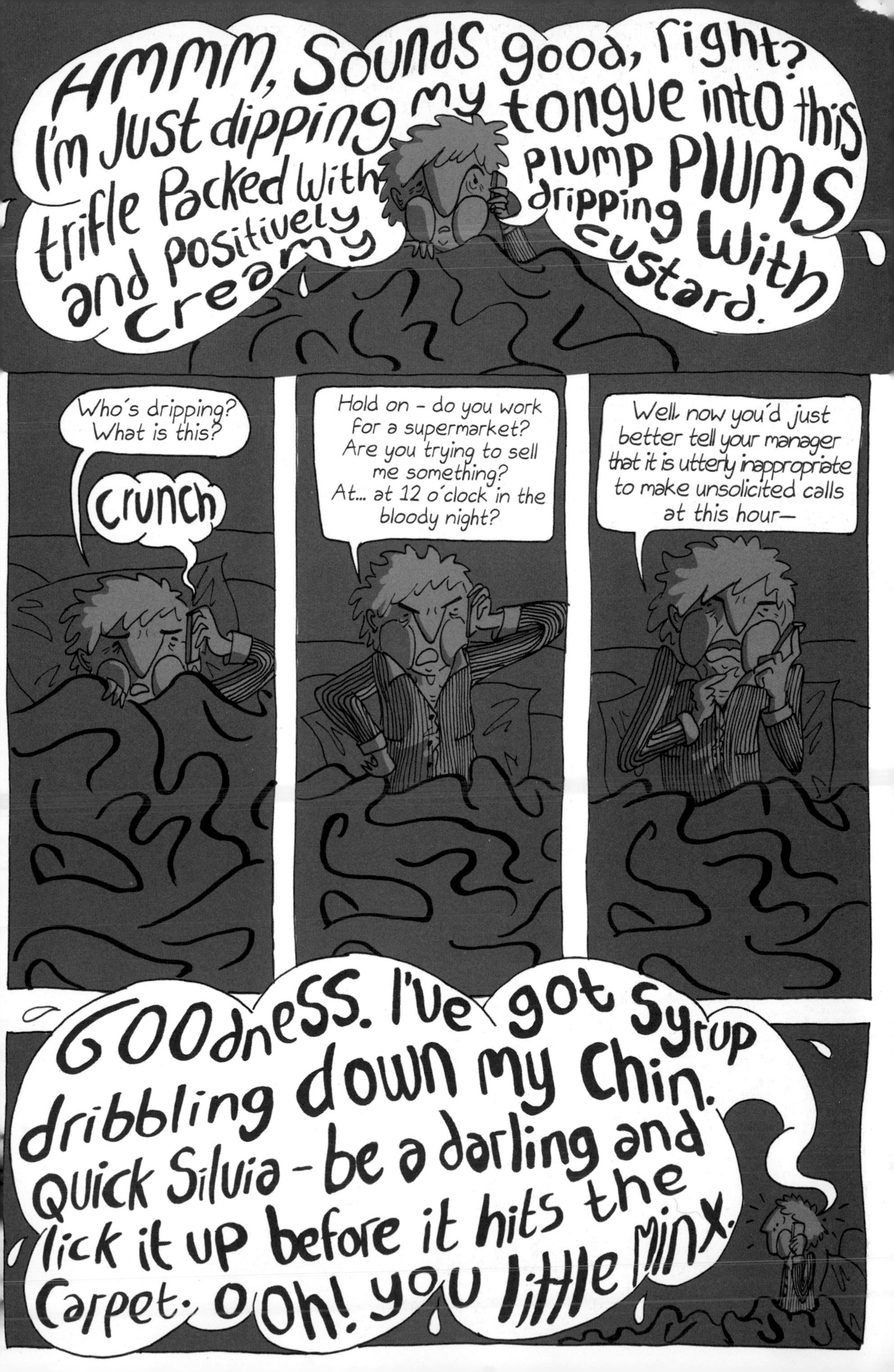
HMMM, SOUNDS good, right? I'm JUST dipping my tongue into this trifle Packed With PLUMP PLUMS and Positively Creamy dripping With custard.
Who's dripping? What is this?
CRUNCH
Hold on - do you work for a supermarket? Are you trying to sell me something? At... at 12 o'clock in the bloody night?
Well now you'd just better tell your manager that it is utterly inappropriate to make unsolicited calls at this hour—
GOOdness. I've got Syrup dribbling down my Chin. Quick Silvia - be a darling and lick it up before it hits the Carpet. OOh! you little Minx.

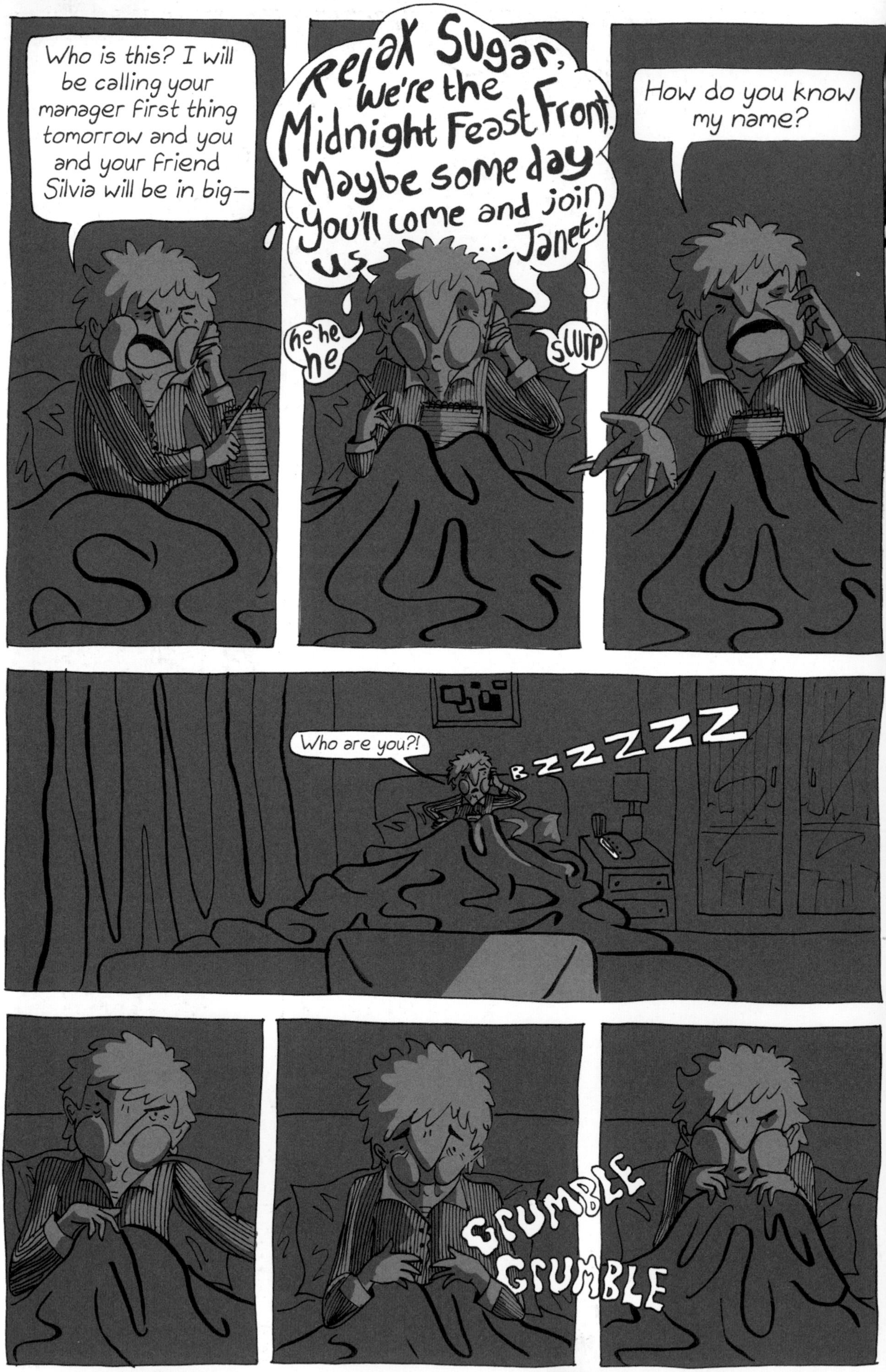

Who is this? I will be calling your manager first thing tomorrow and you and your friend Silvia will be in big–
Relax Sugar, we're the Midnight Feast Front. Maybe some day you'll come and join us ... Janet.
he he he
SLURP
How do you know my name?
Who are you?!
BZZZZZZ
GRUMBLE
GRUMBLE

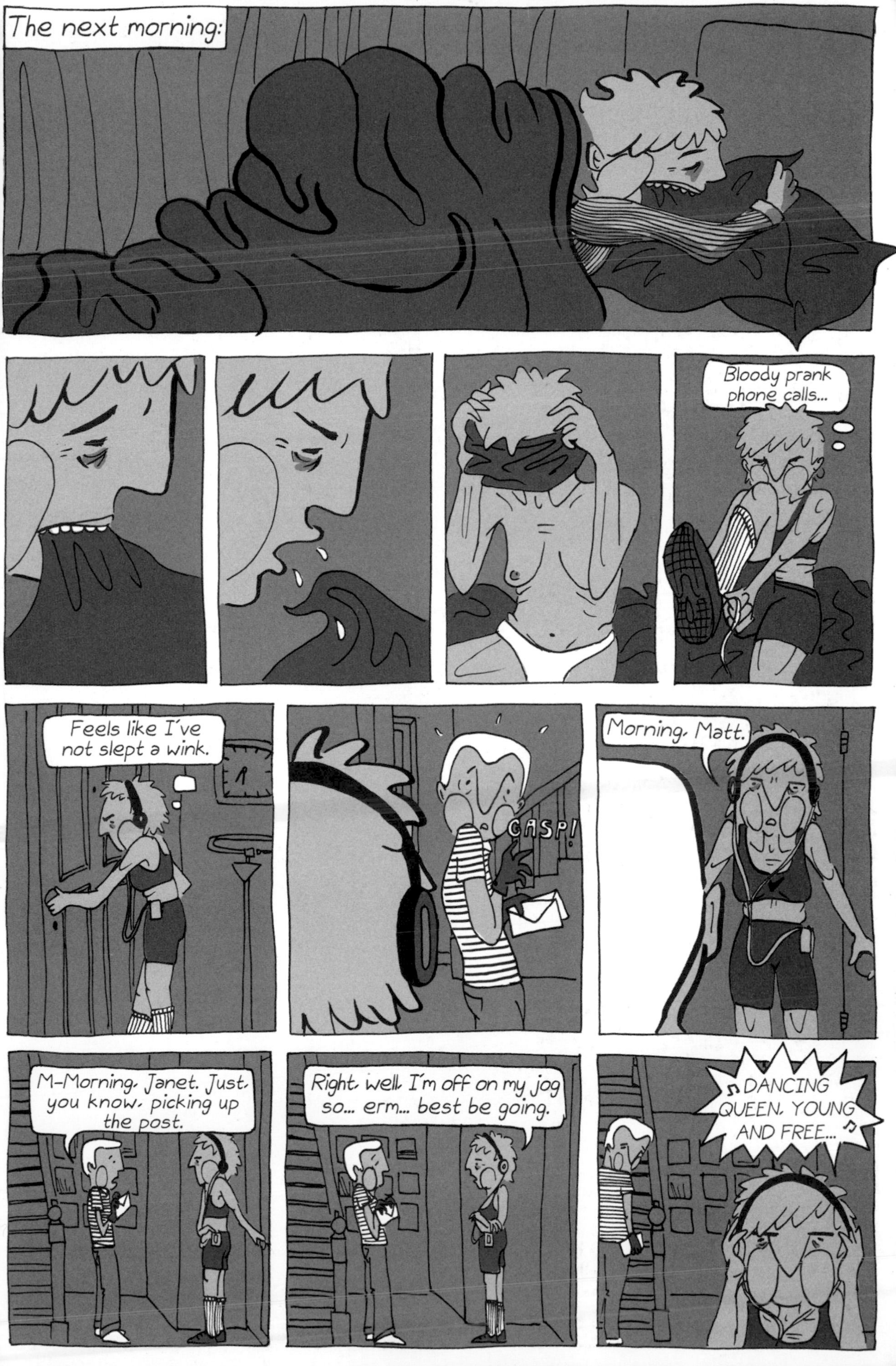
The next morning:
Bloody prank phone calls...
Feels like I've not slept a wink.
GASP!
Morning, Matt.
M-Morning, Janet. Just, you know, picking up the post.
Right, well I'm off on my jog so... erm... best be going.
♫ DANCING QUEEN, YOUNG AND FREE... ♫

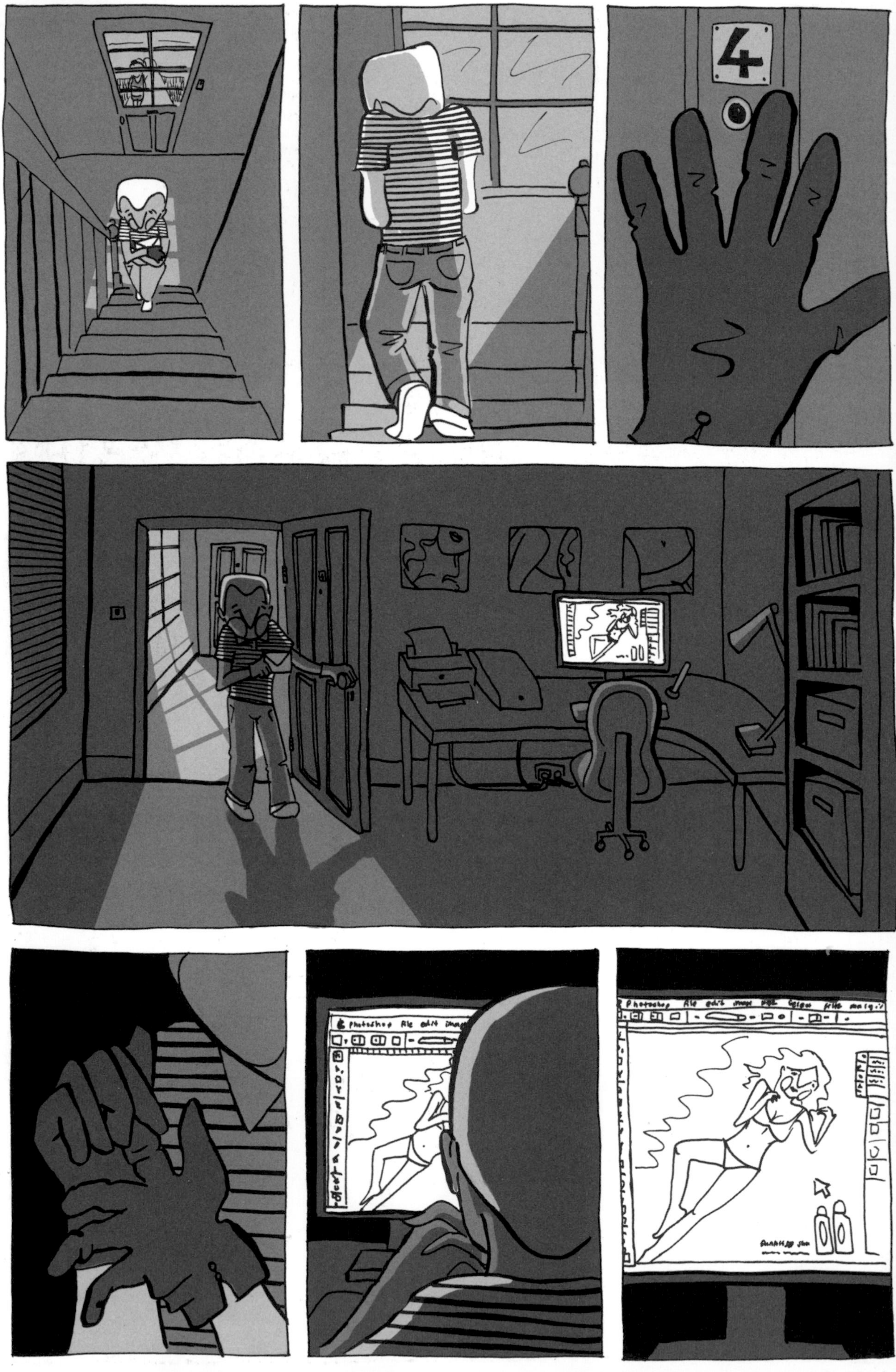
4

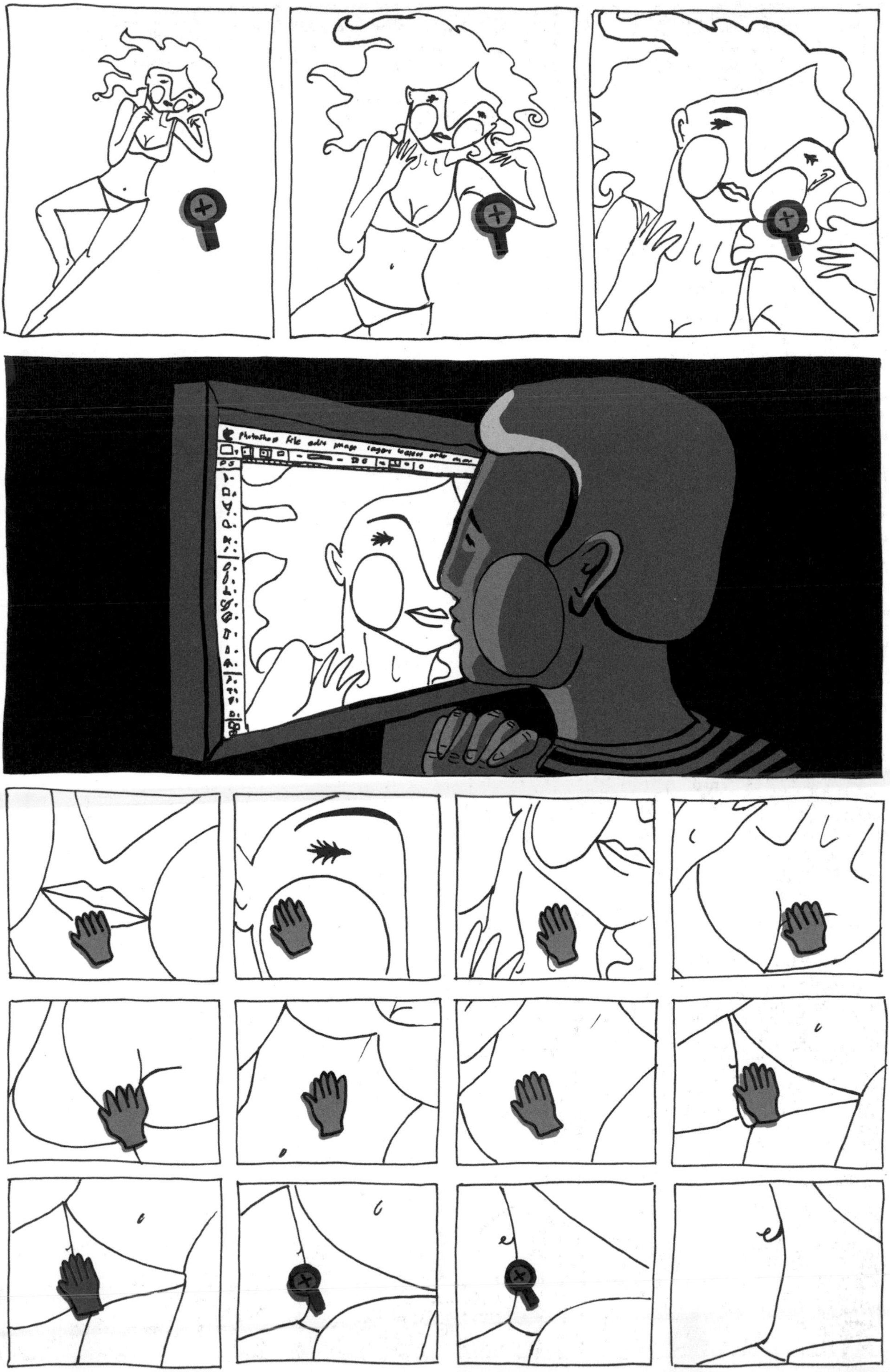
Photoshop file

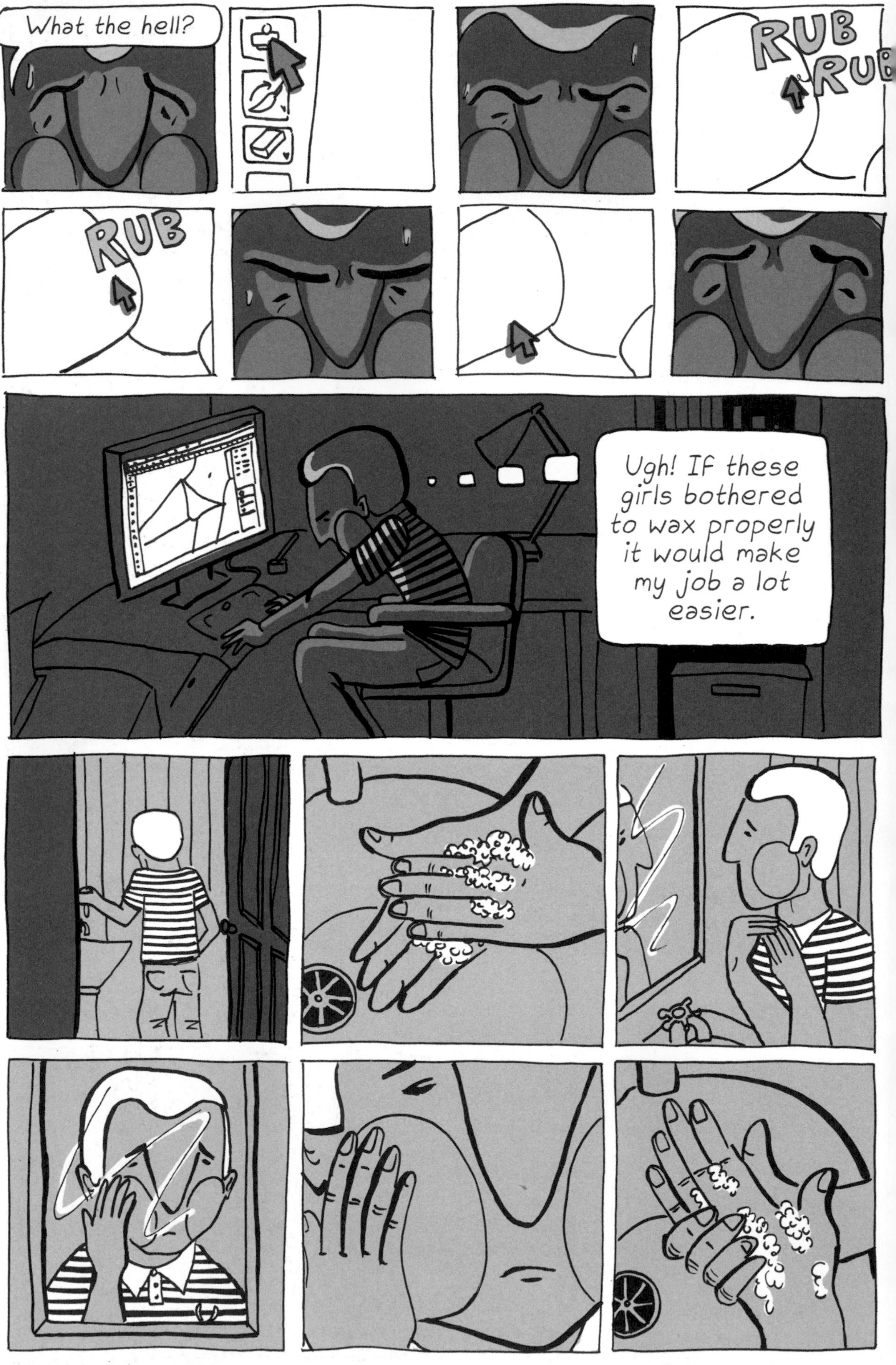
What the hell?
RUB RUB
RUB
Ugh! If these girls bothered to wax properly it would make my job a lot easier.

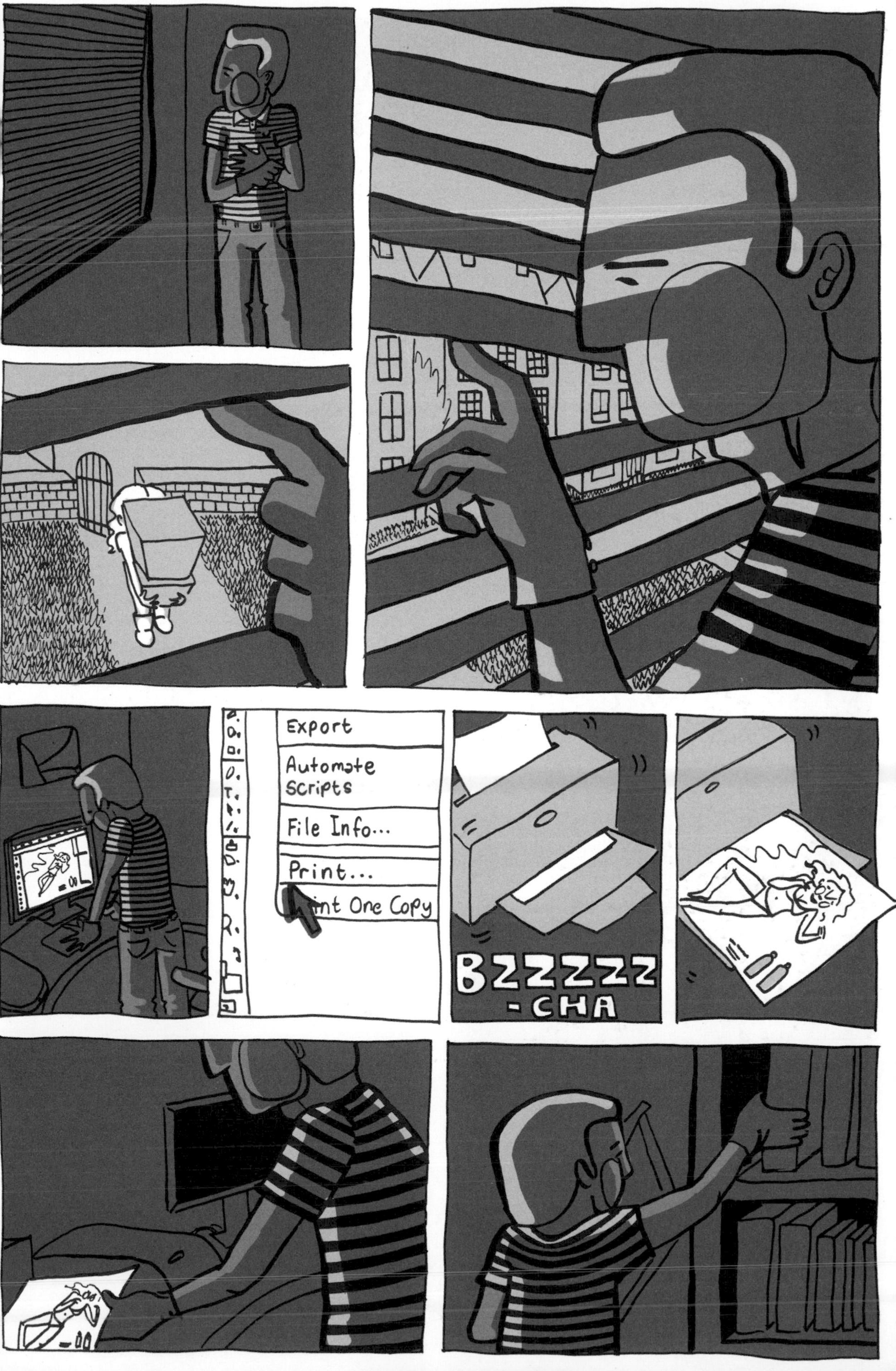
Export
Automate Scripts
File Info...
Print...
Print One Copy
BZZZZZ
-CHA

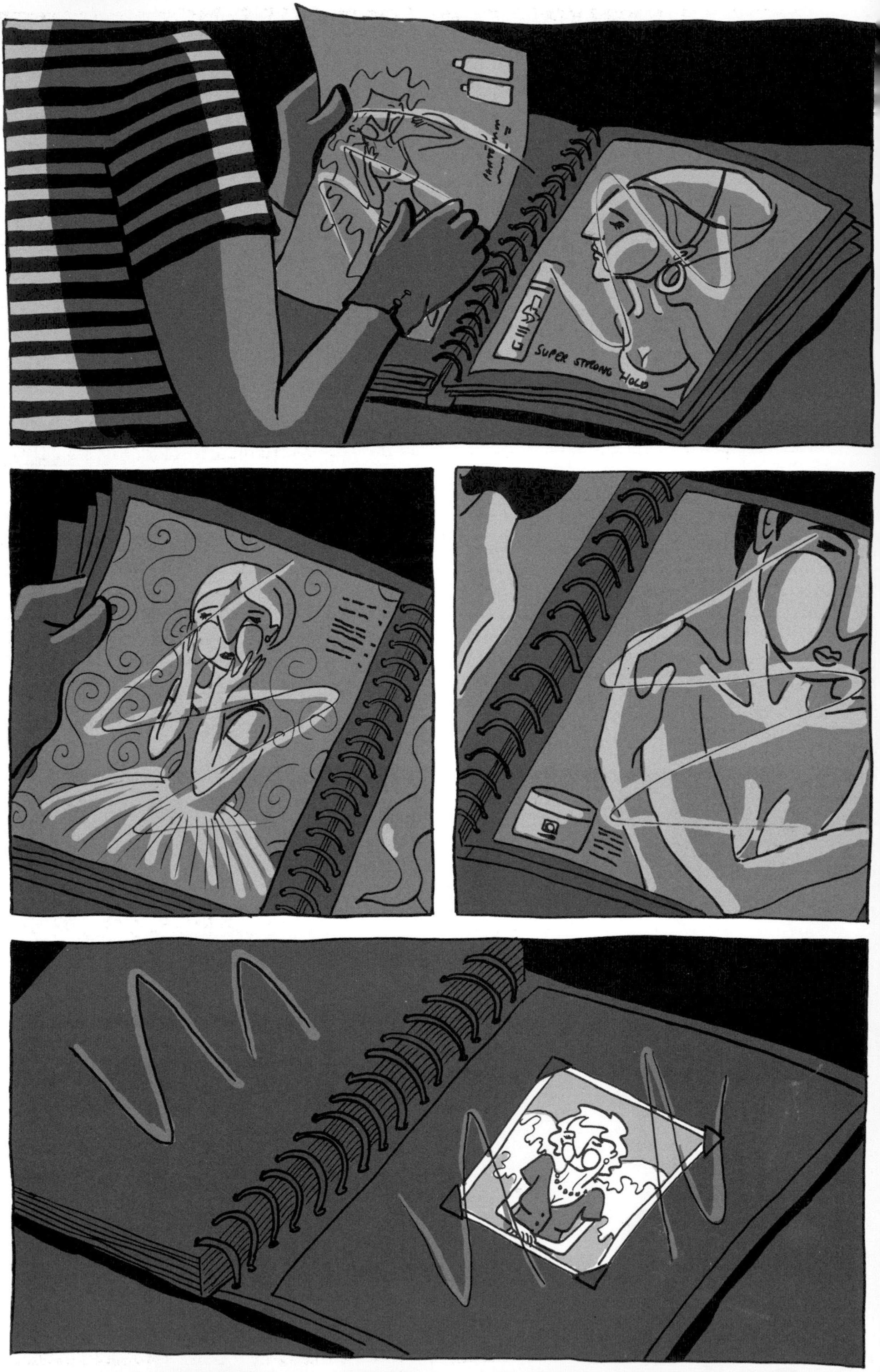
SUPER STRONG HOLD

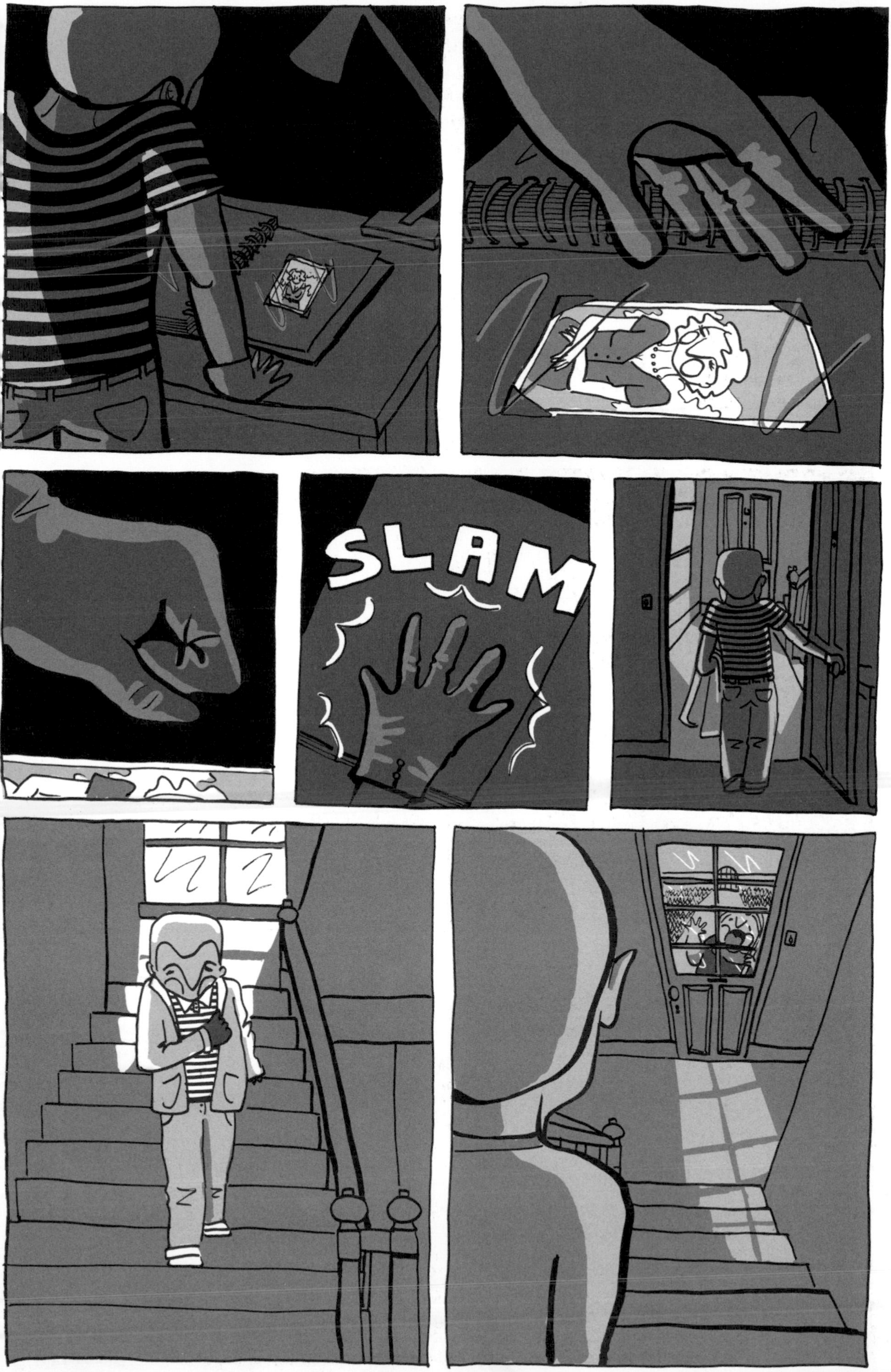
SLAM

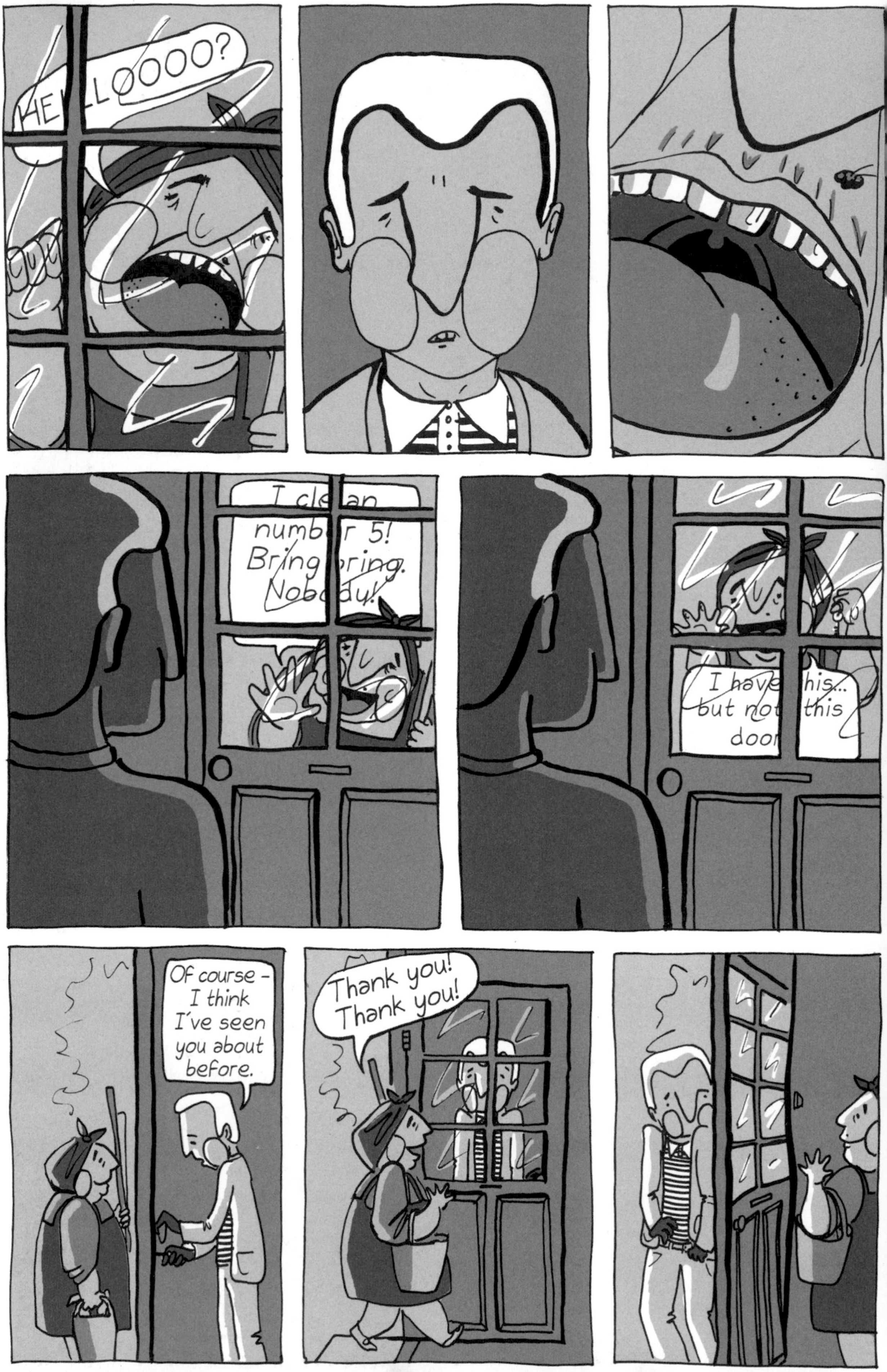
HELLOOOO?
I clean number 5! Bring bring. Nobody!
I have this... but not this door
Of course - I think I've seen you about before.
Thank you! Thank you!

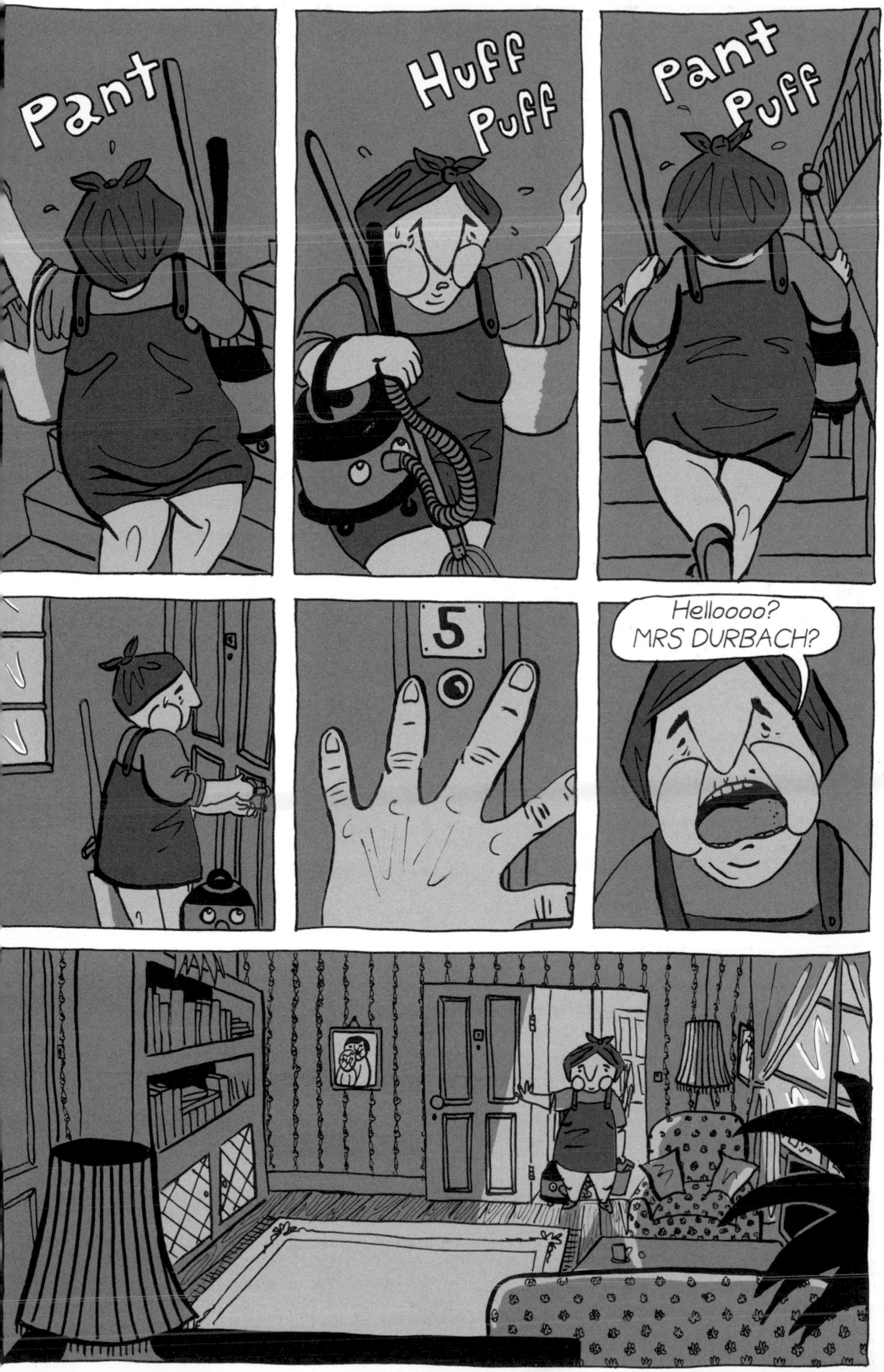
Pant
Huff
Puff
Pant
Puff
5
Helloooo?
MRS DURBACH?

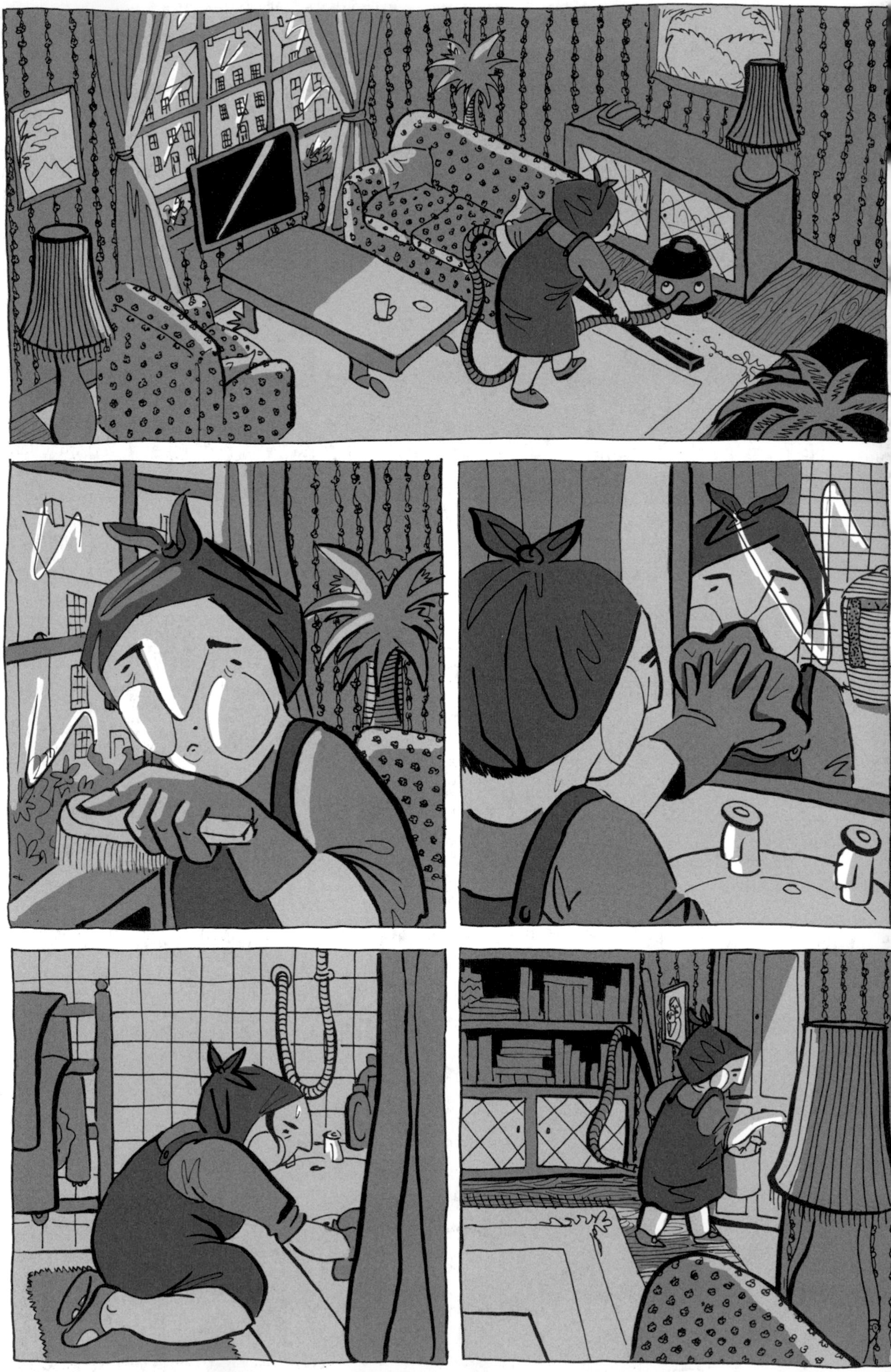

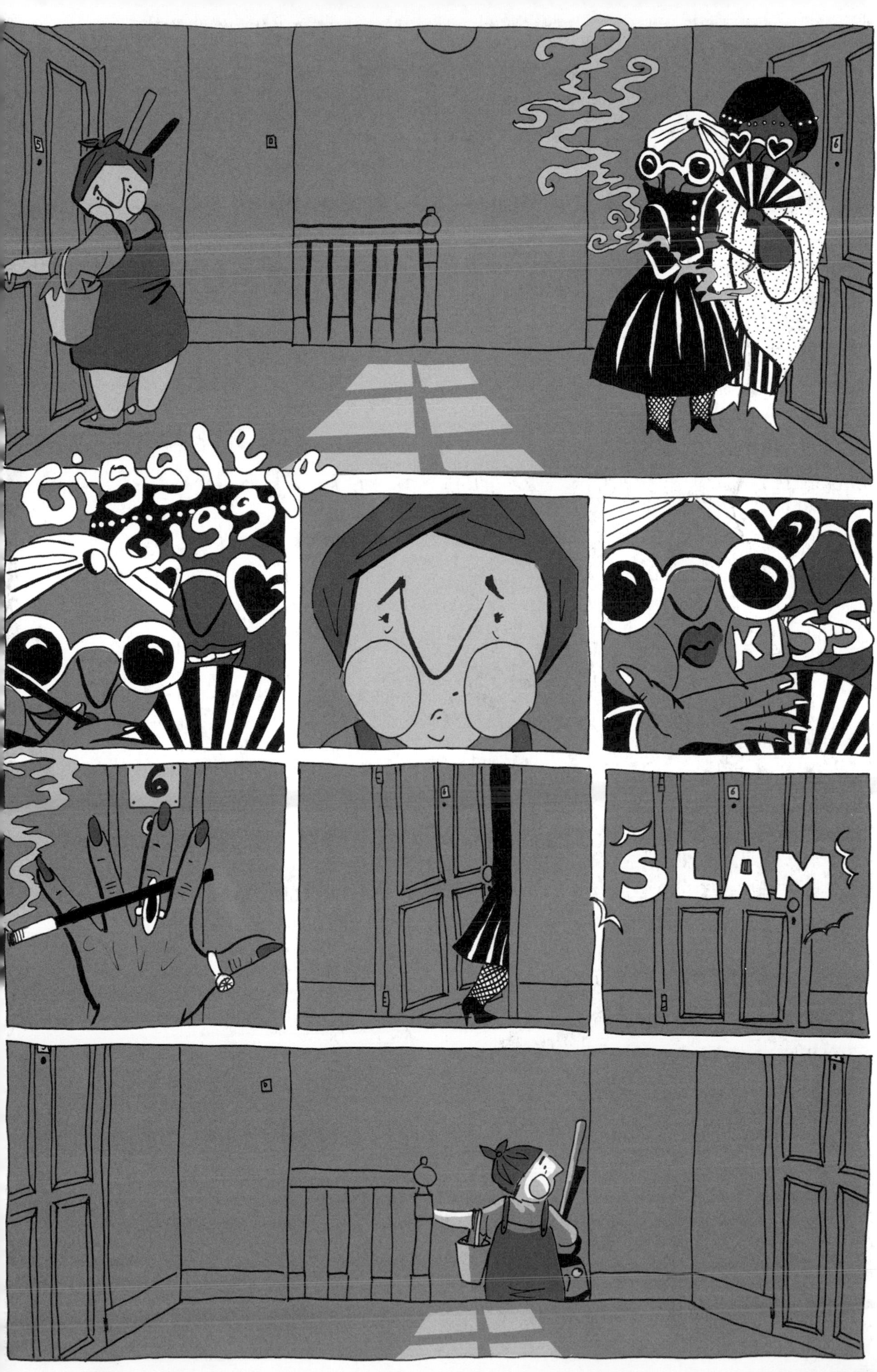
Giggle
Giggle
KISS
SLAM

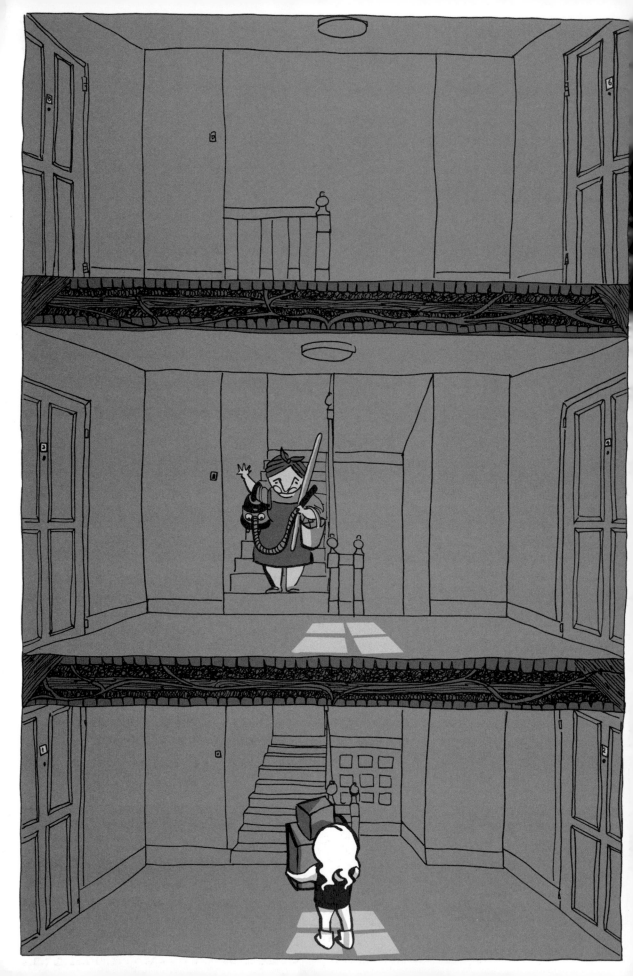

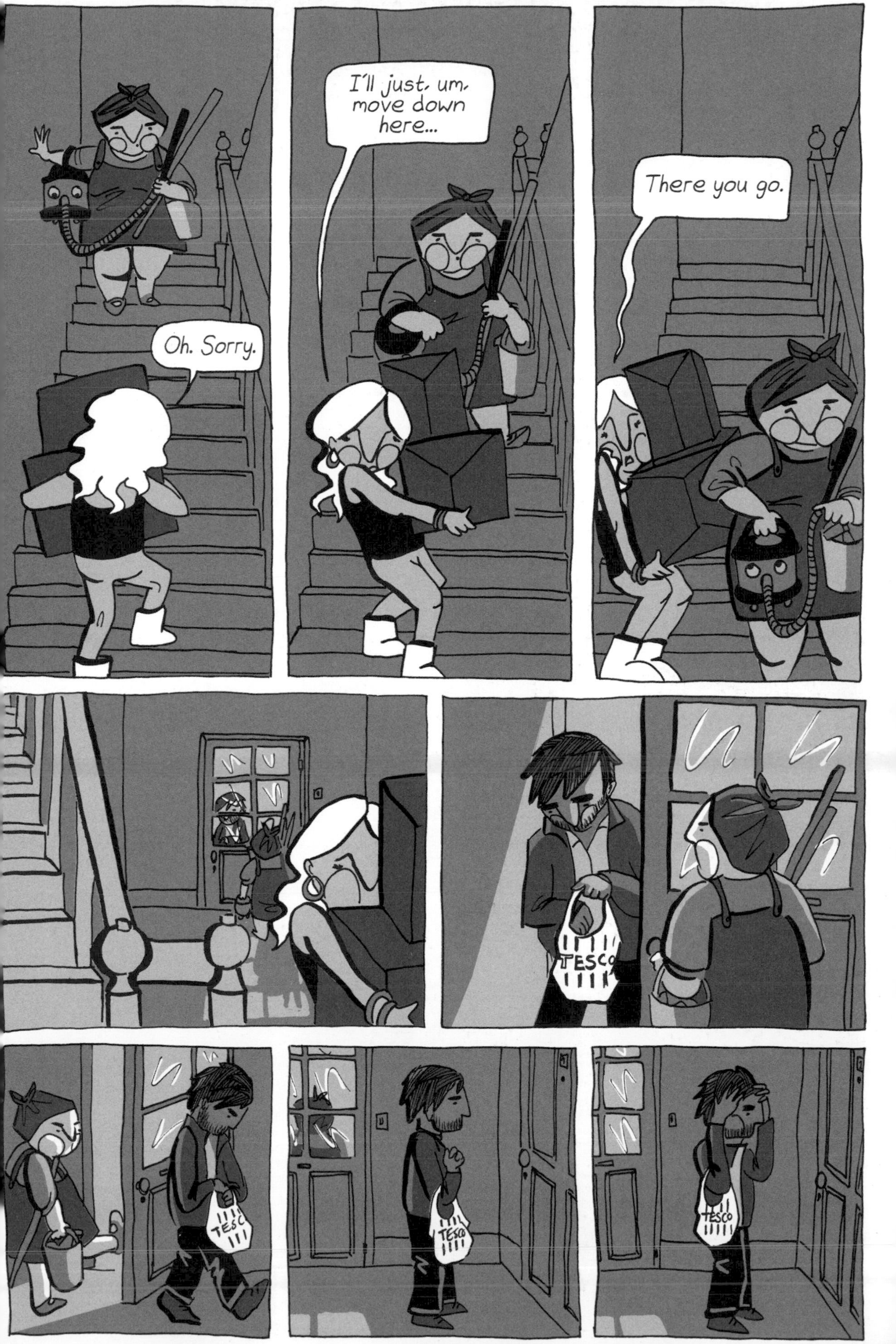
Oh. Sorry.
I'll just, um, move down here...
There you go.
TESCO
TESCO
TESCO
TESCO

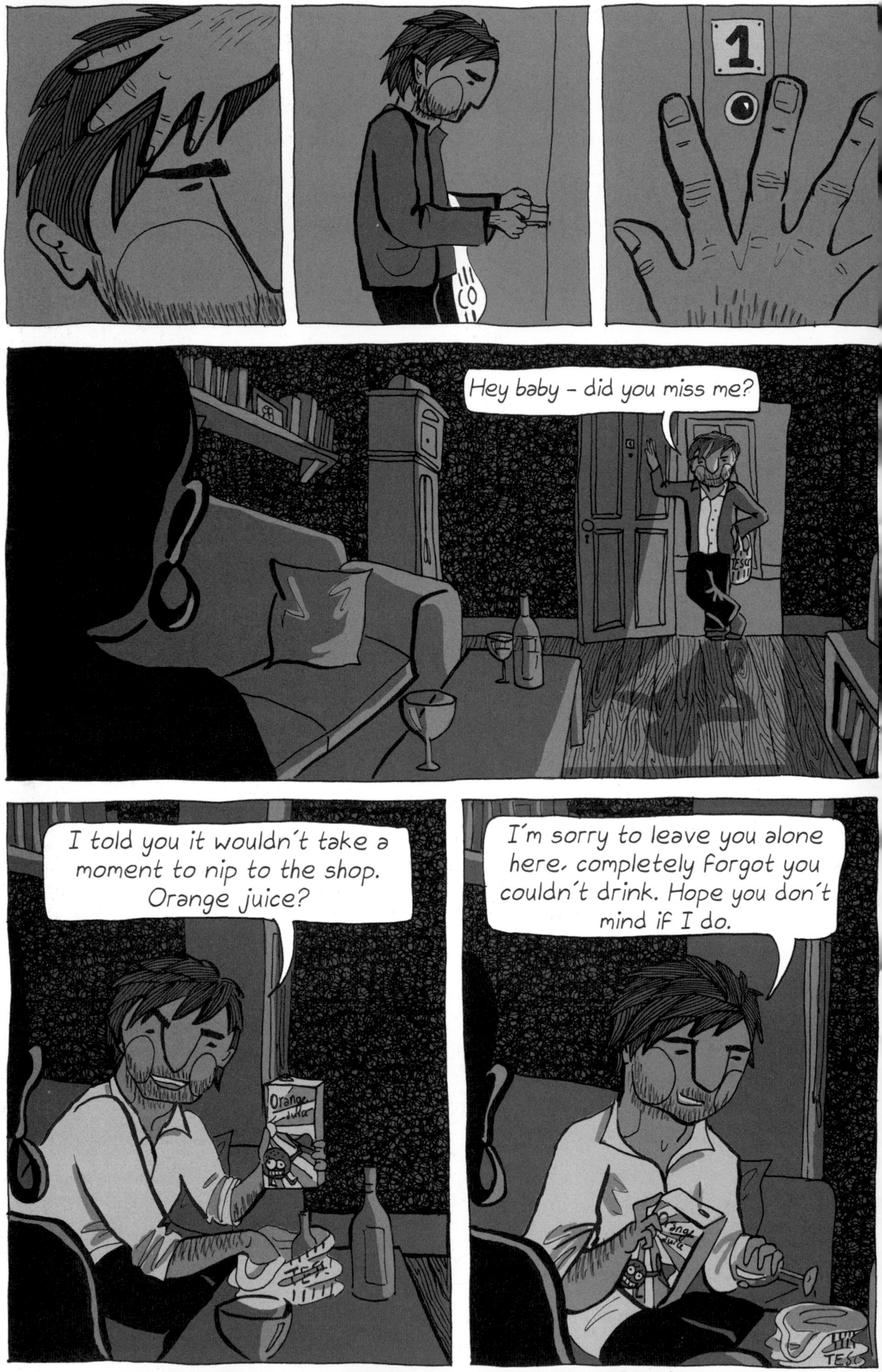
1
Hey baby – did you miss me?
I told you it wouldn't take a moment to nip to the shop. Orange juice?
I'm sorry to leave you alone here, completely forgot you couldn't drink. Hope you don't mind if I do.

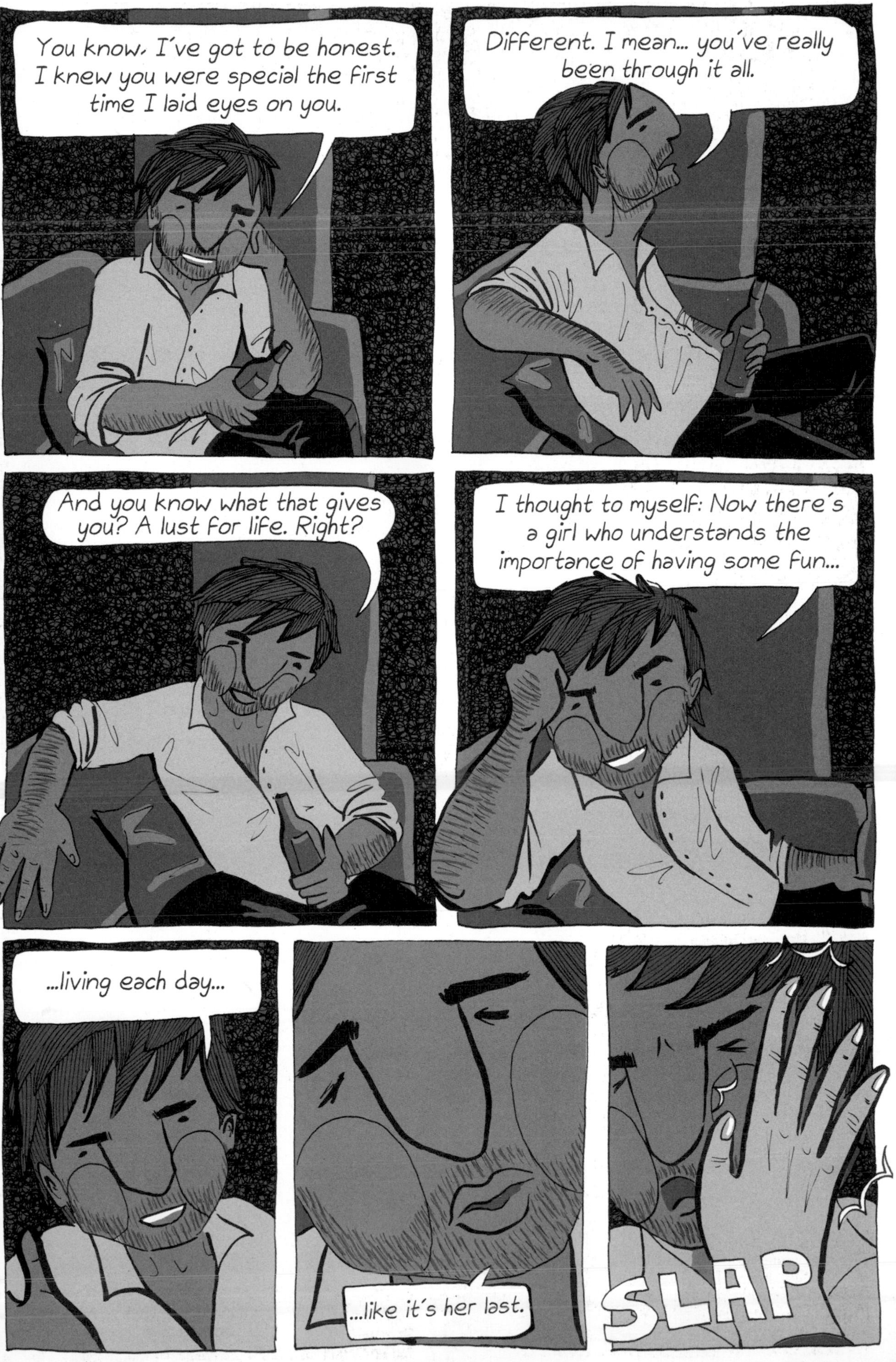
You know, I've got to be honest. I knew you were special the first time I laid eyes on you.
Different. I mean... you've really been through it all.
And you know what that gives you? A lust for life. Right?
I thought to myself: Now there's a girl who understands the importance of having some fun...
...living each day...
...like it's her last.
SLAP

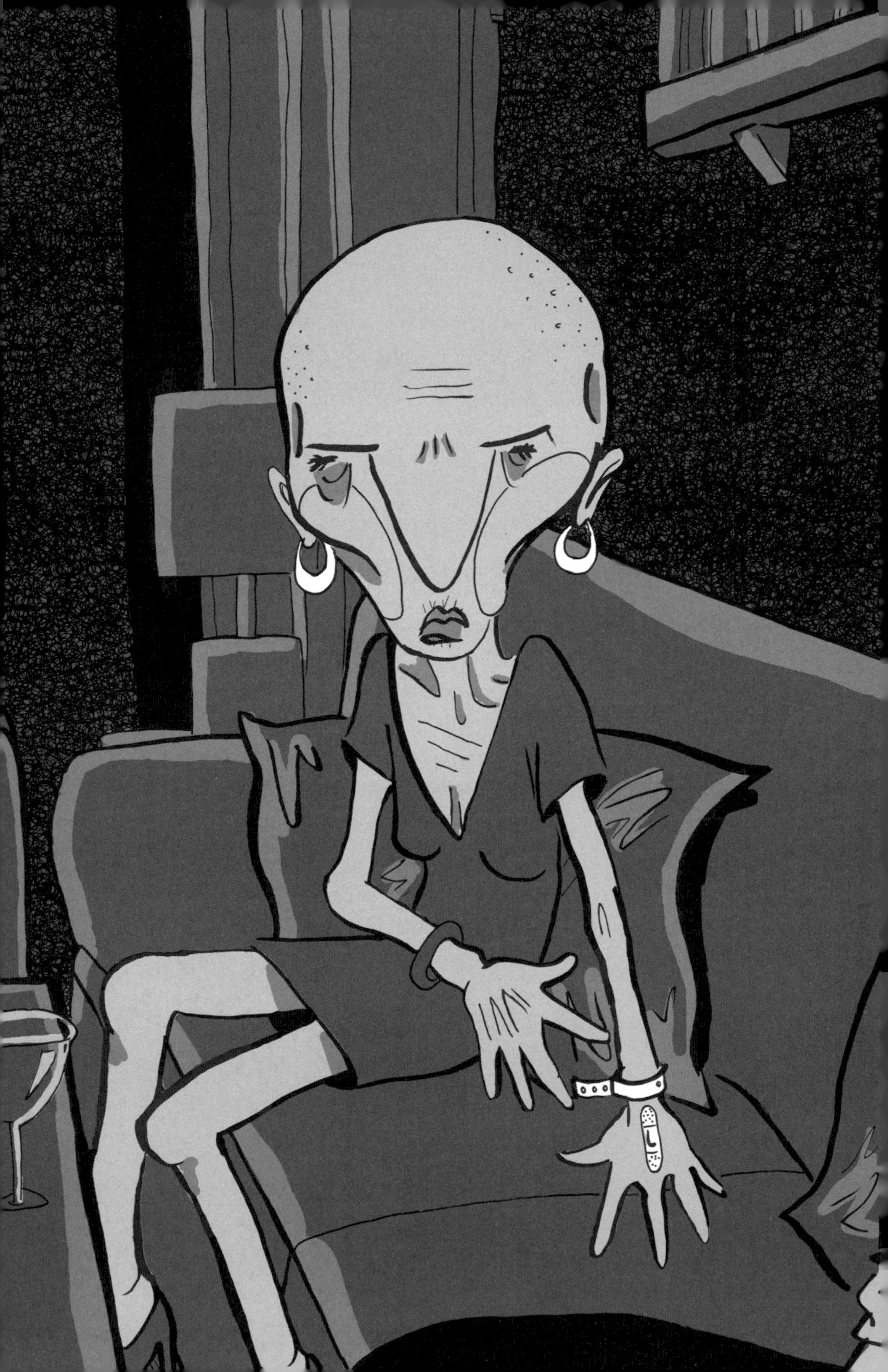

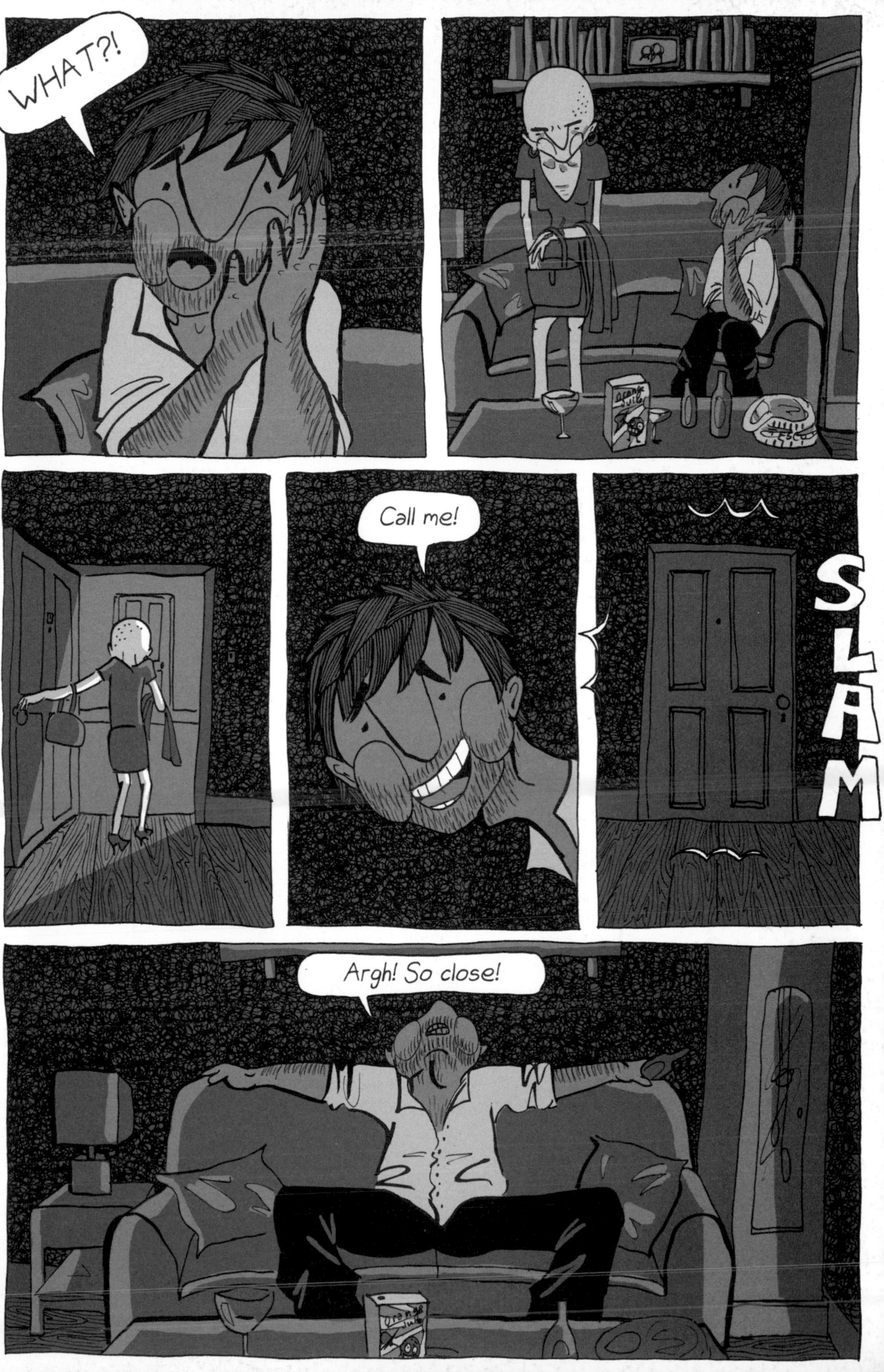
WHAT?!
Call me!
SLAM
Argh! So close!

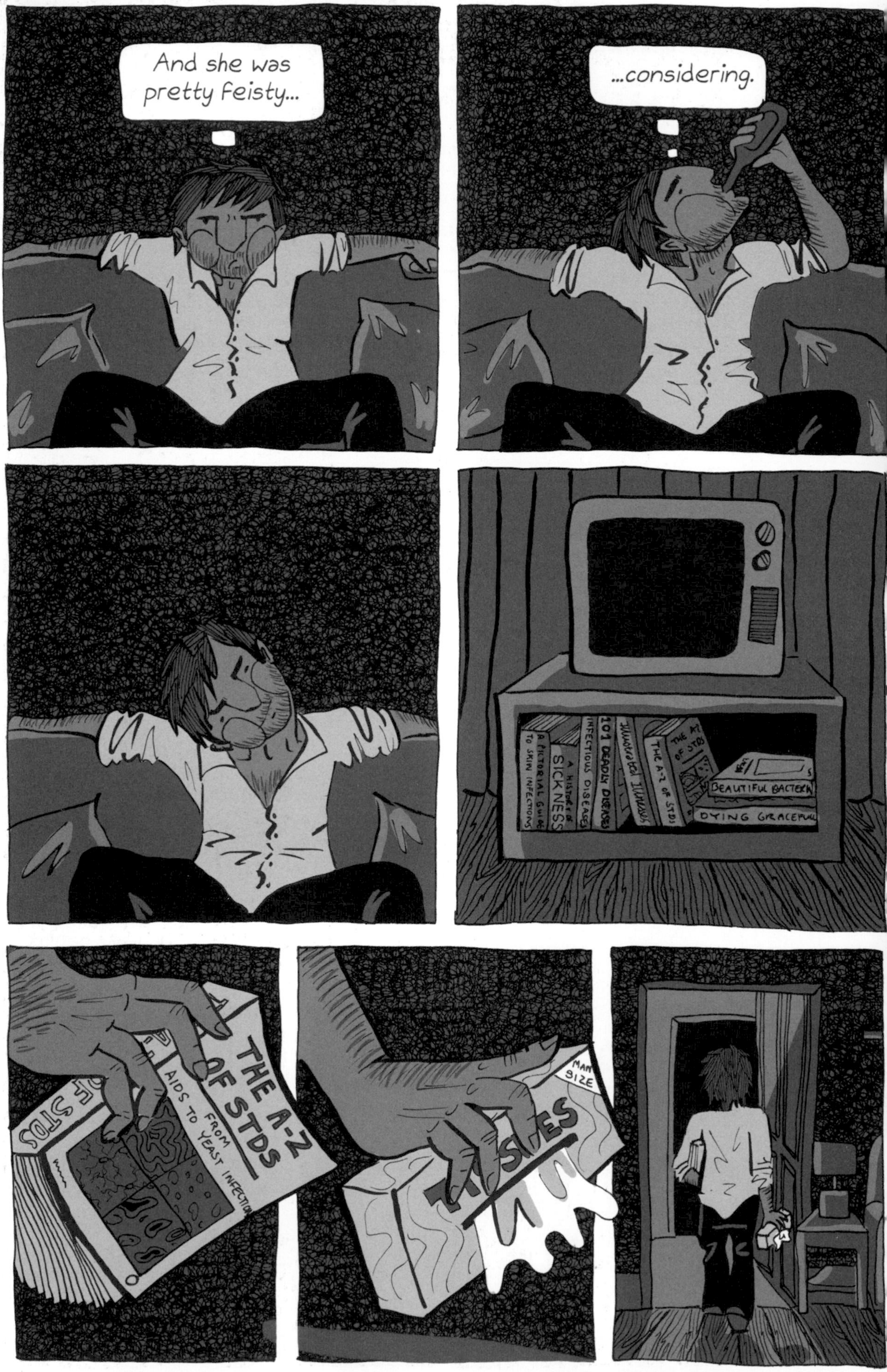
And she was pretty feisty...
...considering.
A PICTORIAL GUIDE TO SKIN INFECTIONS
A HISTORY OF SICKNESS
INFECTIOUS DISEASES
101 DEADLY DISEASES
THE A-Z OF STDS
DYING GRACEFULLY
THE A-Z OF STDS
FROM AIDS TO YEAST
MAN SIZE

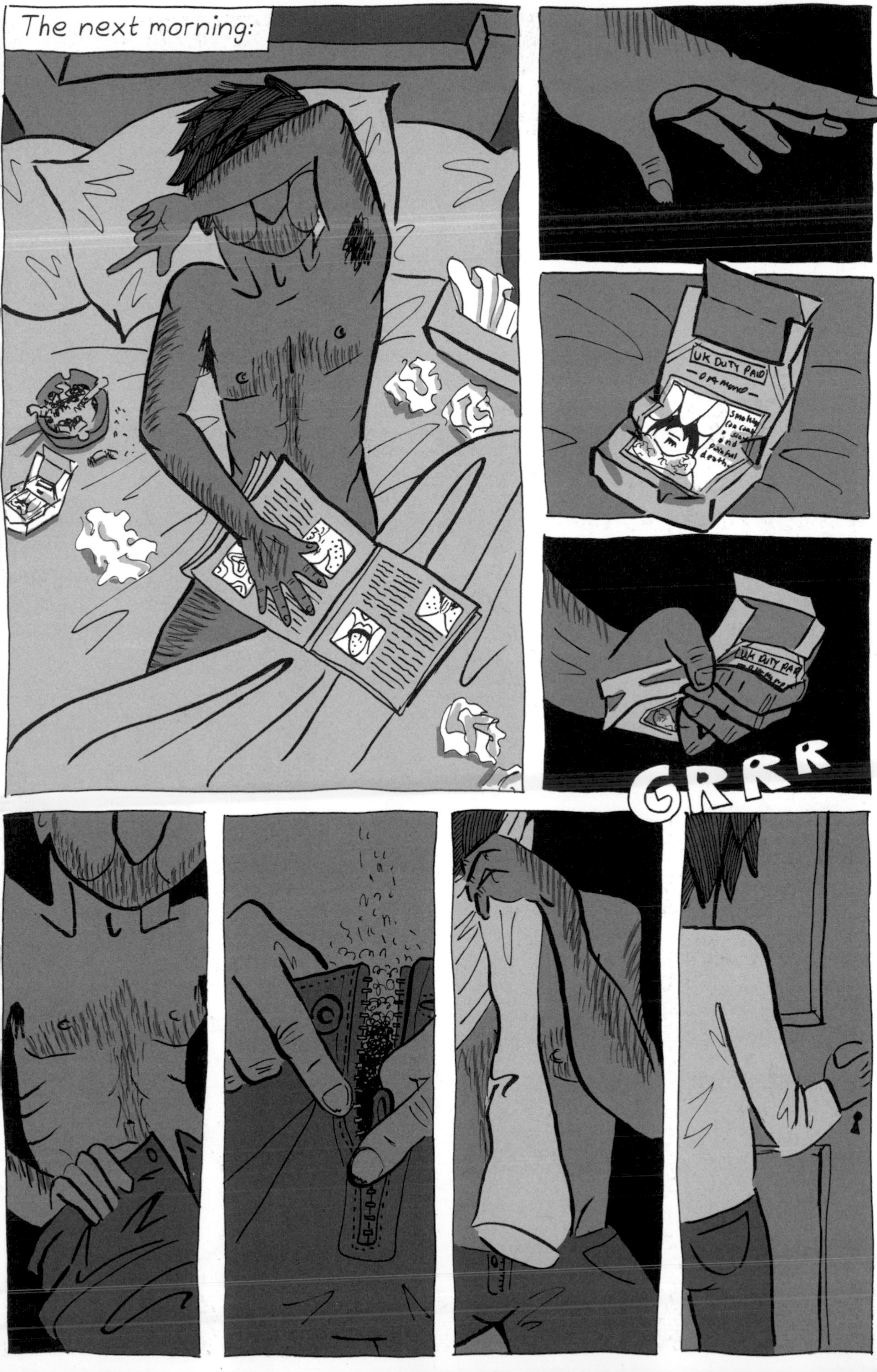
The next morning:
UK DUTY PAID
Smoking can cause a slow and painful death.
GRRR

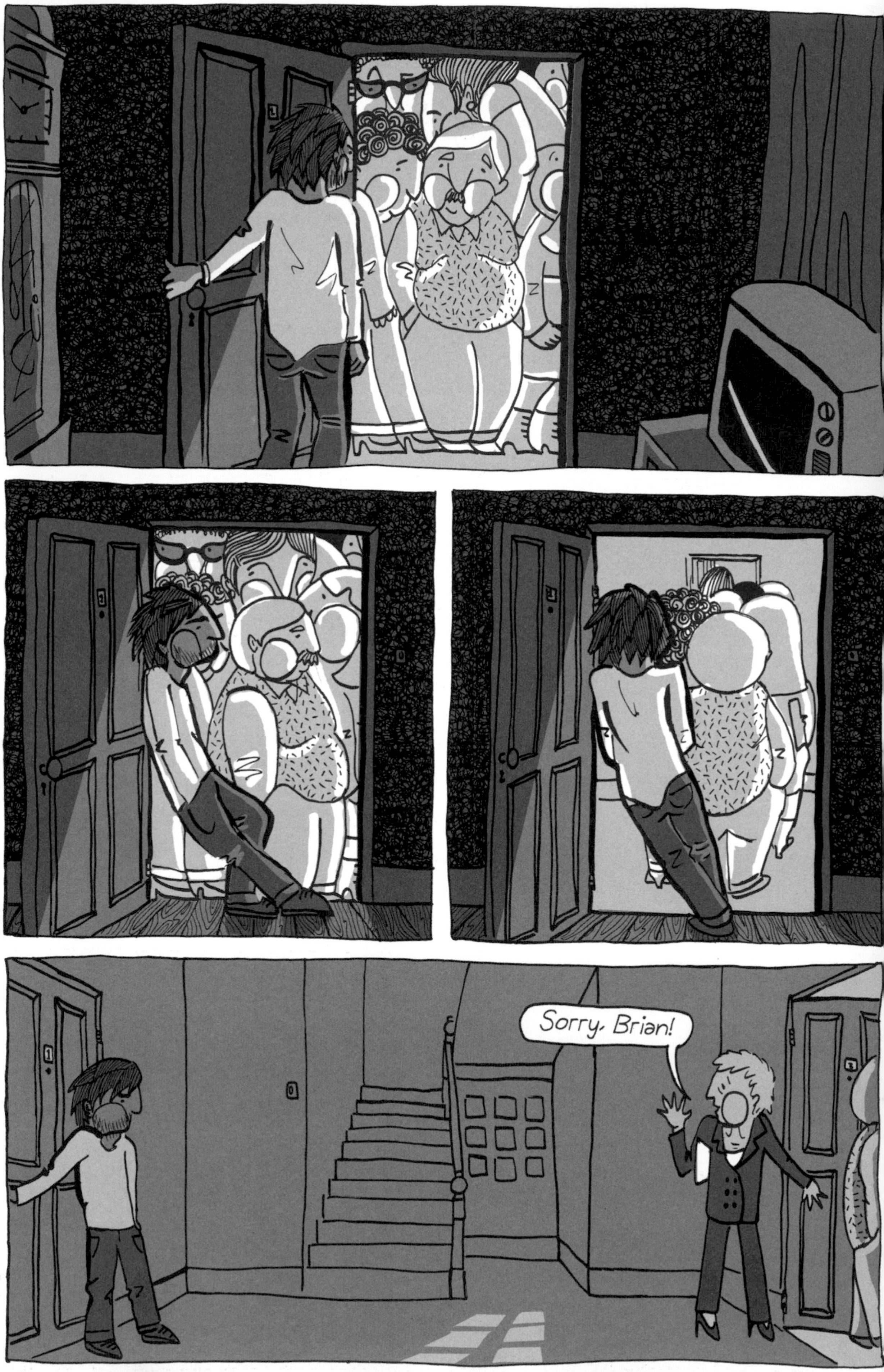
Sorry, Brian!

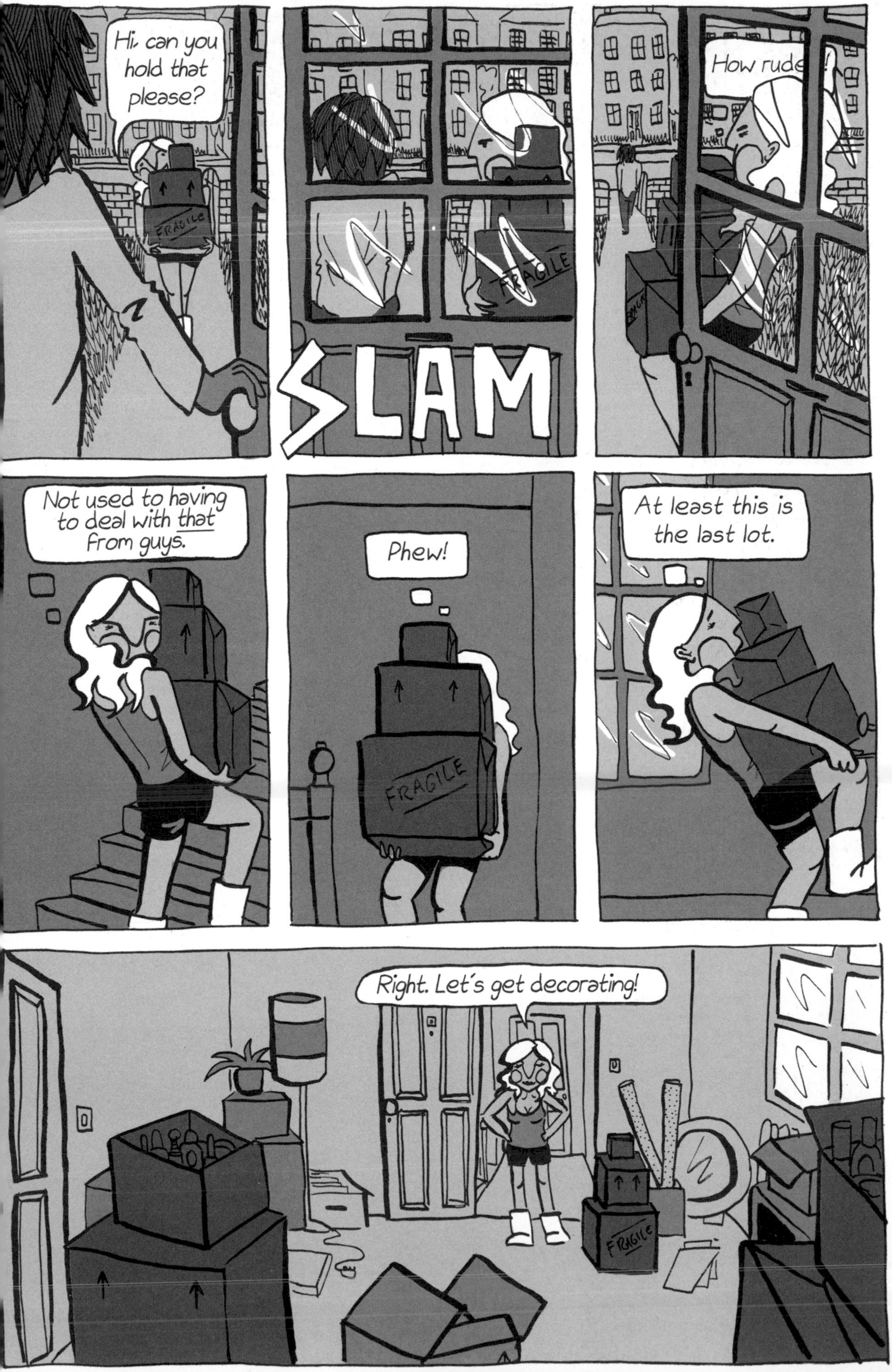
Hi, can you hold that please?
SLAM
How rude!
Not used to having to deal with that from guys.
Phew!
At least this is the last lot.
Right. Let's get decorating!

Chapter Two

Riiiip

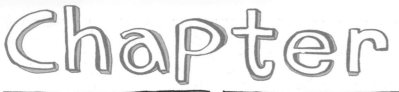

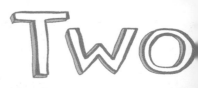

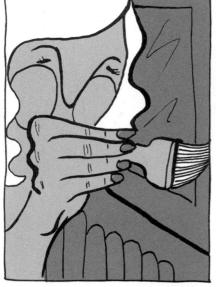

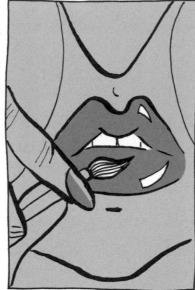

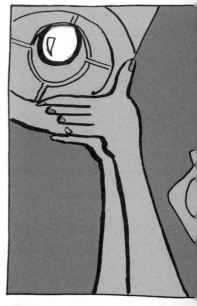

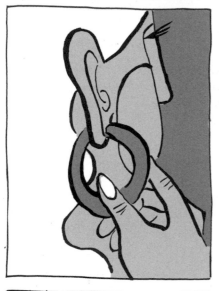

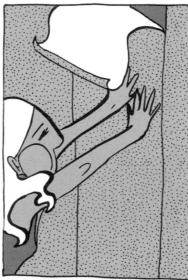

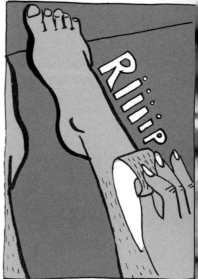

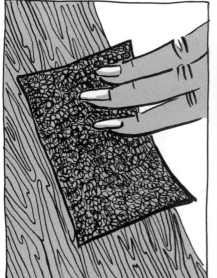

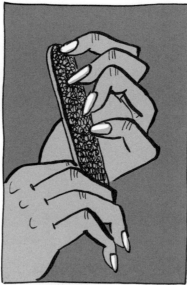

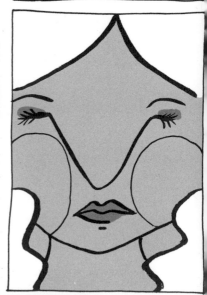

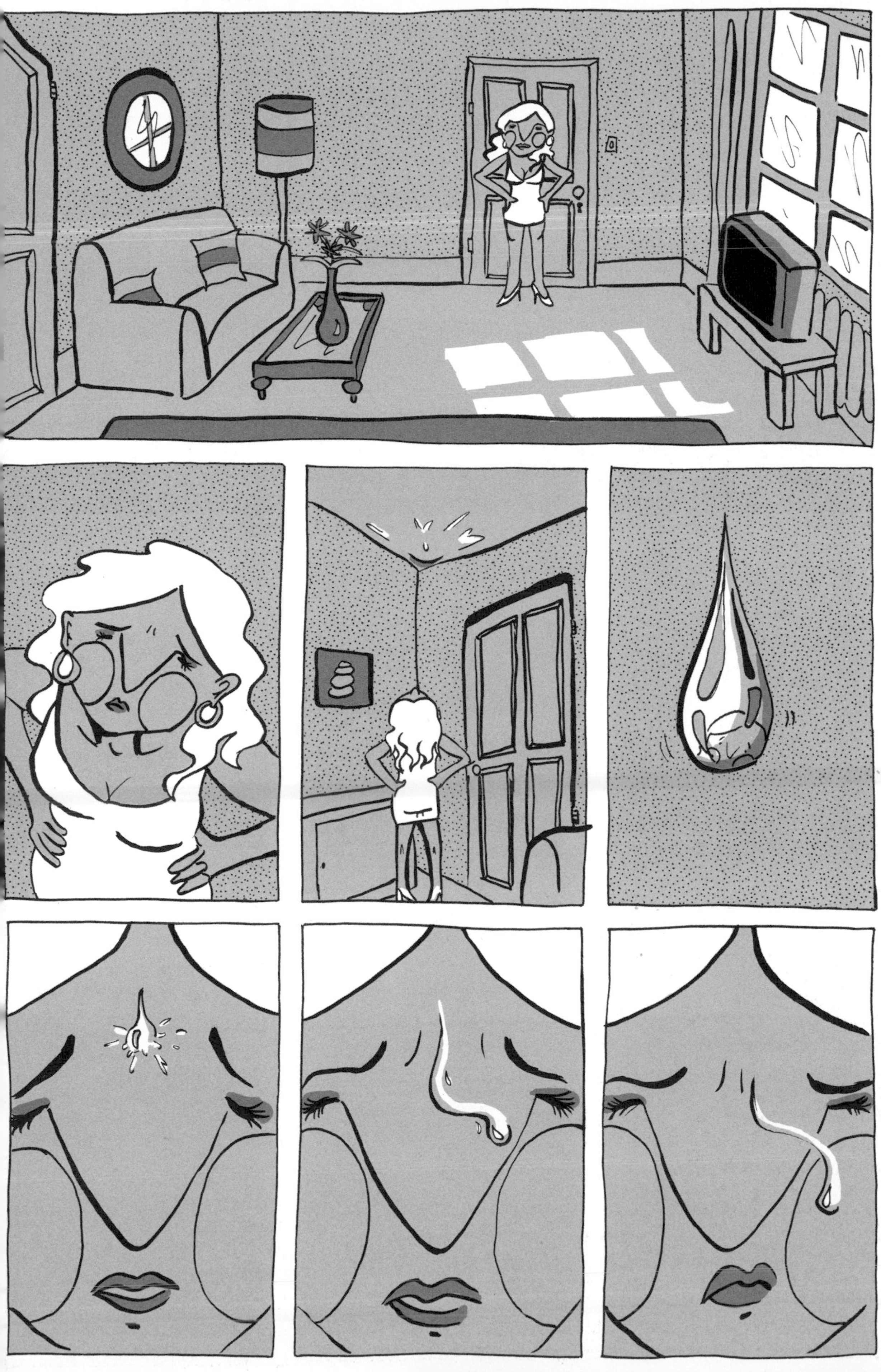

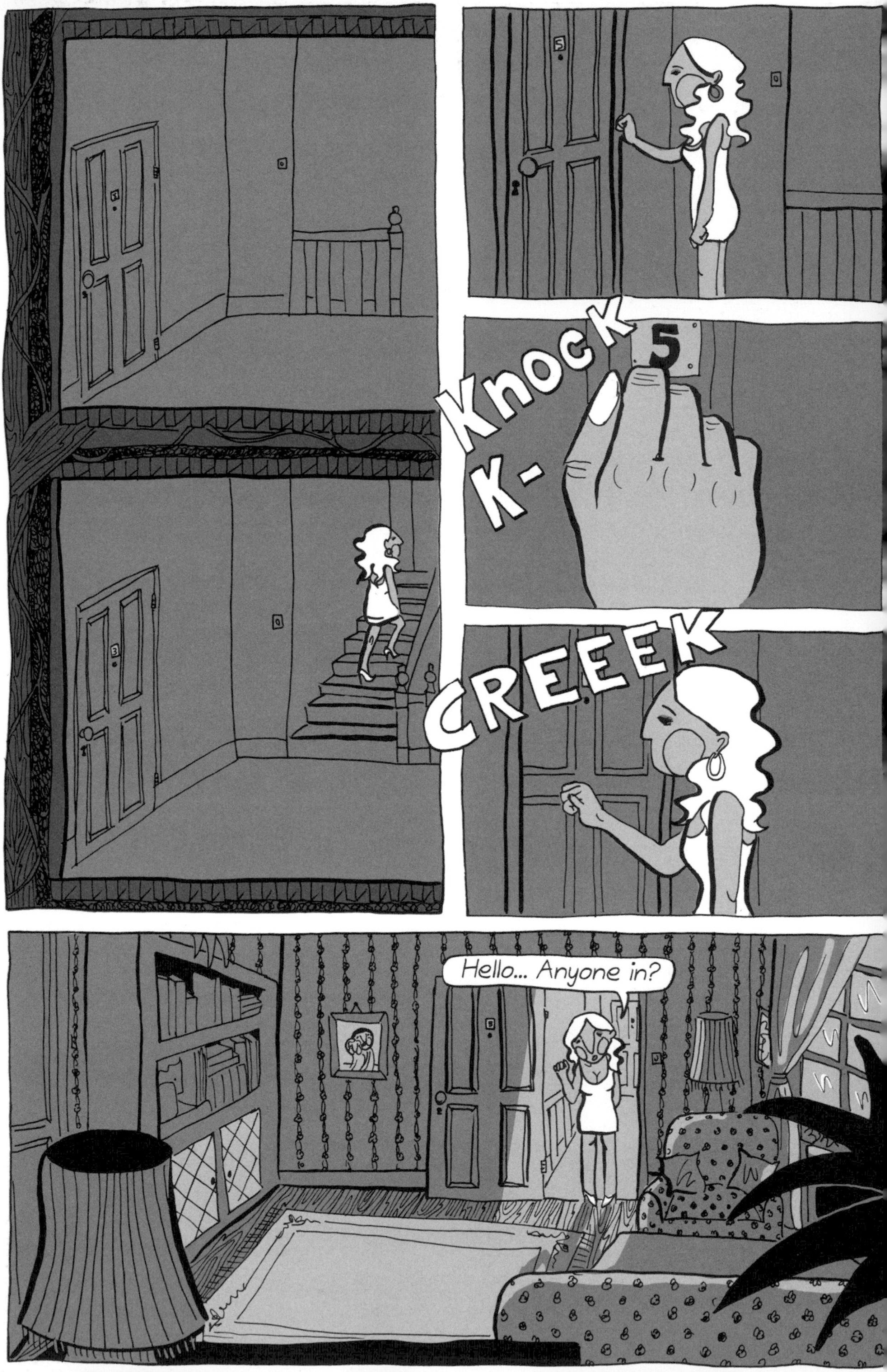
Knock
K-
CREEEK
Hello... Anyone in?

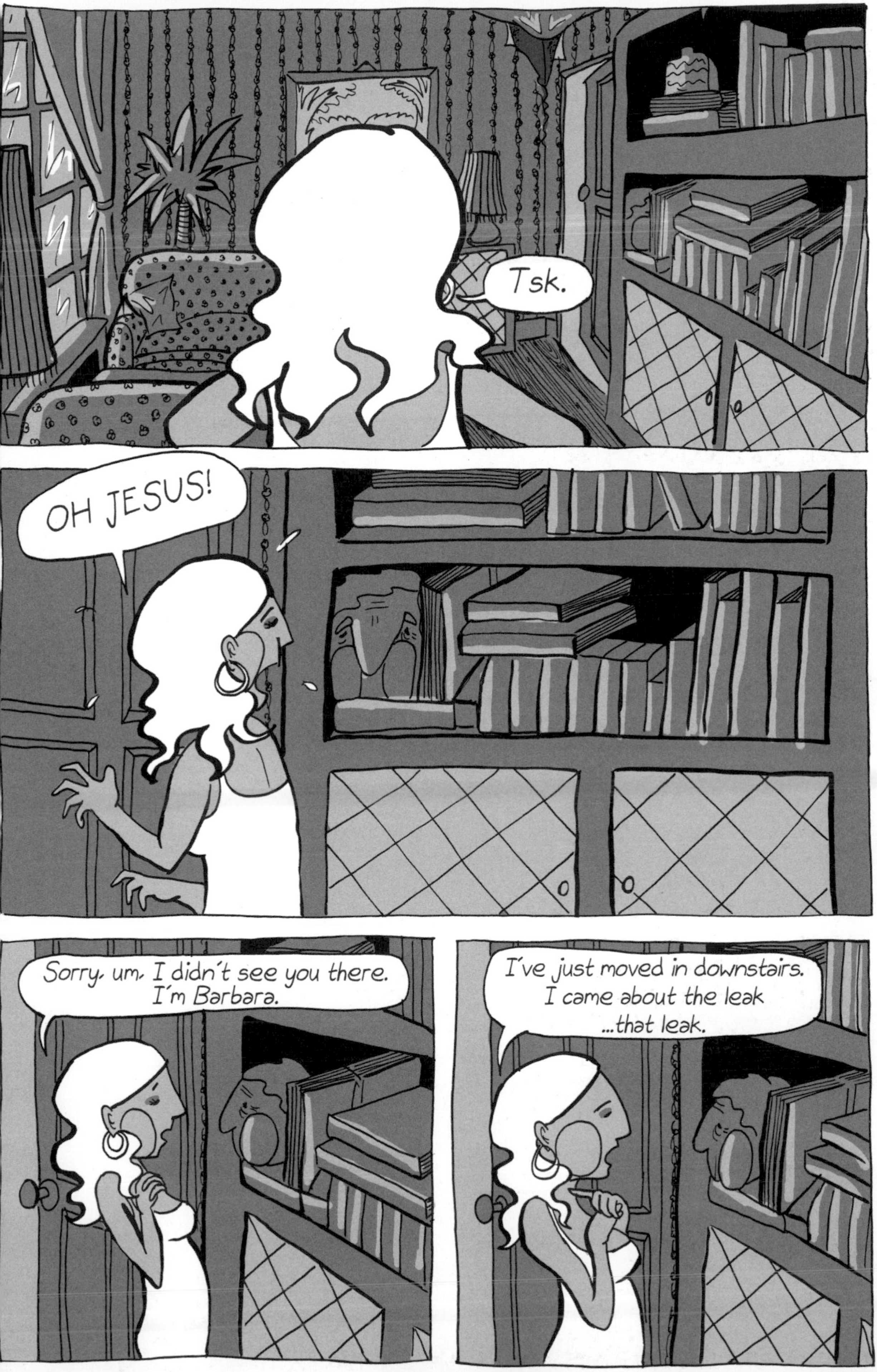
Tsk.
OH JESUS!
Sorry, um, I didn't see you there. I'm Barbara.
I've just moved in downstairs. I came about the leak ...that leak.

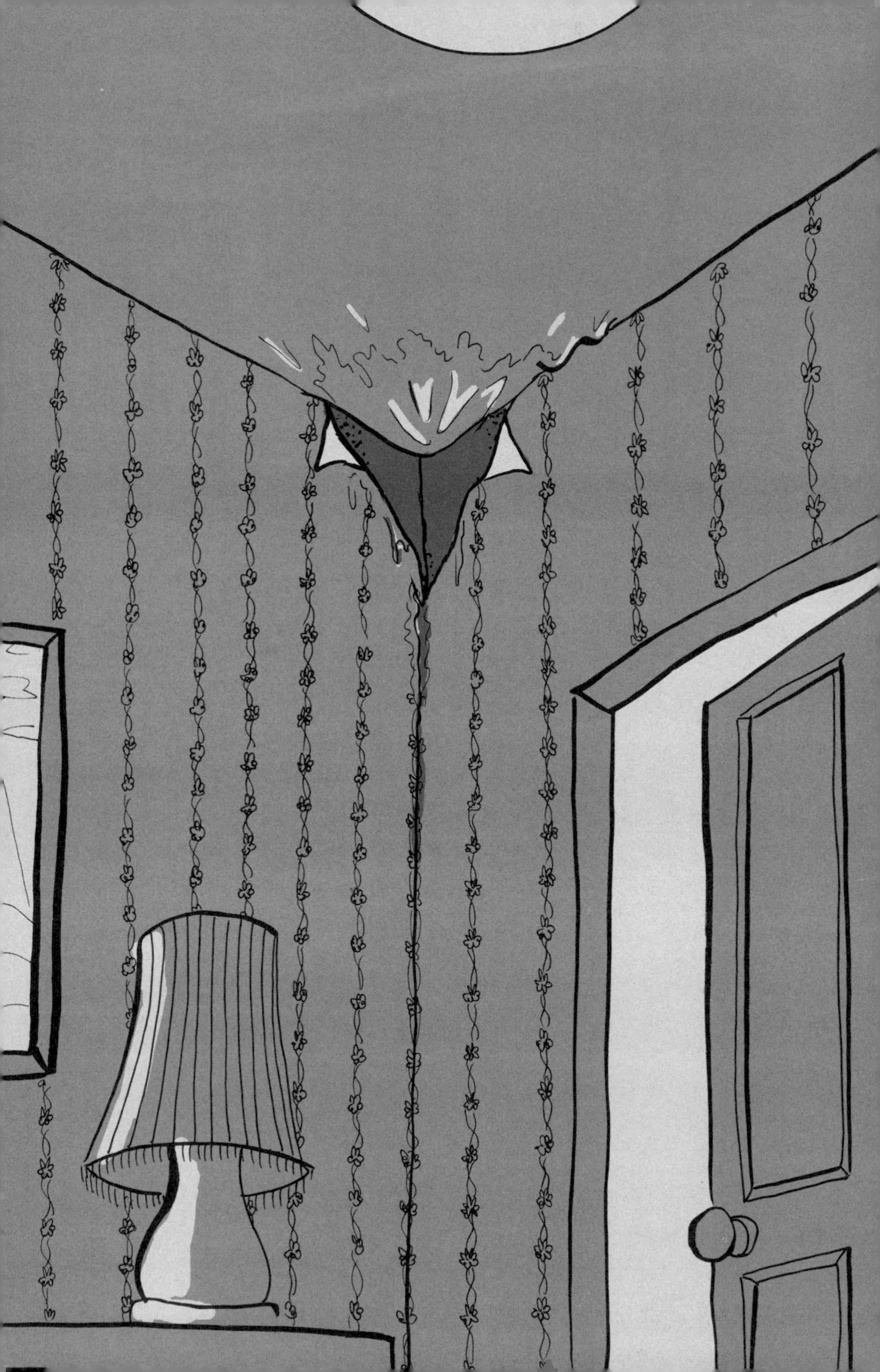

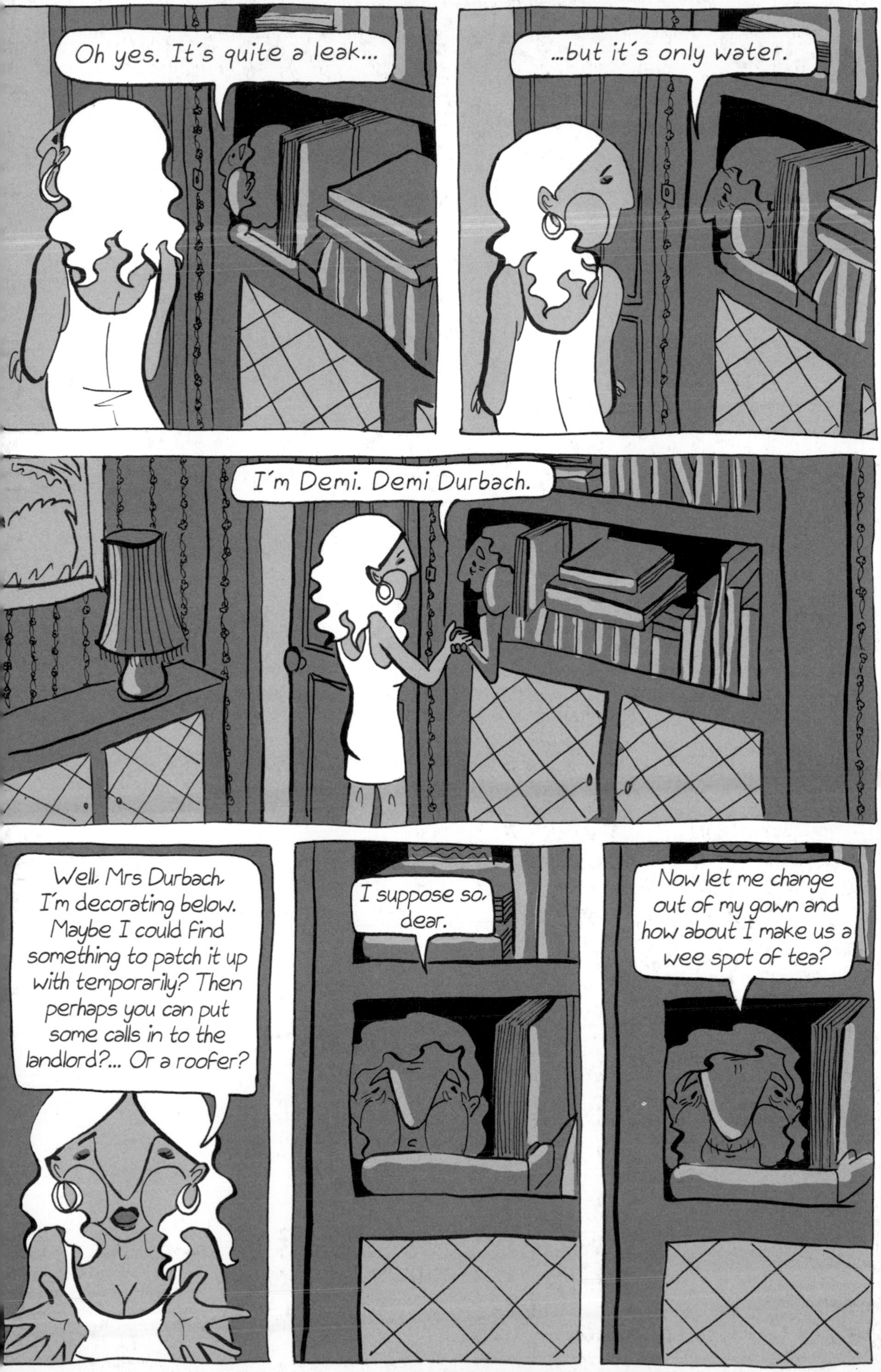

Oh yes. It's quite a leak...
...but it's only water.
I'm Demi. Demi Durbach.
Well, Mrs Durbach, I'm decorating below. Maybe I could find something to patch it up with temporarily? Then perhaps you can put some calls in to the landlord?... Or a roofer?
I suppose so, dear.
Now let me change out of my gown and how about I make us a wee spot of tea?

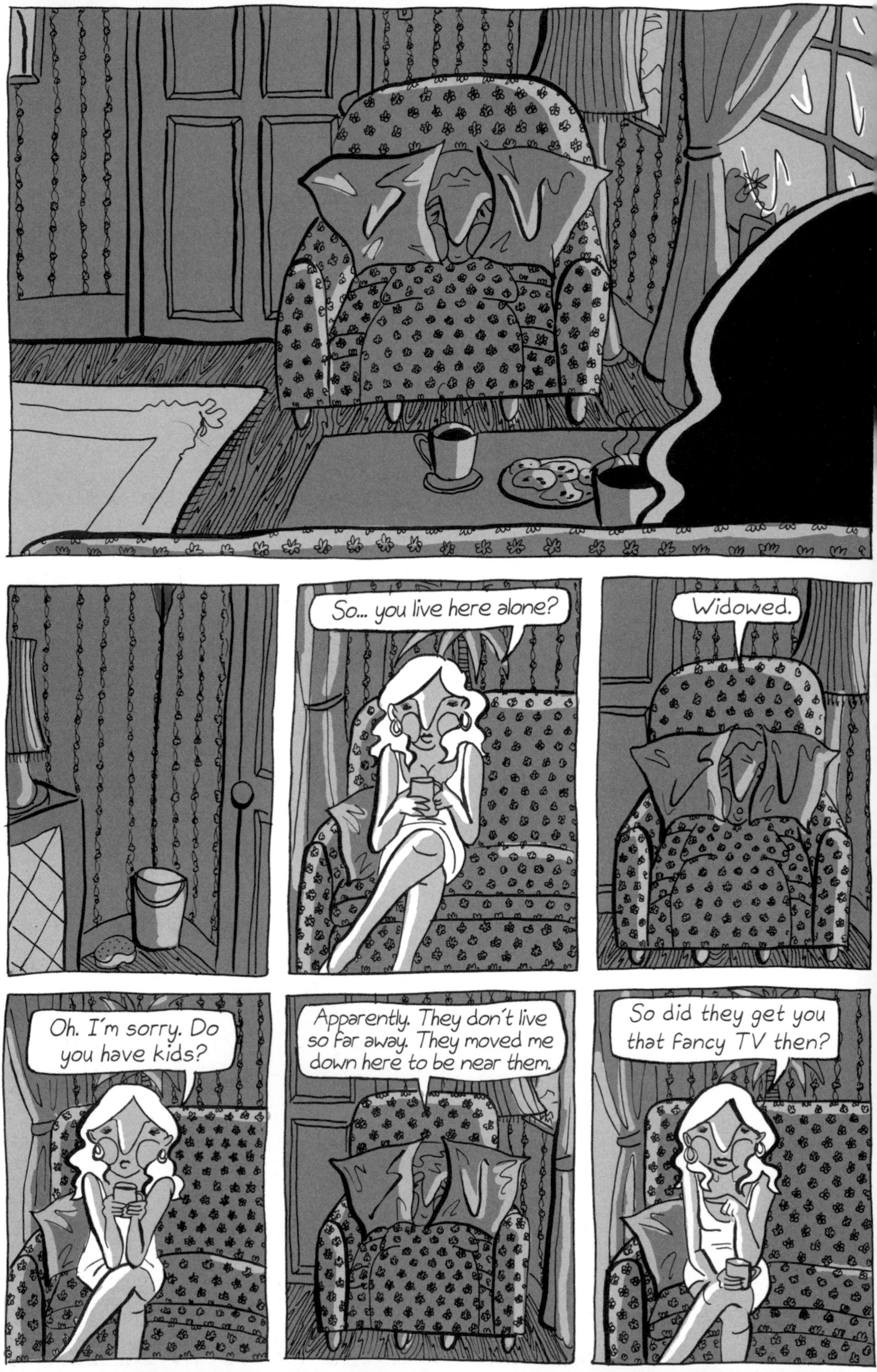
So... you live here alone?
Widowed.
Oh. I'm sorry. Do you have kids?
Apparently. They don't live so far away. They moved me down here to be near them.
So did they get you that fancy TV then?

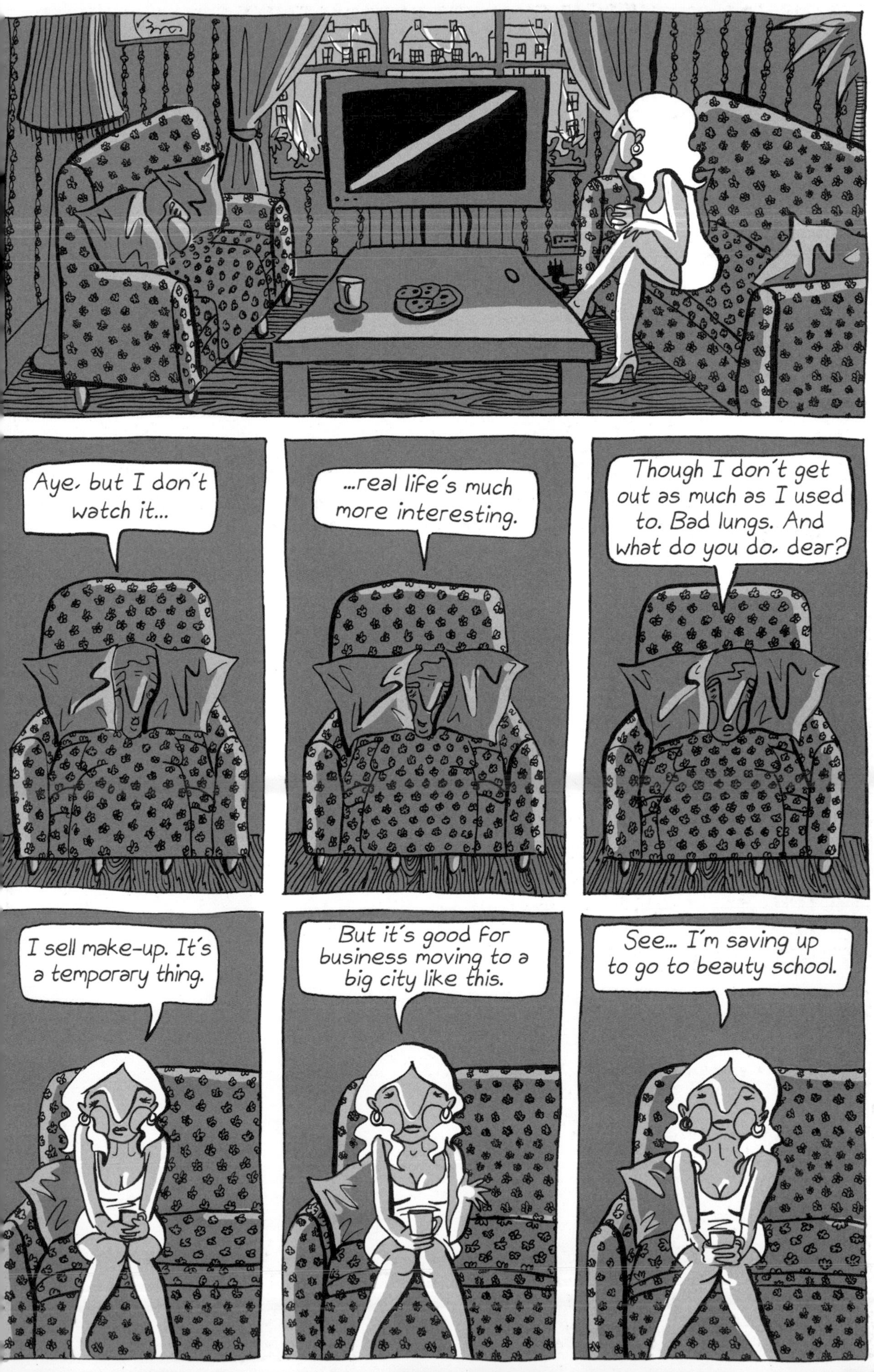
Aye, but I don't watch it...
...real life's much more interesting.
Though I don't get out as much as I used to. Bad lungs. And what do you do, dear?
I sell make-up. It's a temporary thing.
But it's good for business moving to a big city like this.
See... I'm saving up to go to beauty school.

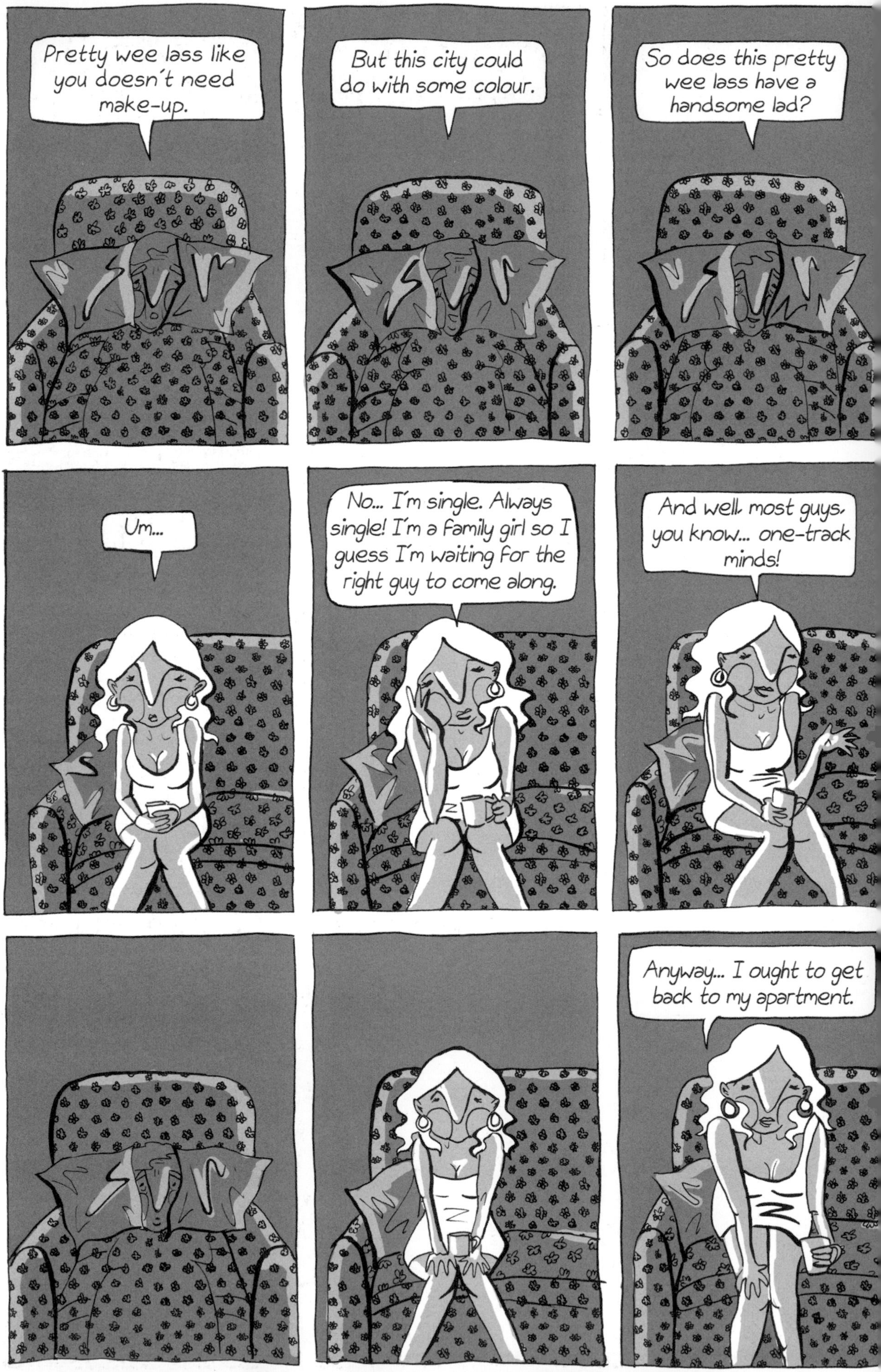
Pretty wee lass like you doesn't need make-up.
But this city could do with some colour.
So does this pretty wee lass have a handsome lad?
Um...
No... I'm single. Always single! I'm a family girl so I guess I'm waiting for the right guy to come along.
And well, most guys, you know... one-track minds!
Anyway... I ought to get back to my apartment.

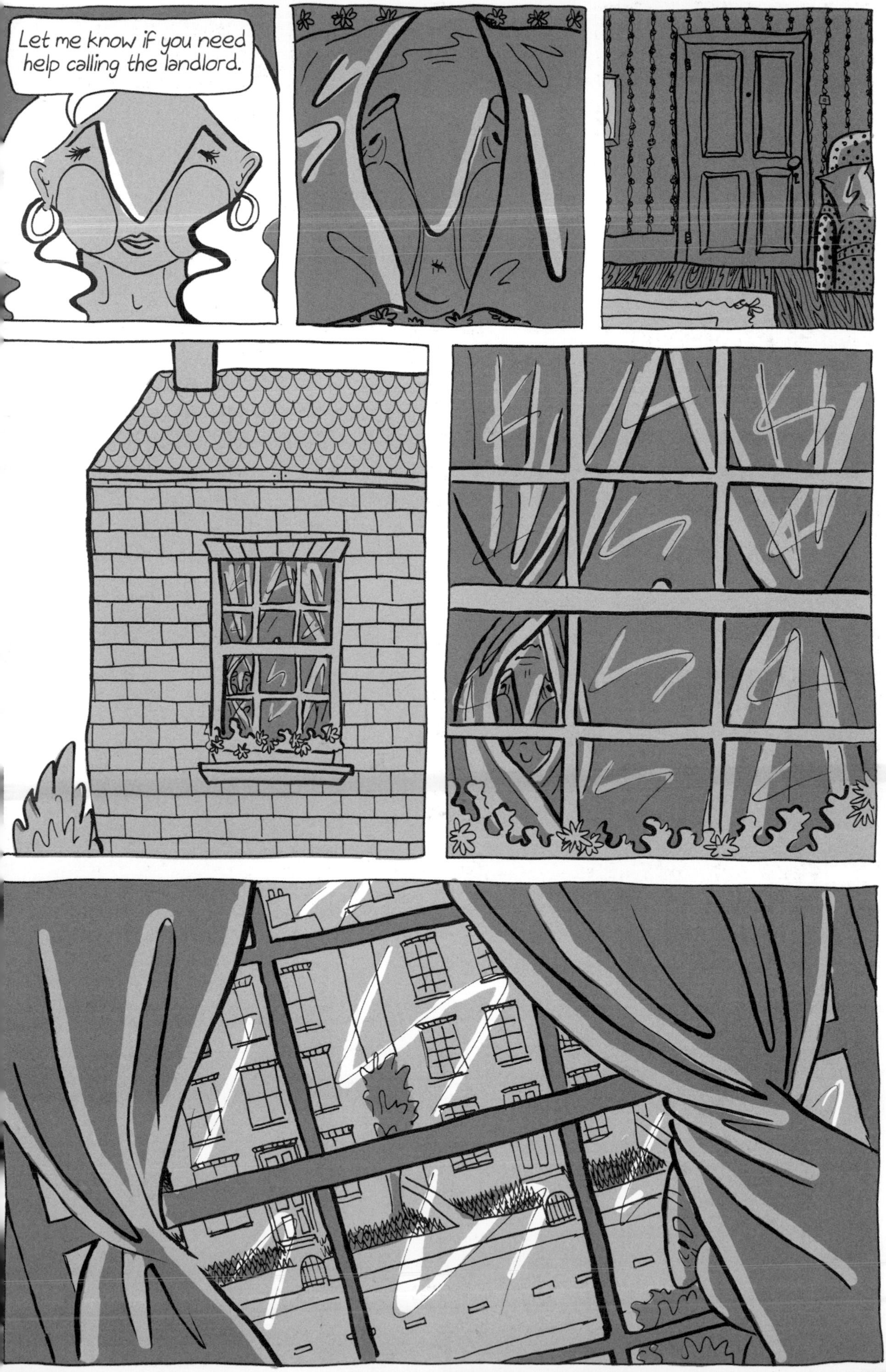
Let me know if you need help calling the landlord.

The Building of Rottin Road, 1865.

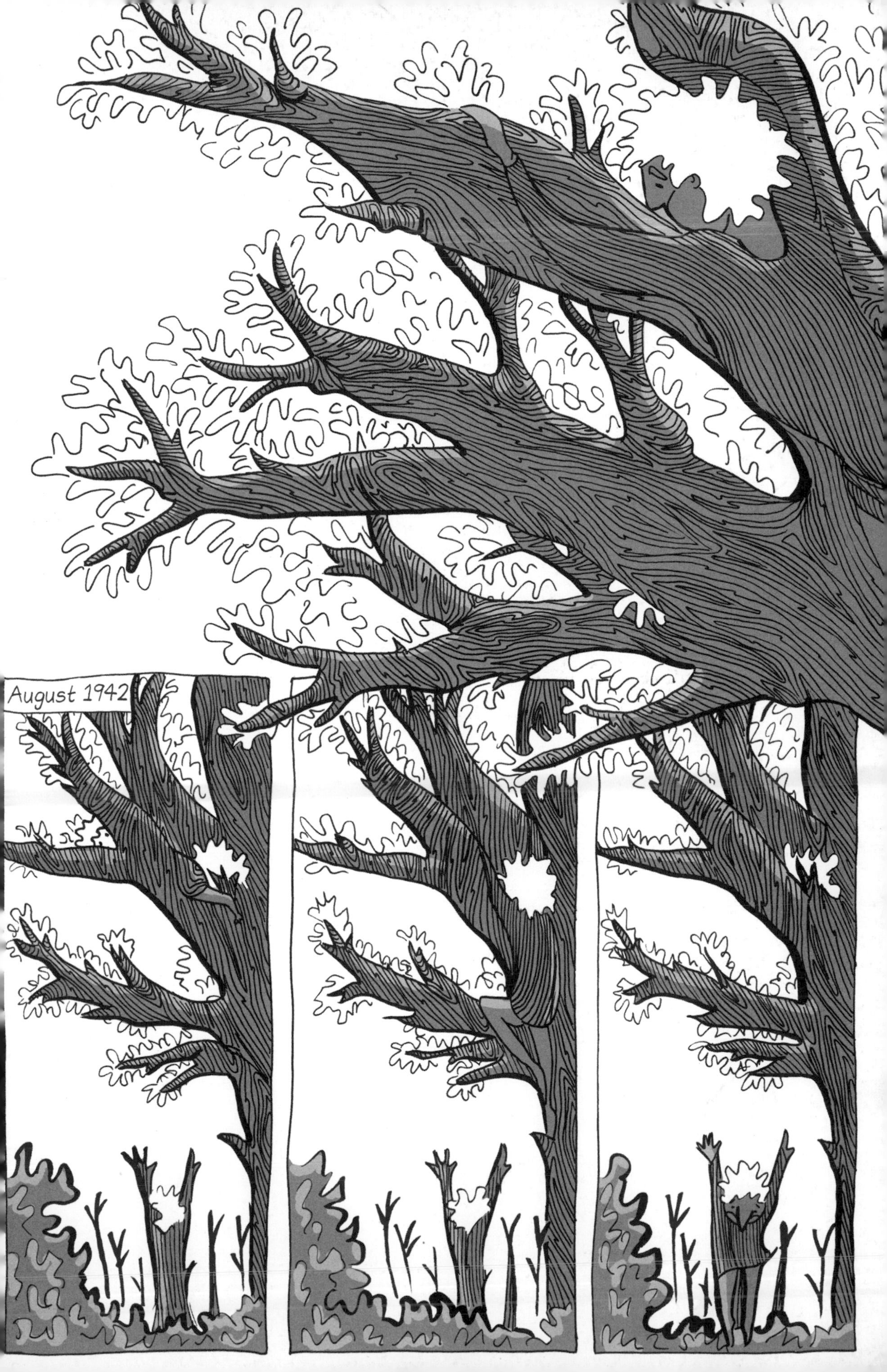
August 1942

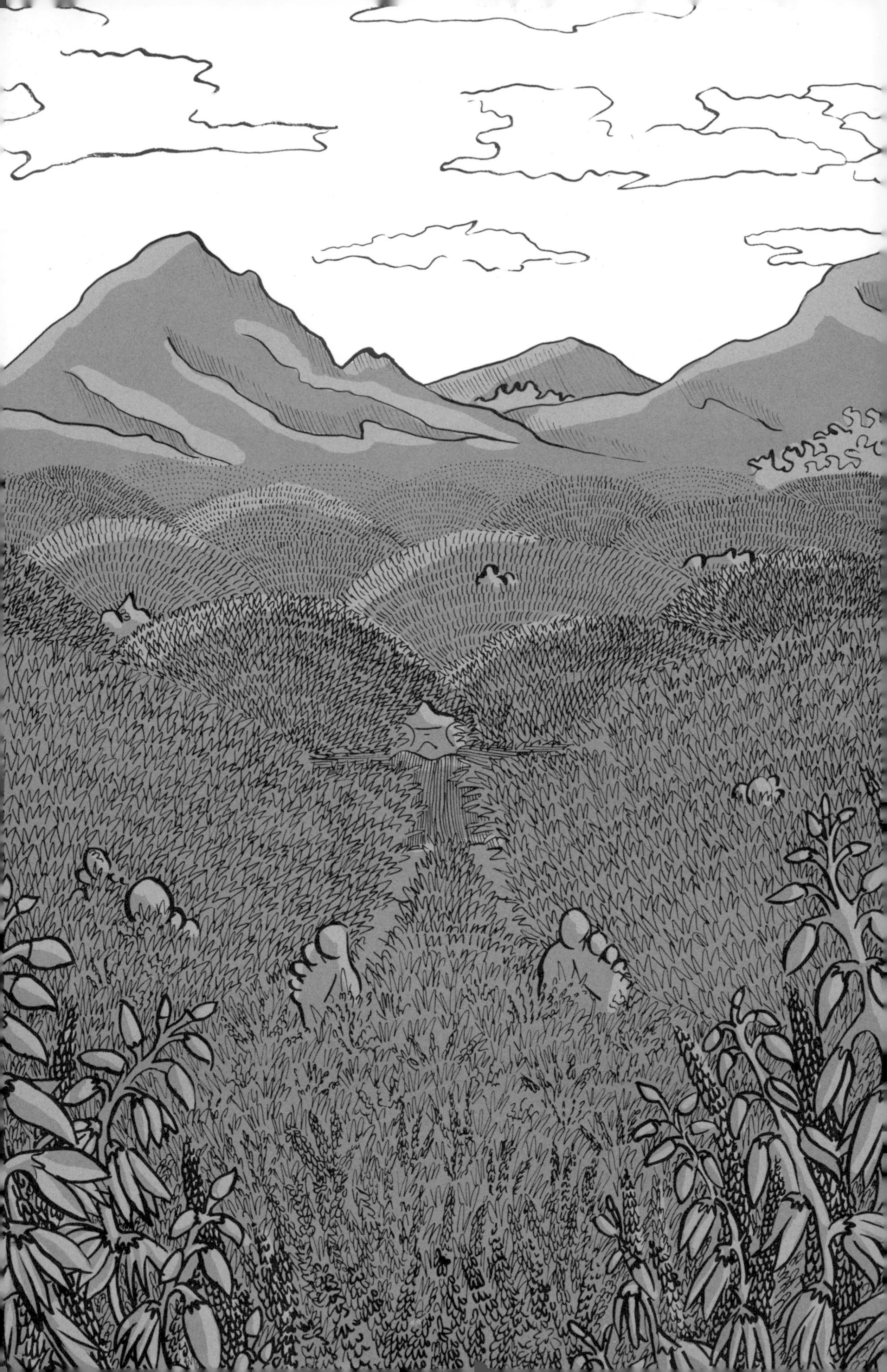

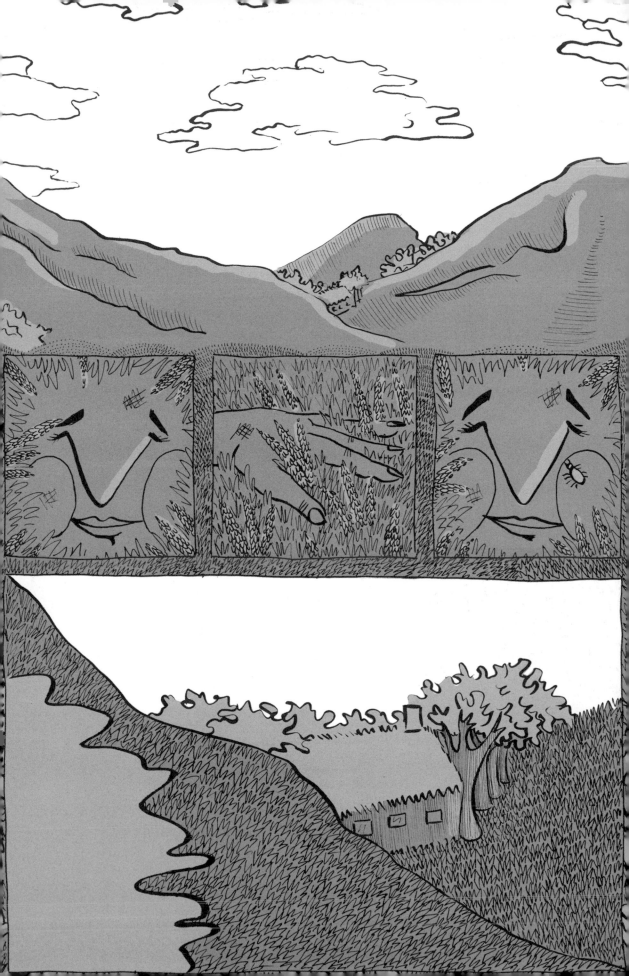

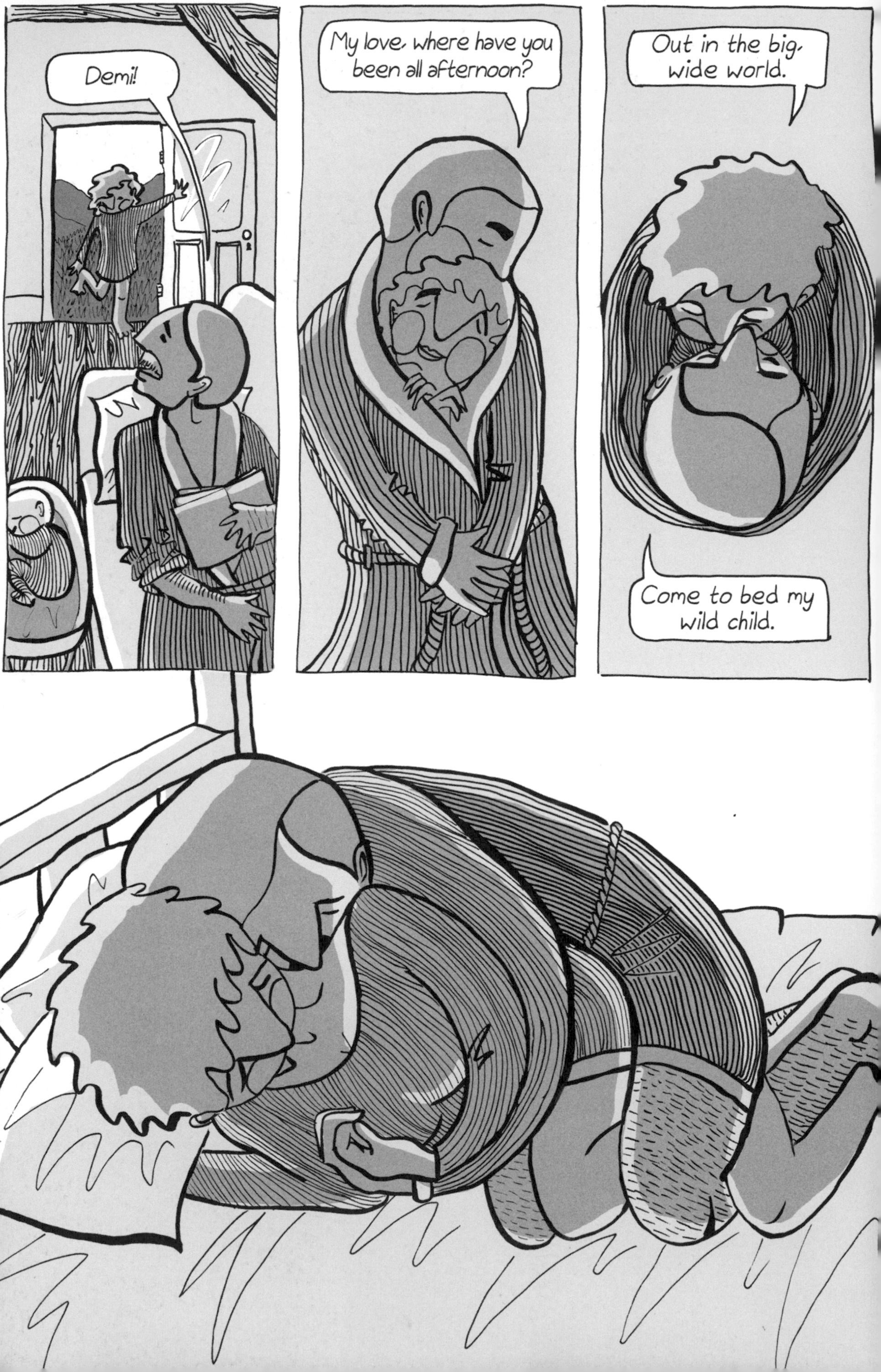
Demi!
My love, where have you been all afternoon?
Out in the big, wide world.
Come to bed my wild child.

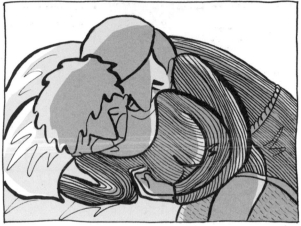

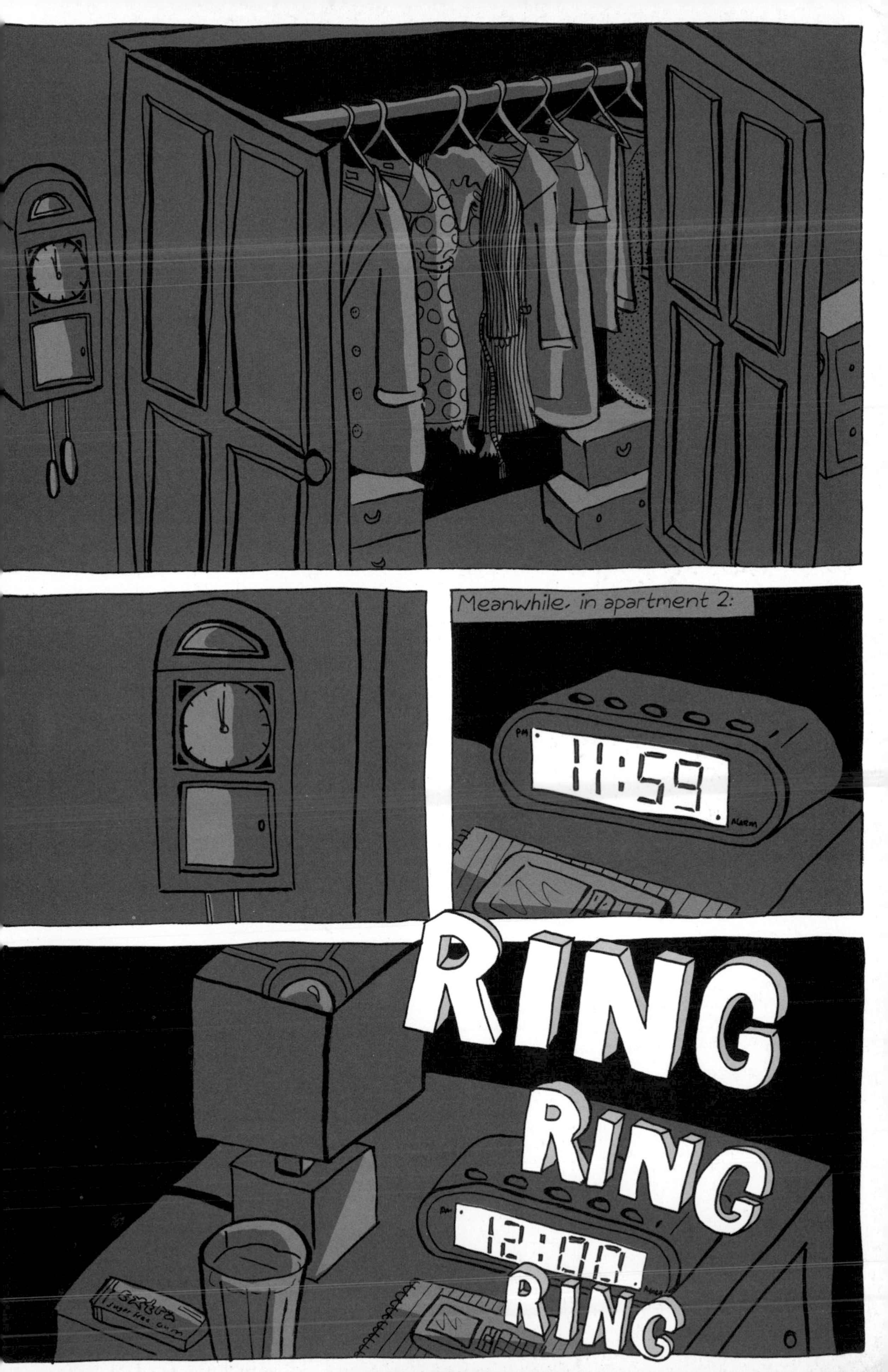
Meanwhile, in apartment 2:
11:59
RING
RING
12:00
RING

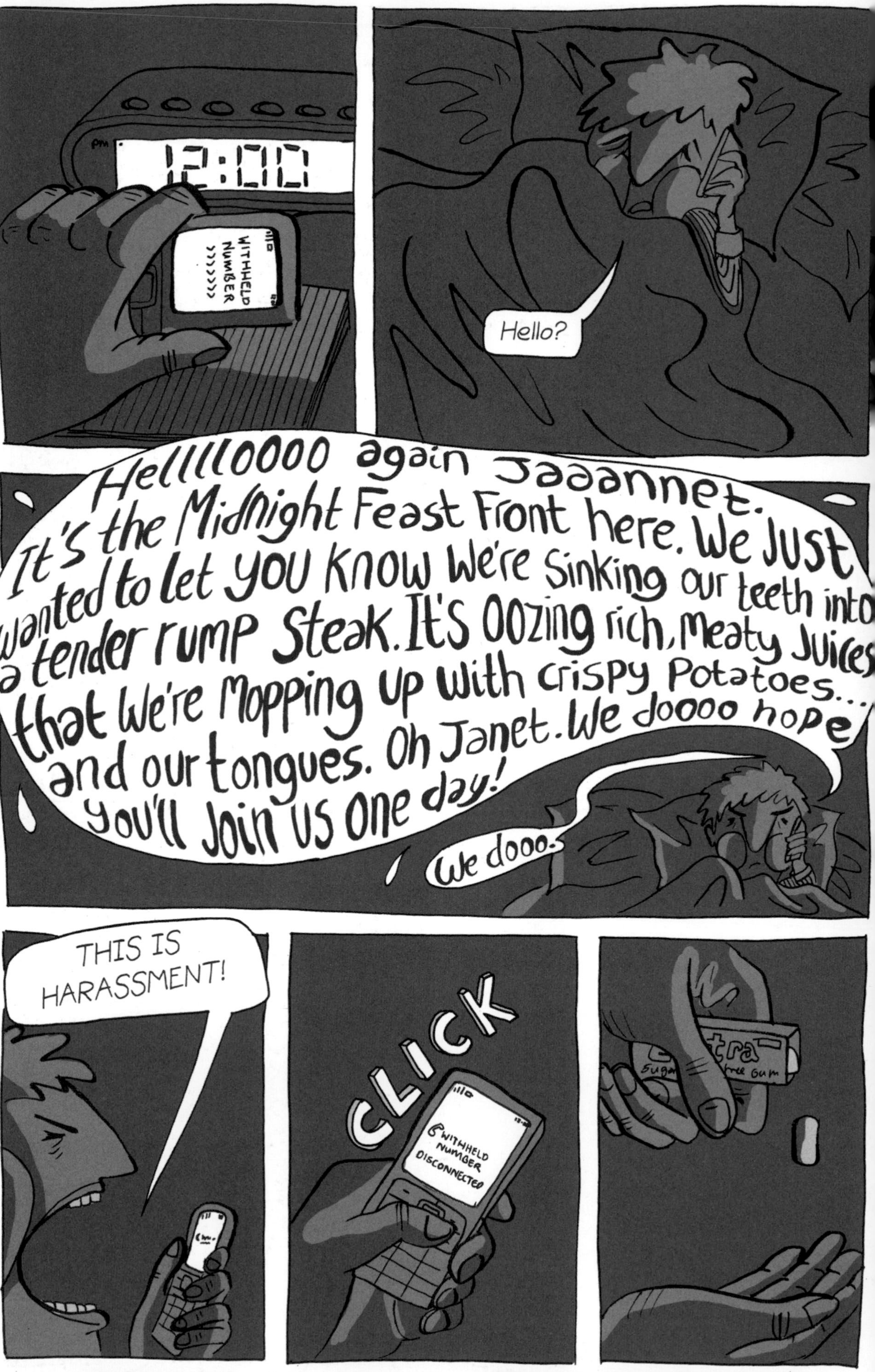
12:00
WITHHELD NUMBER
Hello?
Hellllooooo again Jaaannet. It's the Midnight Feast Front here. We just wanted to let you know we're sinking our teeth into a tender rump steak. It's oozing rich, meaty juices that we're mopping up with crispy potatoes... and our tongues. Oh Janet. We doooo hope you'll join us one day!
We dooo.
THIS IS HARASSMENT!
CLICK
WITHHELD NUMBER DISCONNECTED
Extra
Sugar free gum

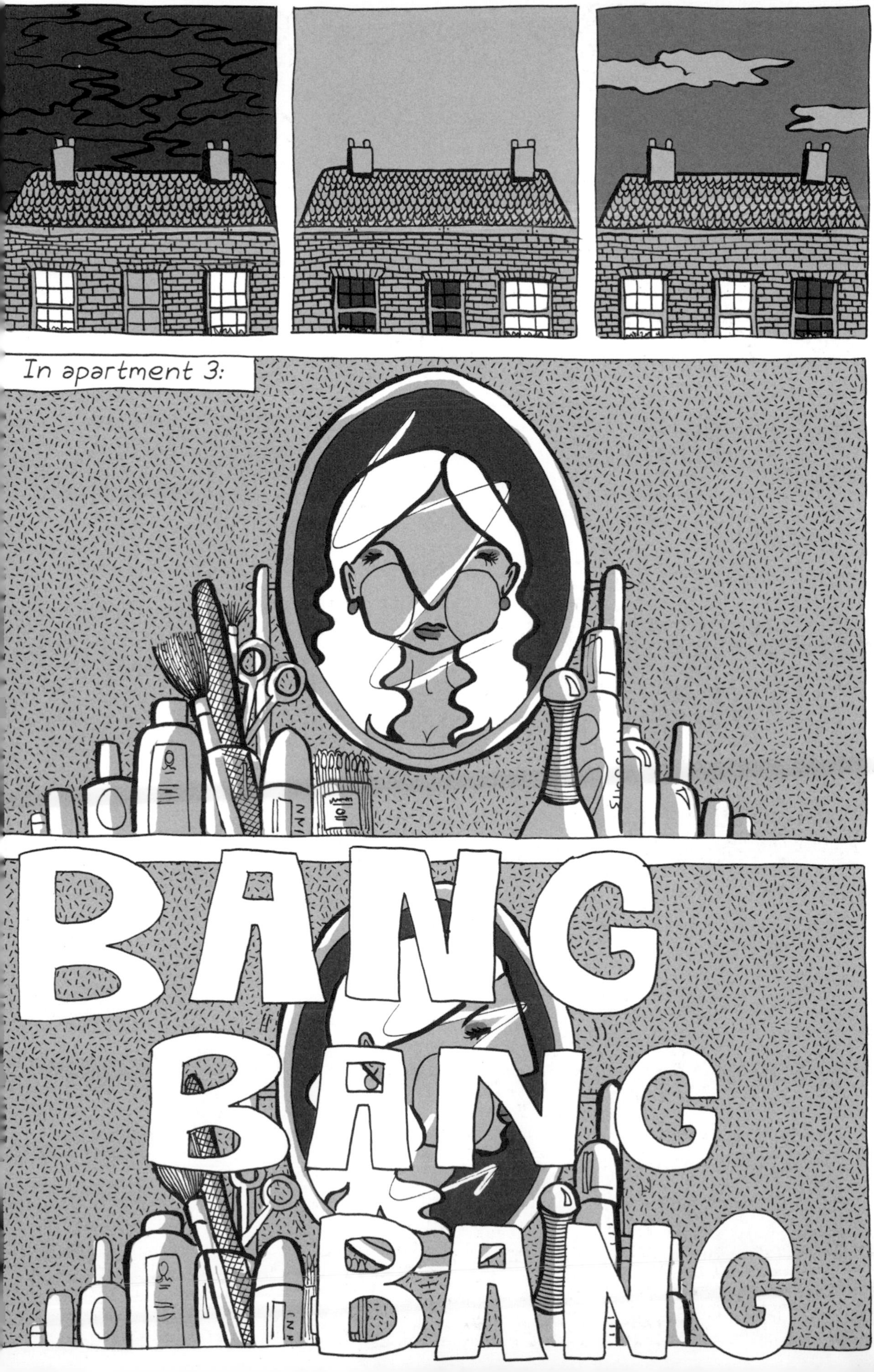
In apartment 3:
BANG
BANG
BANG

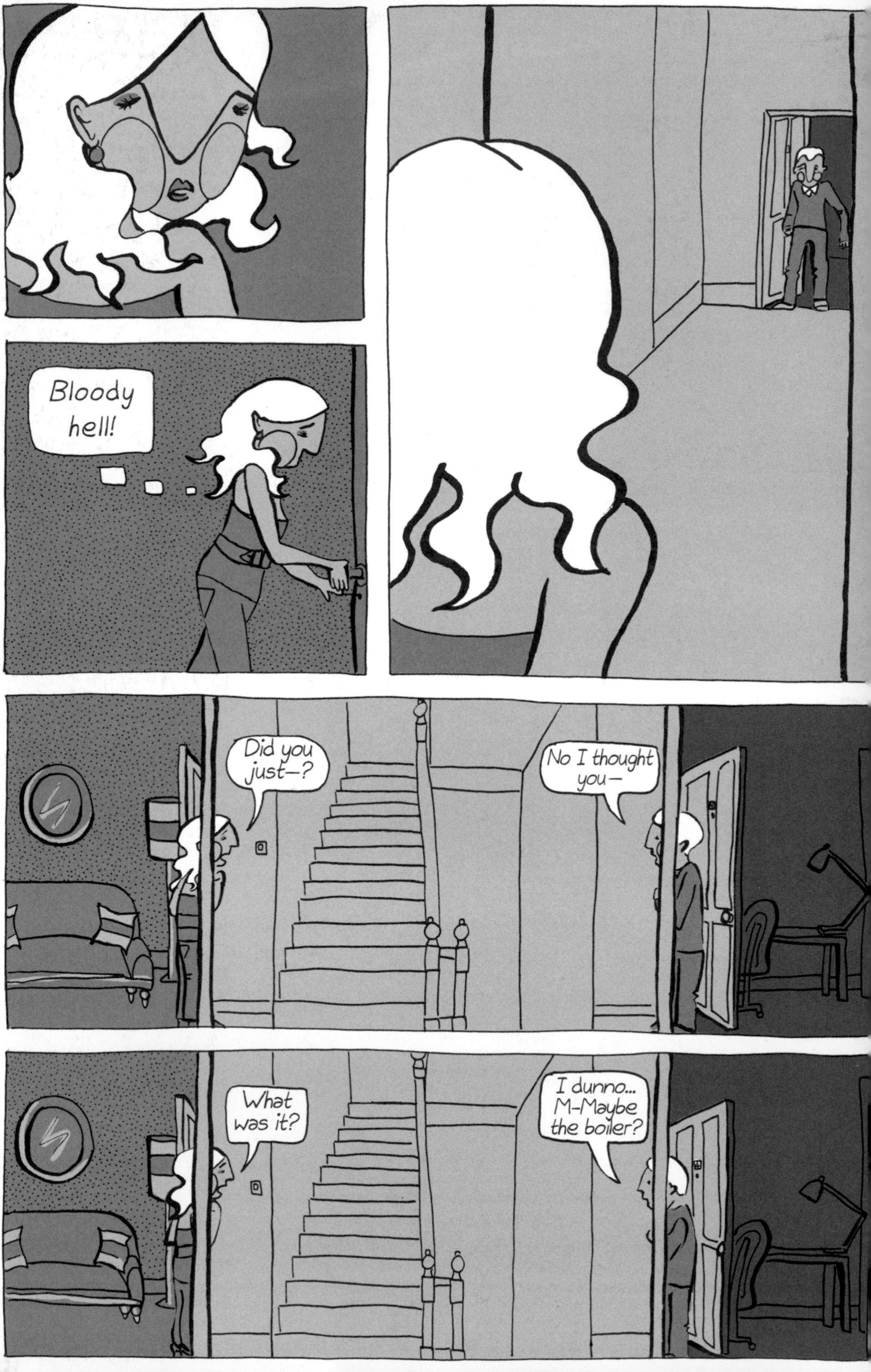
Bloody hell!
Did you just—?
No I thought you—
What was it?
I dunno... M-Maybe the boiler?

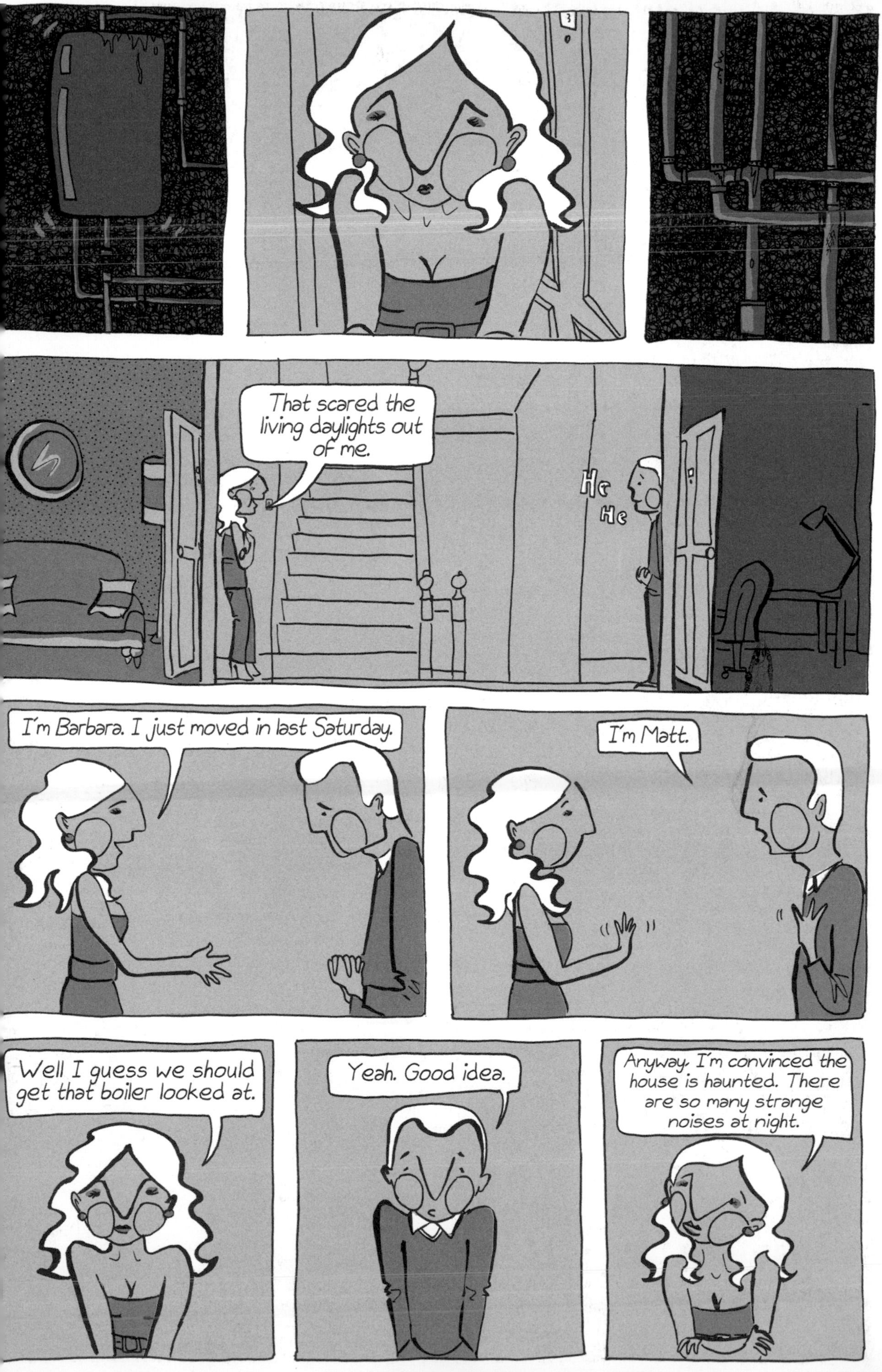

That scared the living daylights out of me.
He He
I'm Barbara. I just moved in last Saturday.
I'm Matt.
Well I guess we should get that boiler looked at.
Yeah. Good idea.
Anyway. I'm convinced the house is haunted. There are so many strange noises at night.

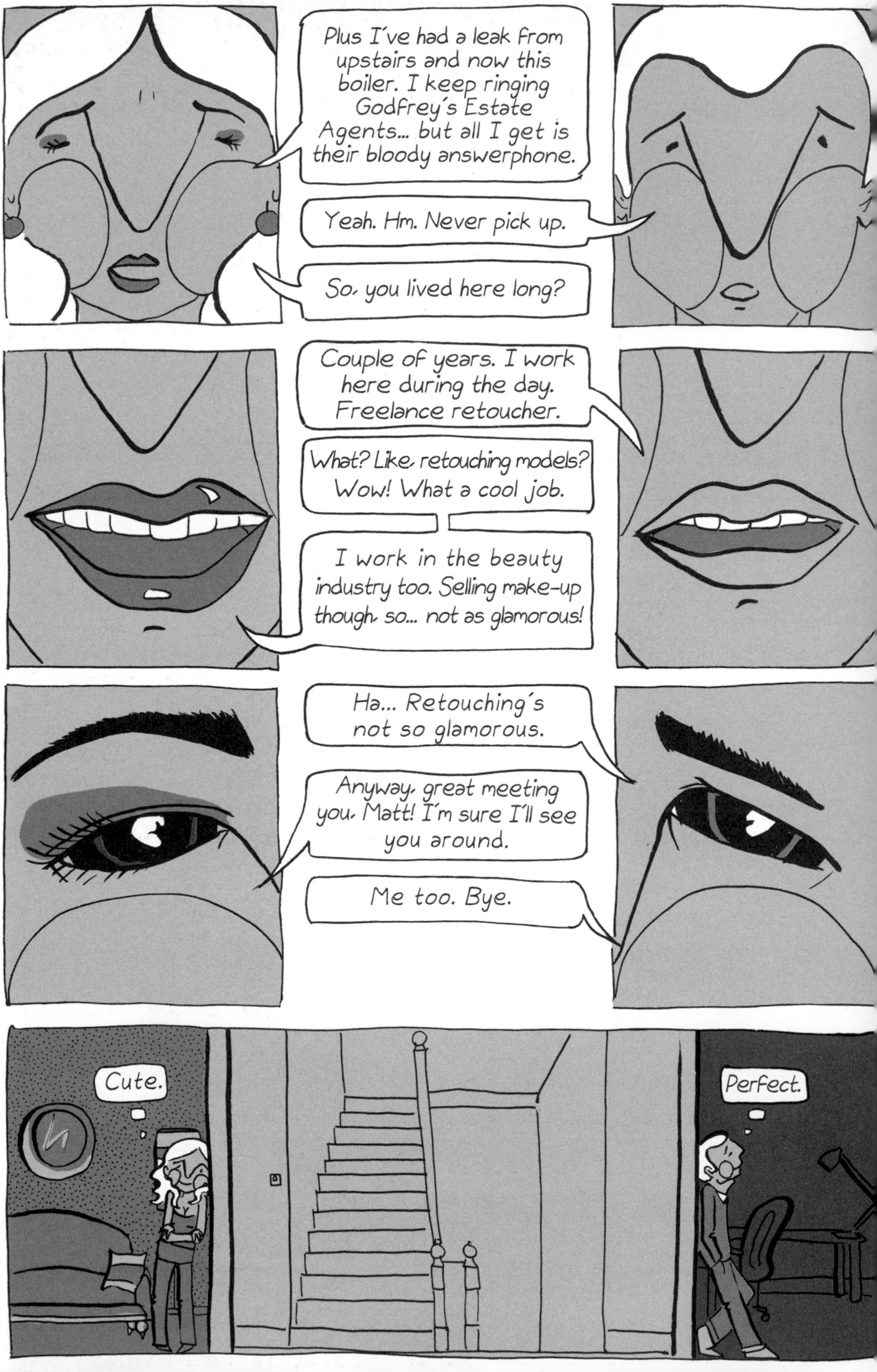
Plus I've had a leak from upstairs and now this boiler. I keep ringing Godfrey's Estate Agents... but all I get is their bloody answerphone.
Yeah. Hm. Never pick up.
So, you lived here long?
Couple of years. I work here during the day. Freelance retoucher.
What? Like, retouching models? Wow! What a cool job.
I work in the beauty industry too. Selling make-up though, so... not as glamorous!
Ha... Retouching's not so glamorous.
Anyway, great meeting you, Matt! I'm sure I'll see you around.
Me too. Bye.
Cute.
Perfect.

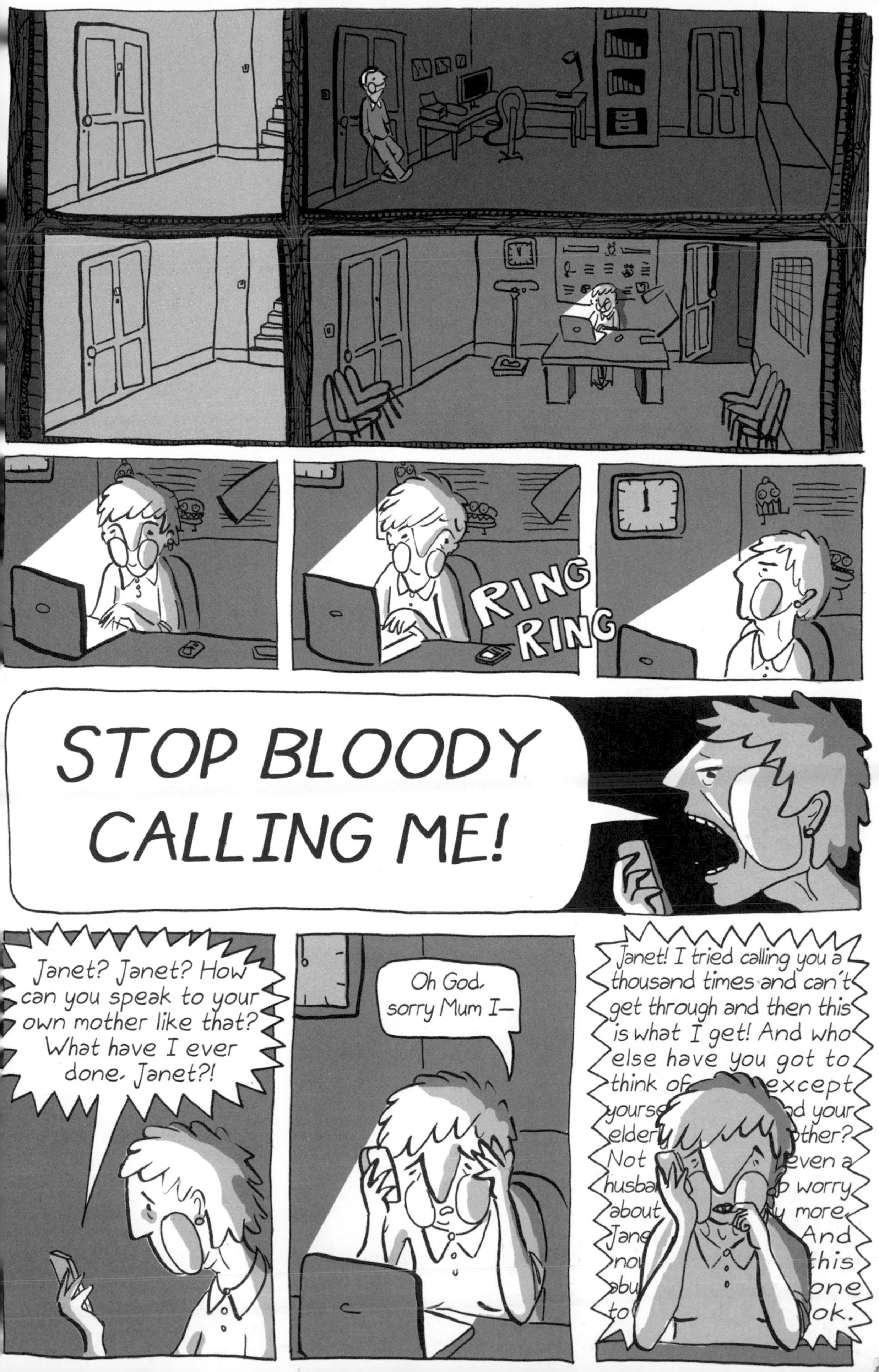
RING
RING
STOP BLOODY CALLING ME!
Janet? Janet? How can you speak to your own mother like that? What have I ever done, Janet?!
Oh God, sorry Mum I—
Janet! I tried calling you a thousand times and can't get through and then this is what I get! And who else have you got to think of except yourse... your elder... Not ... even a husba... worry about ... more. Jane... And no... this abu... one to ... ok.

The Building of Rottin Road, 1865.

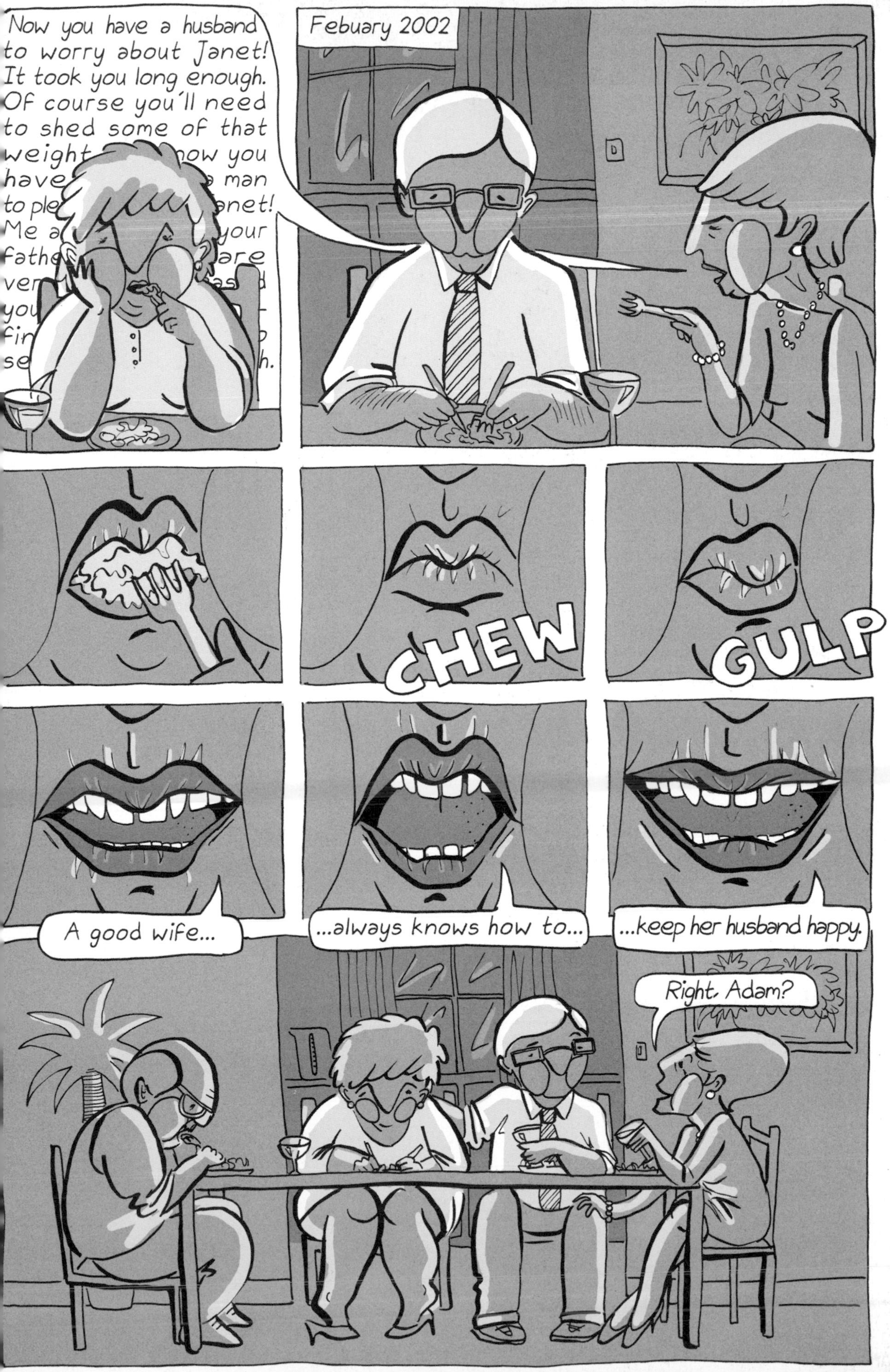
Now you have a husband to worry about Janet! It took you long enough. Of course you´ll need to shed some of that weight
now you
a man
Febuary 2002
CHEW
GULP
A good wife...
...always knows how to...
...keep her husband happy.
Right, Adam?

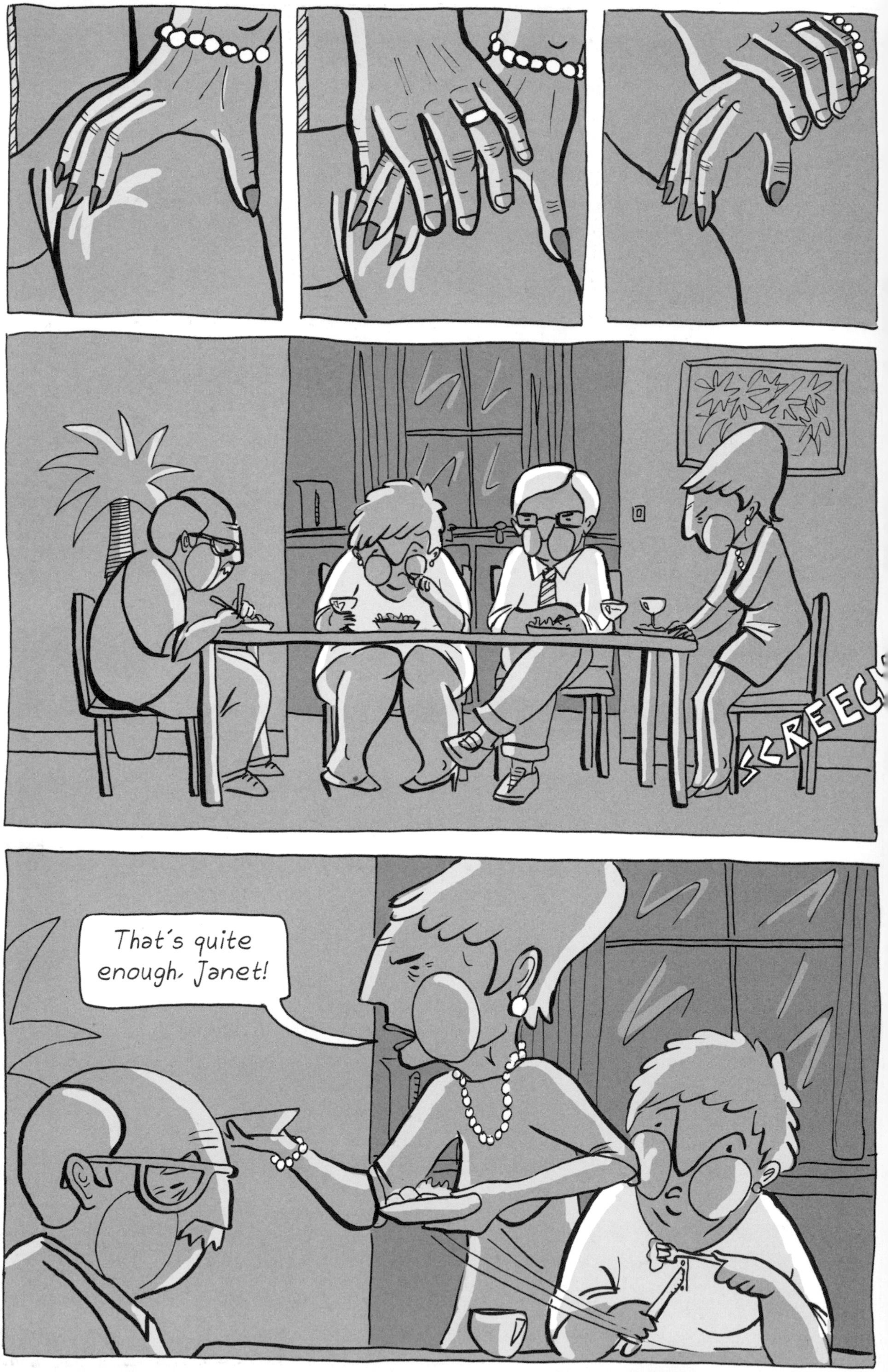
SCREECH
That's quite enough, Janet!

That night:
Your mother's a bit of a bitch.
He
He

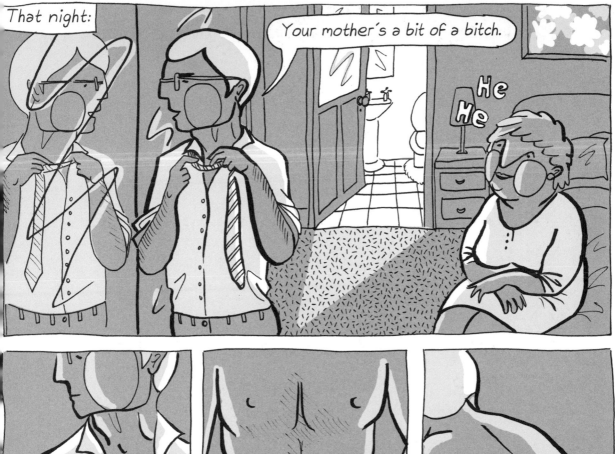

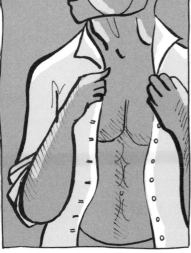

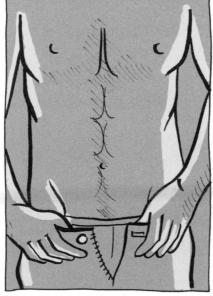

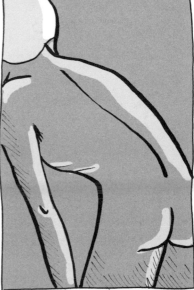

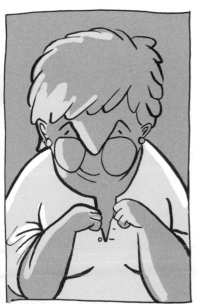

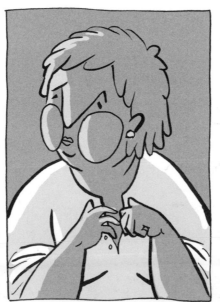

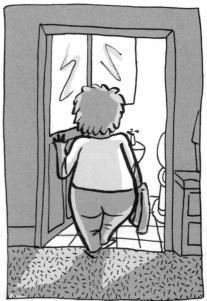

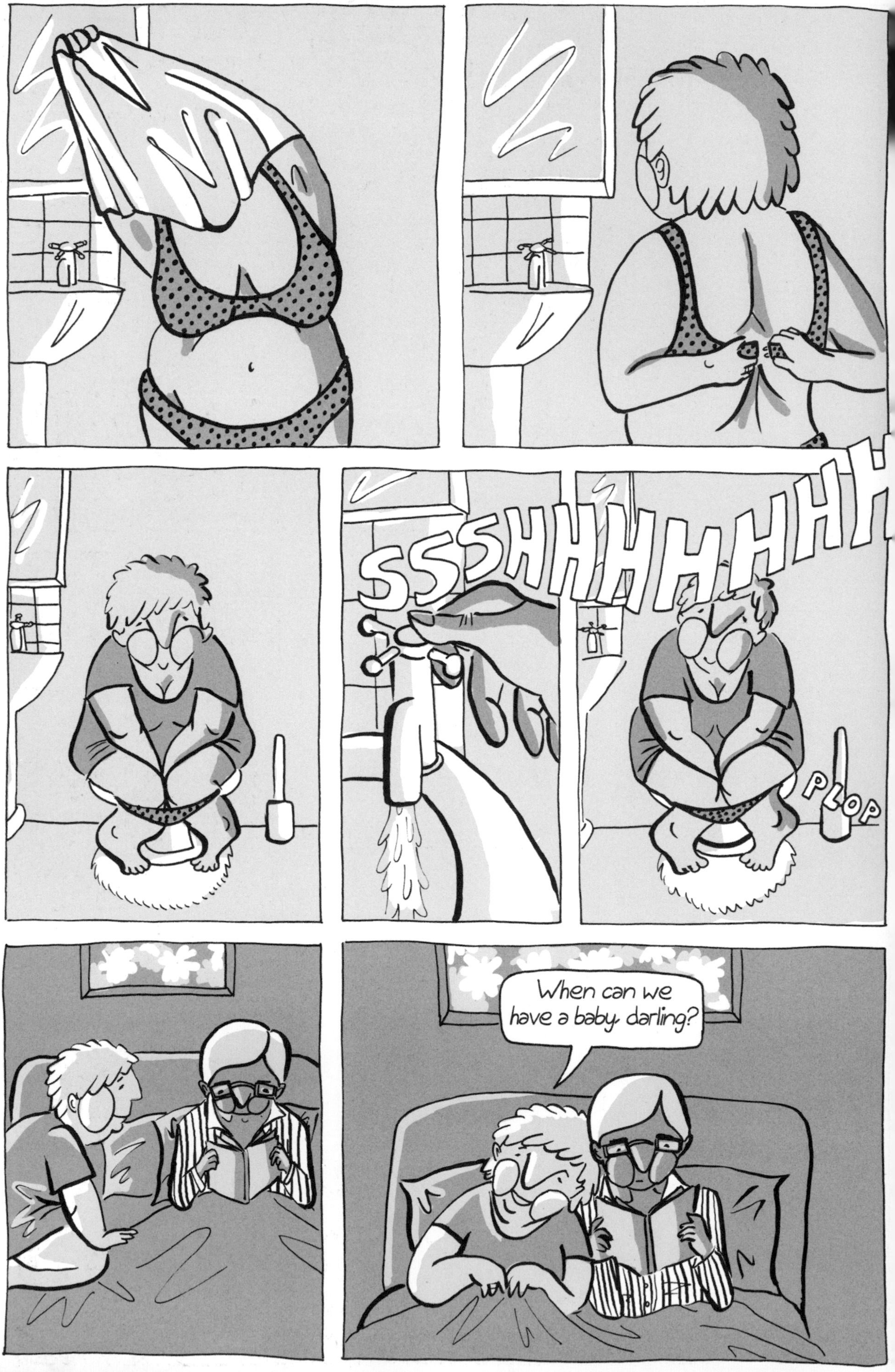
SSSHHHHHHHHH
PLOP
When can we have a baby, darling?

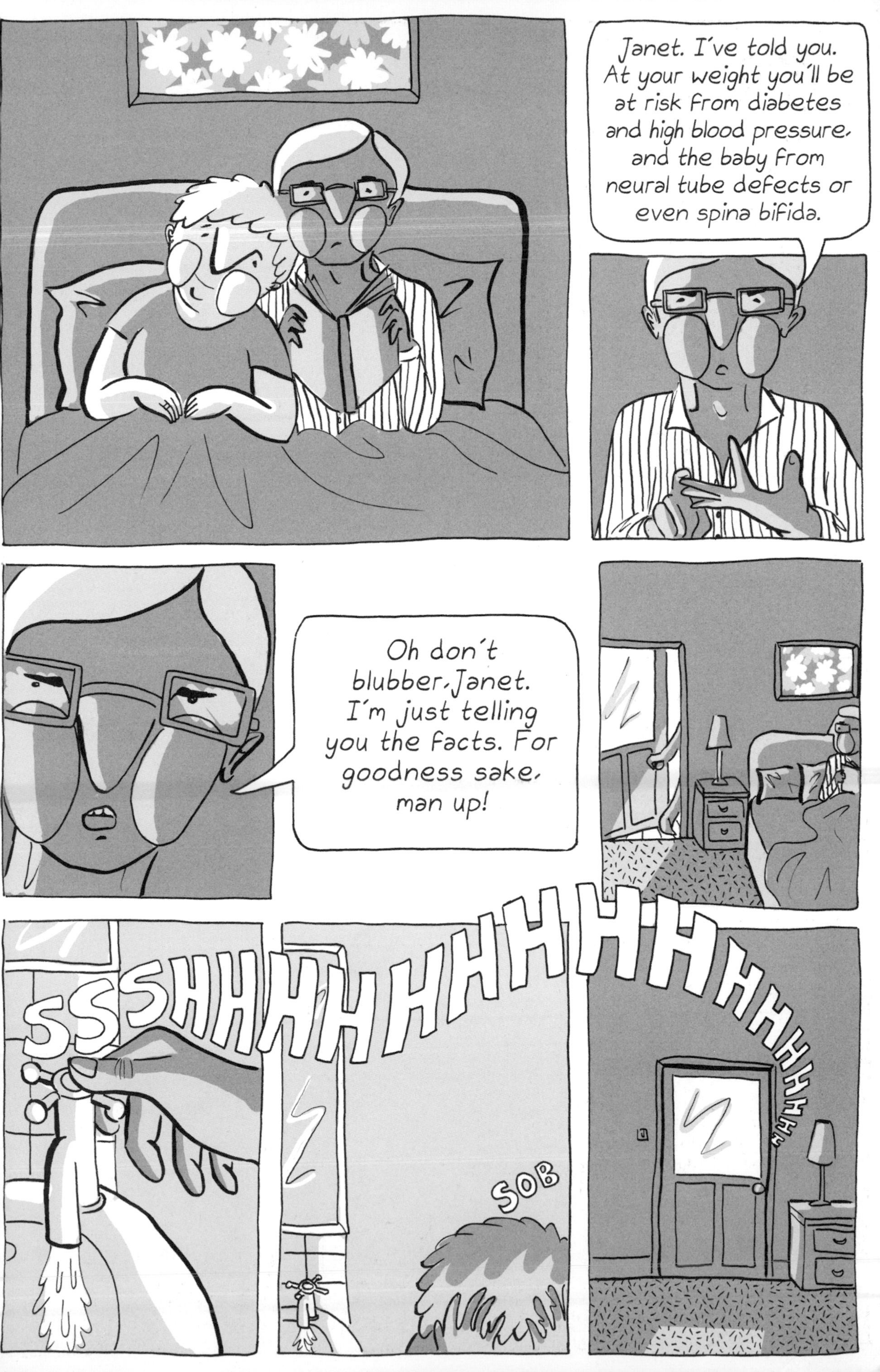
Janet. I've told you. At your weight you'll be at risk from diabetes and high blood pressure, and the baby from neural tube defects or even spina bifida.
Oh don't blubber, Janet. I'm just telling you the facts. For goodness sake, man up!
SSSHHHHHHHHHHHHHHHHHHHHH
SOB

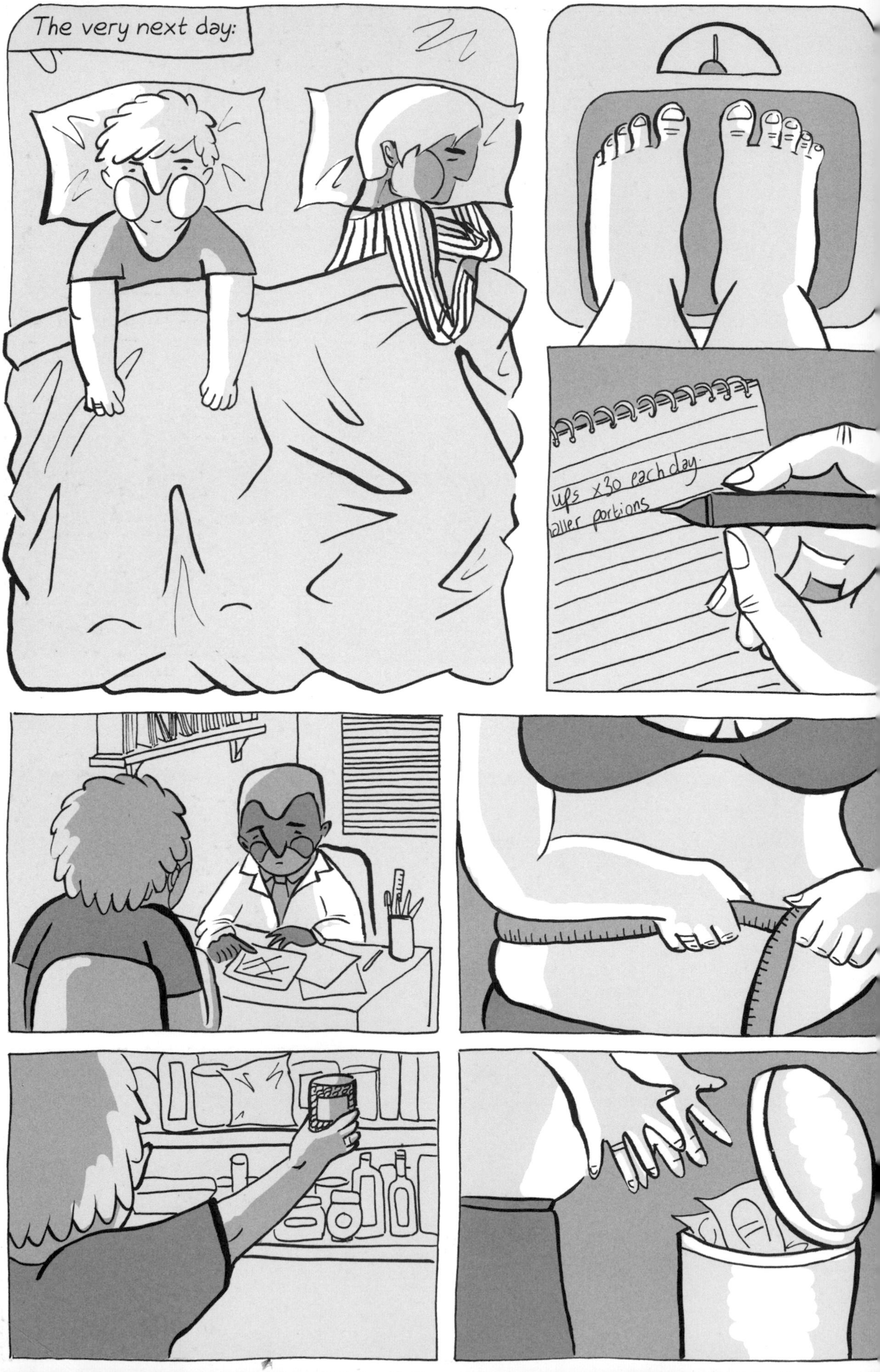
The very next day:
ups x30 each day.
aller portions

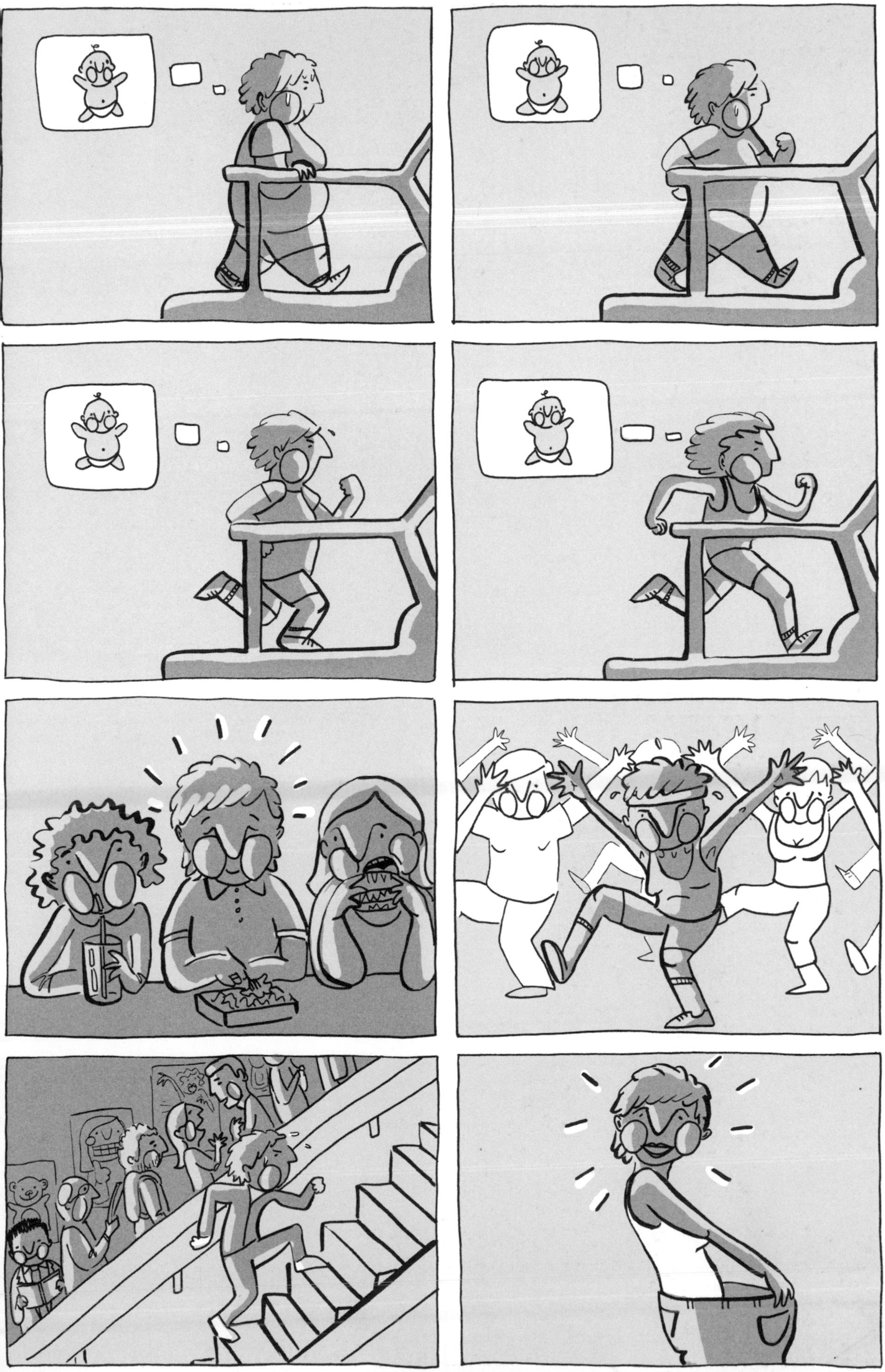

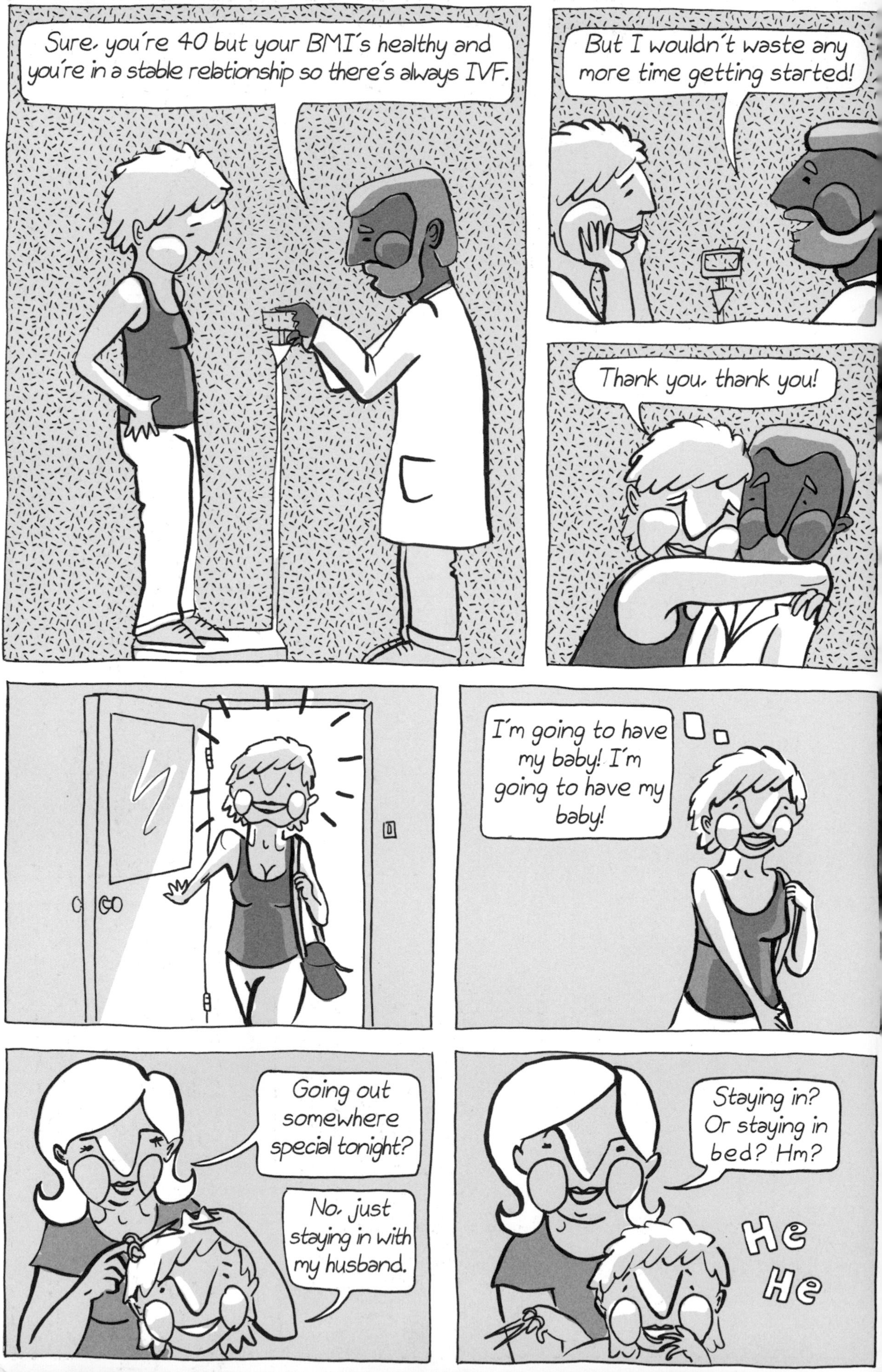
Sure, you're 40 but your BMI's healthy and you're in a stable relationship so there's always IVF.
But I wouldn't waste any more time getting started!
Thank you, thank you!
I'm going to have my baby! I'm going to have my baby!
Going out somewhere special tonight?
No, just staying in with my husband.
Staying in? Or staying in bed? Hm?
He He

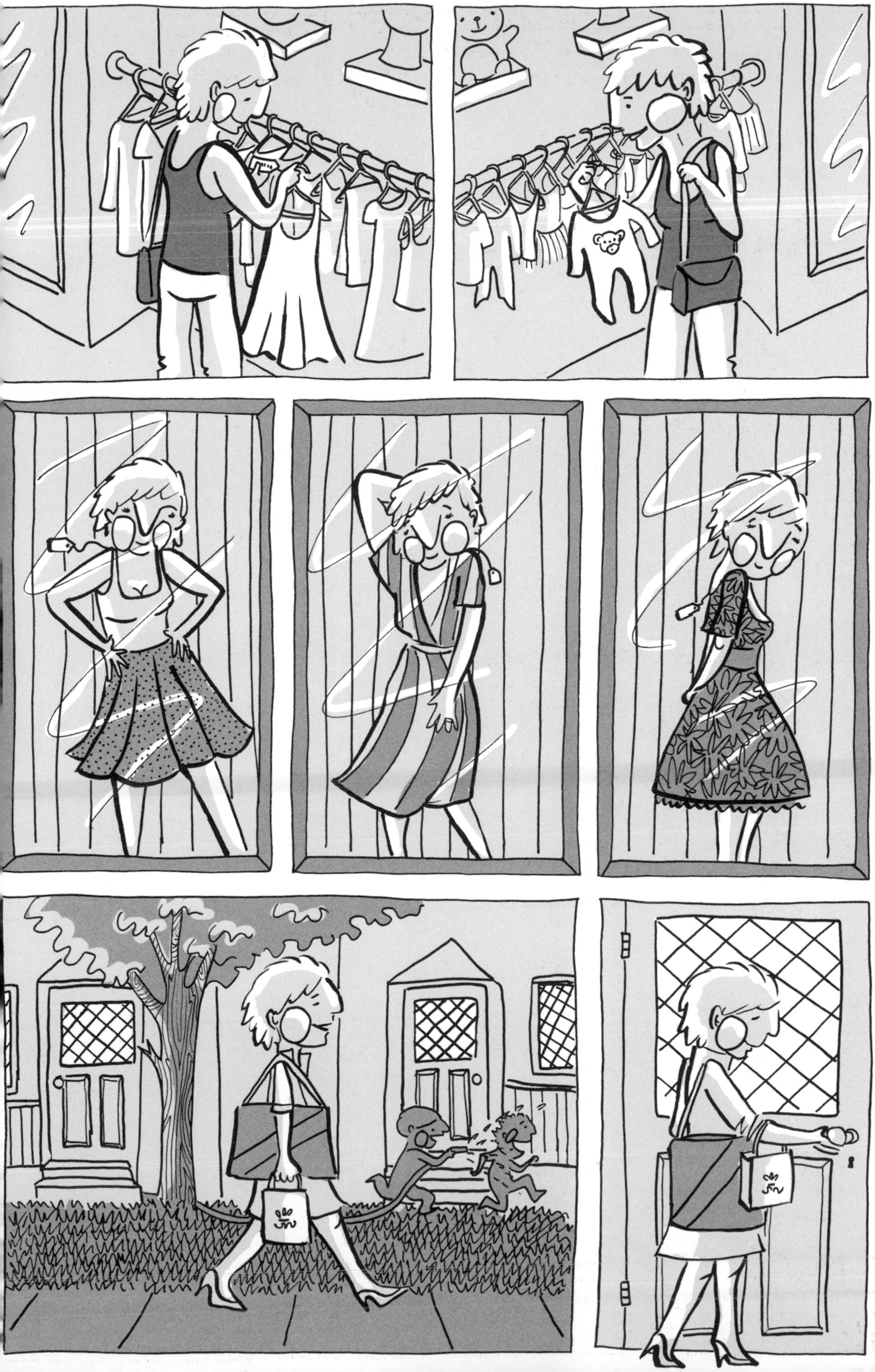

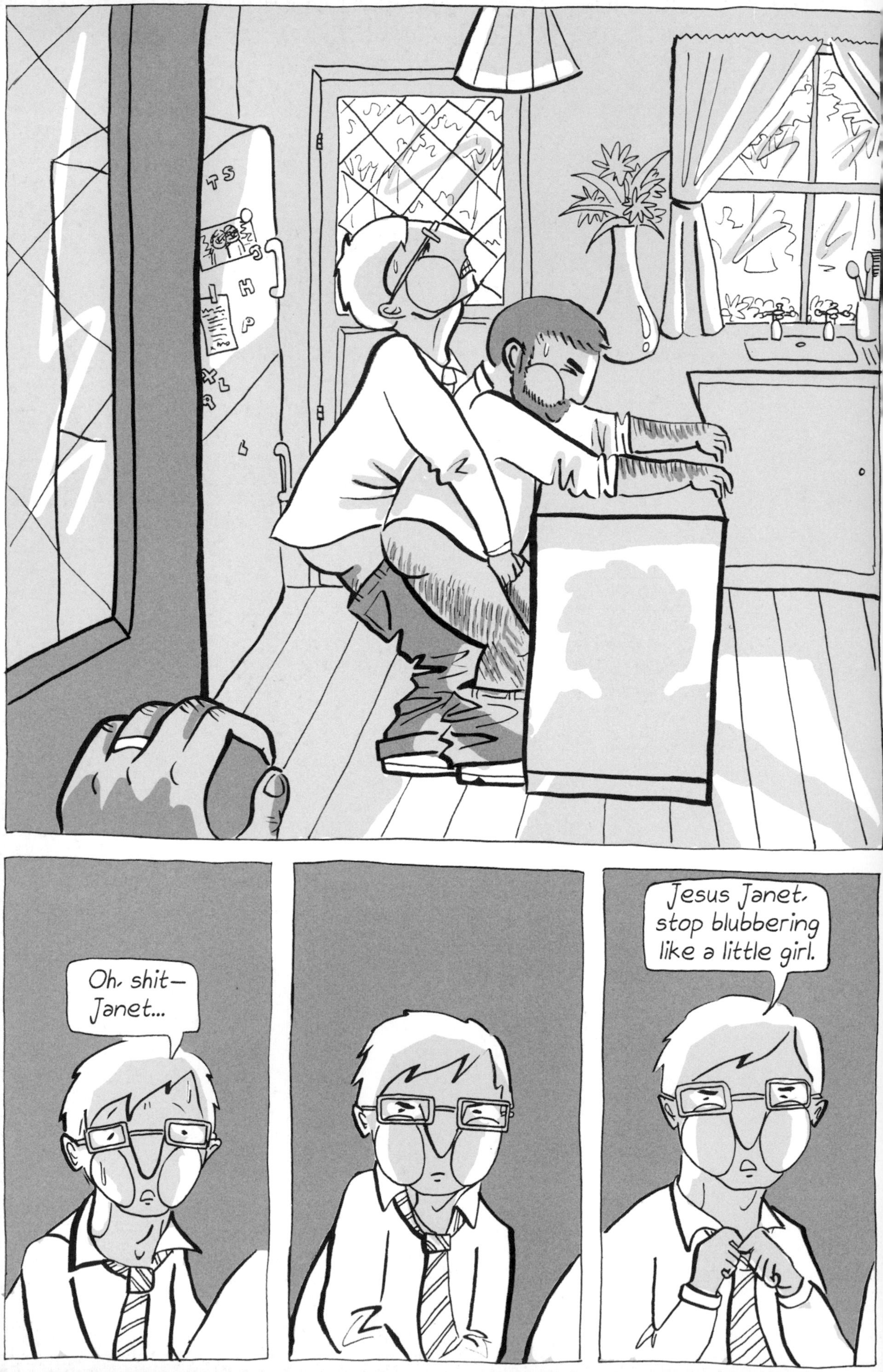
Oh, shit—
Janet...
Jesus Janet, stop blubbering like a little girl.

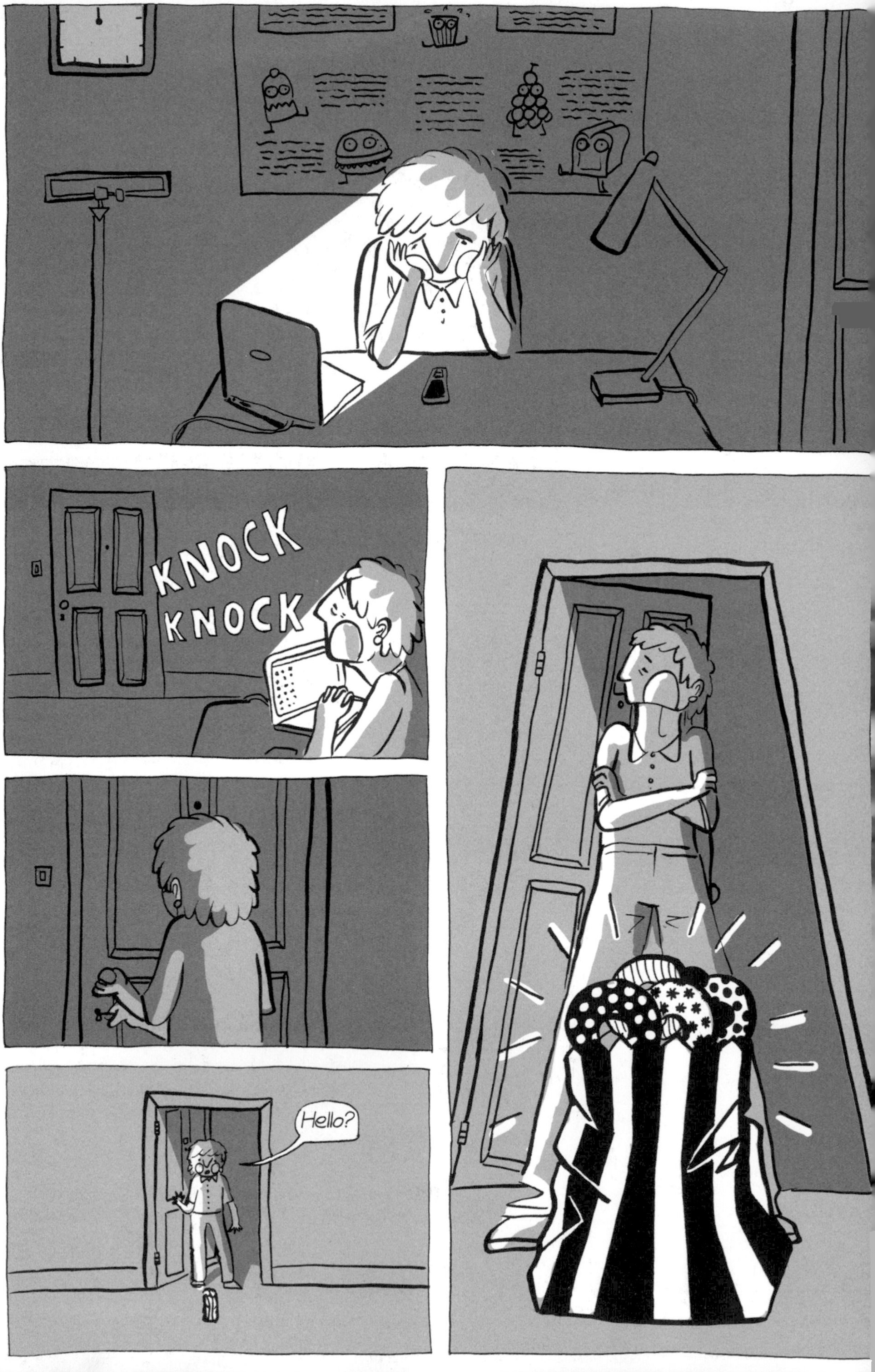
KNOCK
KNOCK
Hello?

Chapter Three

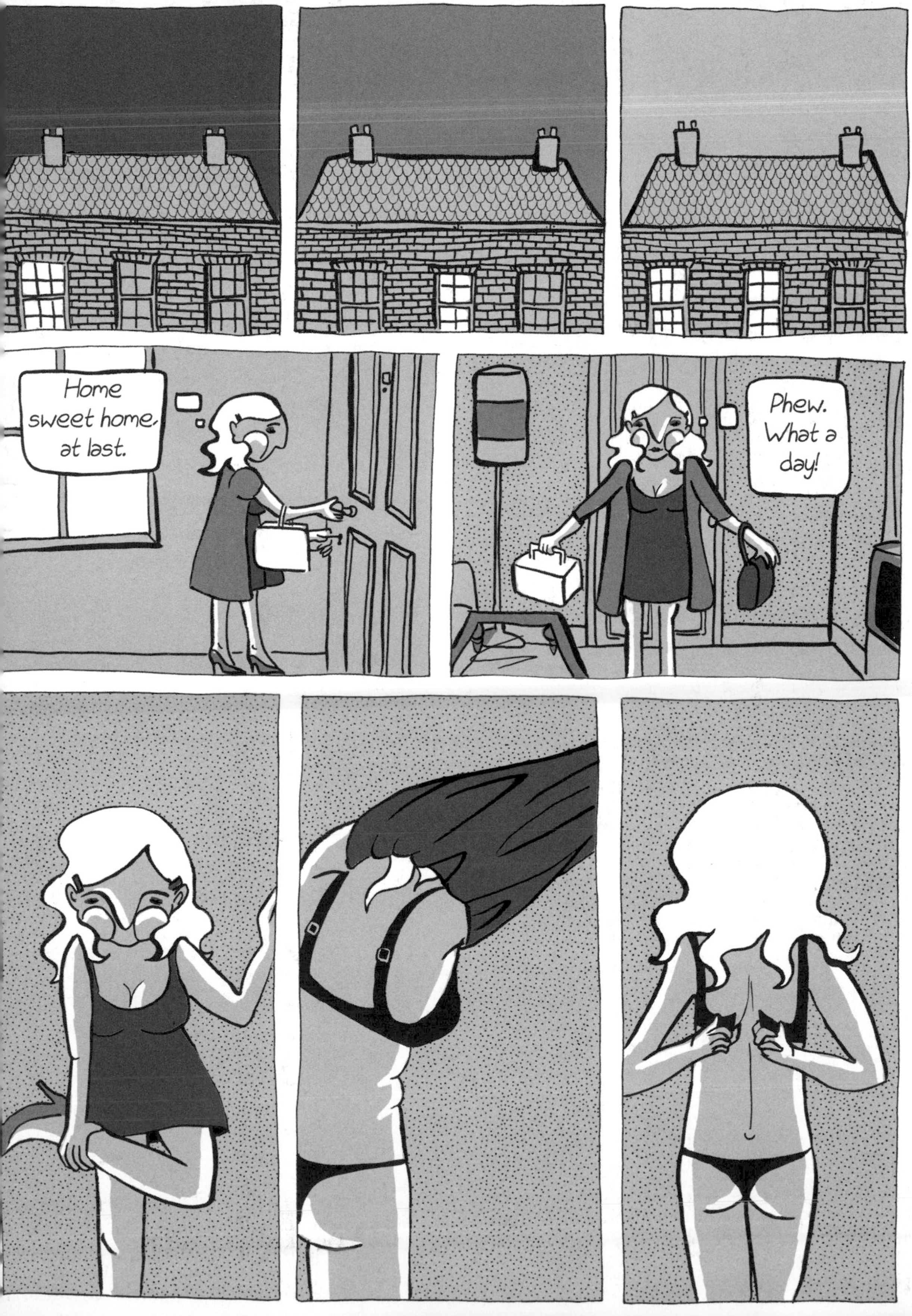
Home sweet home, at last.
Phew. What a day!

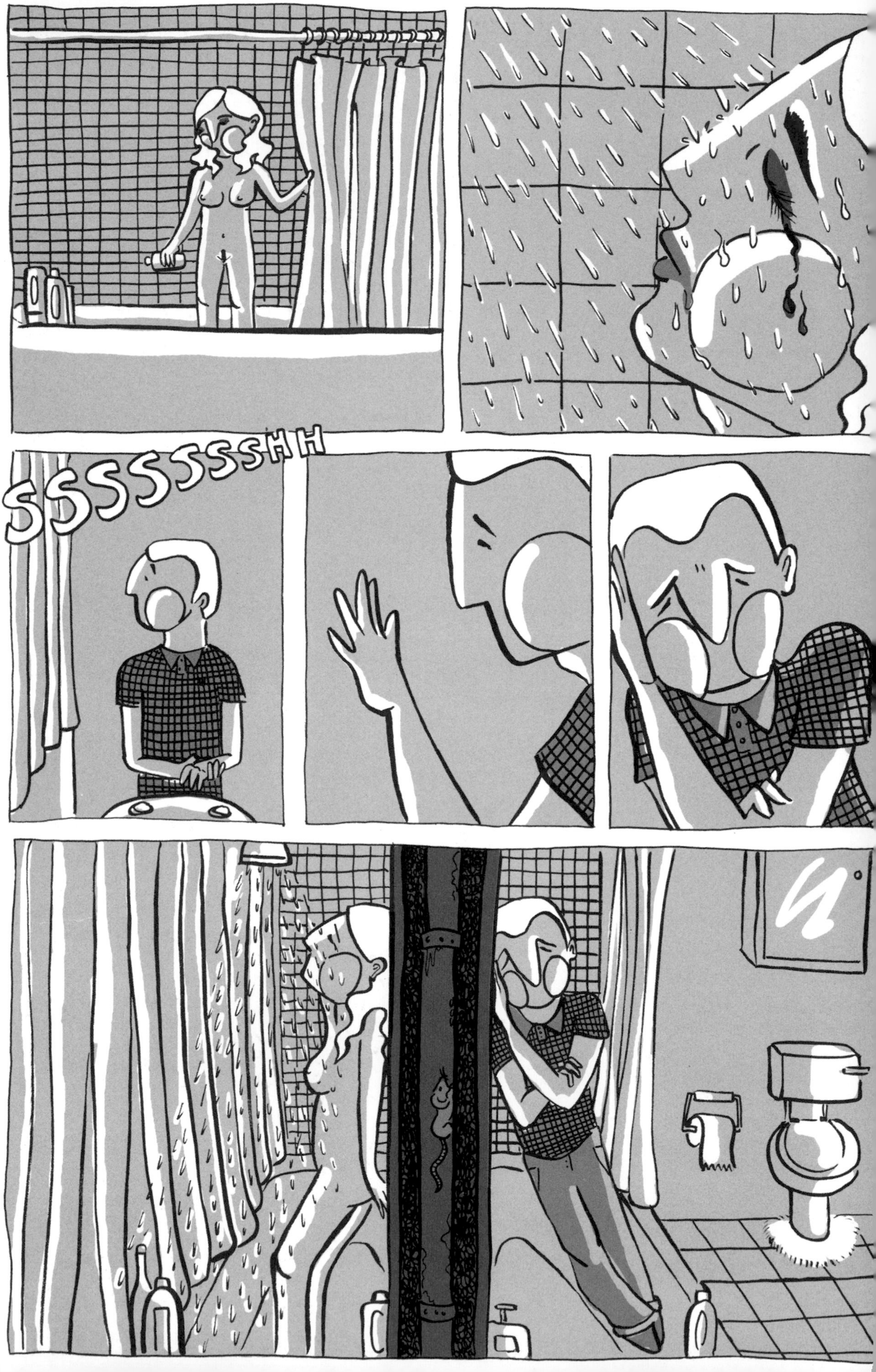
SSSSSSSSHH

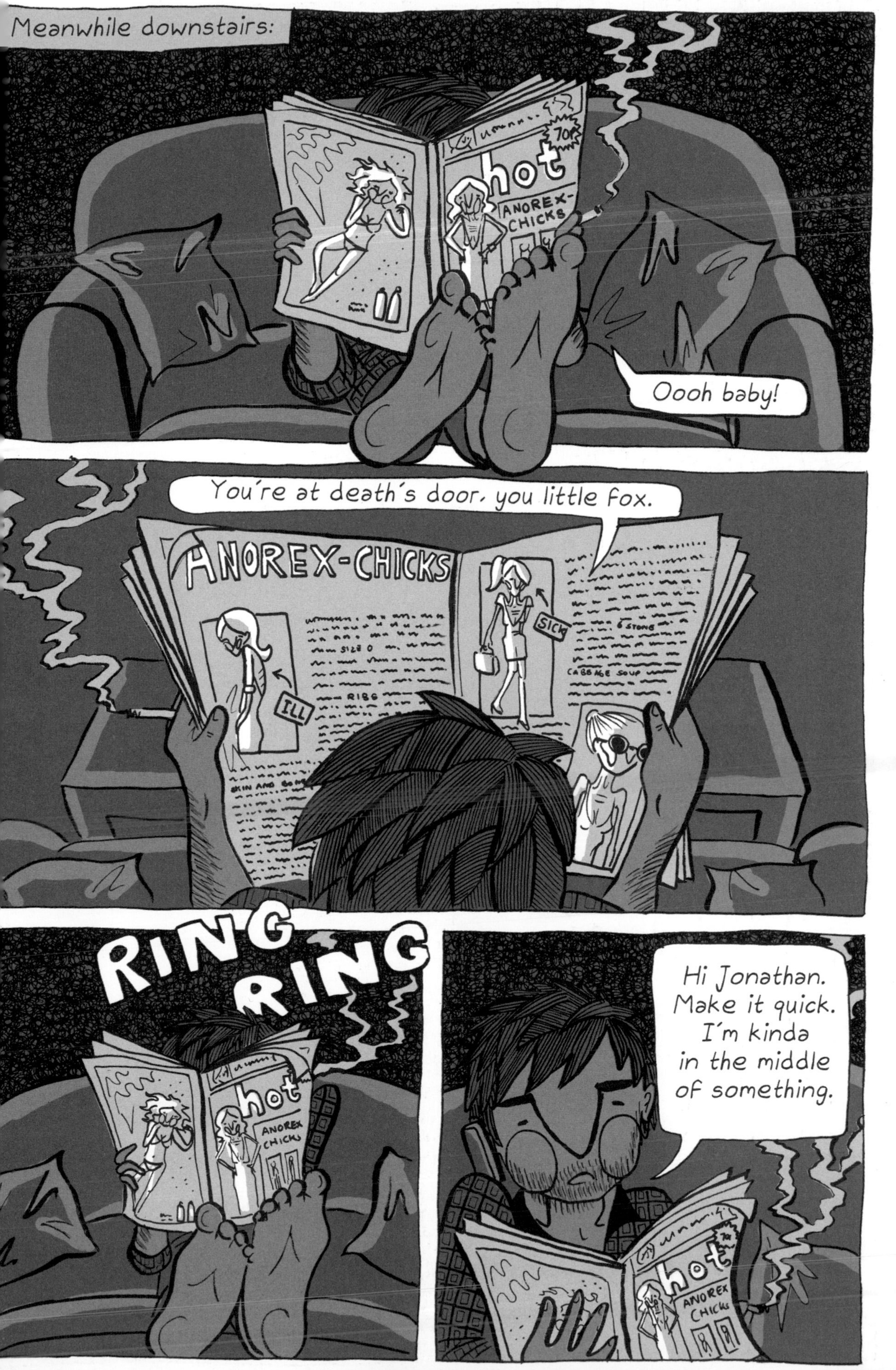
Meanwhile downstairs:
hot
ANOREX-CHICKS
Oooh baby!
You're at death's door, you little fox.
ANOREX-CHICKS
SIZE 0
RIBS
ILL
SICK
6 STONE
CABBAGE SOUP
RING
RING
Hi Jonathan. Make it quick. I'm kinda in the middle of something.

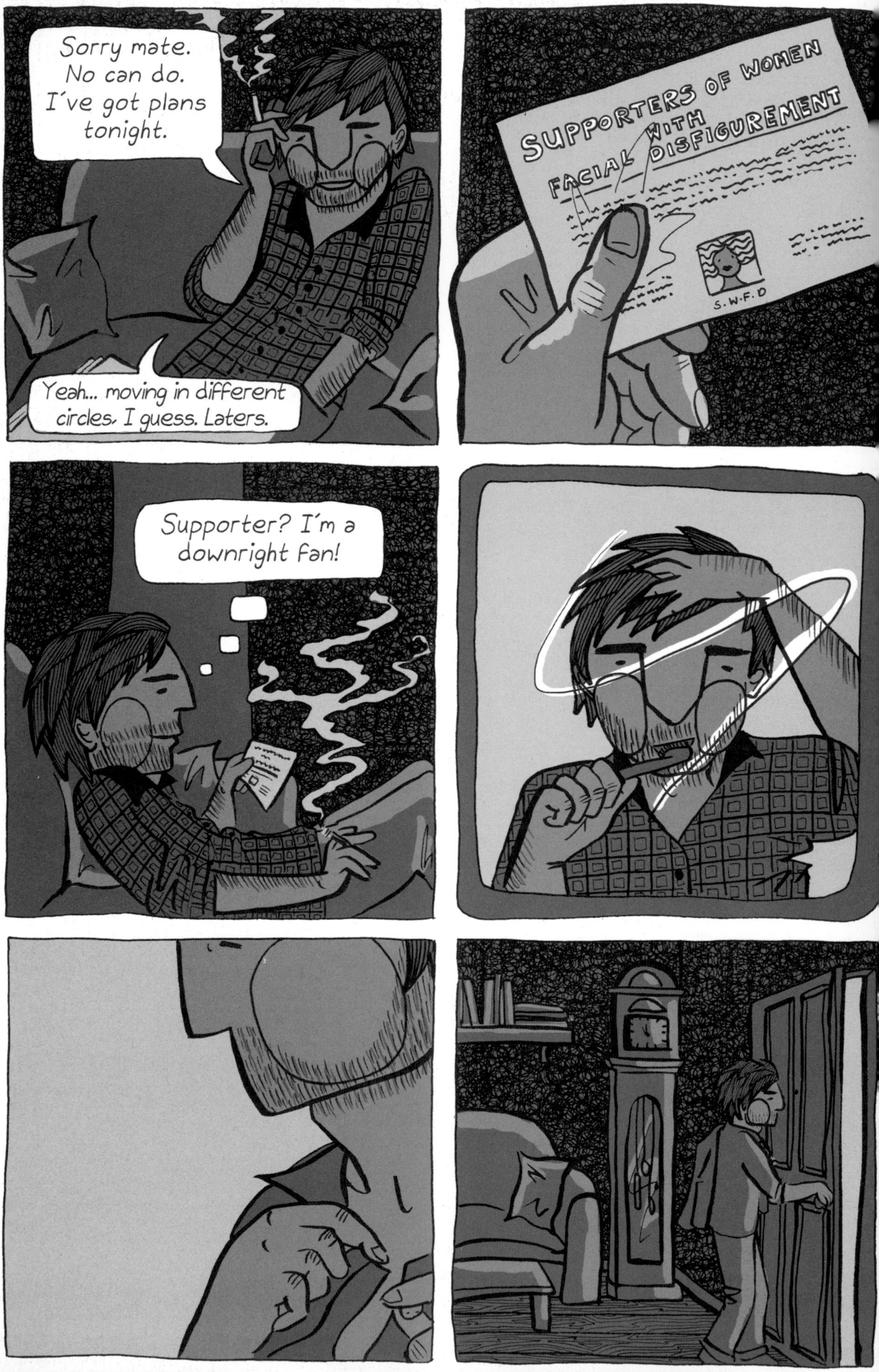
Sorry mate. No can do. I've got plans tonight.
Yeah... moving in different circles, I guess. Laters.
SUPPORTERS OF WOMEN FACIAL WITH DISFIGUREMENT
S.W.F.D
Supporter? I'm a downright fan!

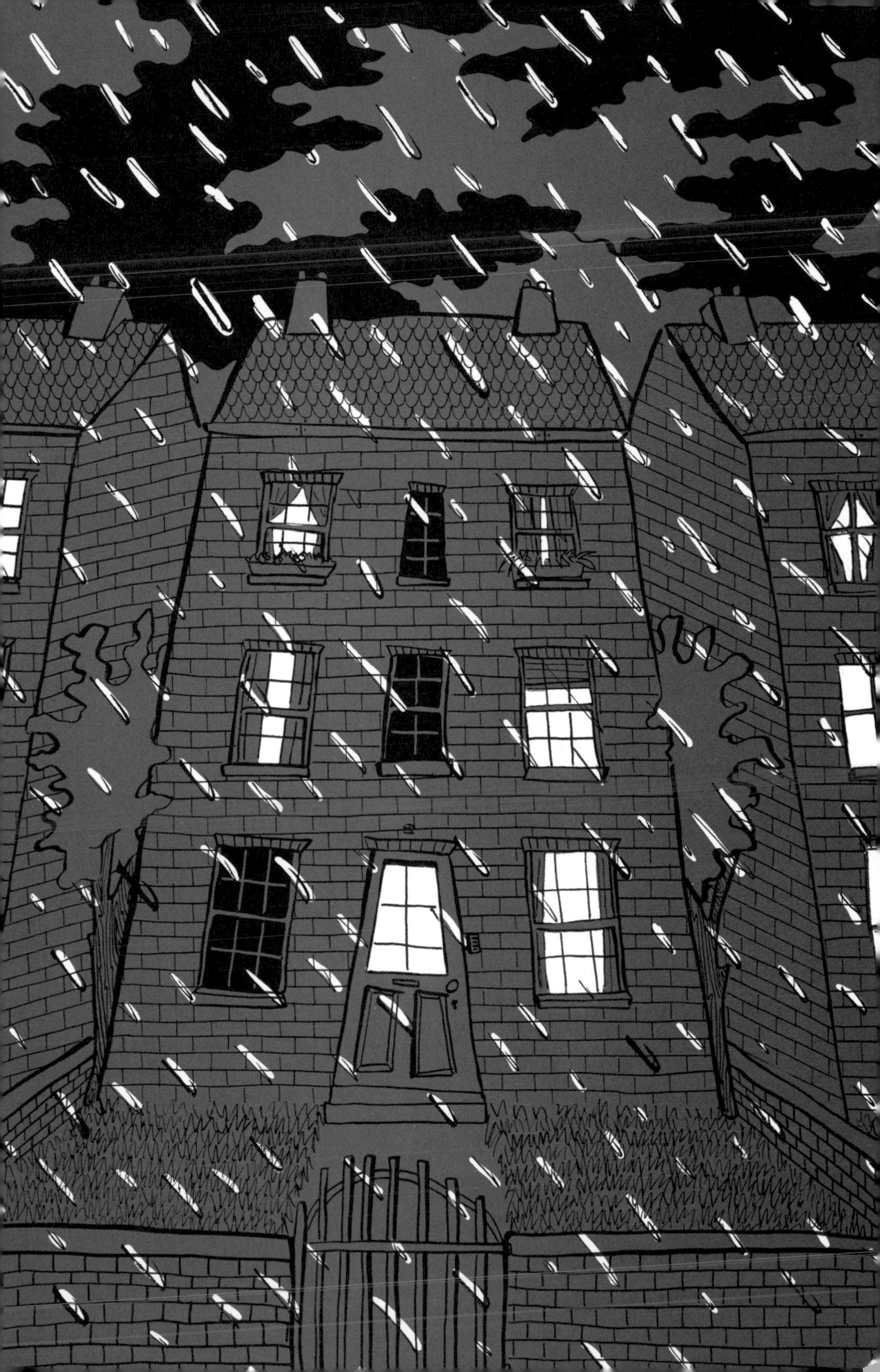

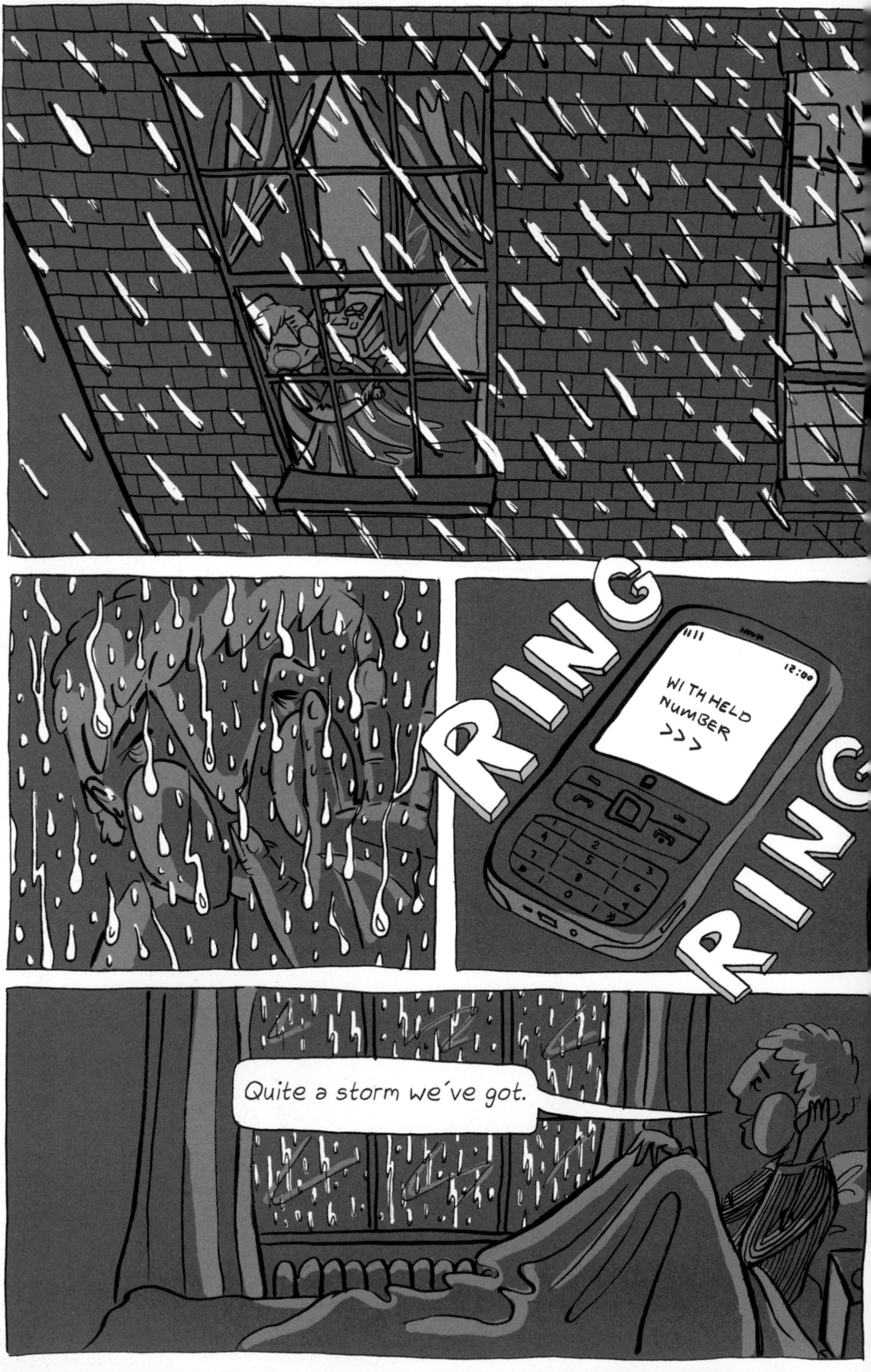
RING
WITHHELD NUMBER >>>
RING
Quite a storm we've got.

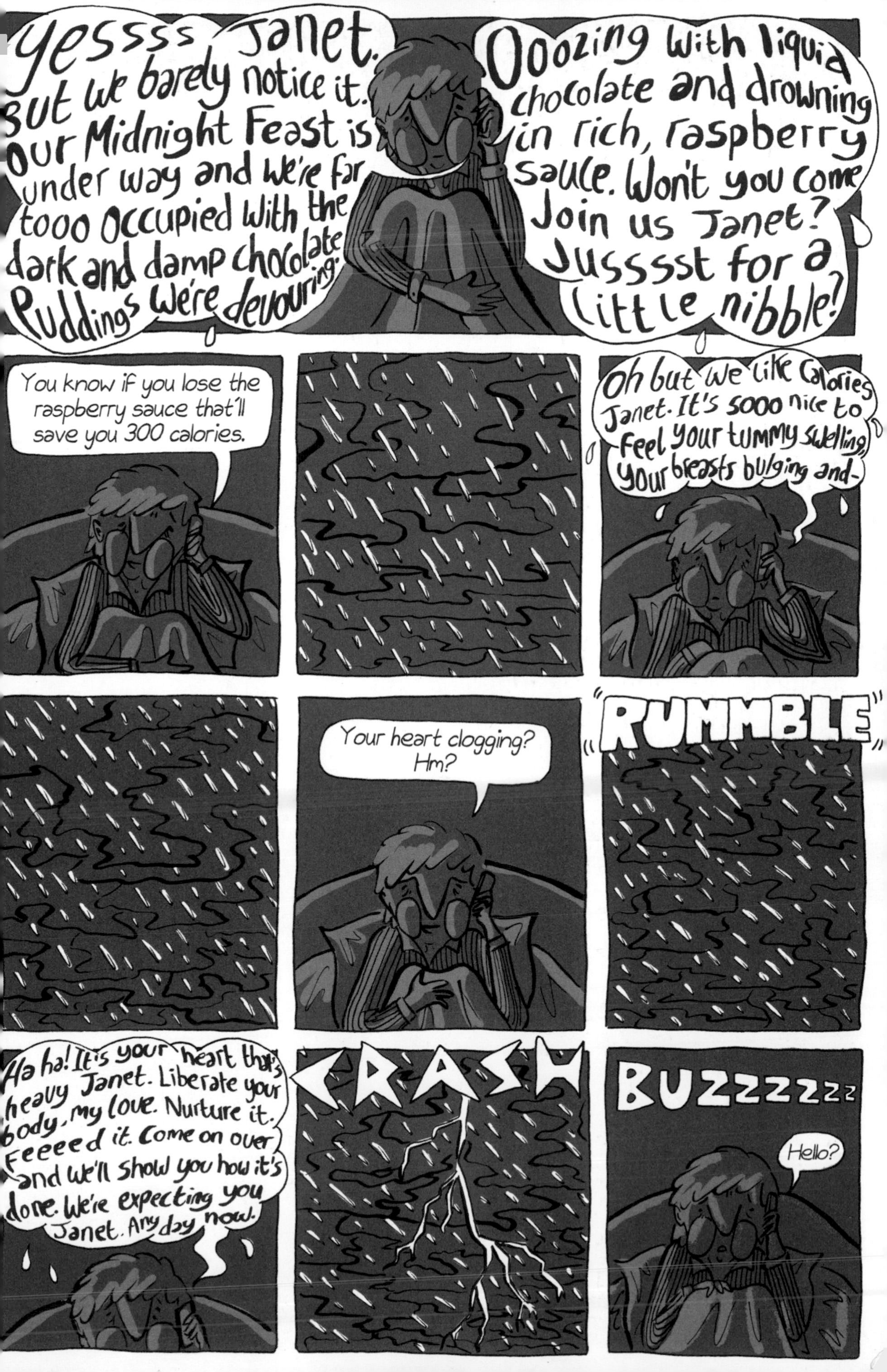

Yessss Janet. But we barely notice it. Our Midnight Feast is under way and we're far tooo occupied with the dark and damp chocolate puddings we're devouring.
Ooozing with liquid chocolate and drowning in rich, raspberry sauce. Won't you come join us Janet? Jusssst for a little nibble?
You know if you lose the raspberry sauce that'll save you 300 calories.
Oh but we like calories Janet. It's sooo nice to feel your tummy swelling, your breasts bulging and-
Your heart clogging? Hm?
"RUMMBLE"
Ha ha! It's your heart that's heavy Janet. Liberate your body, my love. Nurture it. Feeeed it. Come on over and we'll show you how it's done. We're expecting you Janet. Any day now.
CRASH
BUZzzzzzz
Hello?

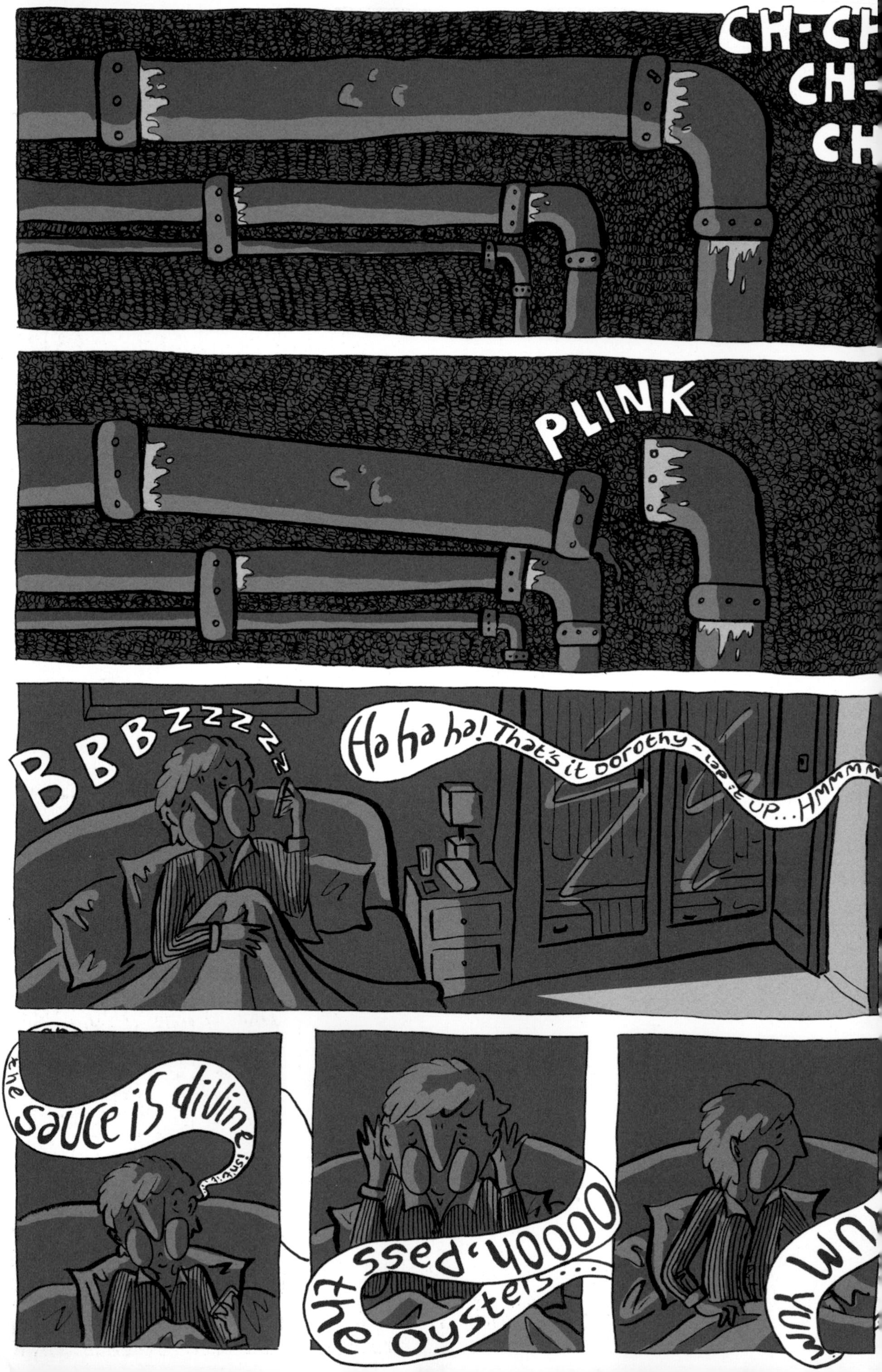
CH-CH
CH-
CH
PLINK
BBBZZZZZZ
Ha ha ha! That's it Dorothy - lap it UP... HMMMM
the sauce is divine isn't it...
Ooooh, pass the oysters...
yum yum

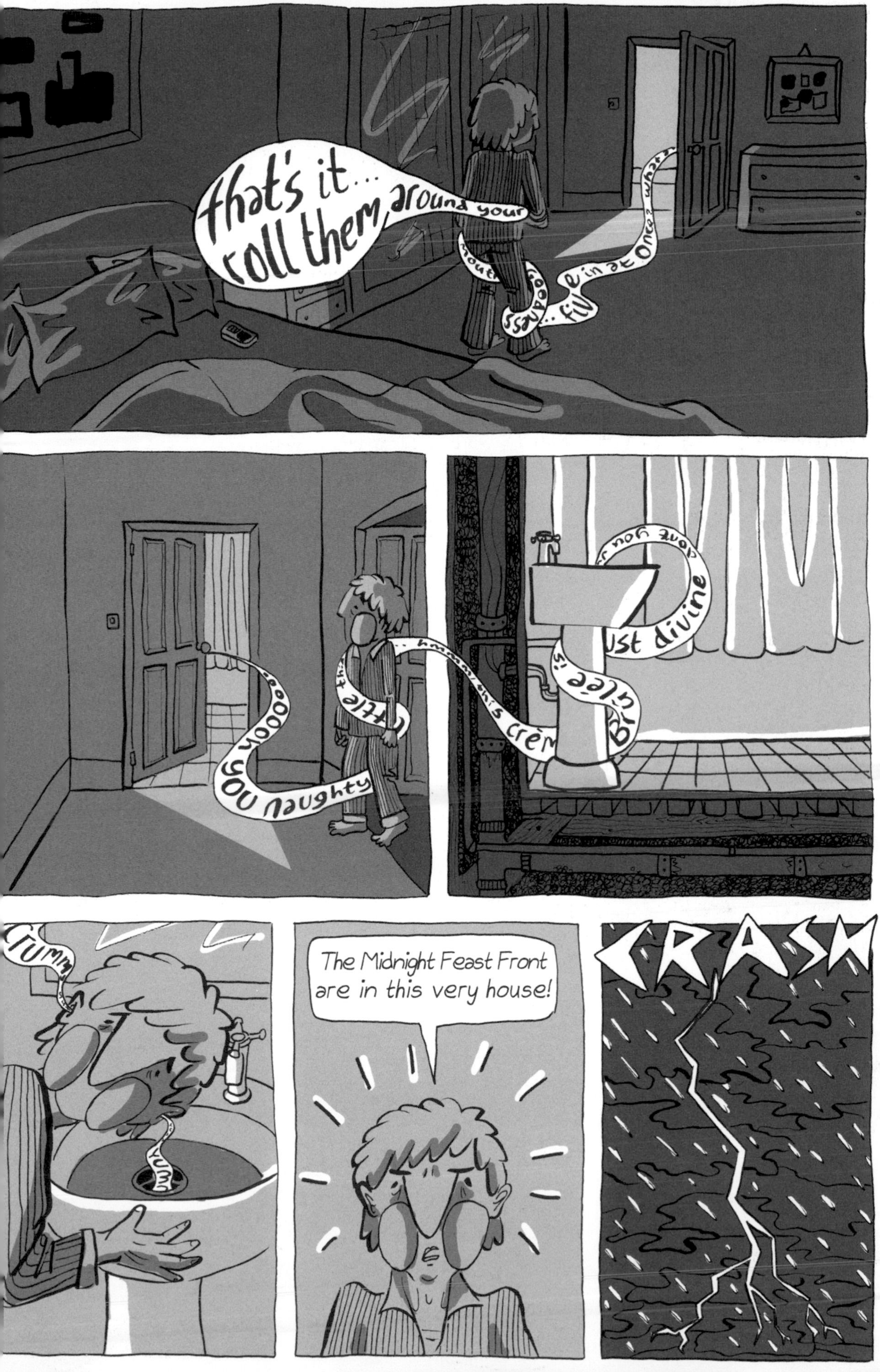
that's it... roll them around your mouth
goodness... five in at once? what
ooooh YOU naughty little
hmmm/this crem
Brulee is
ust divine
dont you
crumm
yumm
The Midnight Feast Front are in this very house!
CRASH

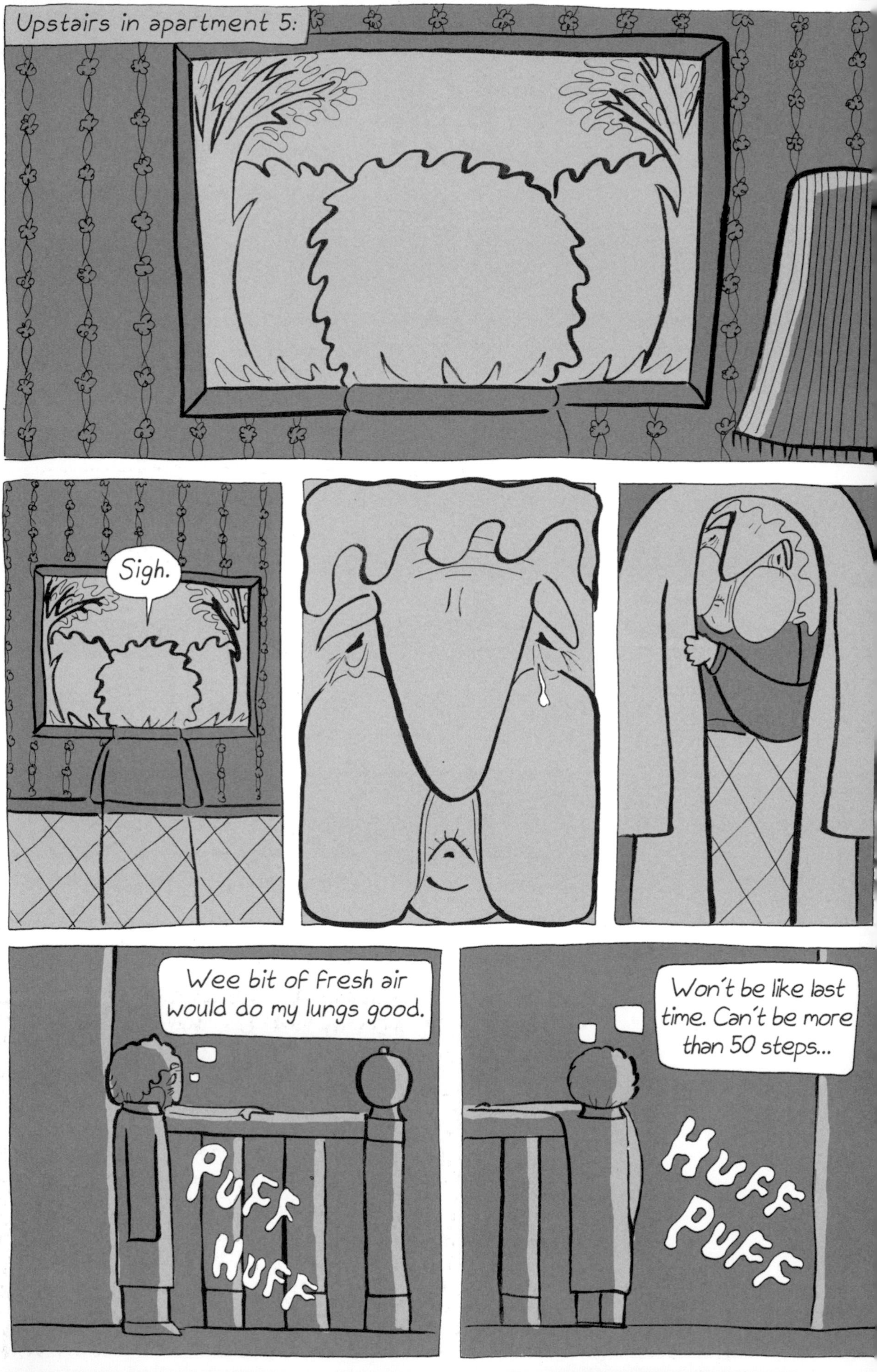
Upstairs in apartment 5:
Sigh.
Wee bit of fresh air would do my lungs good.
PUFF HUFF
Won't be like last time. Can't be more than 50 steps...
HUFF PUFF

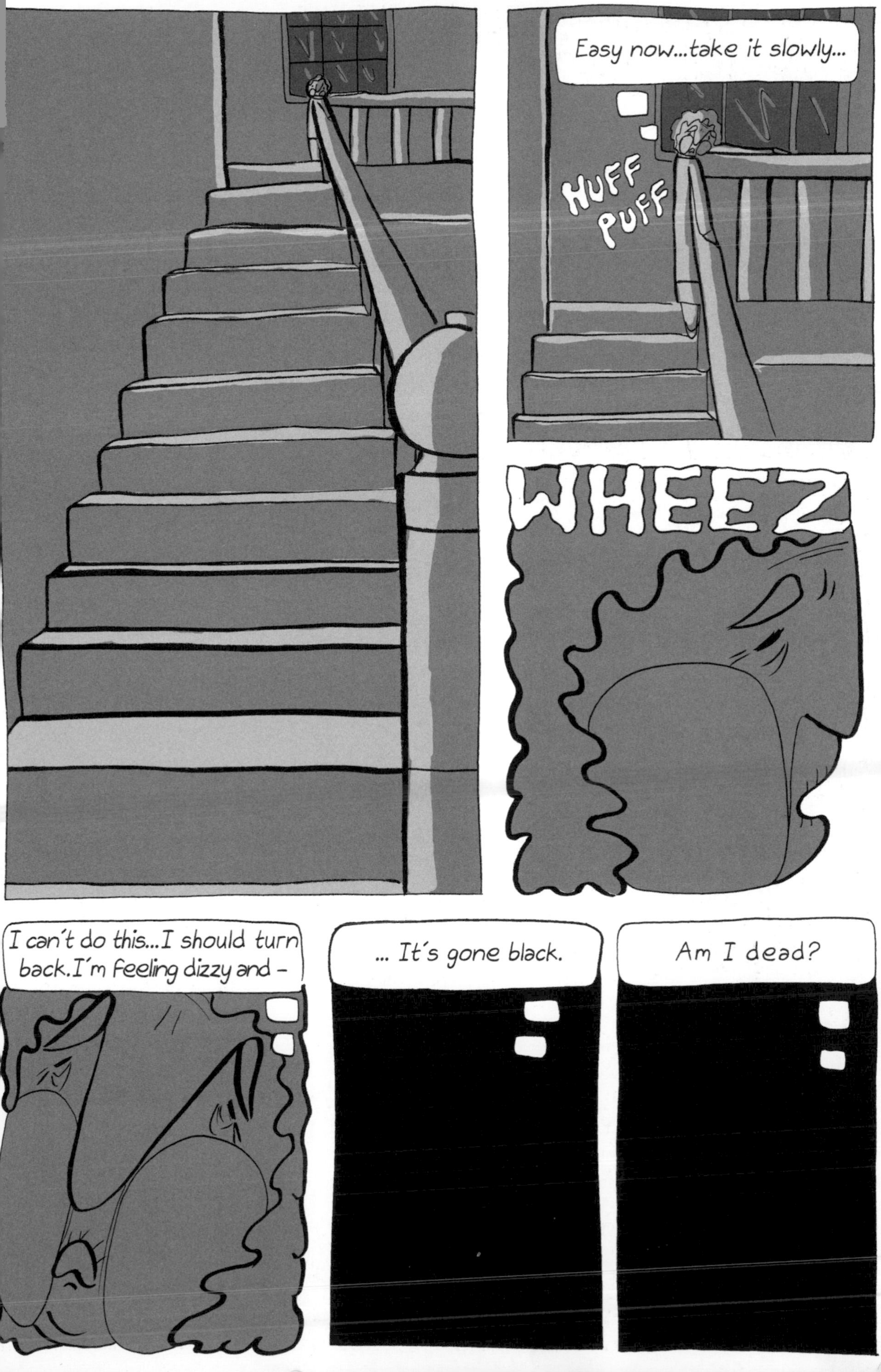
Easy now...take it slowly...
HUFF PUFF
WHEEZ
I can't do this...I should turn back. I'm feeling dizzy and –
... It's gone black.
Am I dead?

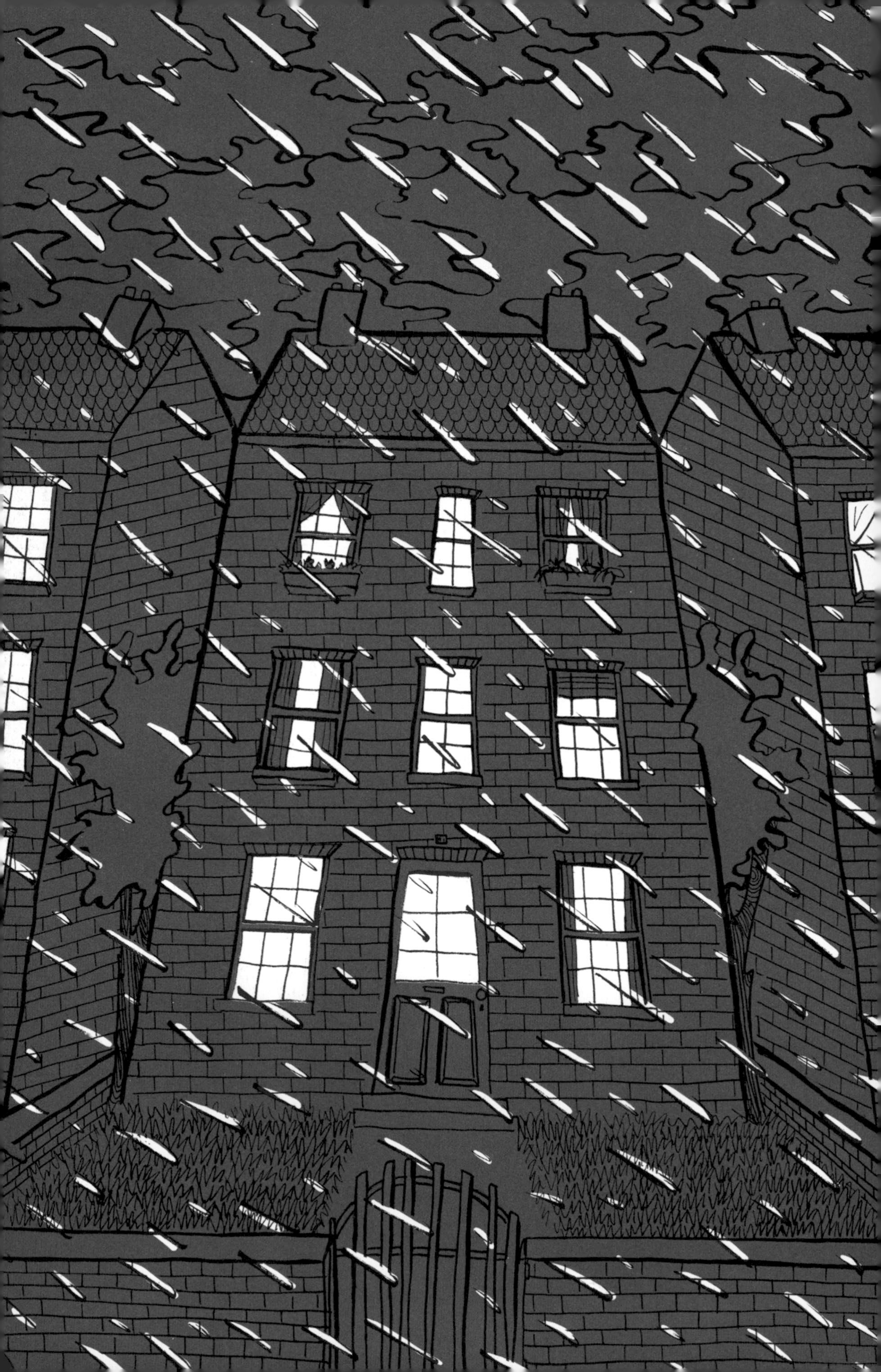

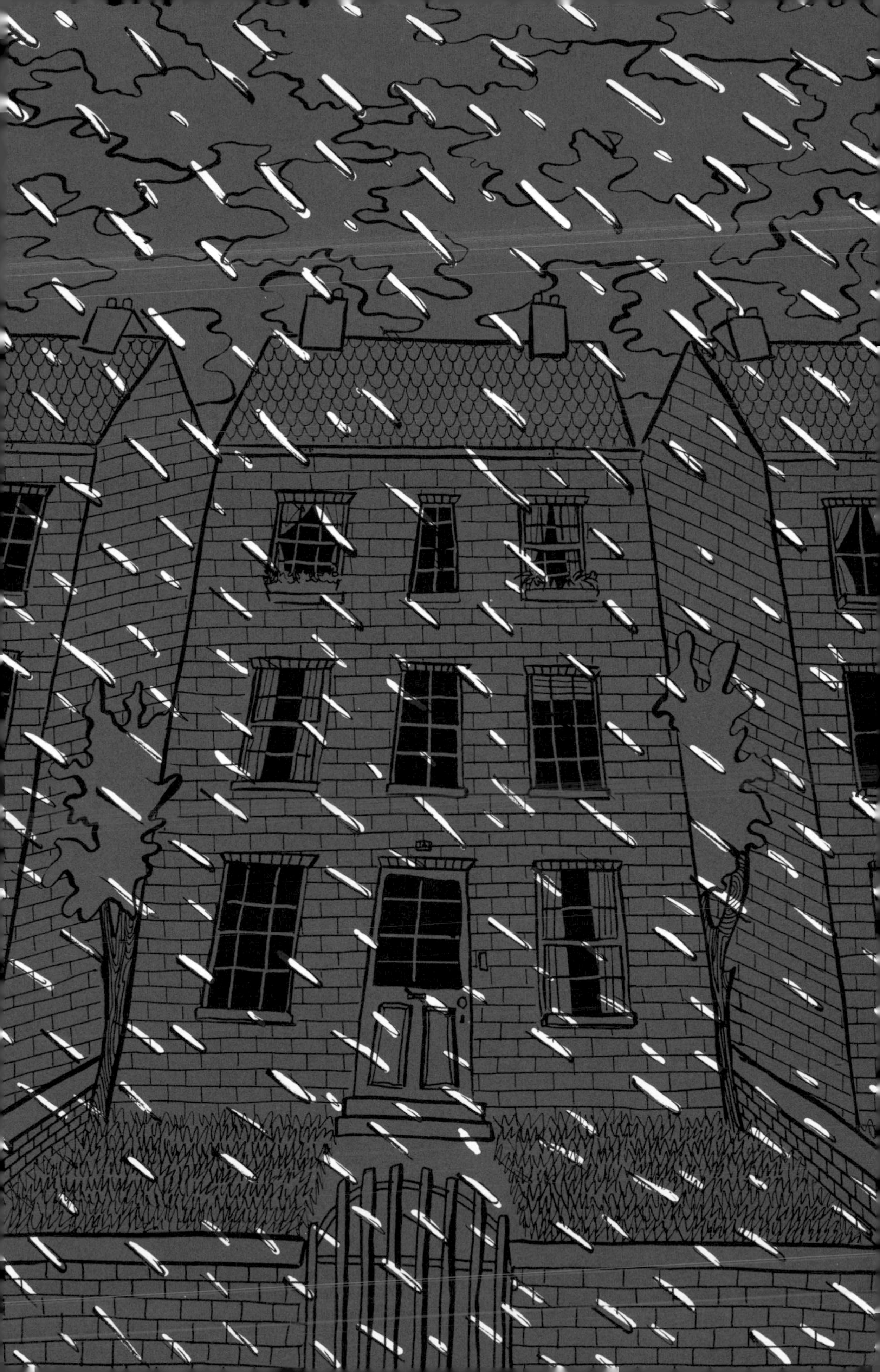

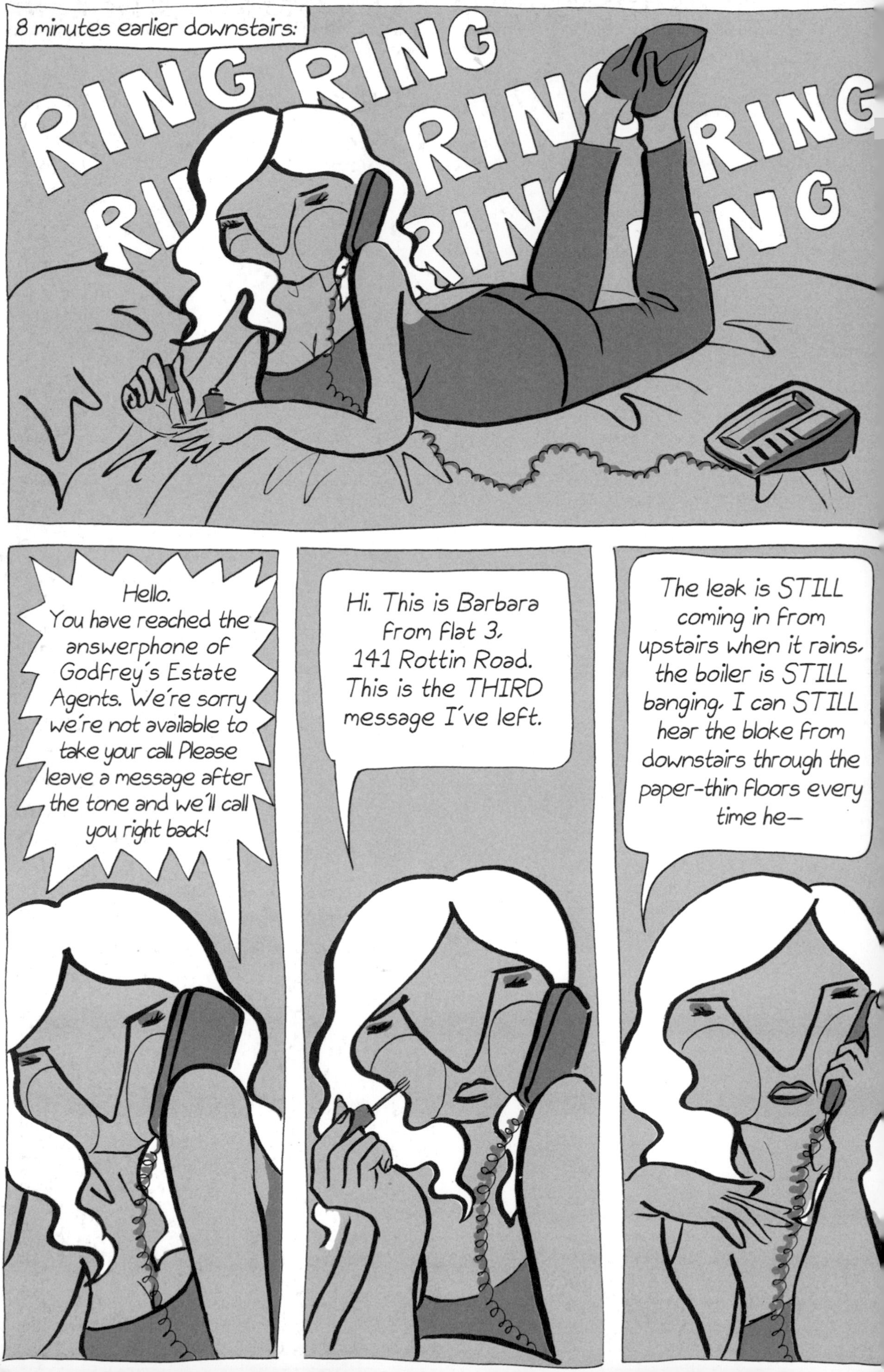
8 minutes earlier downstairs:
RING RING RING RING RING RING RING
Hello.
You have reached the answerphone of Godfrey's Estate Agents. We're sorry we're not available to take your call. Please leave a message after the tone and we'll call you right back!
Hi. This is Barbara from Flat 3, 141 Rottin Road. This is the THIRD message I've left.
The leak is STILL coming in from upstairs when it rains, the boiler is STILL banging, I can STILL hear the bloke from downstairs through the paper-thin floors every time he–

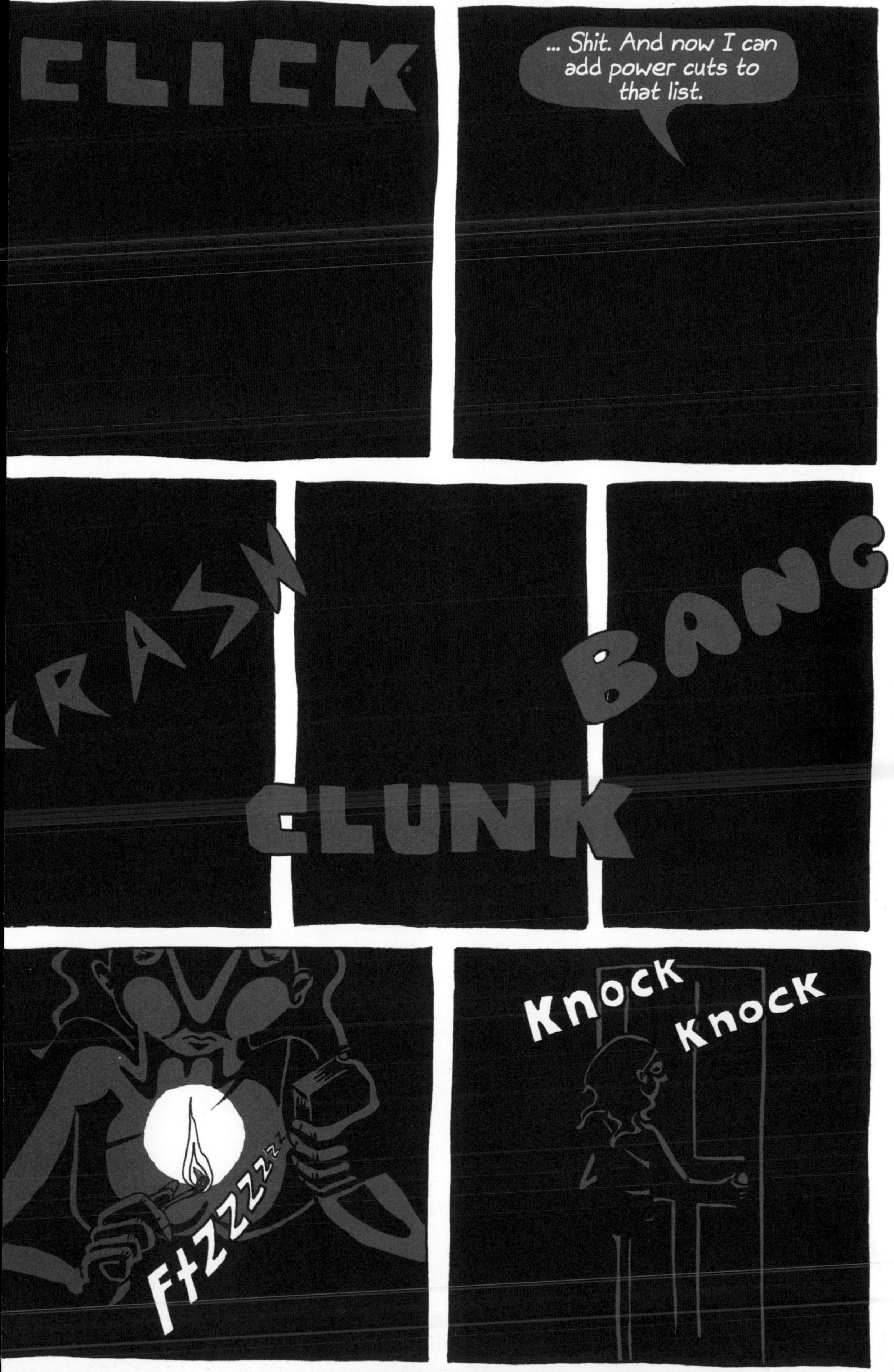
CLICK
... Shit. And now I can add power cuts to that list.
KRASH
CLUNK
BANG
FTZZZZzzz
Knock
Knock

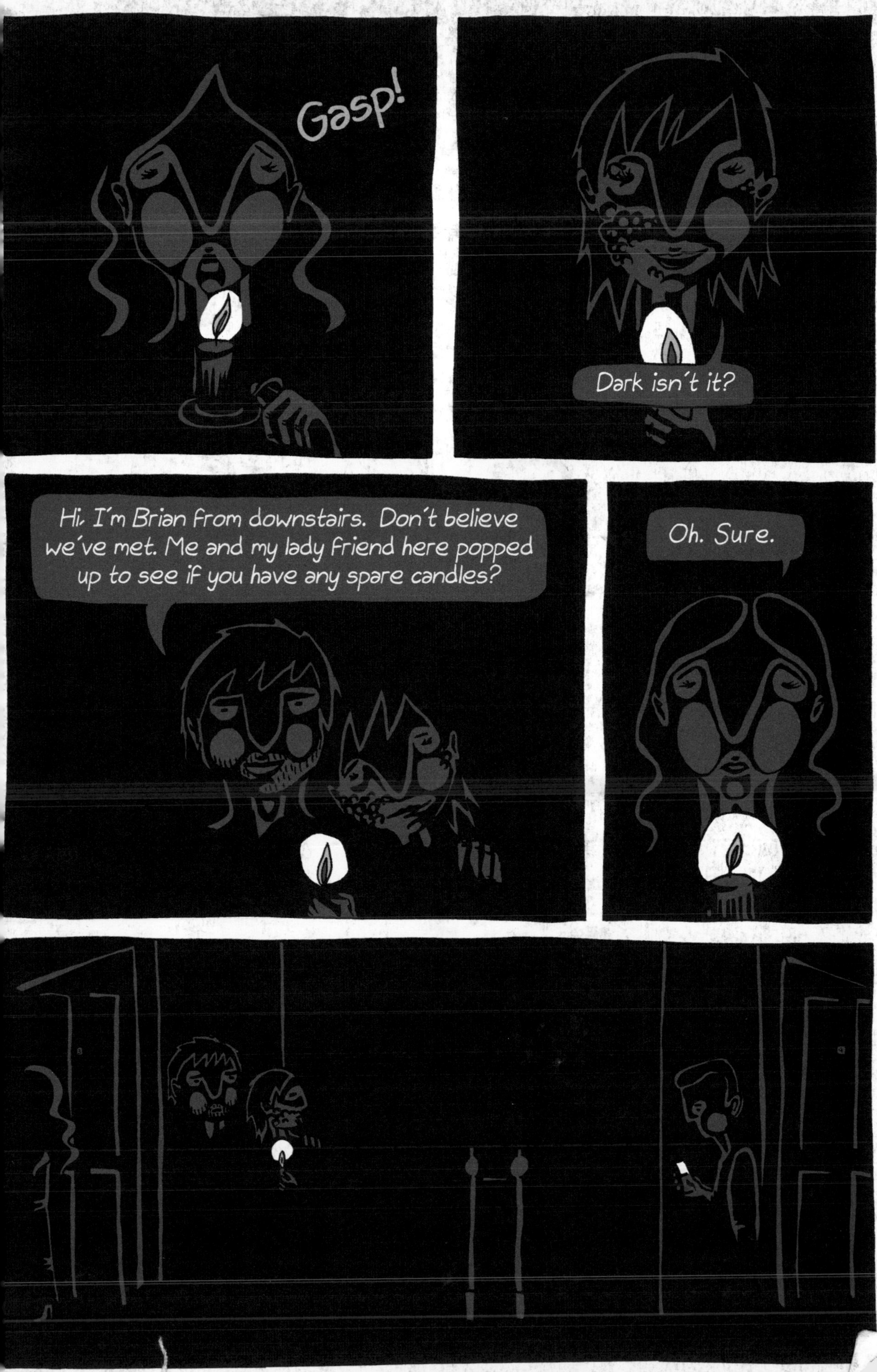
Gasp!
Dark isn't it?
Hi, I'm Brian from downstairs. Don't believe we've met. Me and my lady friend here popped up to see if you have any spare candles?
Oh. Sure.

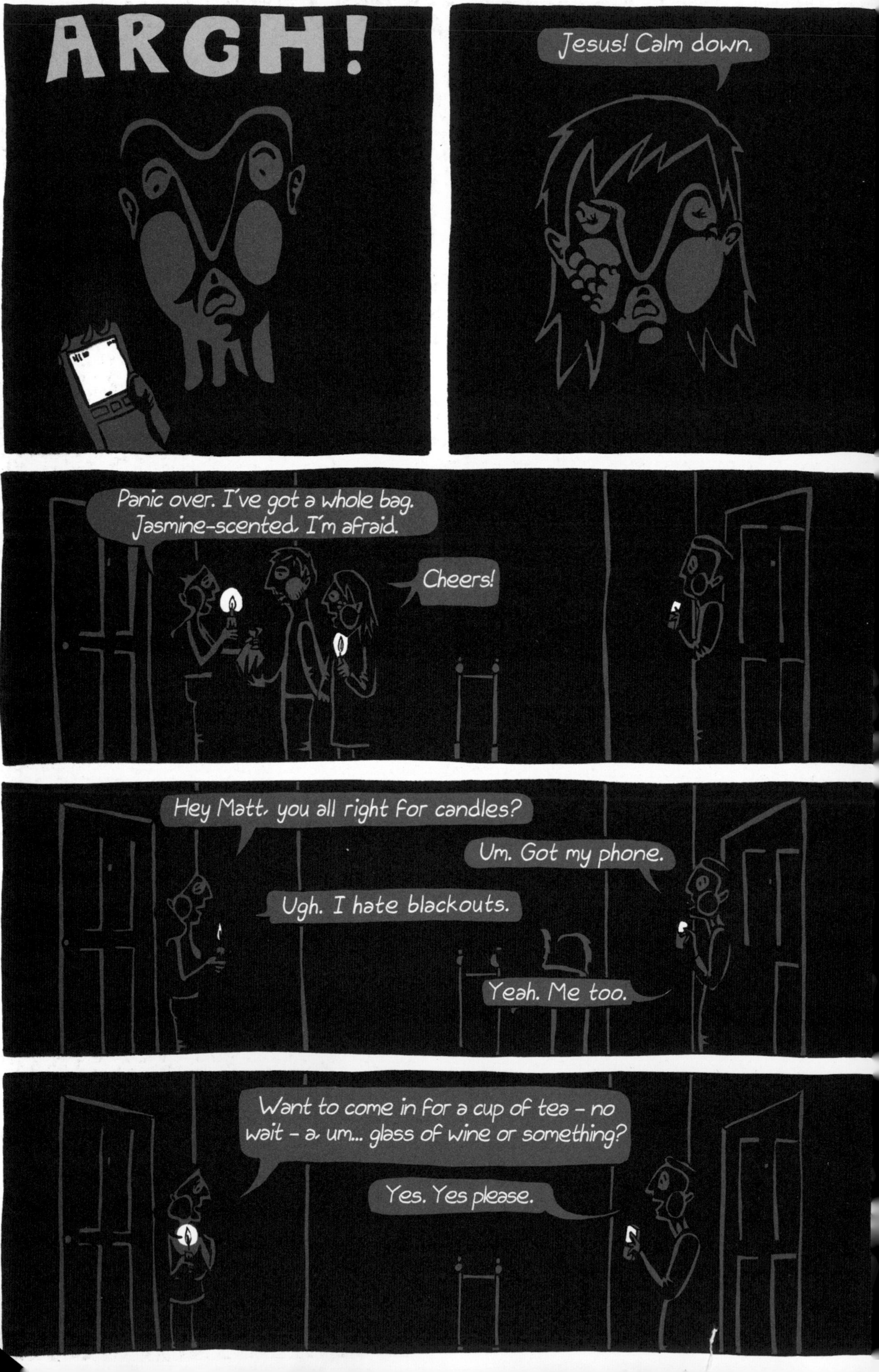
ARGH!
Jesus! Calm down.
Panic over. I've got a whole bag. Jasmine-scented, I'm afraid.
Cheers!
Hey Matt, you all right for candles?
Um. Got my phone.
Ugh. I hate blackouts.
Yeah. Me too.
Want to come in for a cup of tea – no wait – a, um... glass of wine or something?
Yes. Yes please.

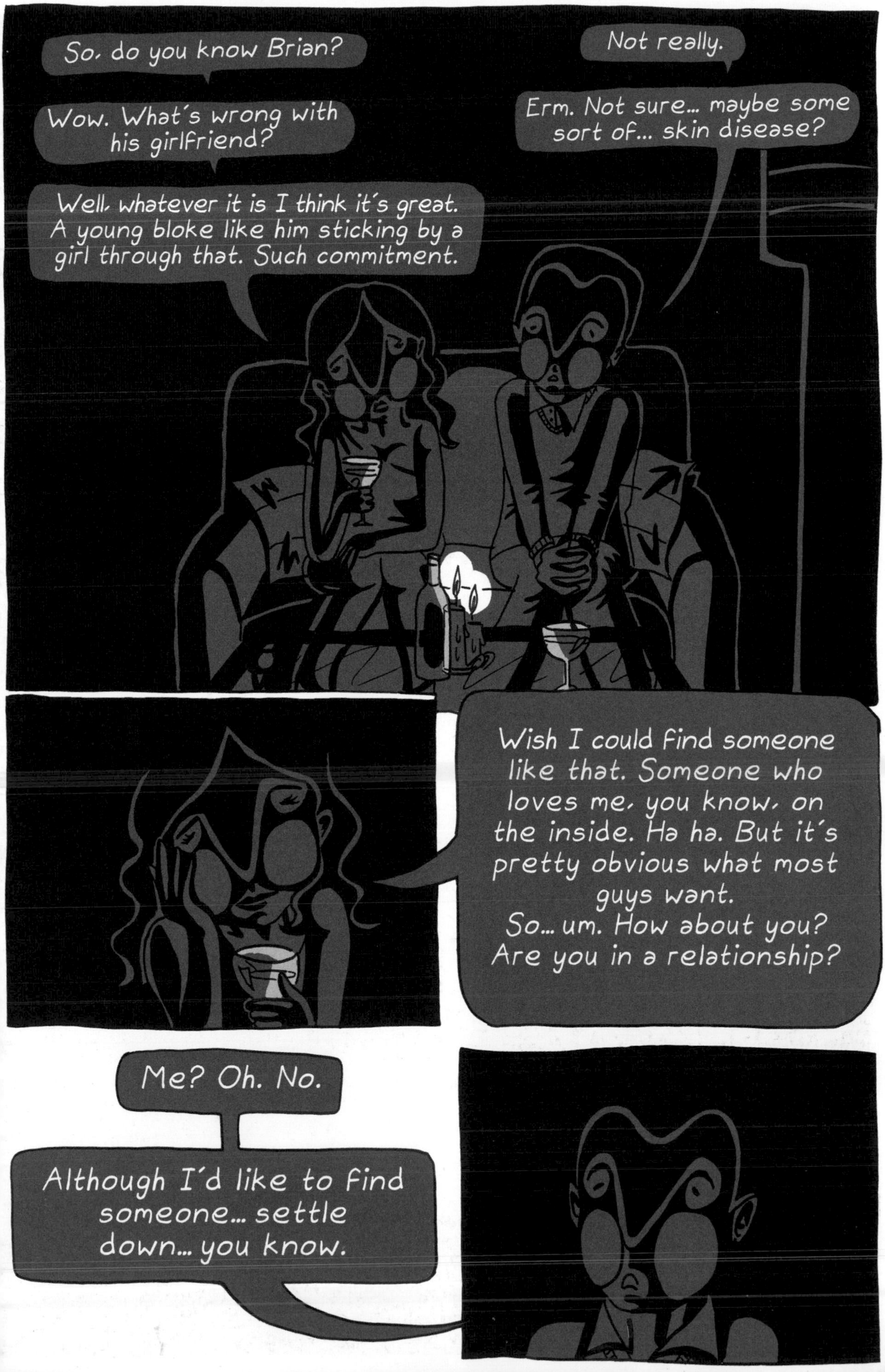
So, do you know Brian?
Not really.
Wow. What's wrong with his girlfriend?
Erm. Not sure... maybe some sort of... skin disease?
Well, whatever it is I think it's great. A young bloke like him sticking by a girl through that. Such commitment.
Wish I could find someone like that. Someone who loves me, you know, on the inside. Ha ha. But it's pretty obvious what most guys want.
So... um. How about you? Are you in a relationship?
Me? Oh. No.
Although I'd like to find someone... settle down... you know.

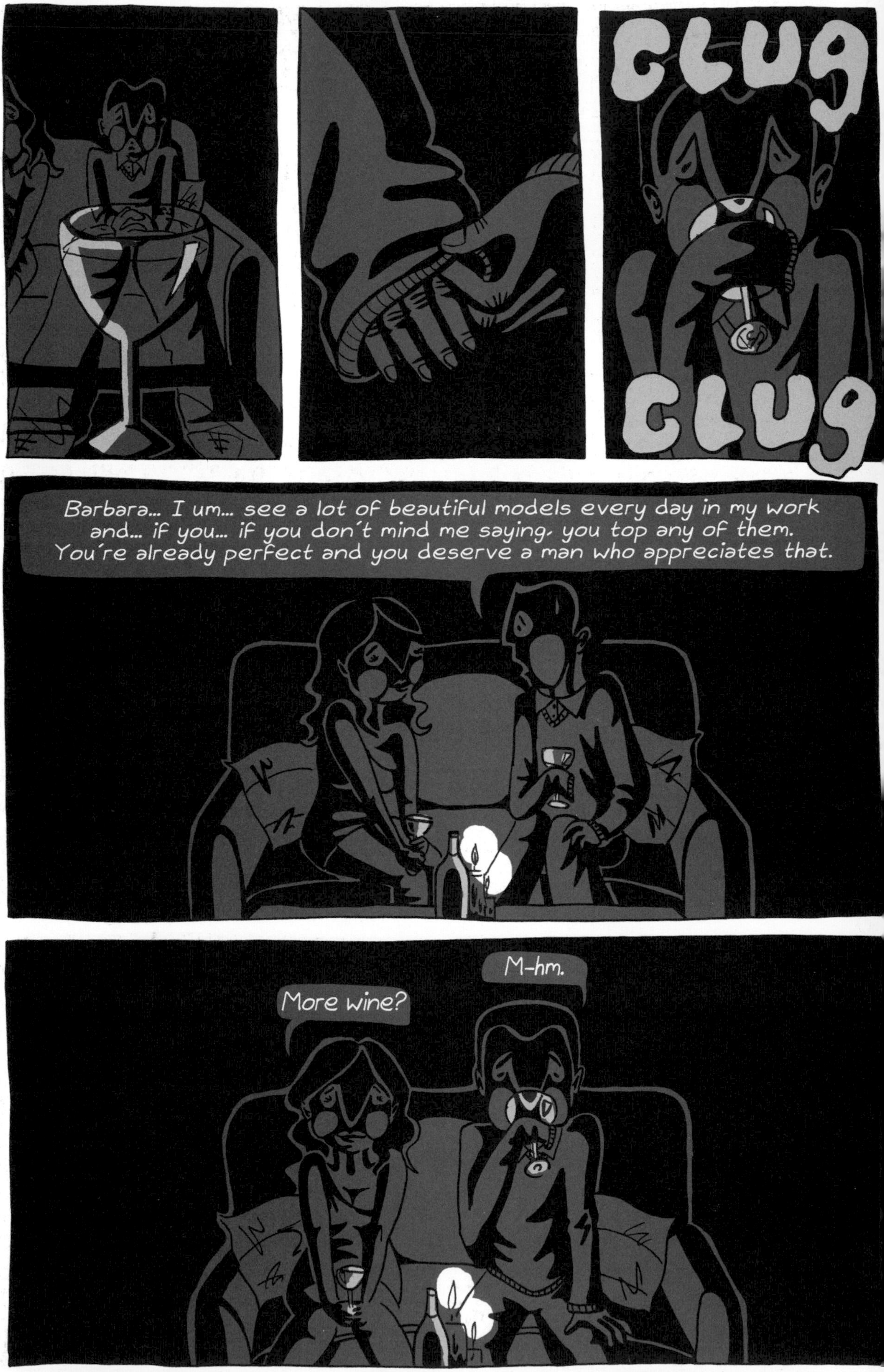
CLUG
CLUG
Barbara... I um... see a lot of beautiful models every day in my work and... if you... if you don't mind me saying, you top any of them. You're already perfect and you deserve a man who appreciates that.
More wine?
M-hm.

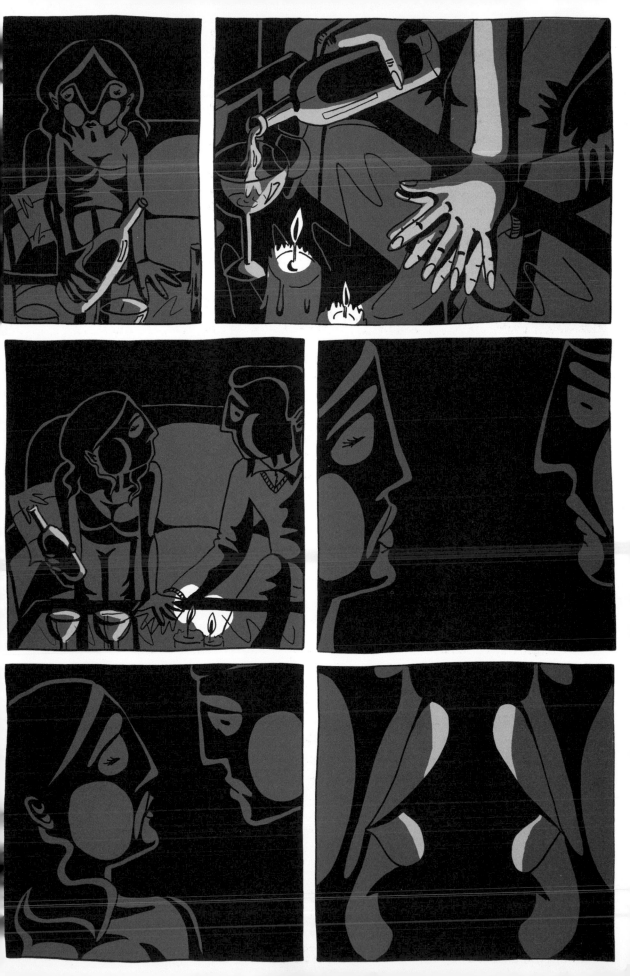

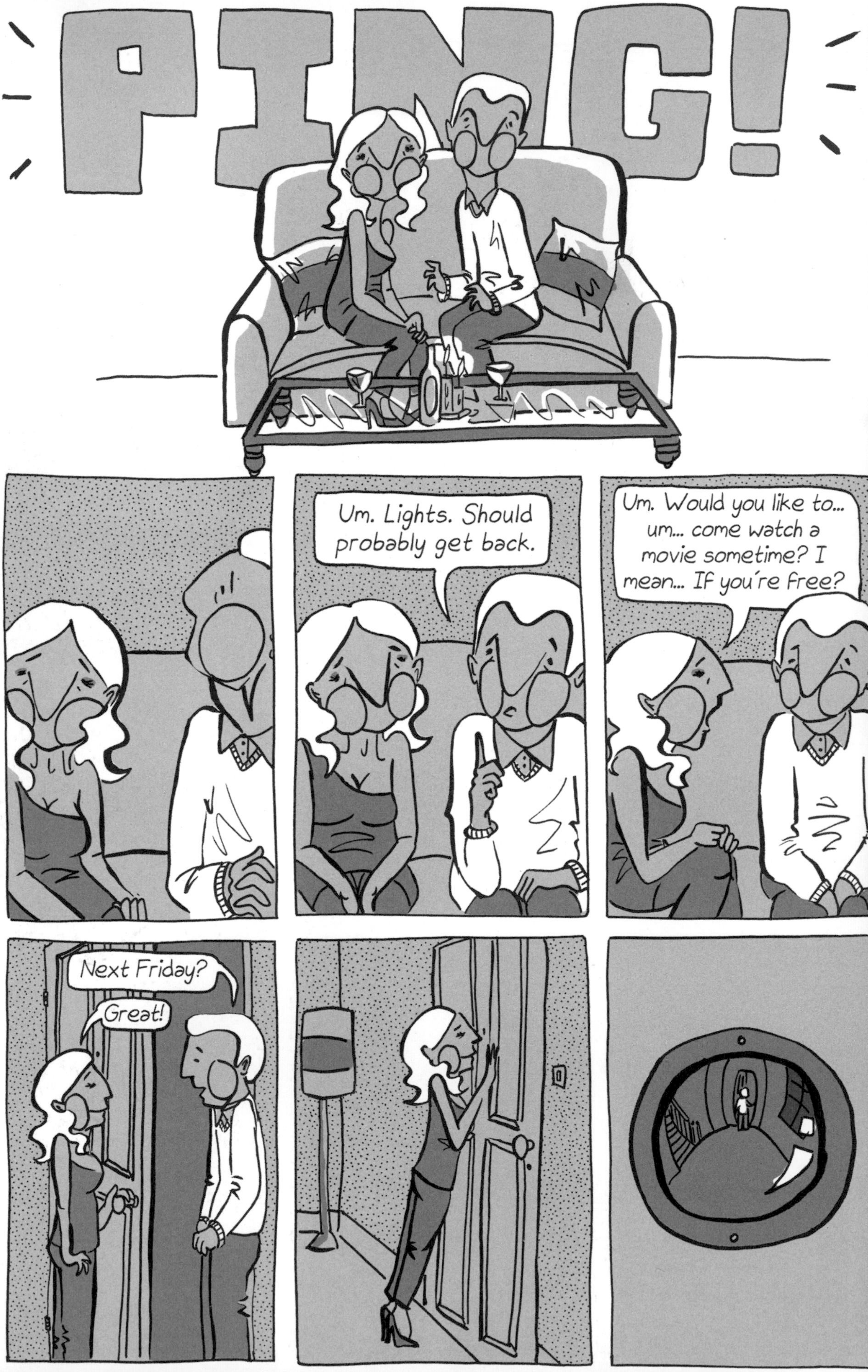
PING!
Um. Lights. Should probably get back.
Um. Would you like to... um... come watch a movie sometime? I mean... If you're free?
Next Friday?
Great!

Chapter Four

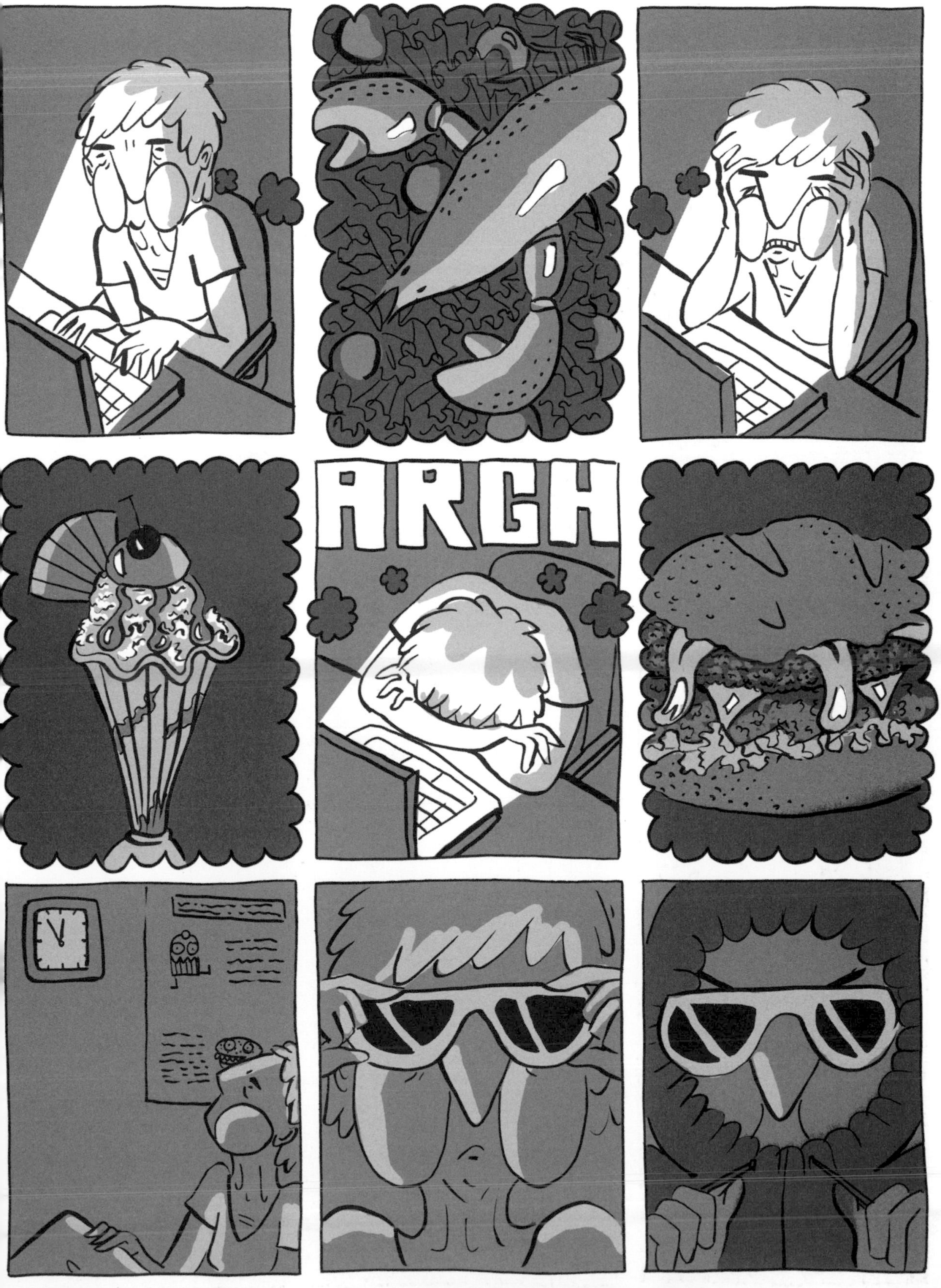
ARGH

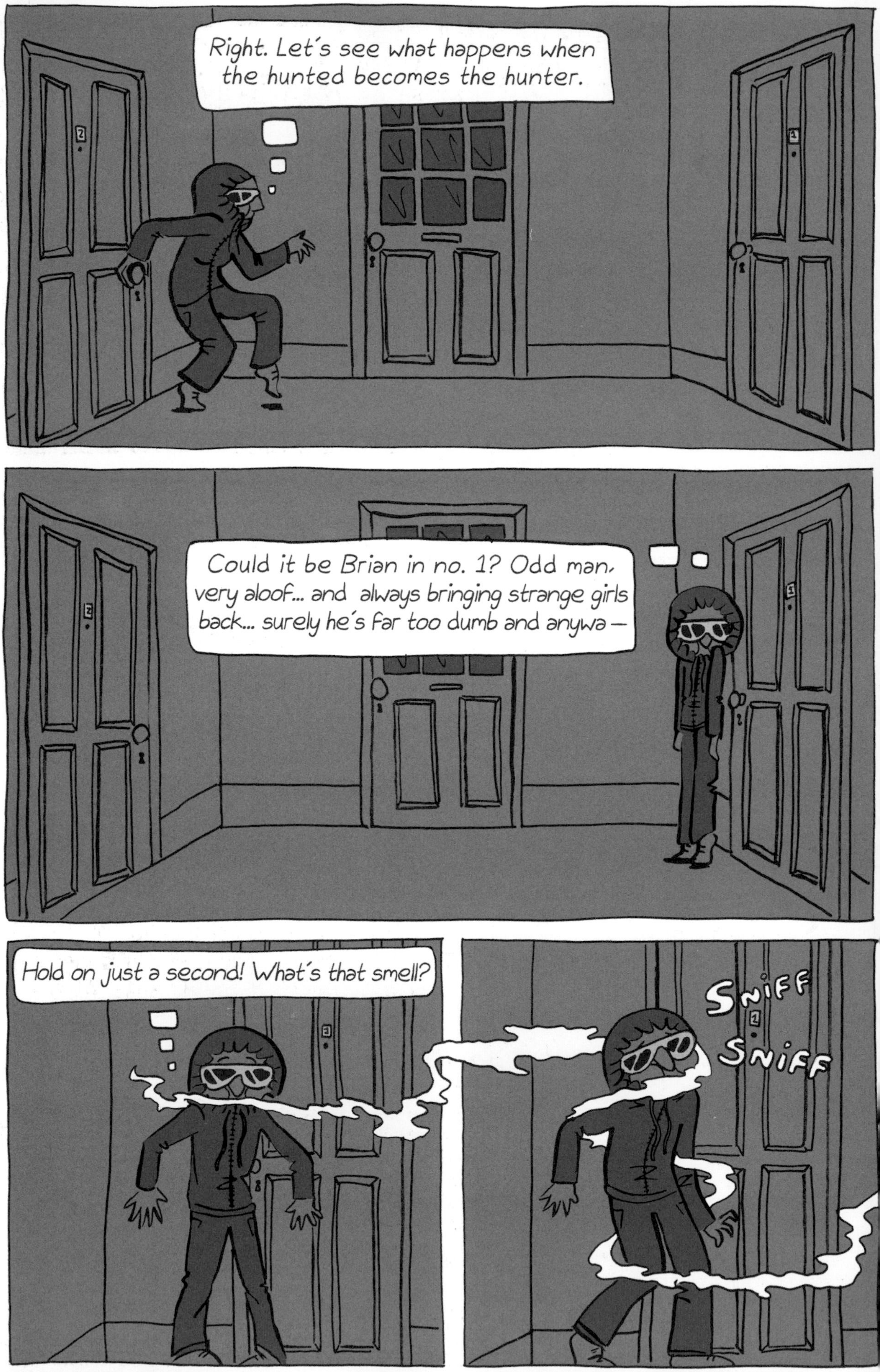
Right. Let's see what happens when the hunted becomes the hunter.
Could it be Brian in no. 1? Odd man, very aloof... and always bringing strange girls back... surely he's far too dumb and anywa –
Hold on just a second! What's that smell?
SNIFF
SNIFF

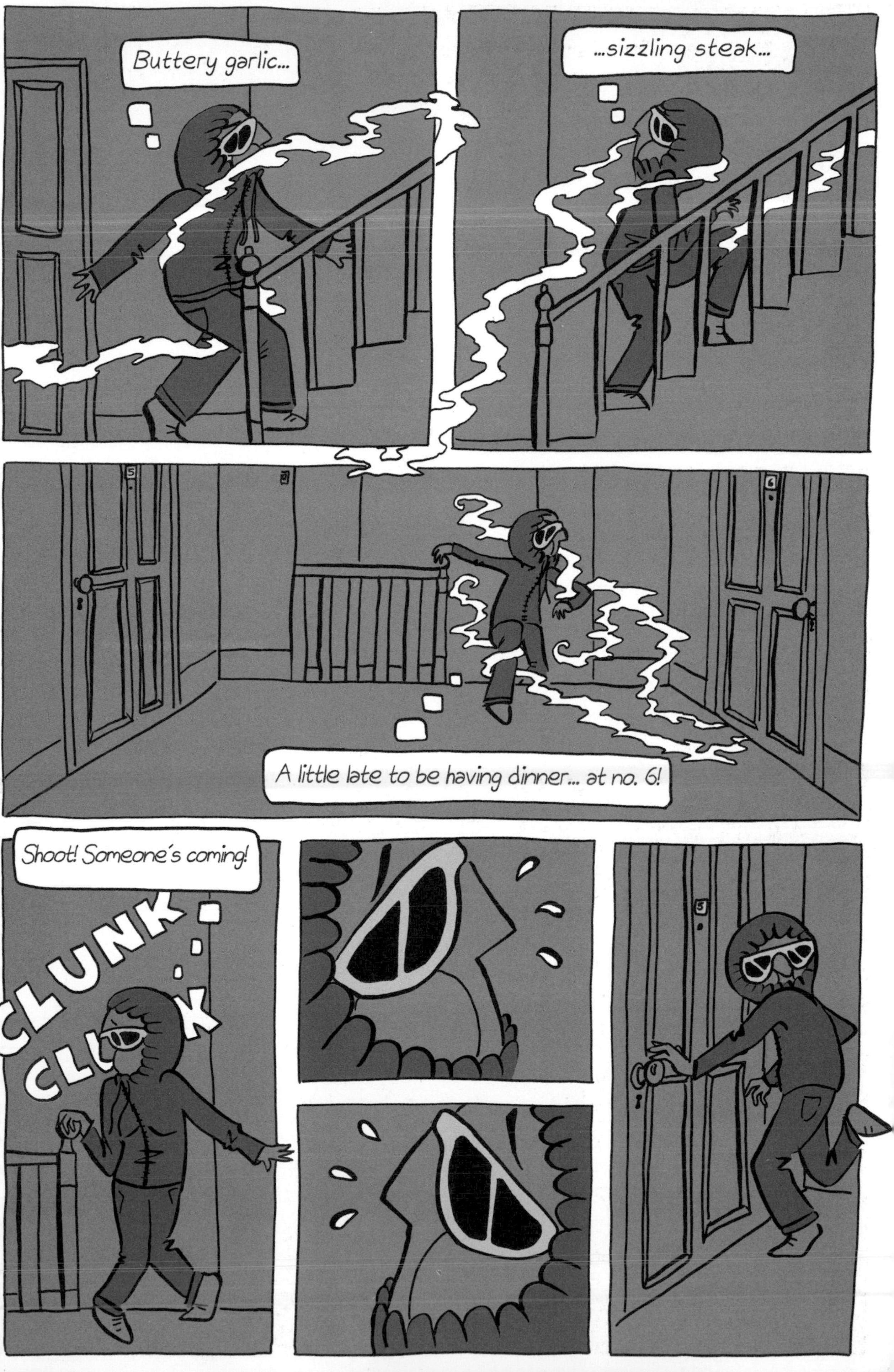
Buttery garlic...
...sizzling steak...
5
6
A little late to be having dinner... at no. 6!
Shoot! Someone's coming!
CLUNK
CLUNK
5

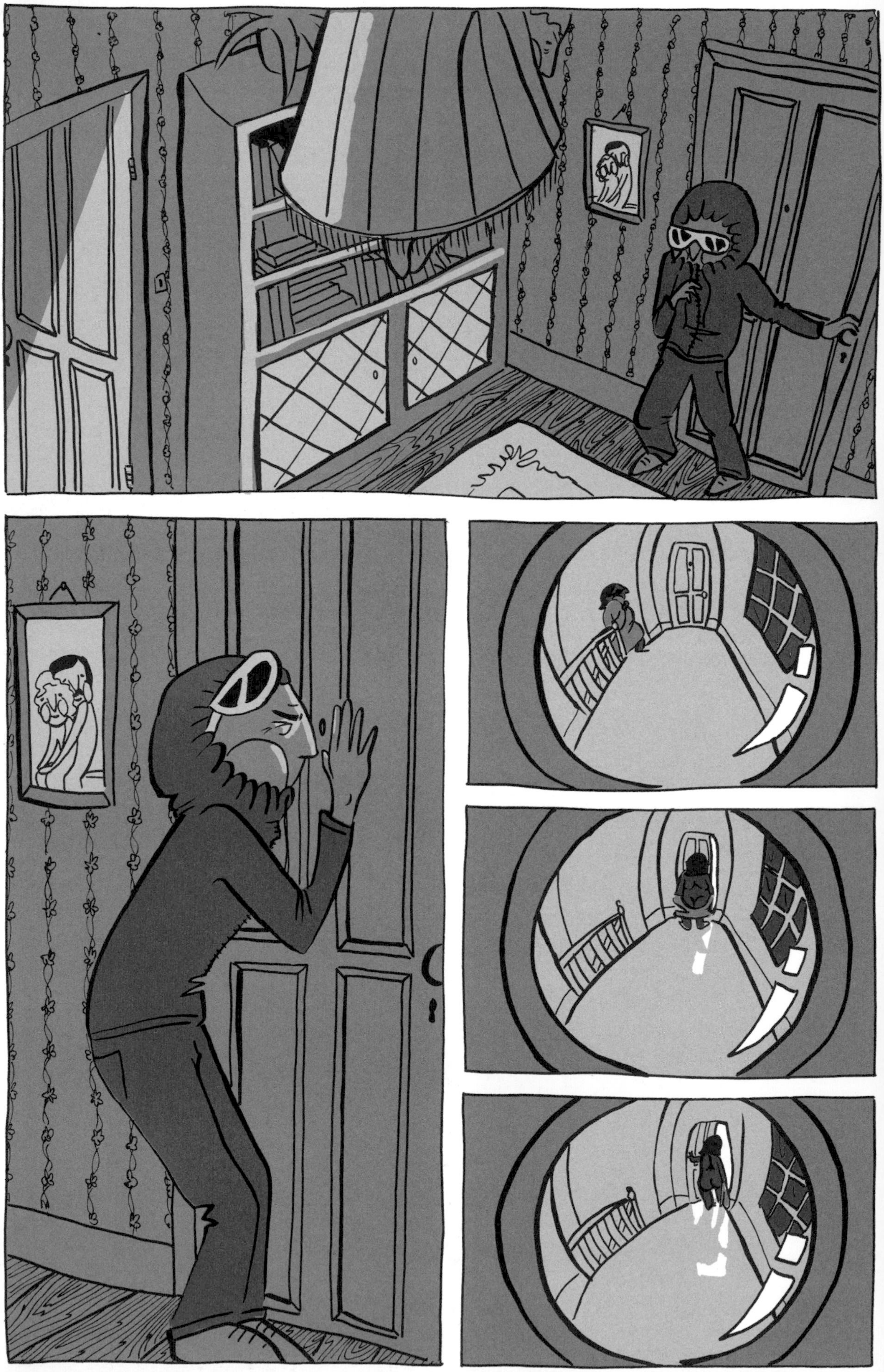

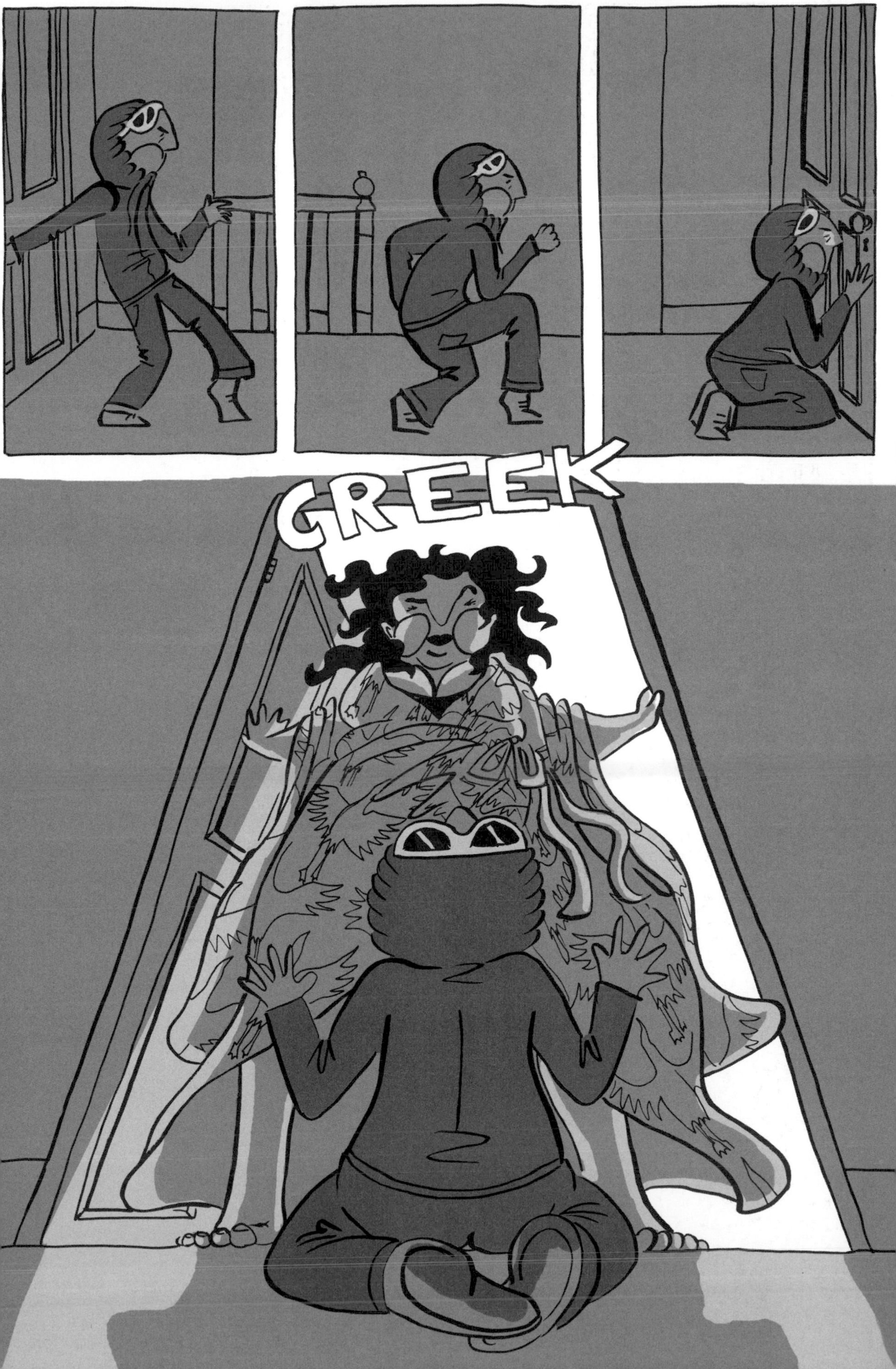
CREEK

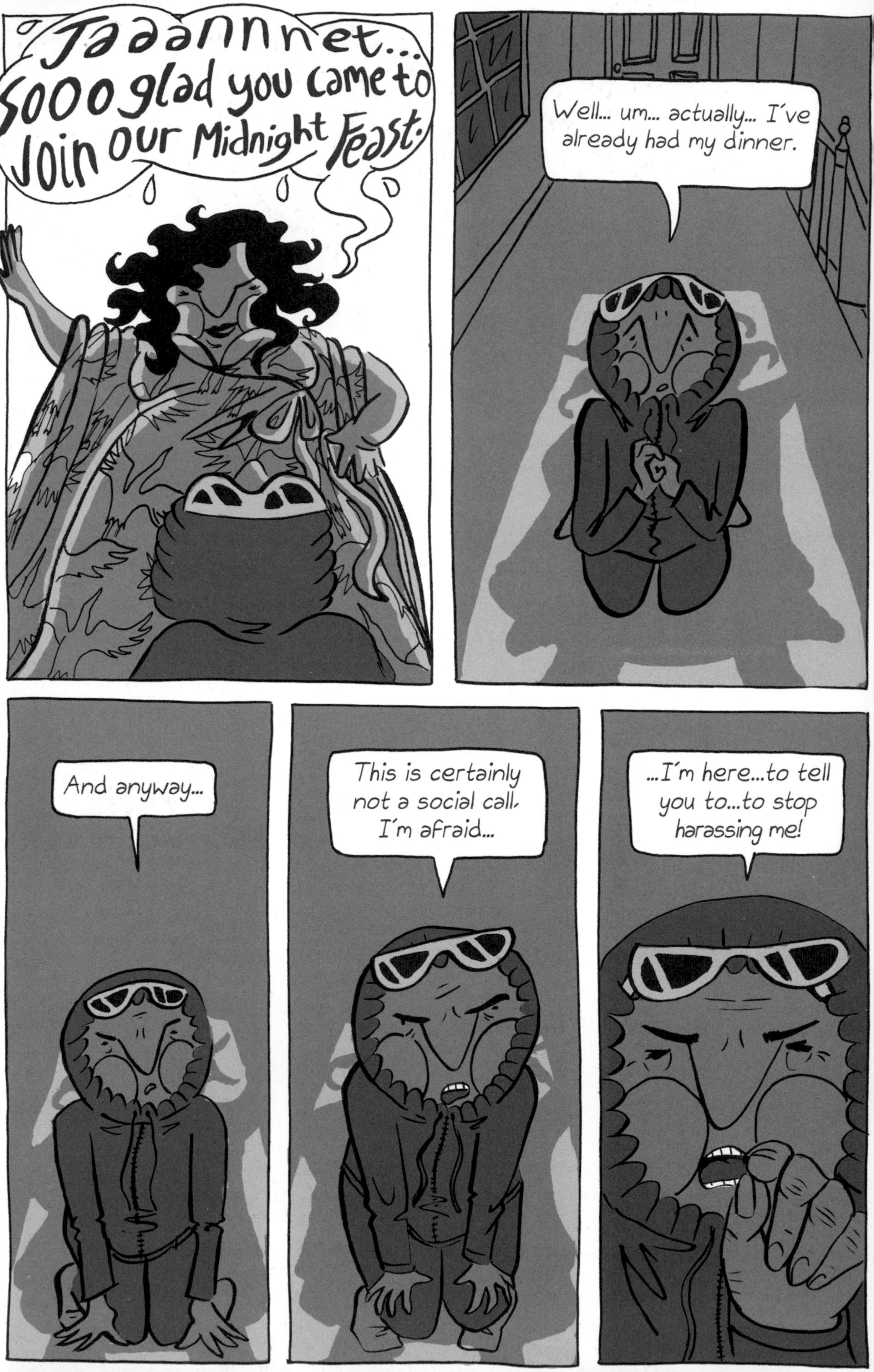
Jaaannnet... Sooo glad you came to Join our Midnight Feast.
Well... um... actually... I've already had my dinner.
And anyway...
This is certainly not a social call, I'm afraid...
...I'm here...to tell you to...to stop harassing me!

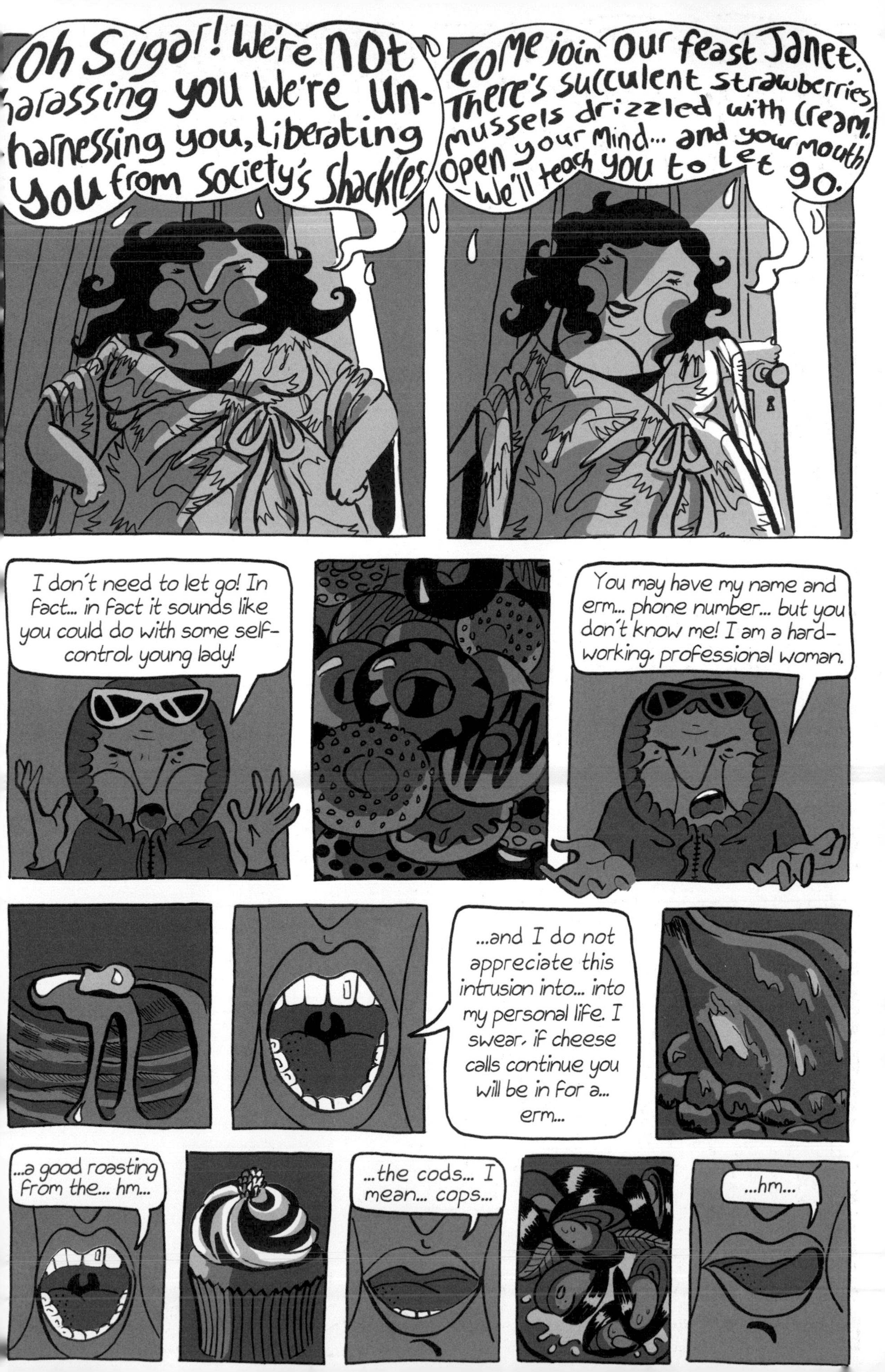

Oh Sugar! We're NOT harassing you we're un-harnessing you, liberating you from society's shackles.
Come join our feast Janet. There's succulent strawberries, mussels drizzled with cream. Open your mind... and your mouth – we'll teach you to let go.
I don't need to let go! In fact... in fact it sounds like you could do with some self-control, young lady!
You may have my name and erm... phone number... but you don't know me! I am a hard-working, professional woman.
...and I do not appreciate this intrusion into... into my personal life. I swear, if cheese calls continue you will be in for a... erm...
...a good roasting from the... hm...
...the cods... I mean... cops...
...hm...

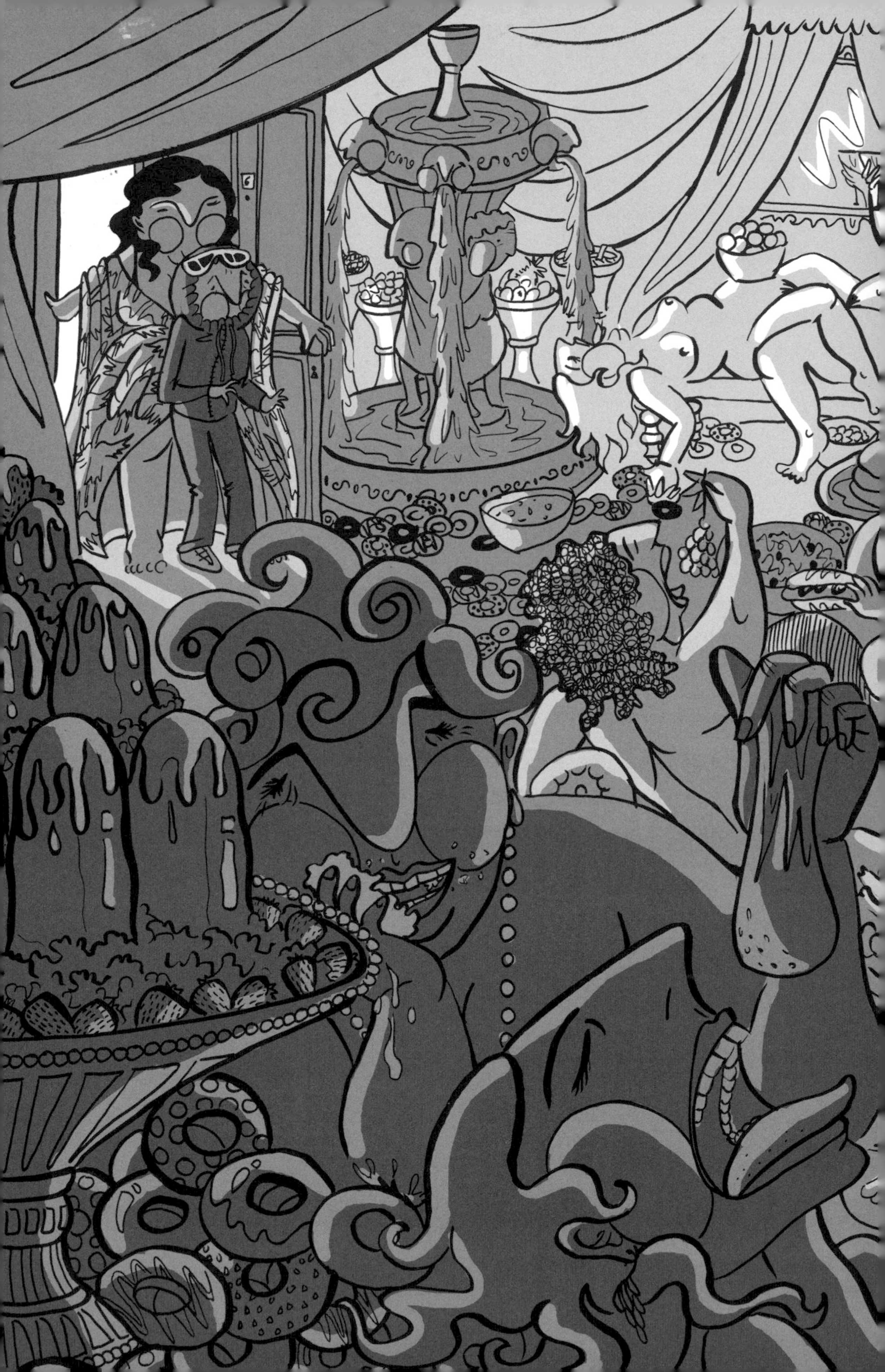

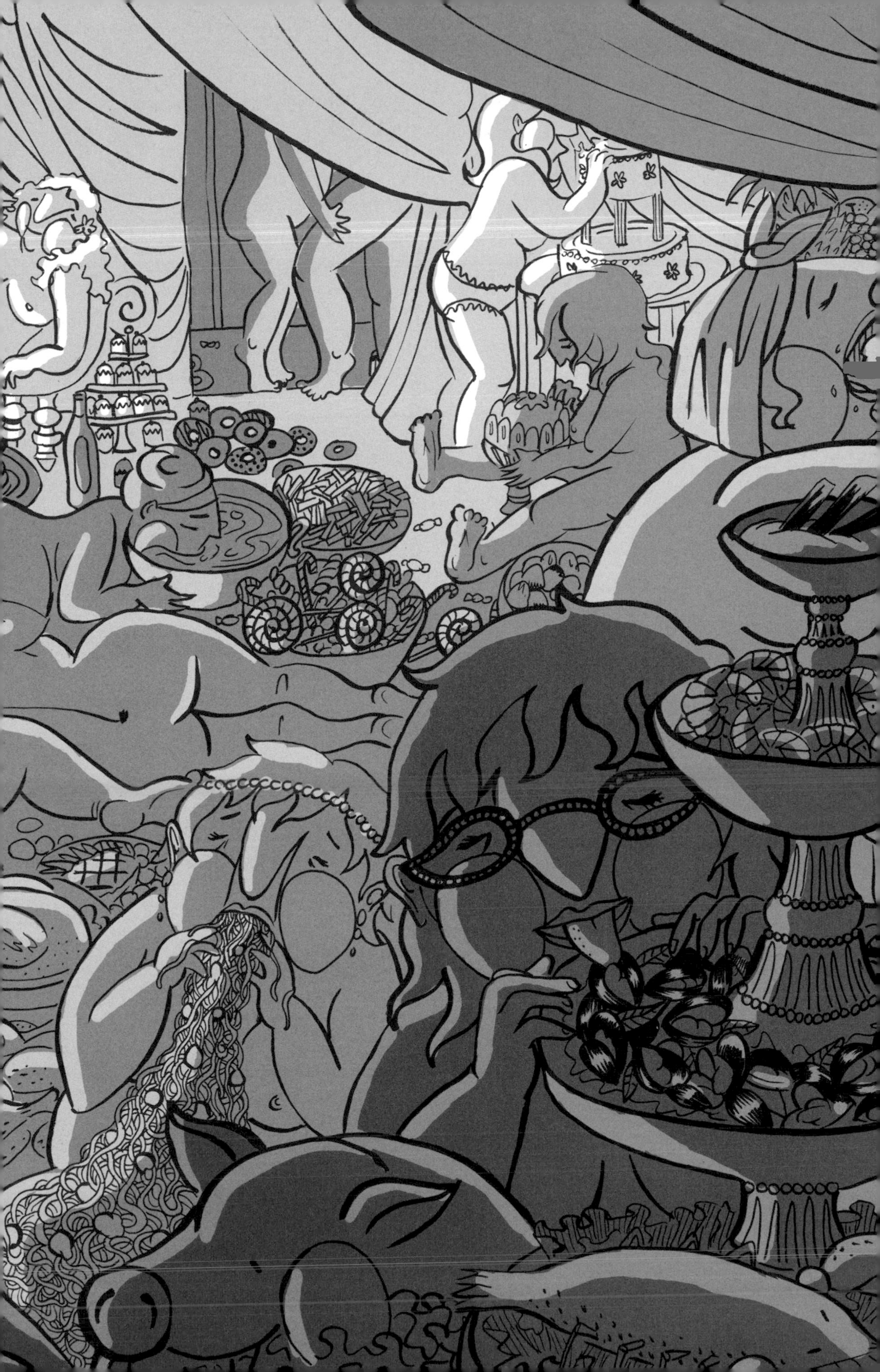

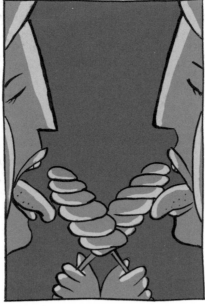
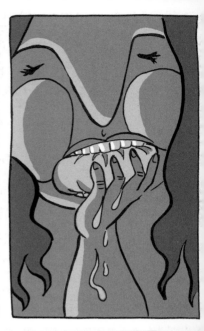

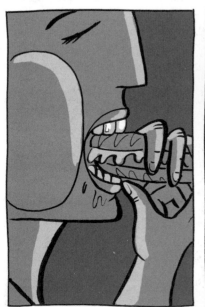

This behaviour is shameful!

And Lizzie! Now I see why you've been missing my classes!

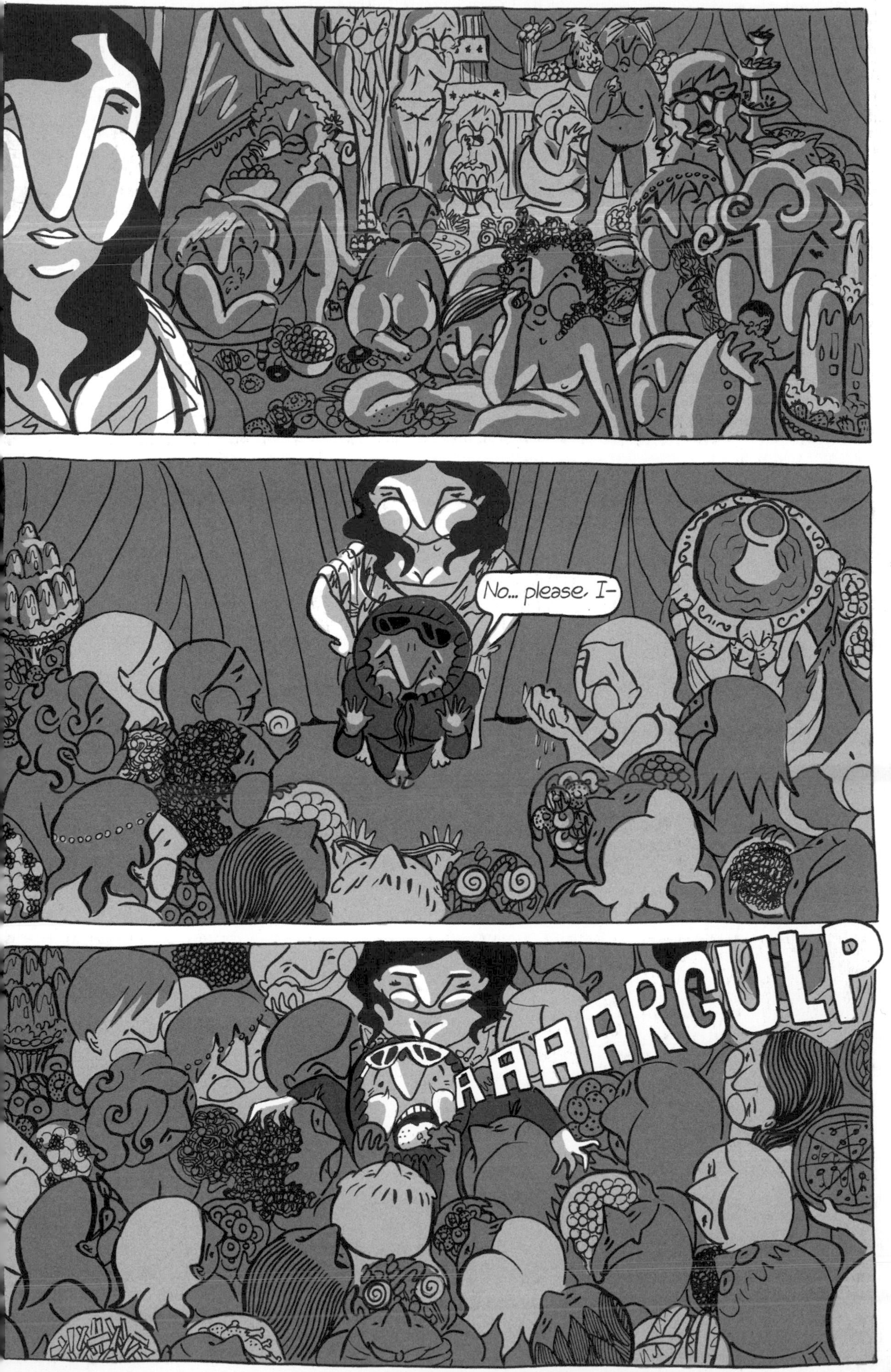
No... please, I-
AAAAARGULP

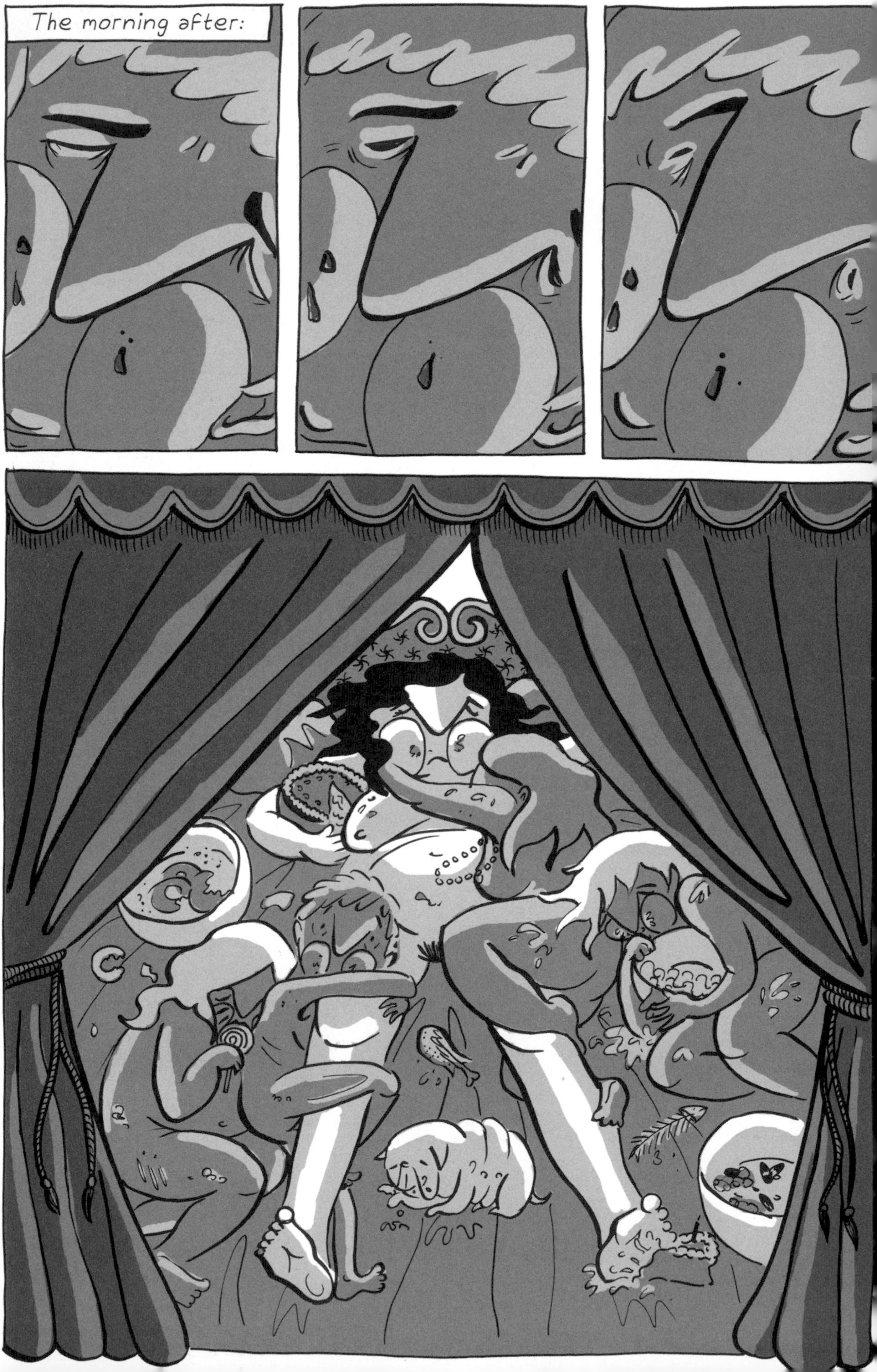
The morning after:

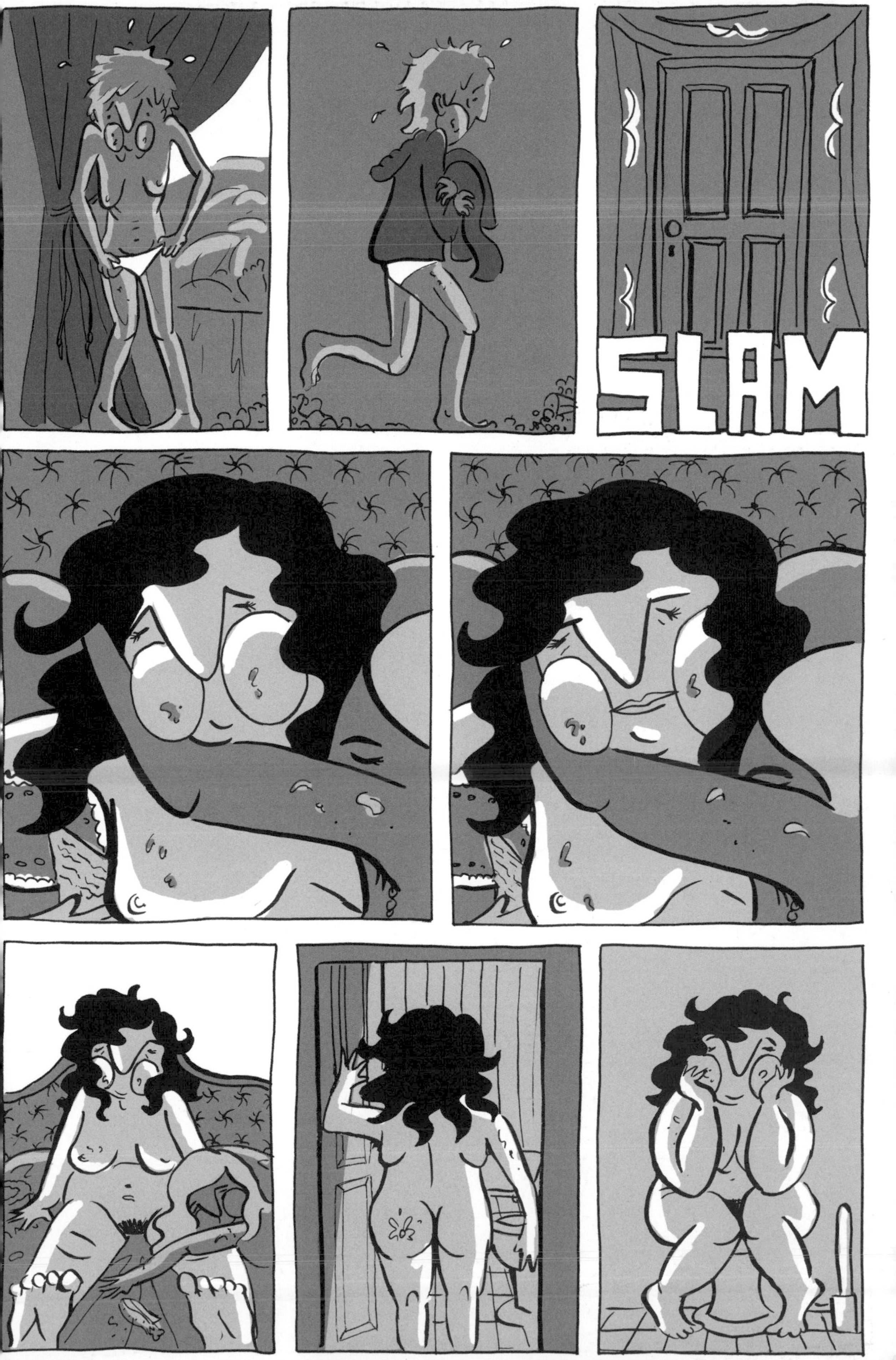
SLAM

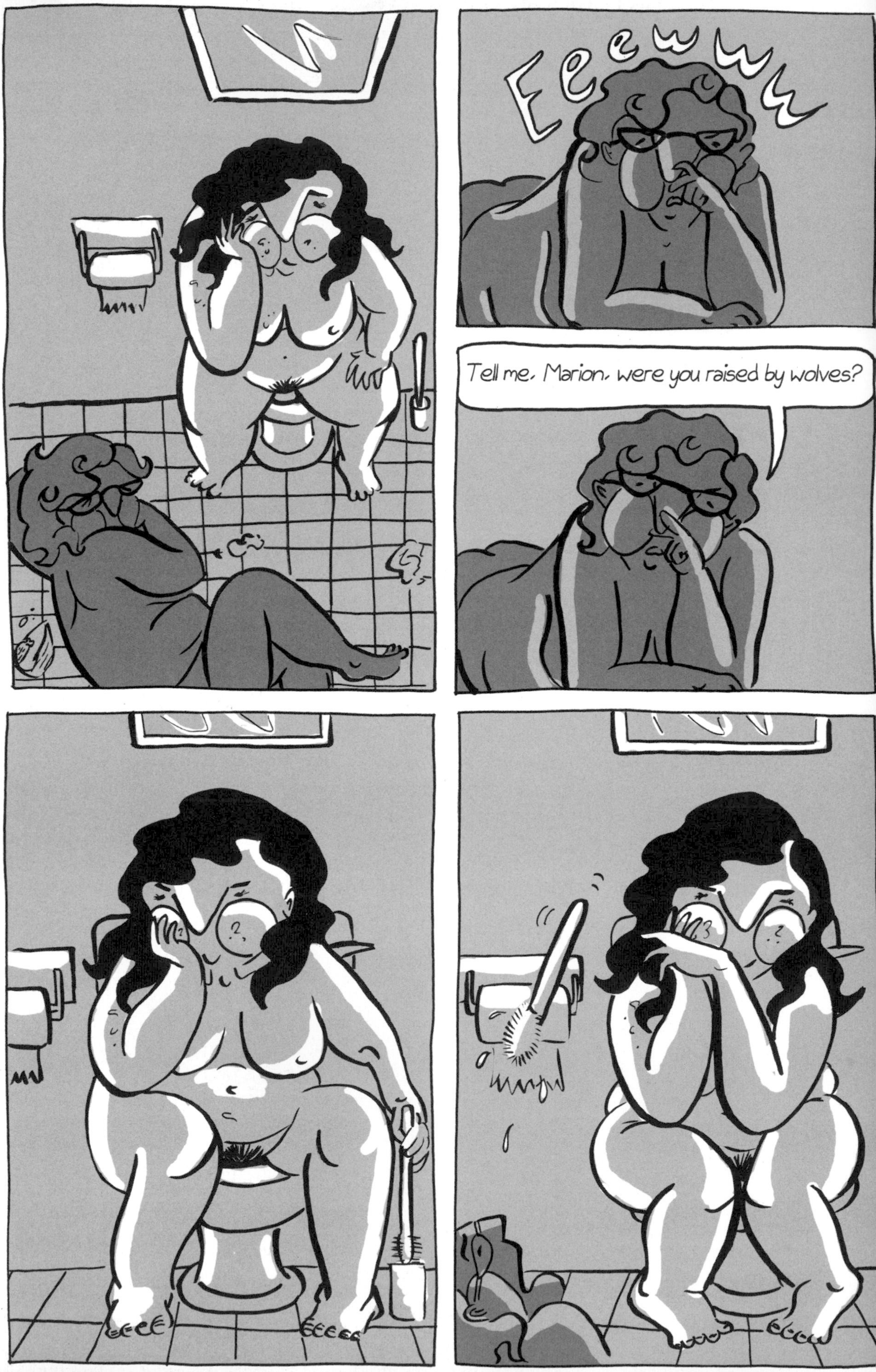
Eeewww
Tell me, Marion, were you raised by wolves?

The Building of Rottin Road, 1865.

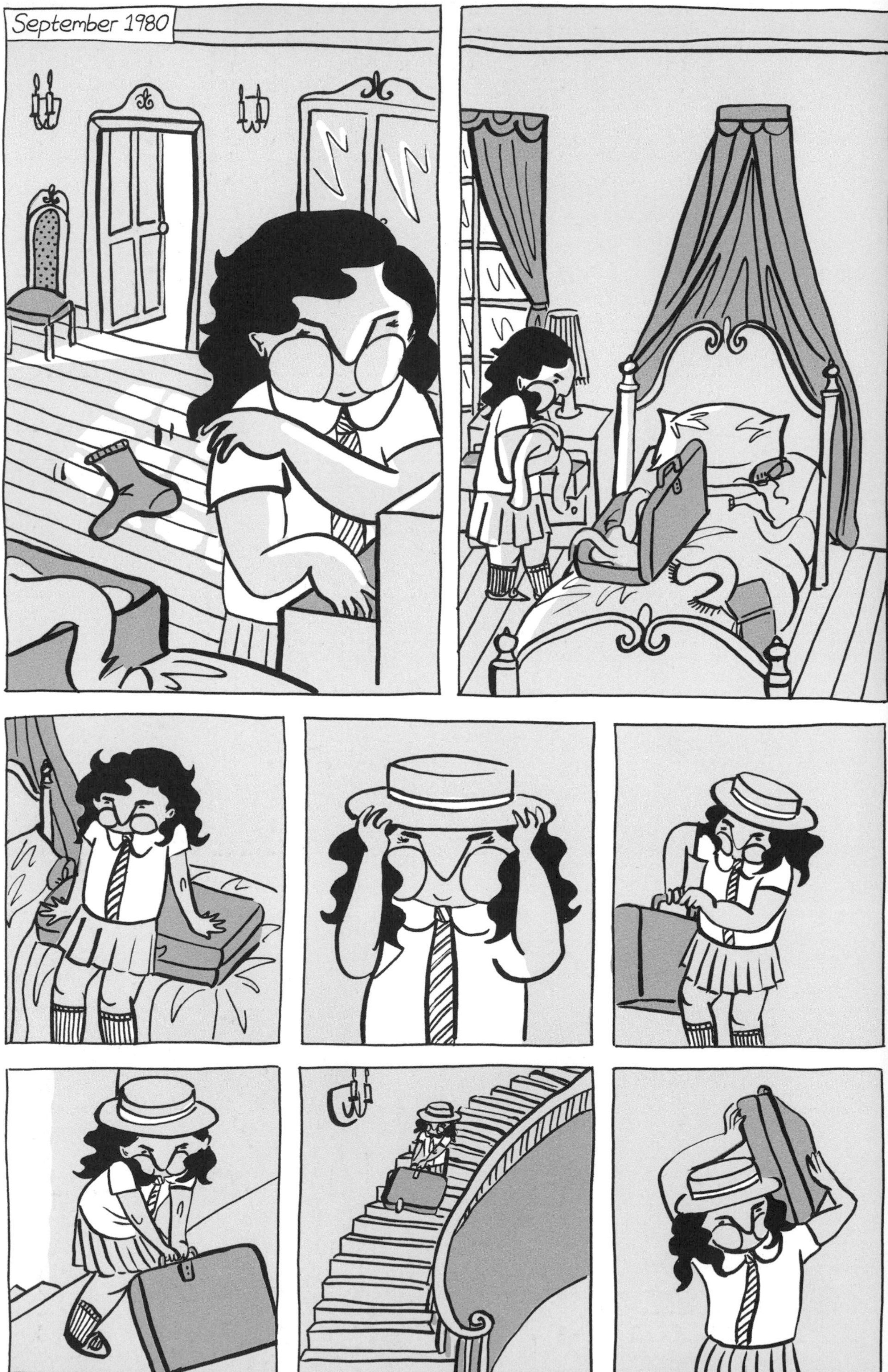
September 1980

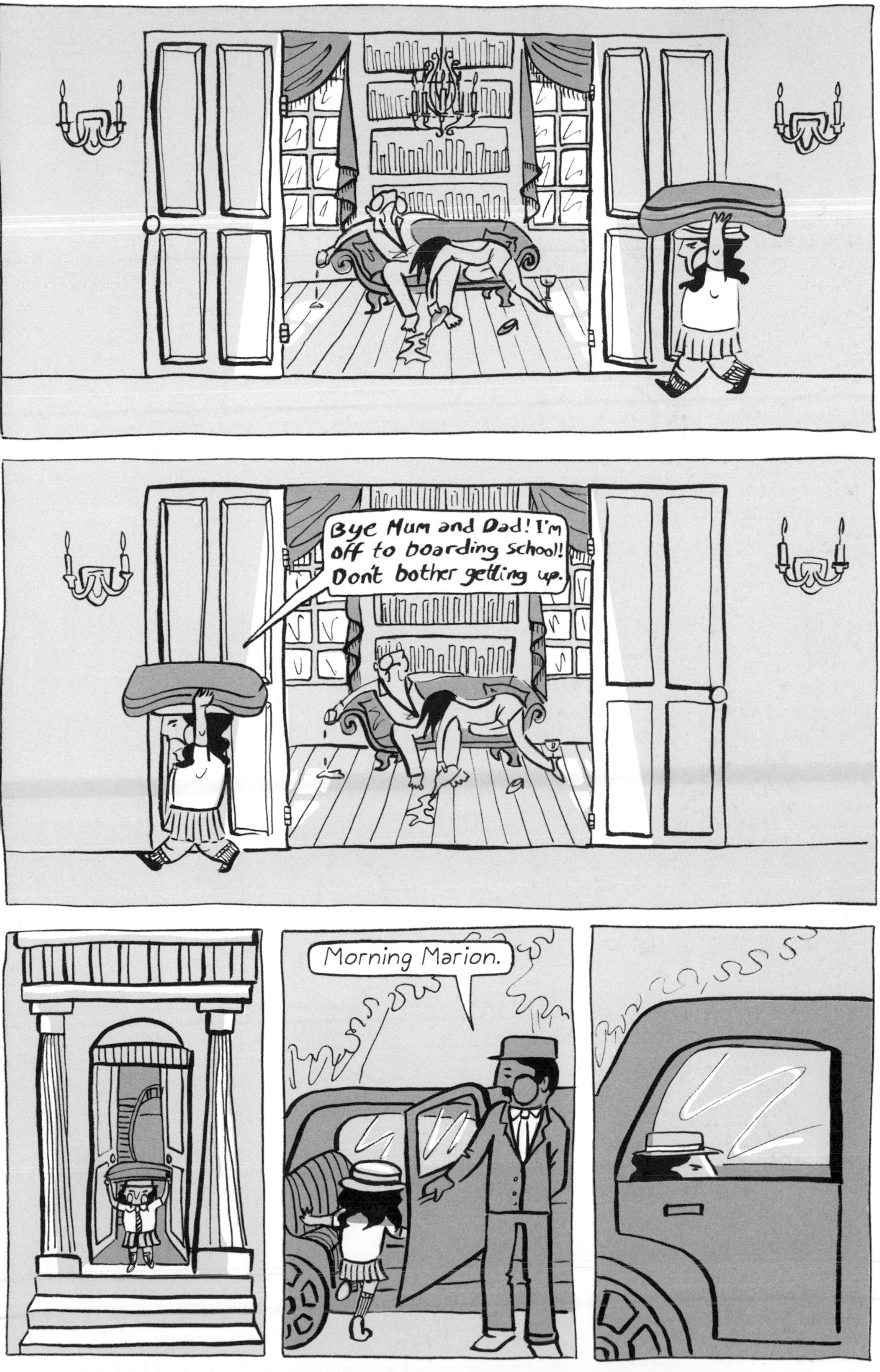
Bye Mum and Dad! I'm off to boarding school! Don't bother getting up.
Morning Marion.

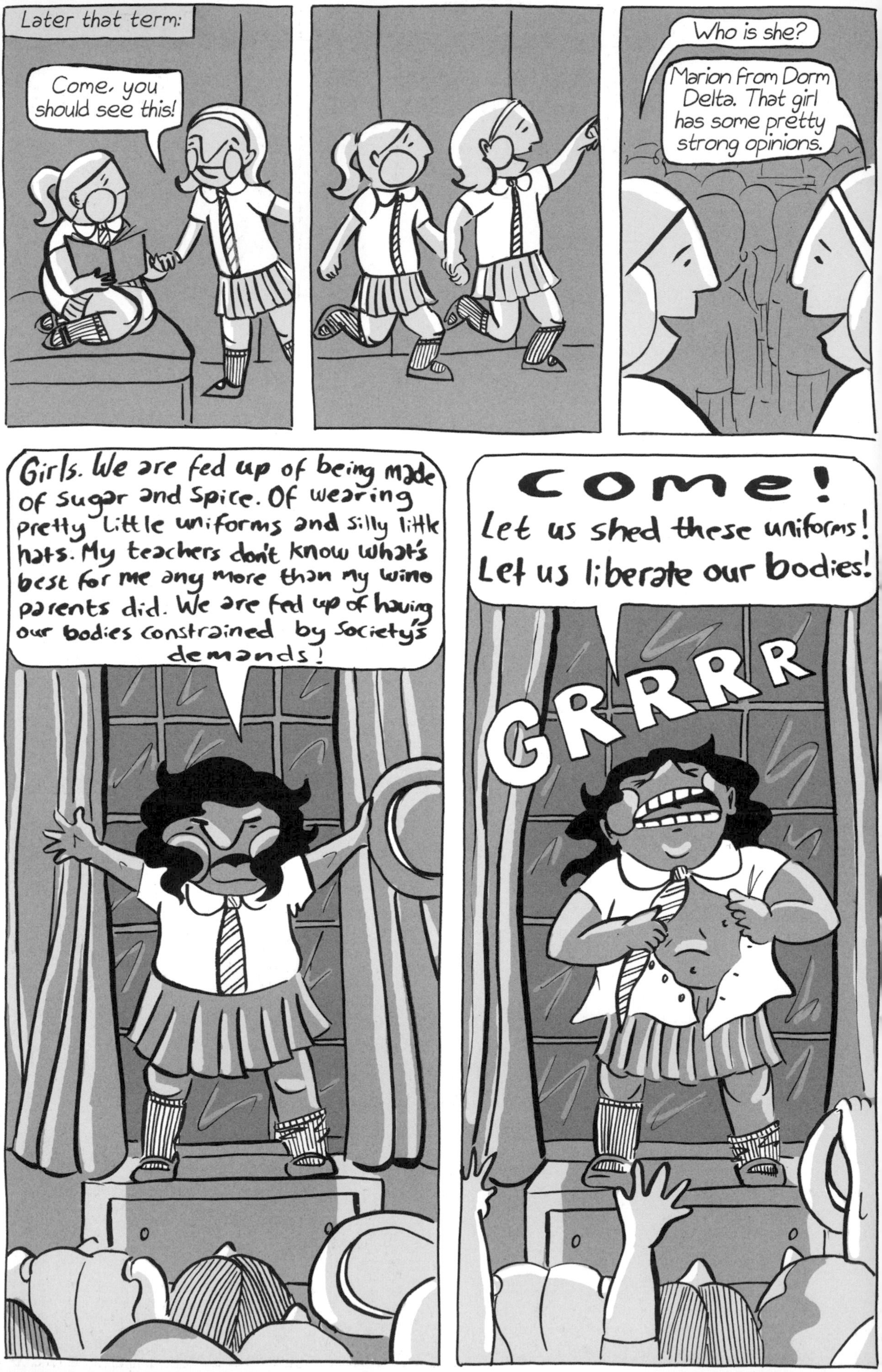
Later that term:
Come, you should see this!
Who is she?
Marion from Dorm Delta. That girl has some pretty strong opinions.
Girls. We are fed up of being made of sugar and spice. Of wearing pretty little uniforms and silly little hats. My teachers don't know what's best for me any more than my wino parents did. We are fed up of having our bodies constrained by society's demands!
COME!
Let us shed these uniforms!
Let us liberate our bodies!
GRRRR

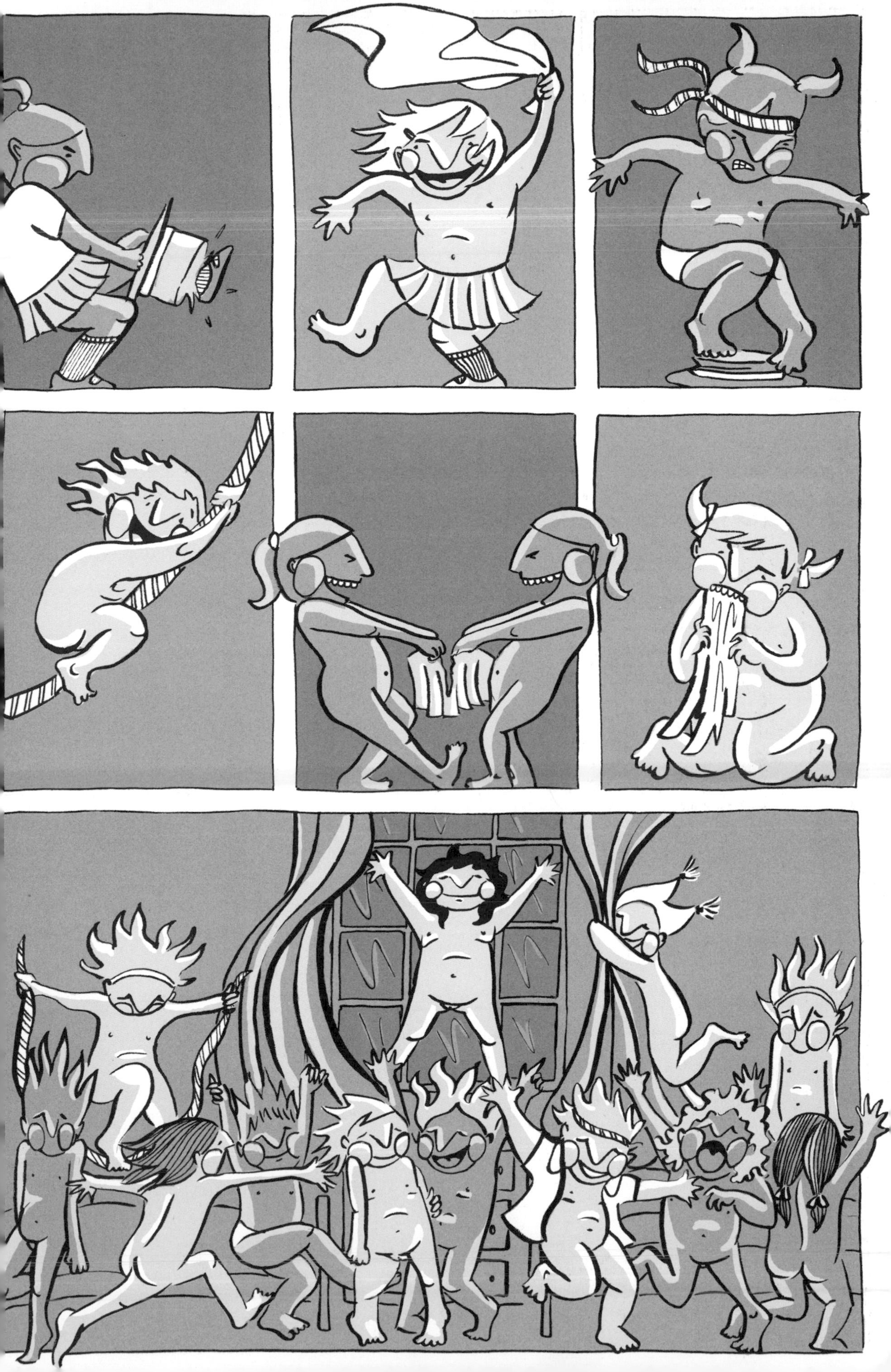

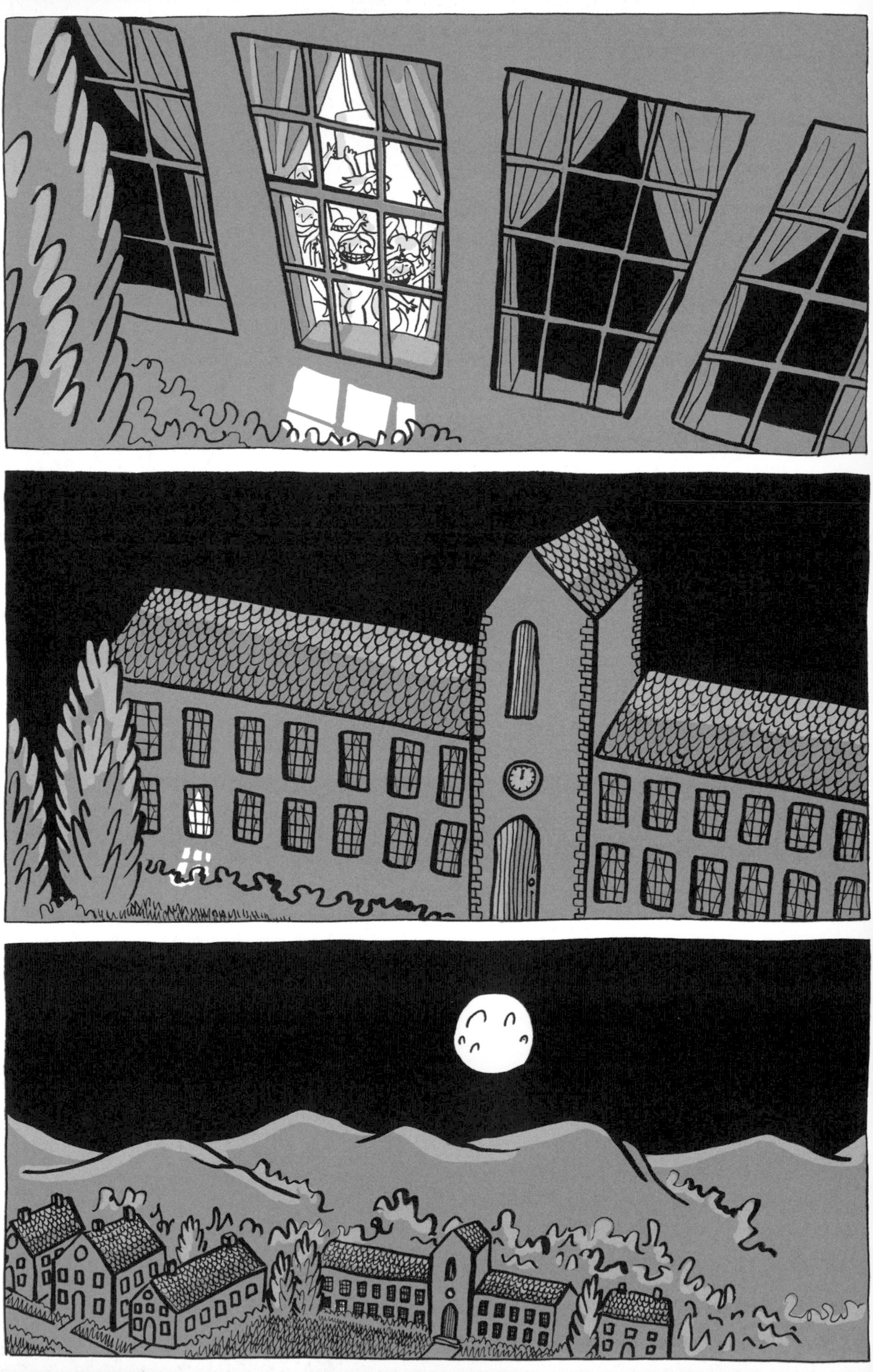

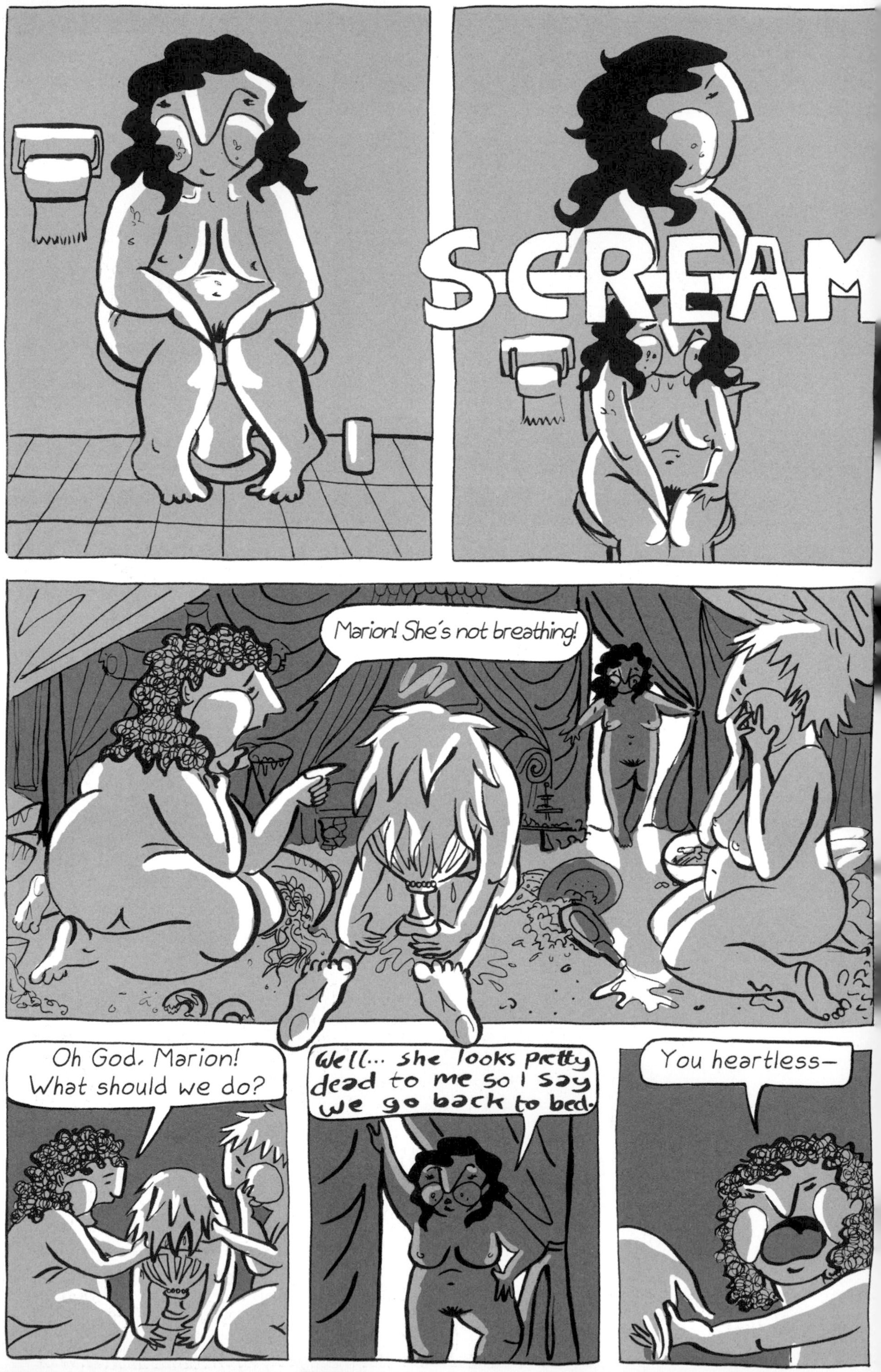
SCREAM
Marion! She's not breathing!
Oh God, Marion! What should we do?
Well... she looks pretty dead to me so I say we go back to bed.
You heartless—

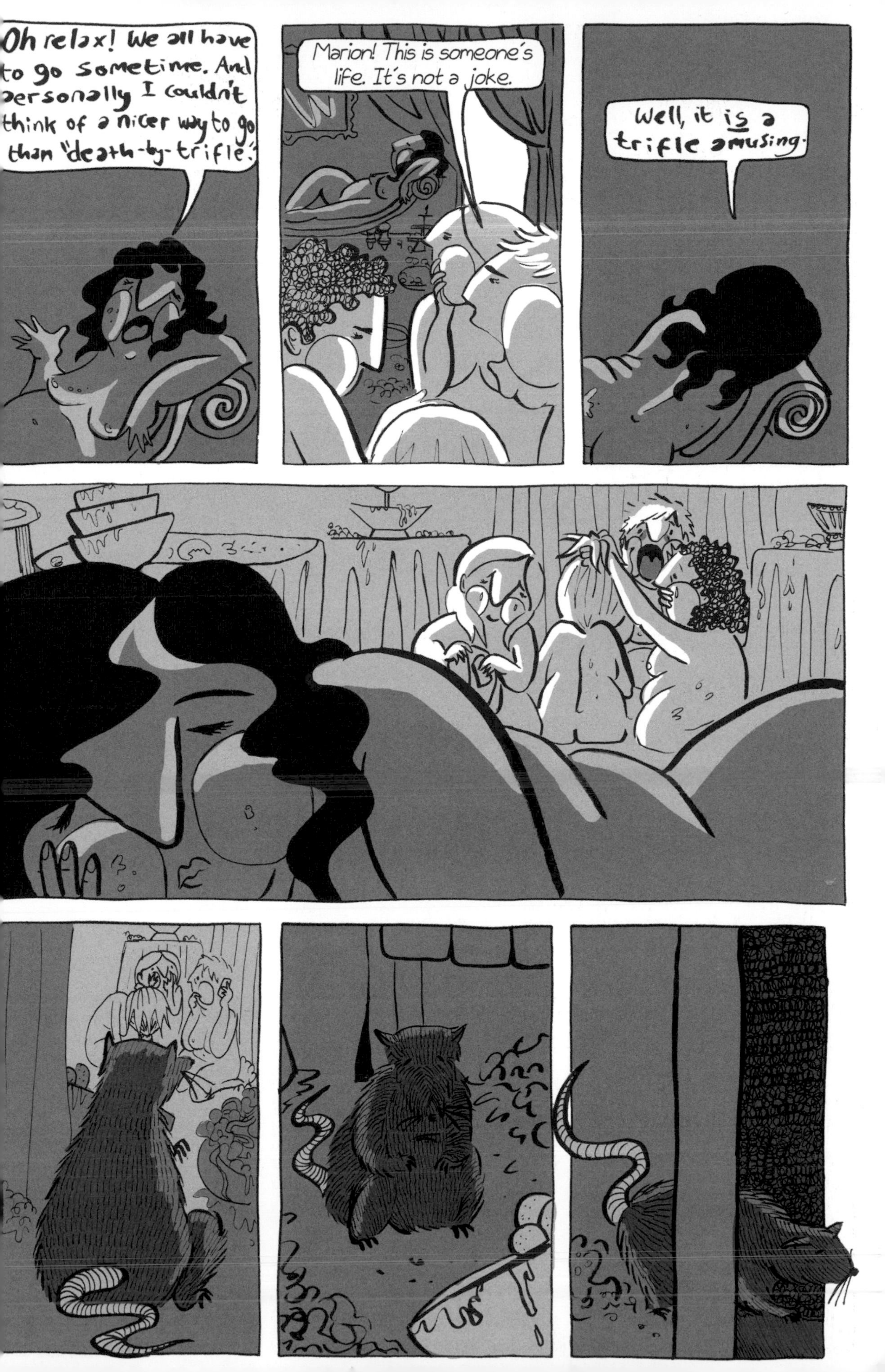
Oh relax! We all have to go sometime. And personally I couldn't think of a nicer way to go than "death-by-trifle".
Marion! This is someone's life. It's not a joke.
Well, it is a trifle amusing.

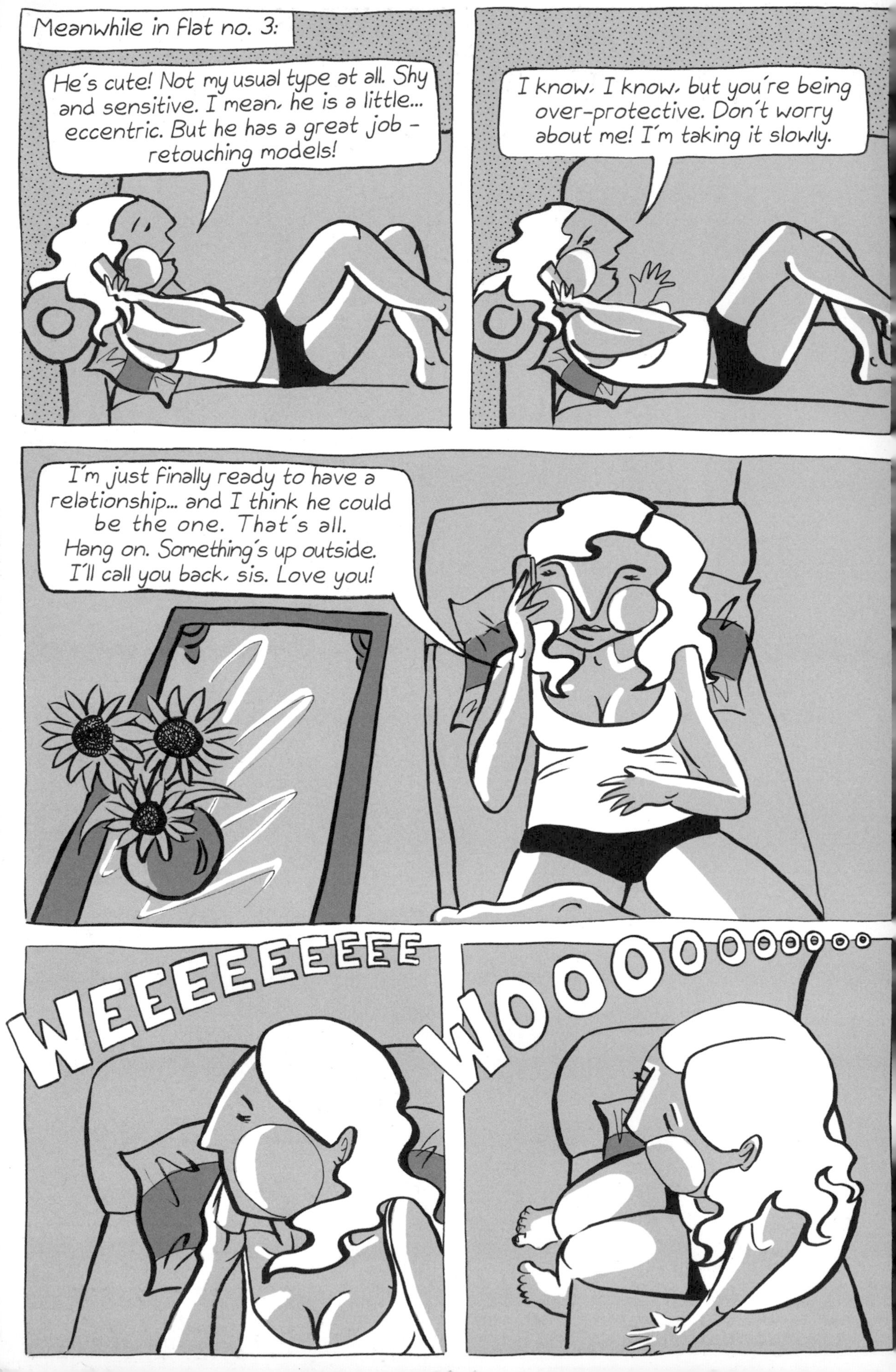
Meanwhile in flat no. 3:
He's cute! Not my usual type at all. Shy and sensitive. I mean, he is a little... eccentric. But he has a great job - retouching models!
I know, I know, but you're being over-protective. Don't worry about me! I'm taking it slowly.
I'm just finally ready to have a relationship... and I think he could be the one. That's all. Hang on. Something's up outside. I'll call you back, sis. Love you!
WEEEEEEEEEE
WOOOOOOOOOOO

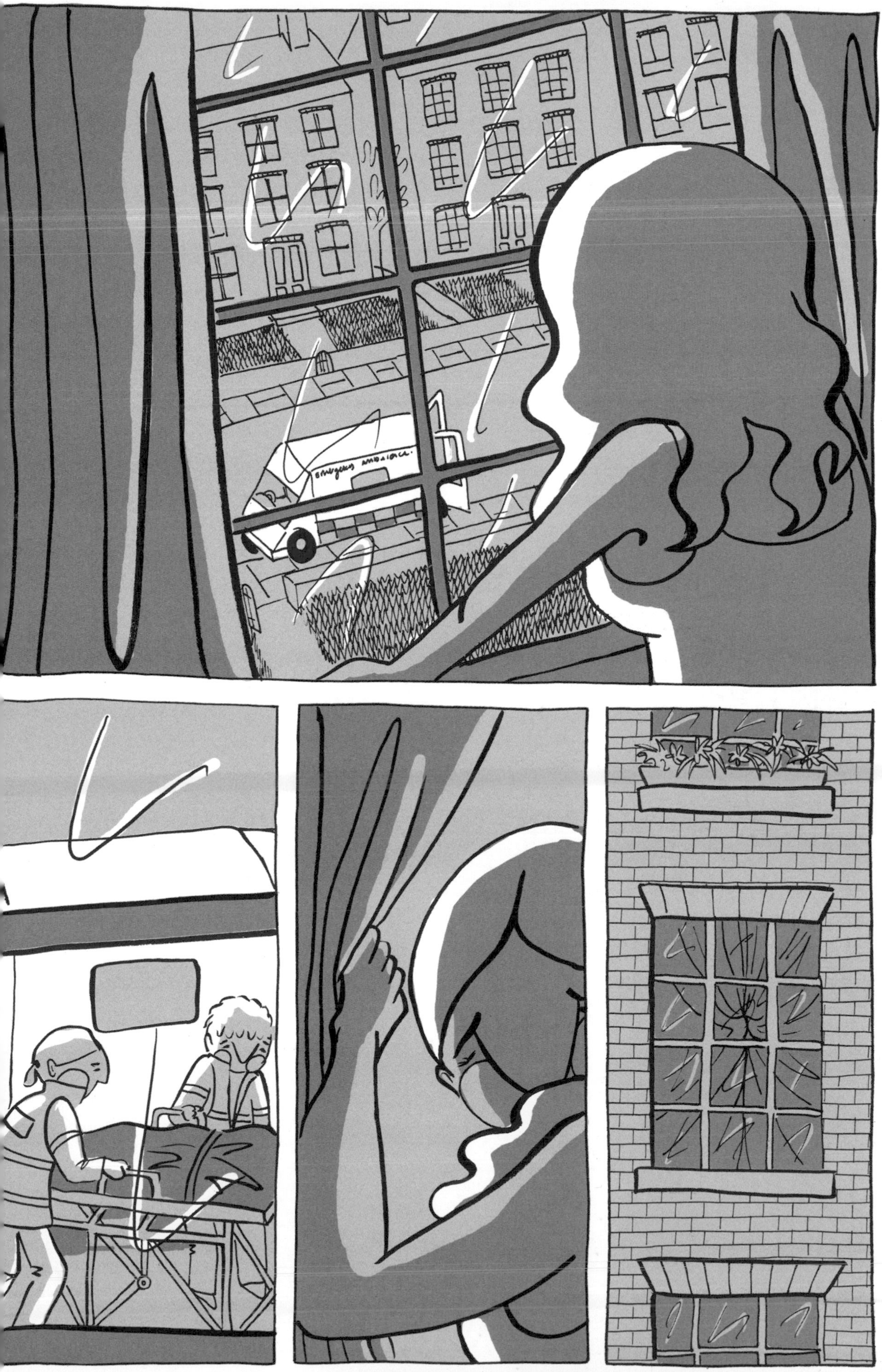

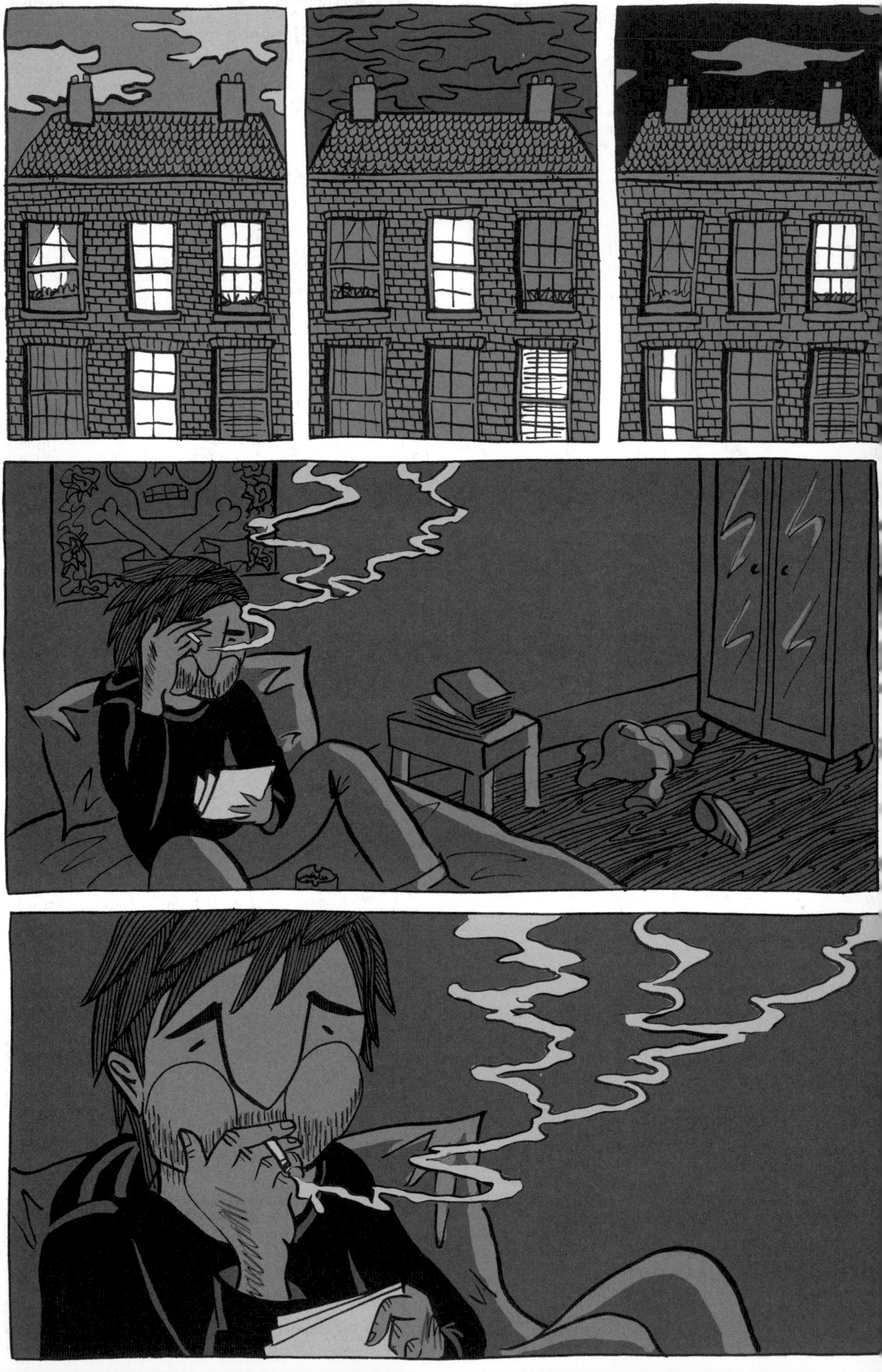

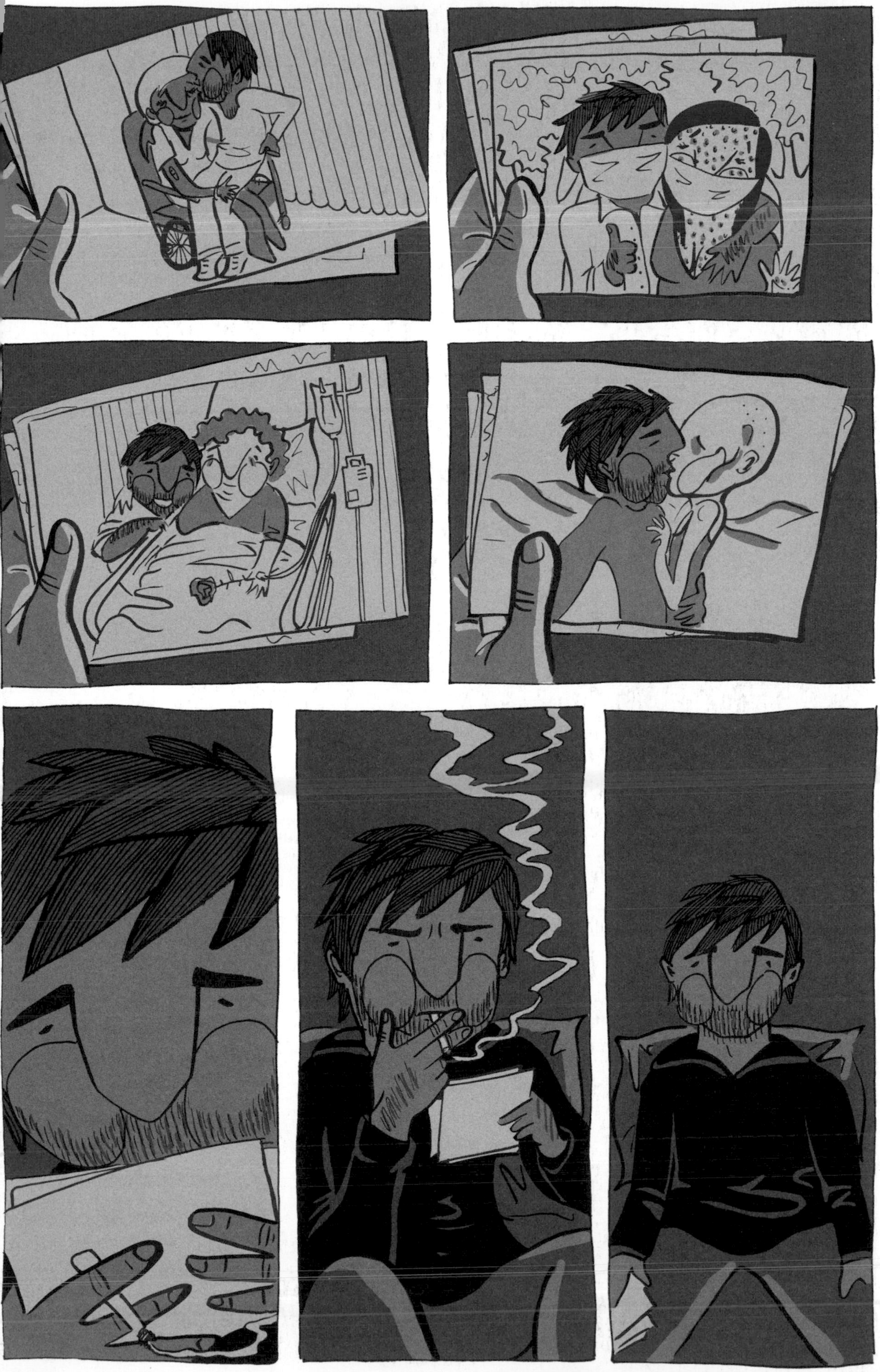

The Building of Rottin Road, 1865.

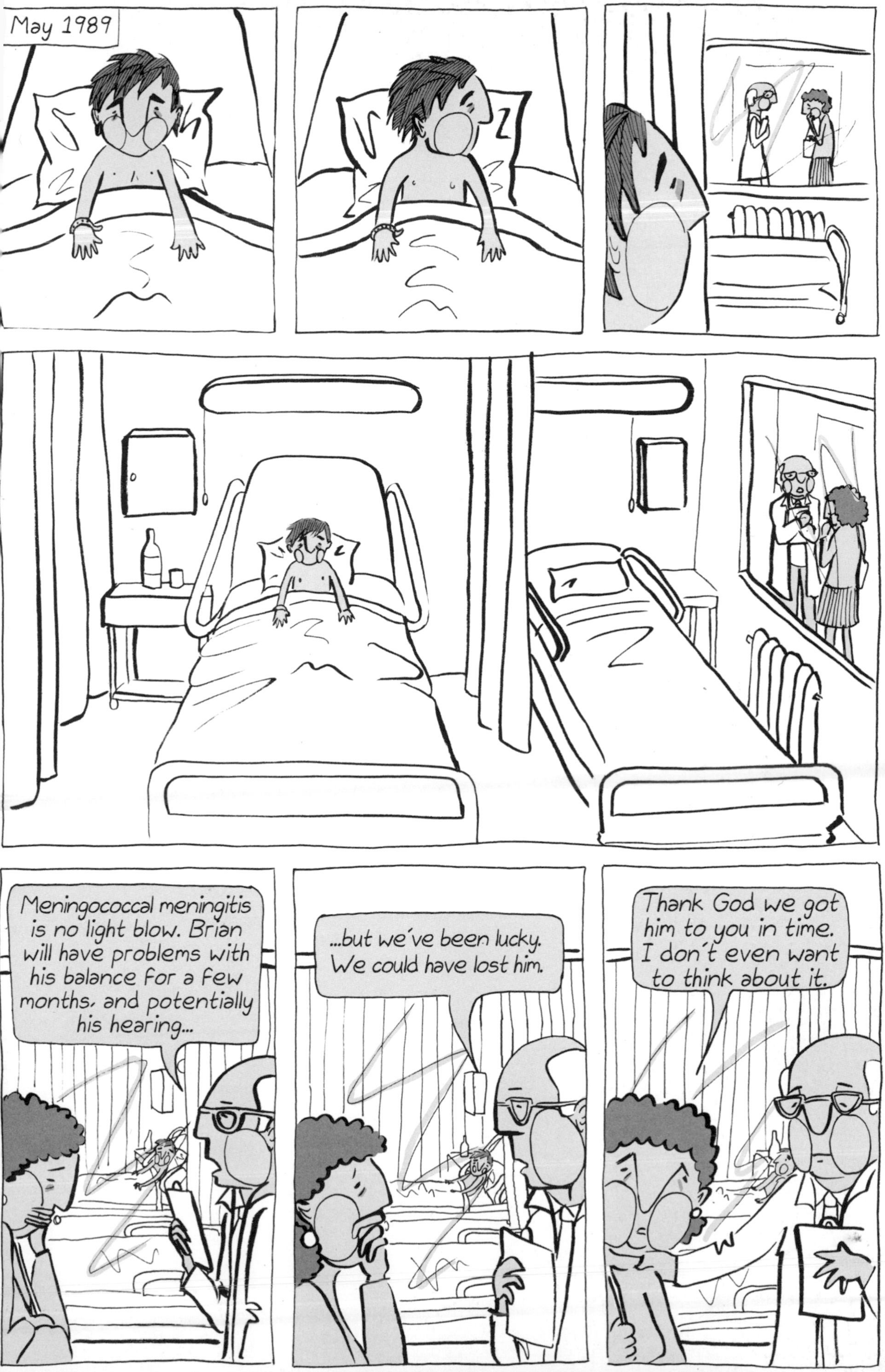
May 1989
Meningococcal meningitis is no light blow. Brian will have problems with his balance for a few months, and potentially his hearing...
...but we've been lucky. We could have lost him.
Thank God we got him to you in time. I don't even want to think about it.

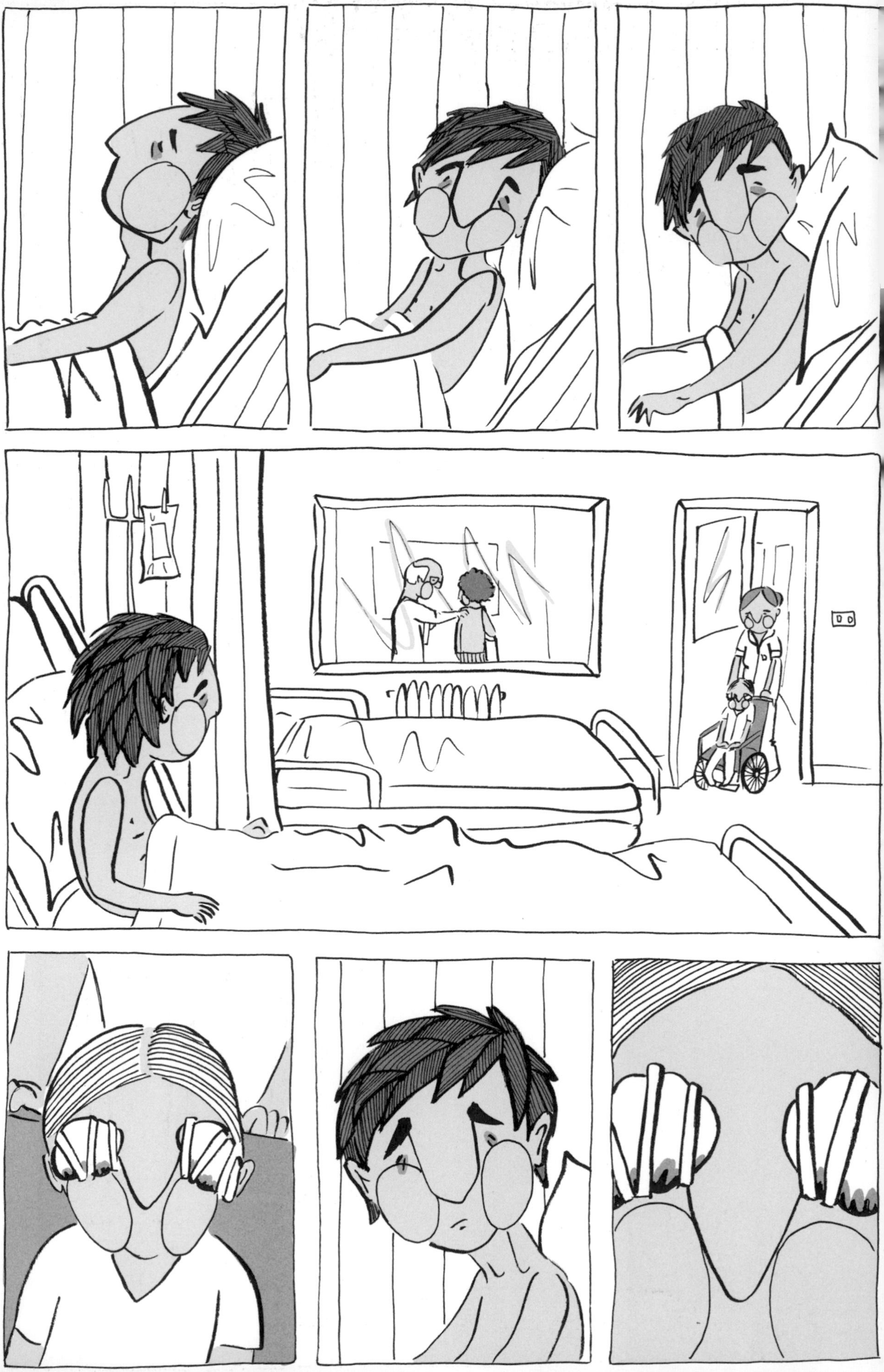

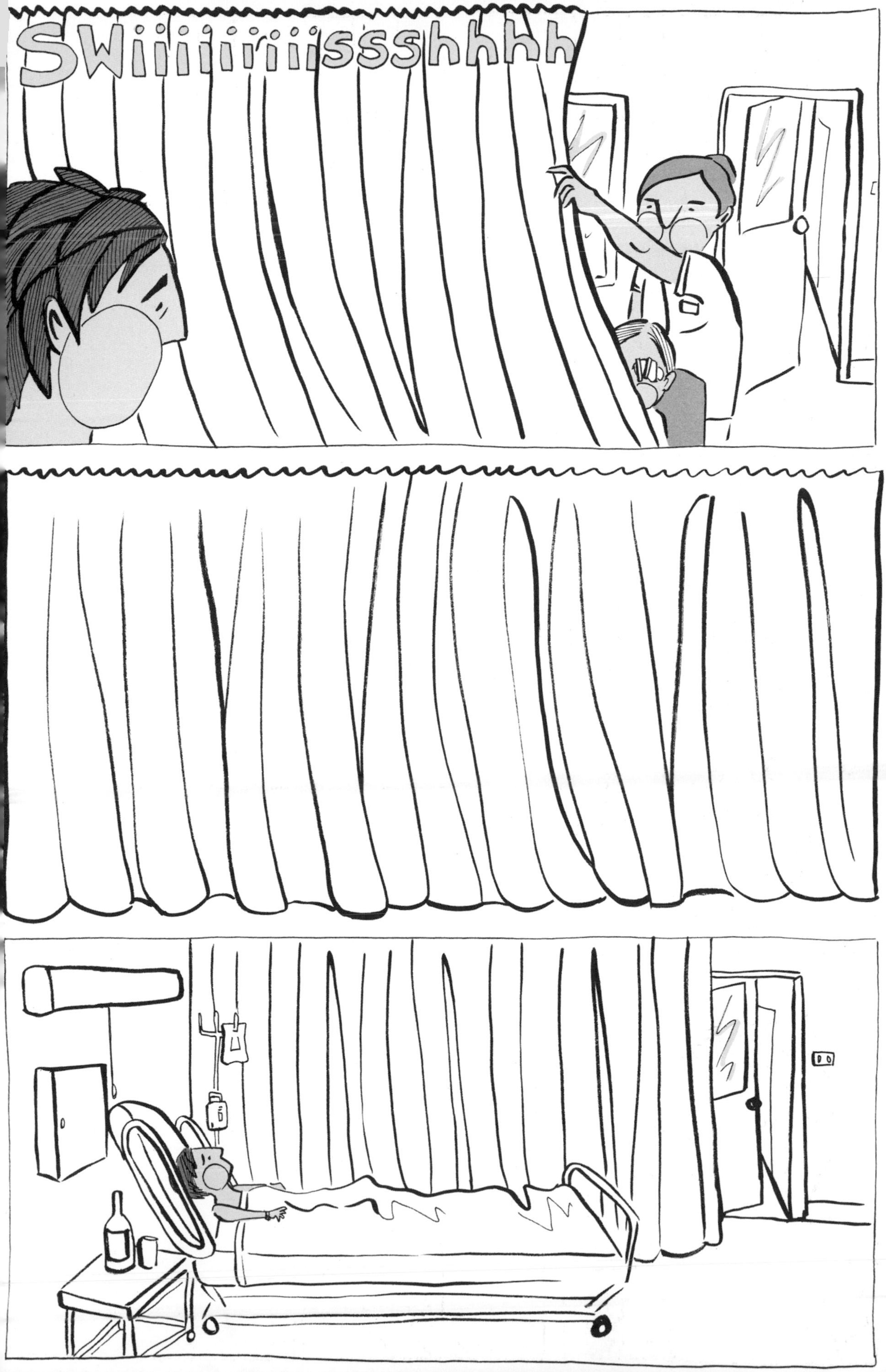
SWiiiiiiiiiiissshhhh

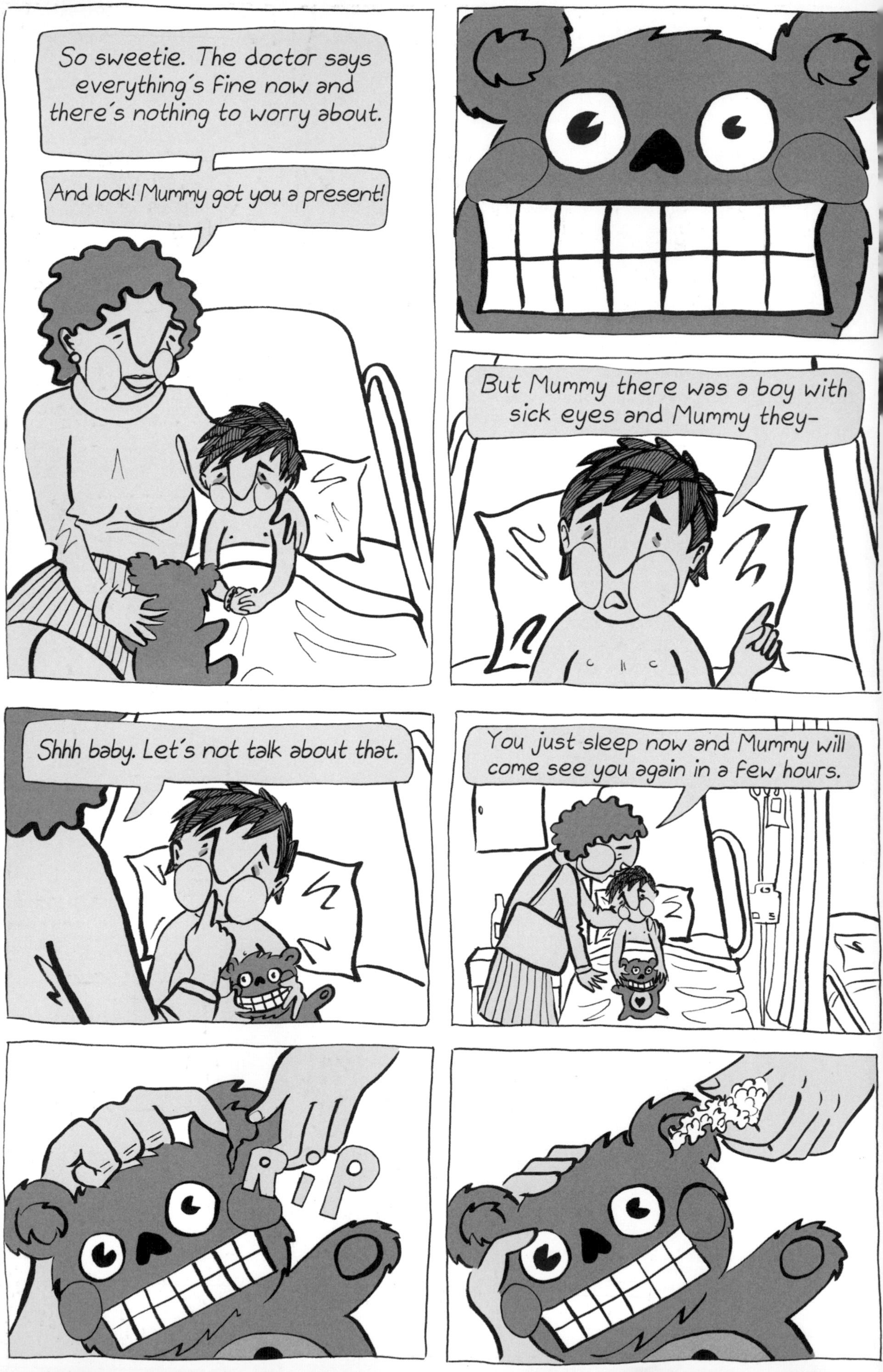
So sweetie. The doctor says everything's fine now and there's nothing to worry about.
And look! Mummy got you a present!
But Mummy there was a boy with sick eyes and Mummy they-
Shhh baby. Let's not talk about that.
You just sleep now and Mummy will come see you again in a few hours.
RiP

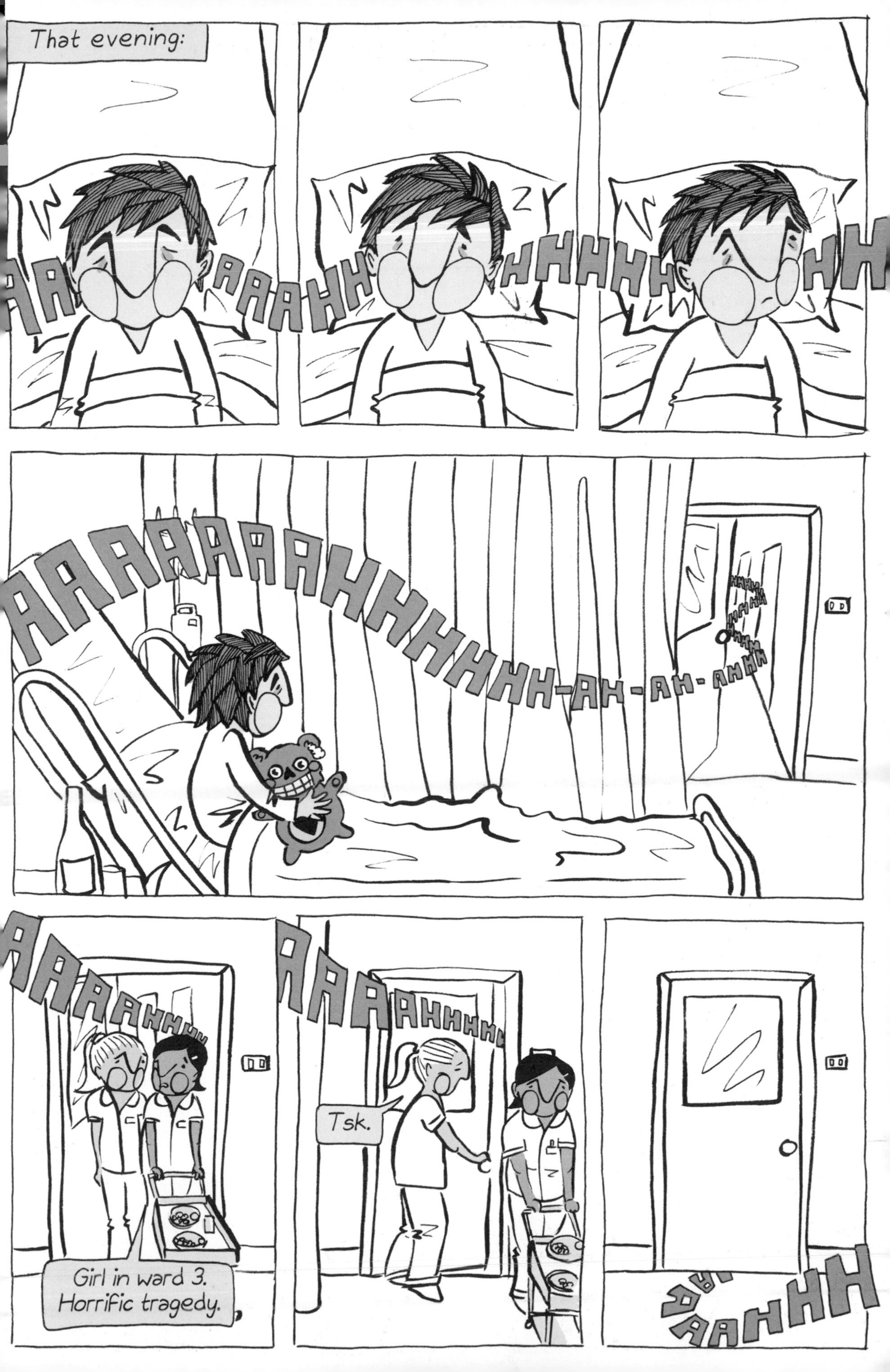

That evening:
AAAAAAAHHHHHHHHHH
AAAAAAAAAHHHHHHHHH-AH-AH-AHHH
AAAAHHHHH
Girl in ward 3. Horrific tragedy.
AAAAHHHHHH
Tsk.
AAAAHHH

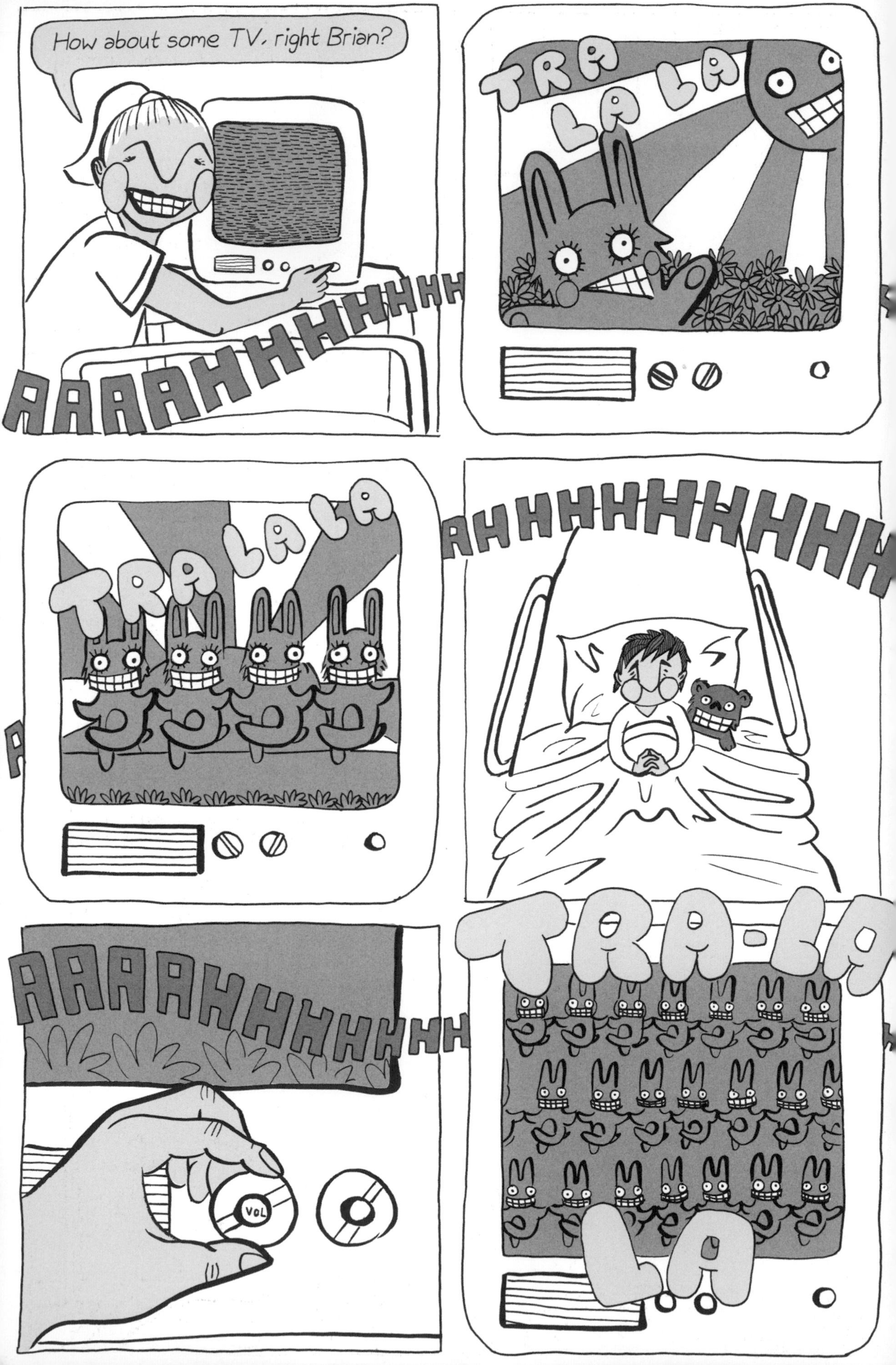
How about some TV, right Brian?
AAAAHHHHHHHHH
TRA LA LA
TRA LA LA
AHHHHHHHHHHH
AAAAHHHHHHHHH
VOL
TRA-LA
LA

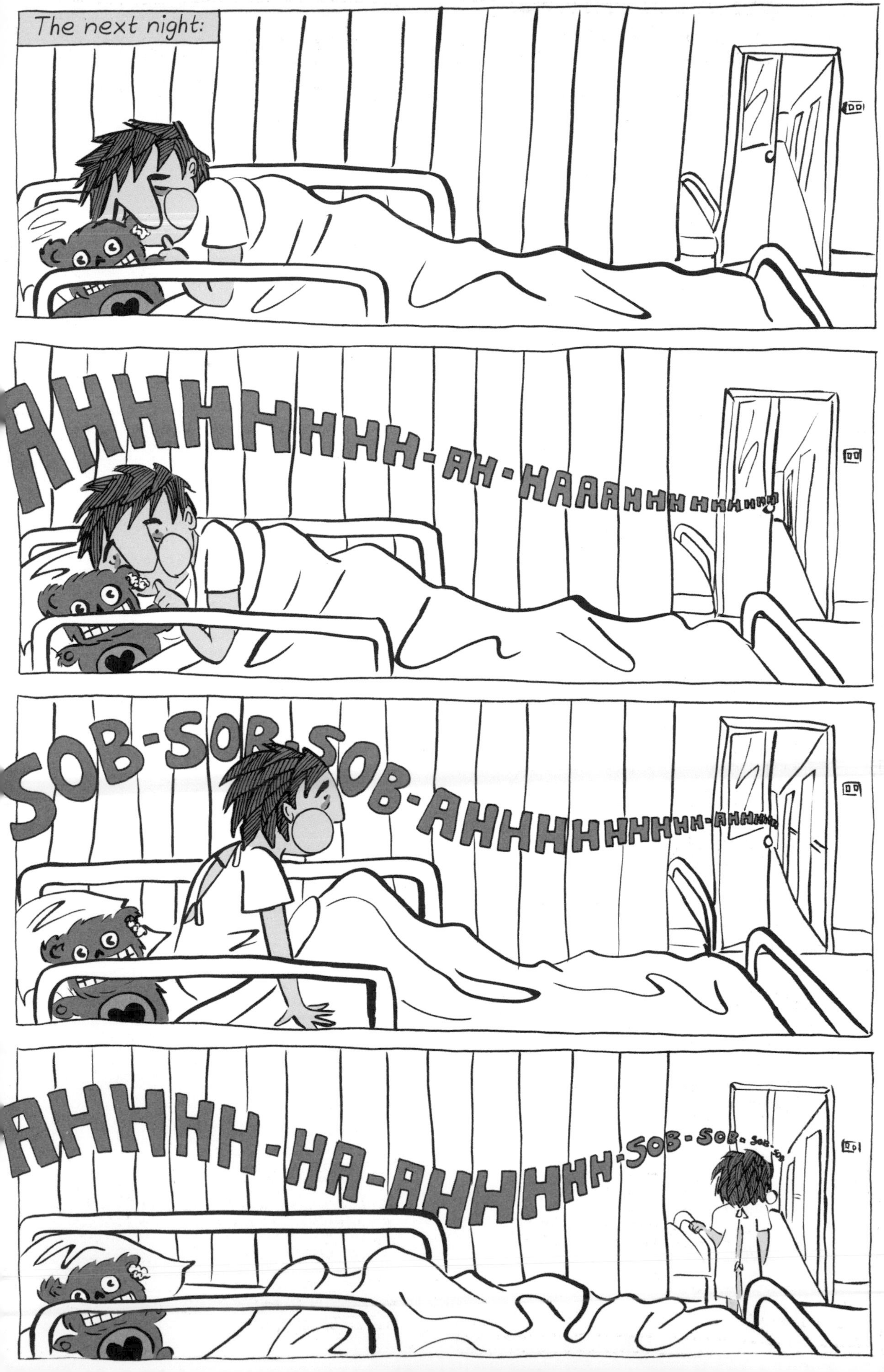

The next night:
AHHHHHHHH-AH-HAAAHHHHHHHHH
SOB-SOB-SOB-AHHHHHHHHHH-AHHHHH
AHHHH-HA-AHHHHH-SOB-SOB-SOB-SOB

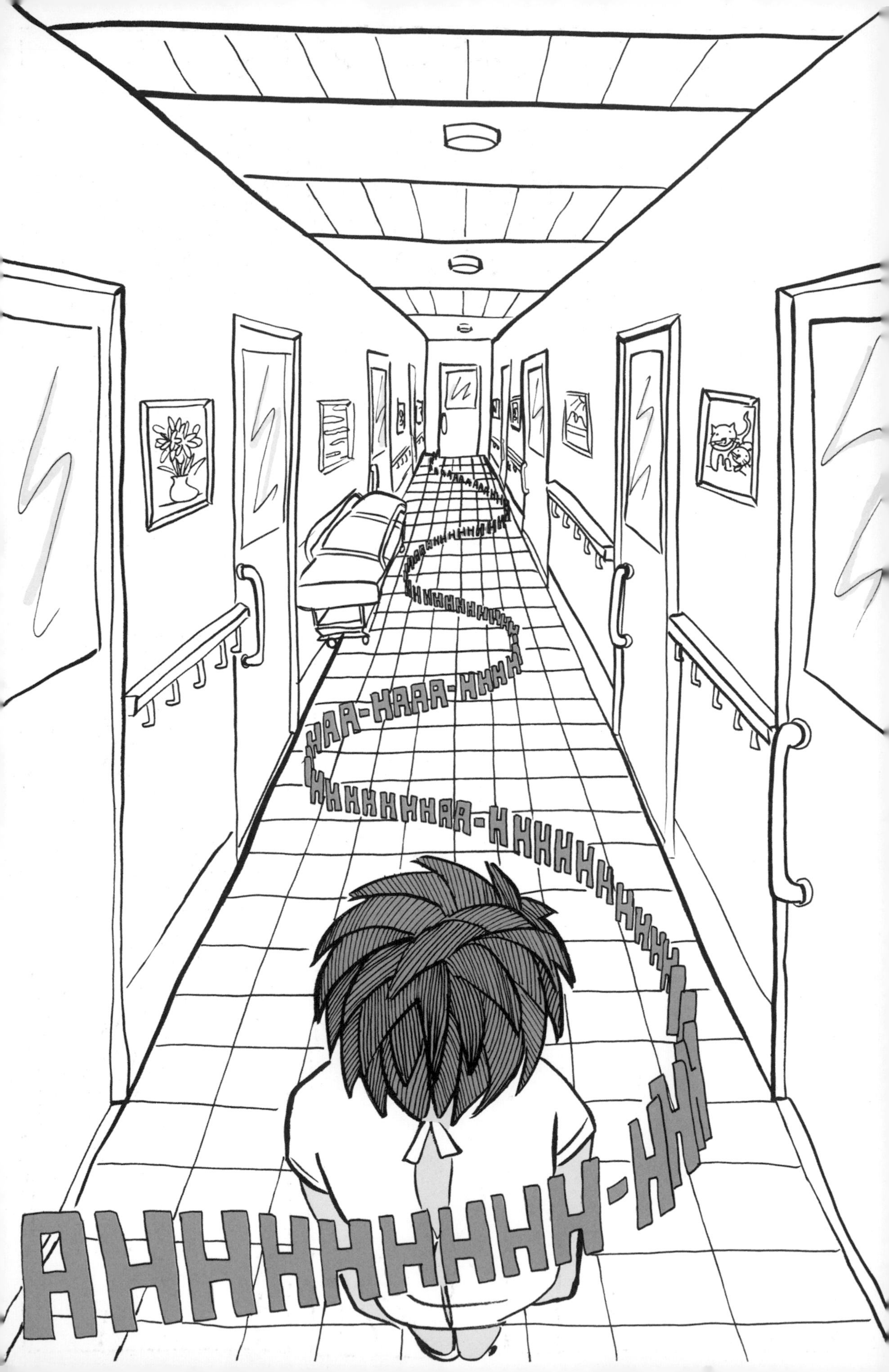

AHHHHHHHH-HHH
HHHHHHHHAA-HHHHHHHH
HAA-HAAA-HHHH

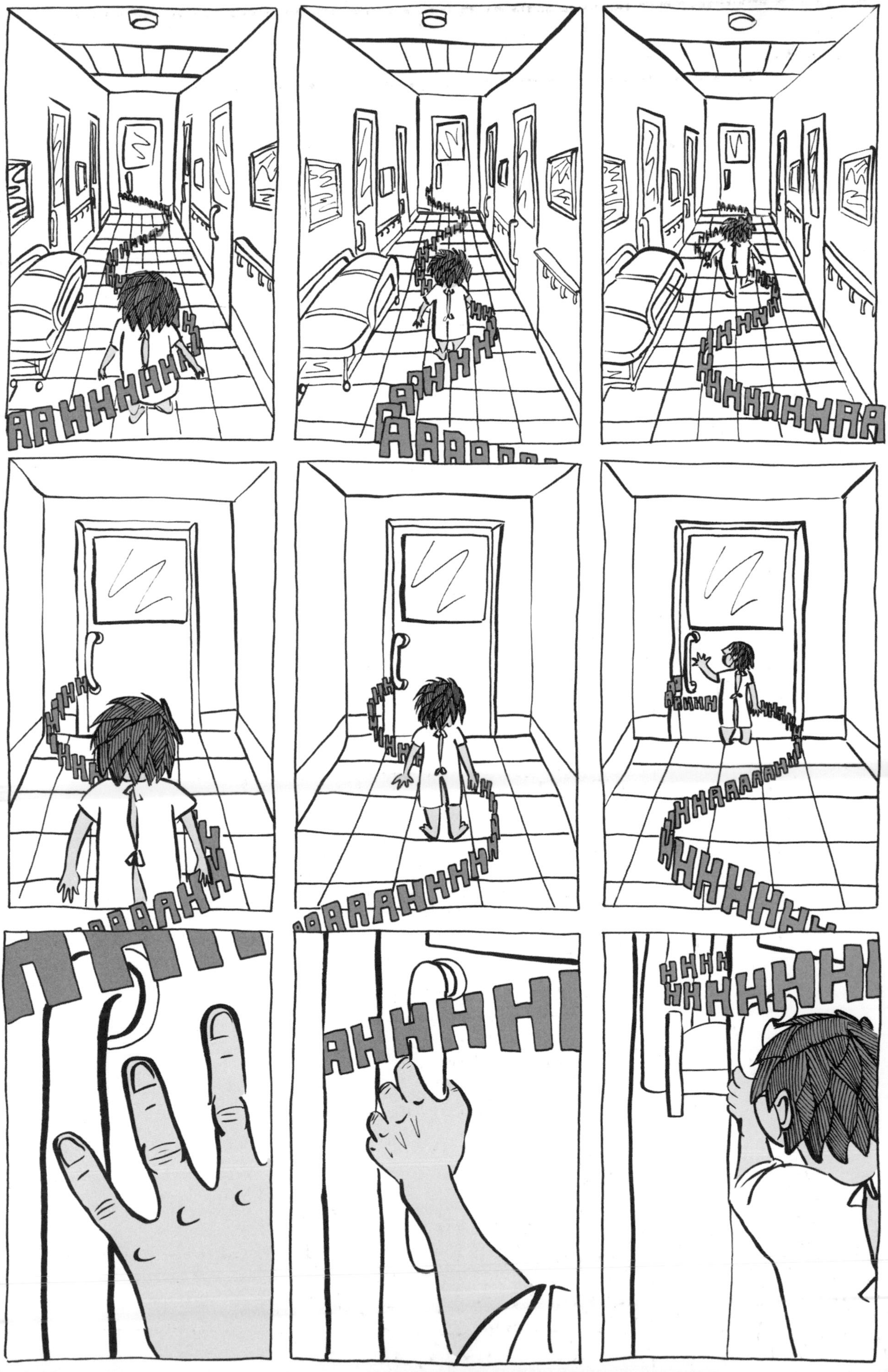

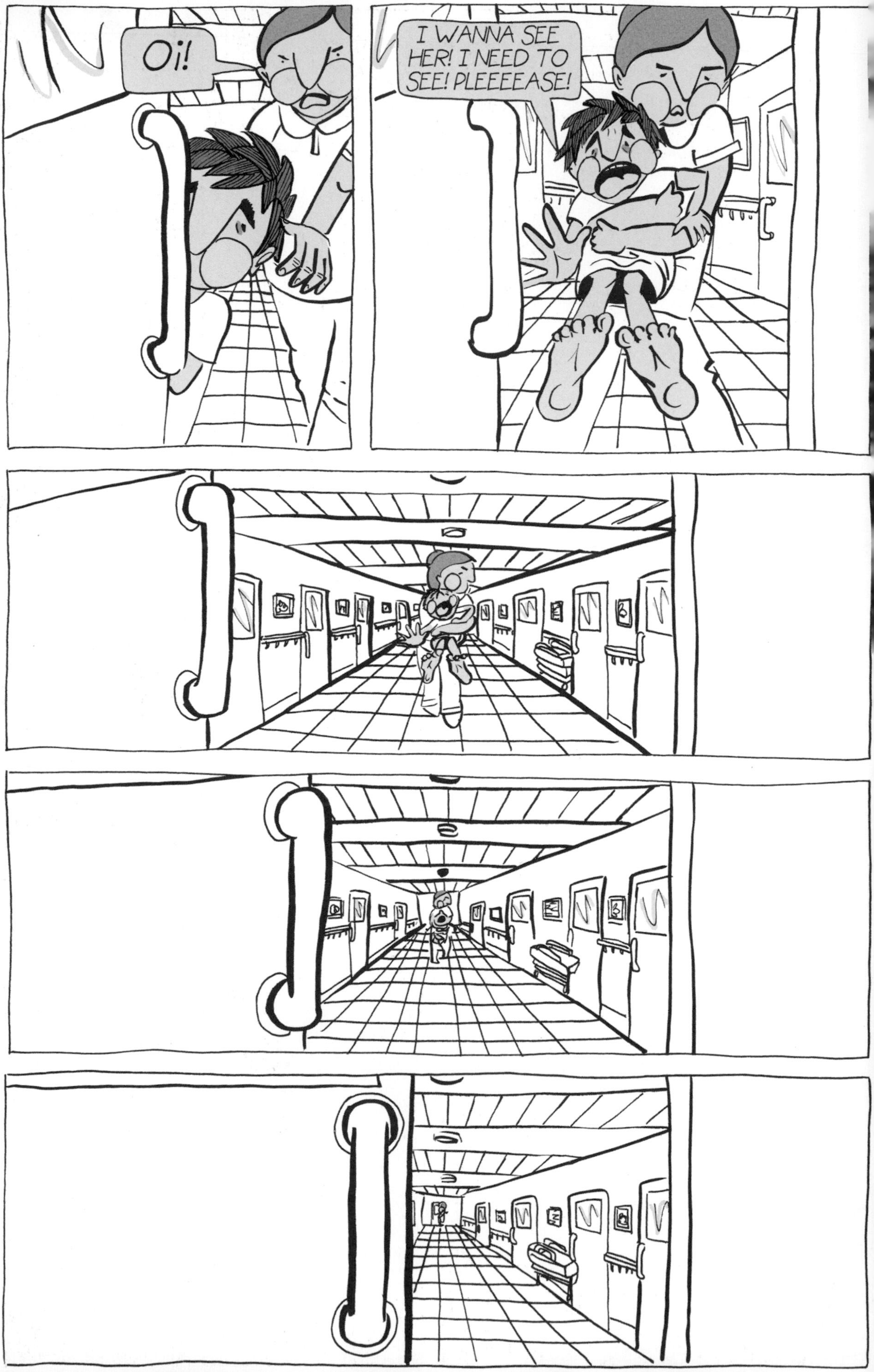
Oi!
I WANNA SEE HER! I NEED TO SEE! PLEEEEASE!

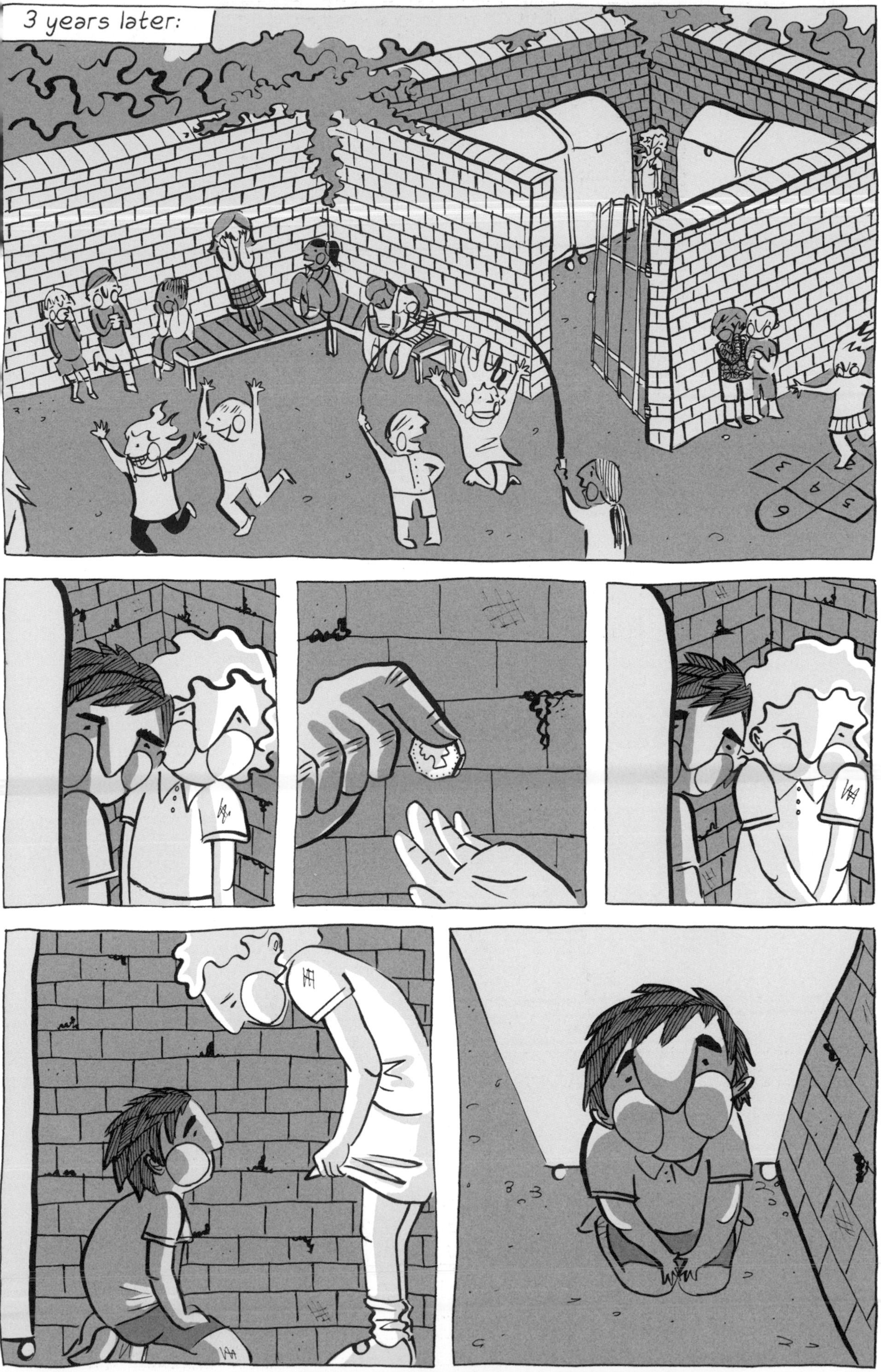
3 years later:

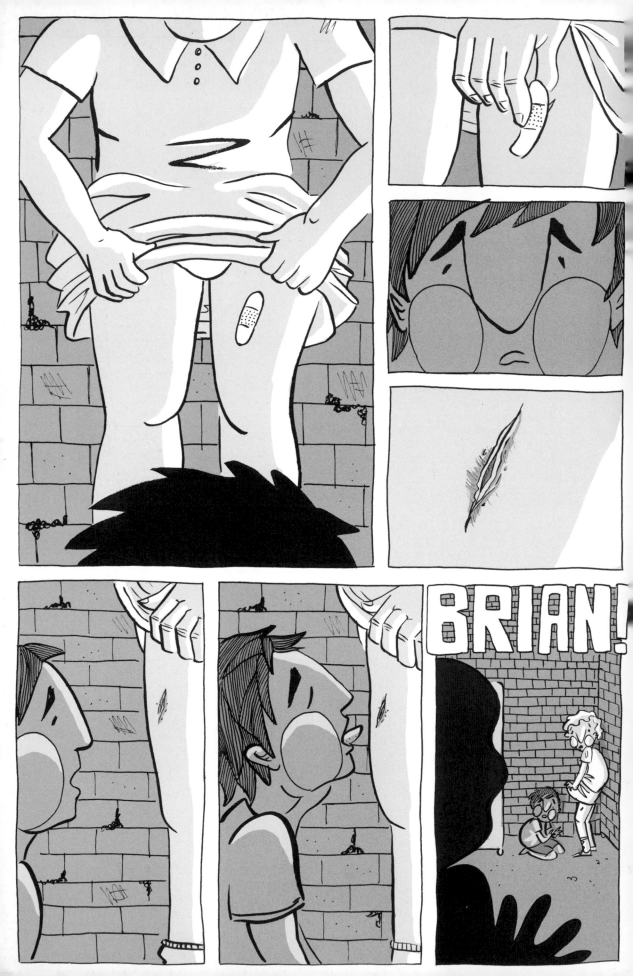

BRIAN!

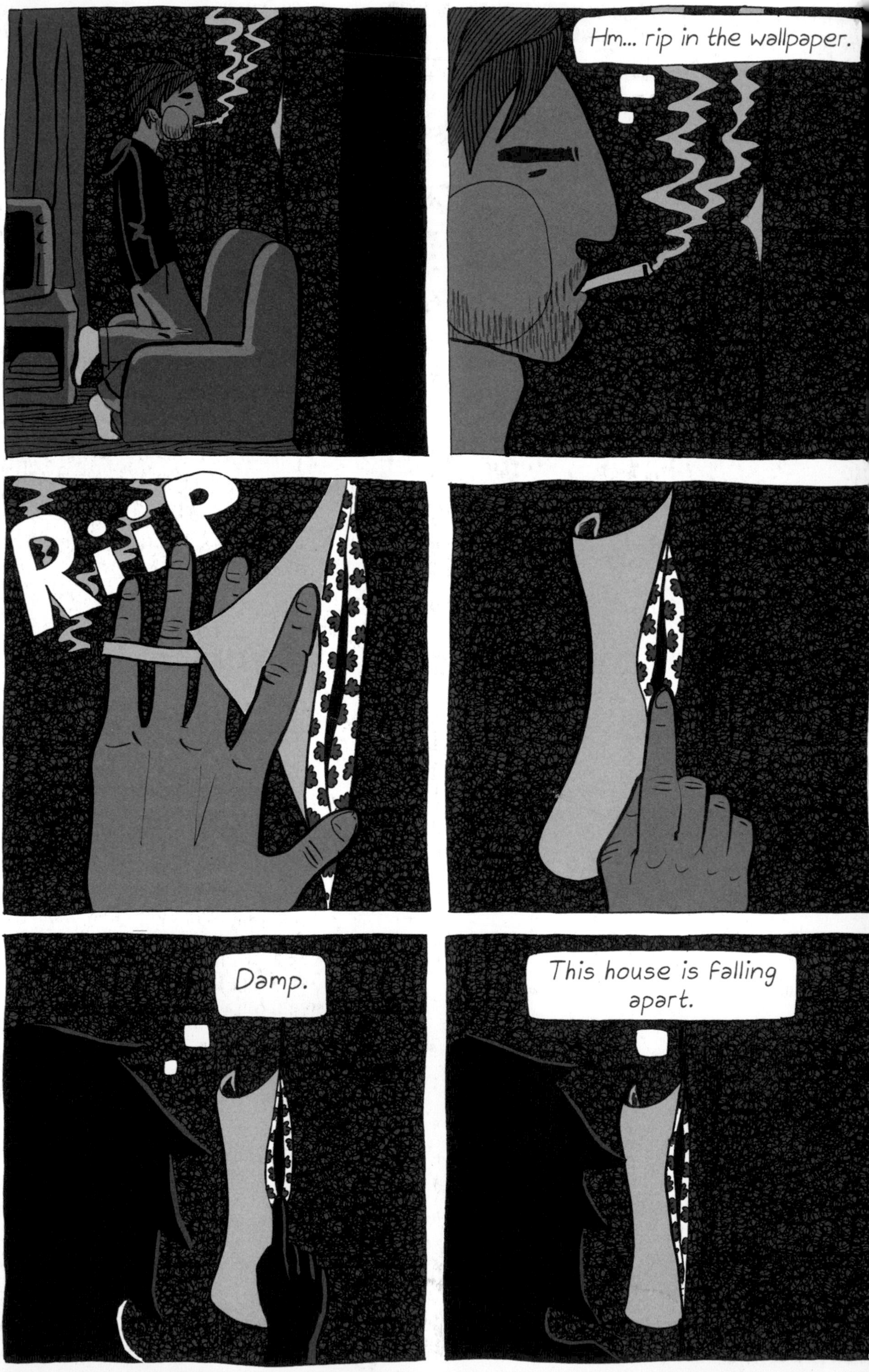
Hm... rip in the wallpaper.
RIIP
Damp.
This house is falling apart.

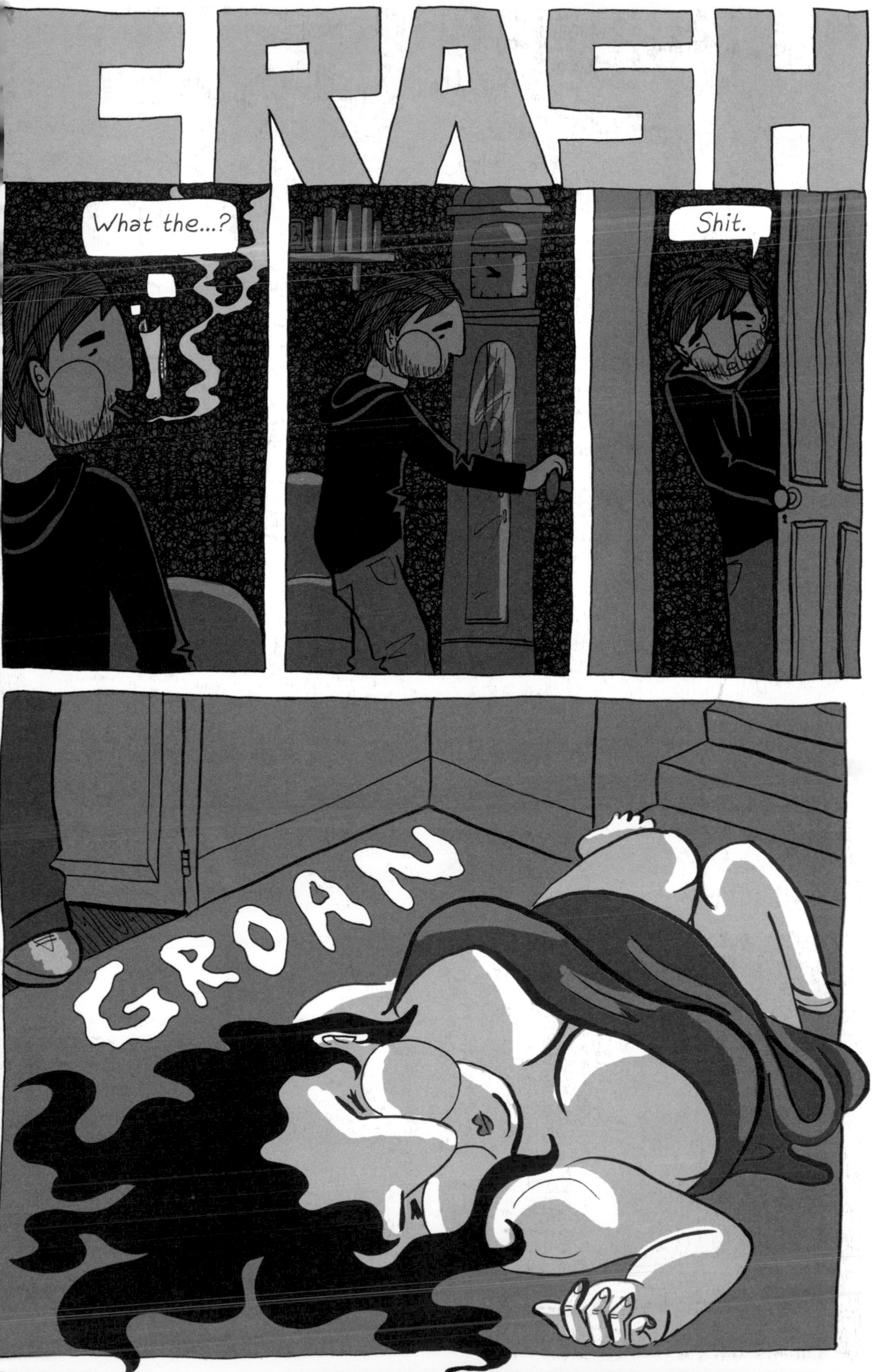
CRASH
What the...?
Shit.
GROAN

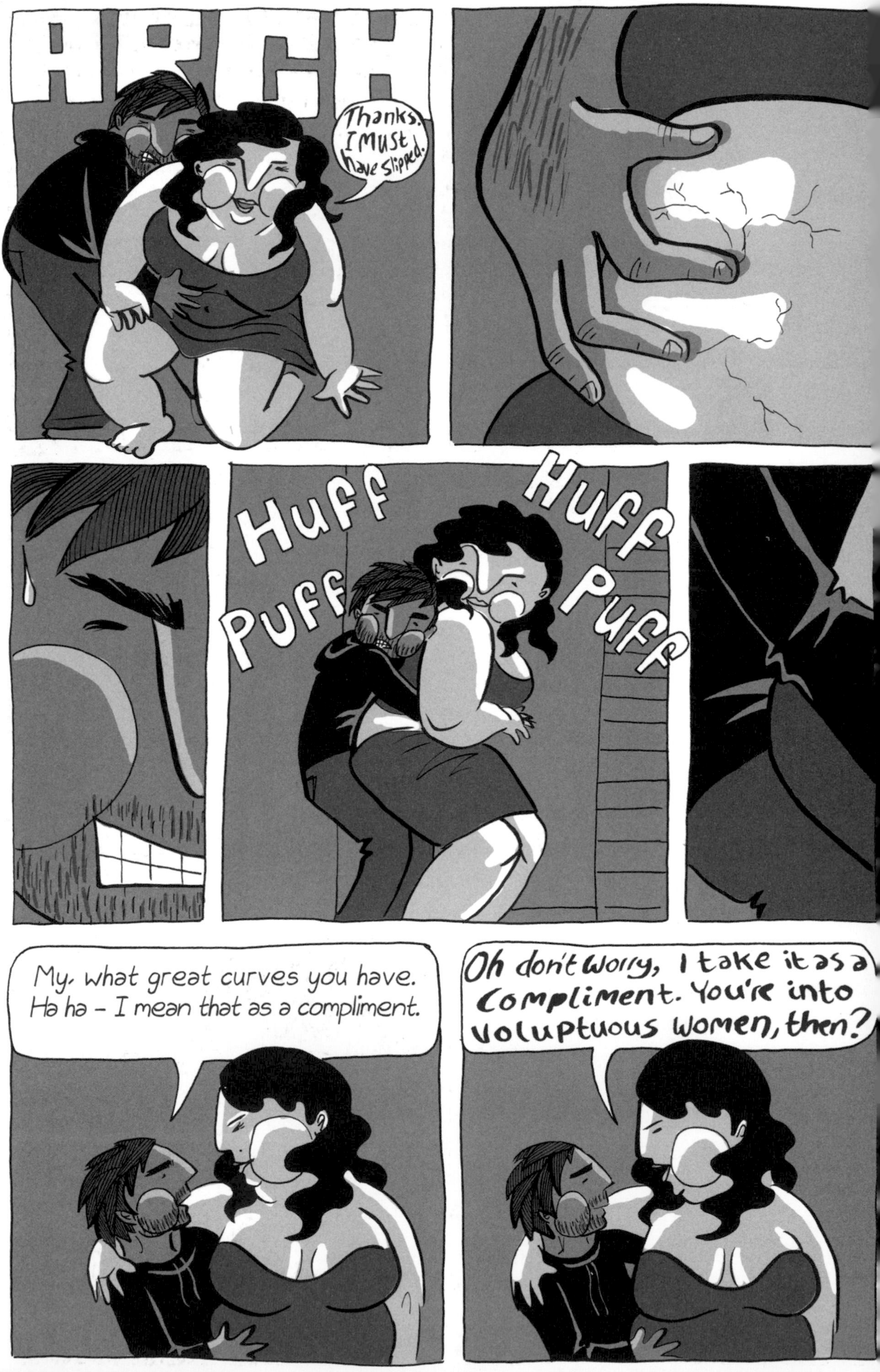
ARCH
Thanks. I must have slipped.
Huff Puff
Huff Puff
My, what great curves you have. Ha ha – I mean that as a compliment.
Oh don't worry, I take it as a compliment. You're into voluptuous women, then?

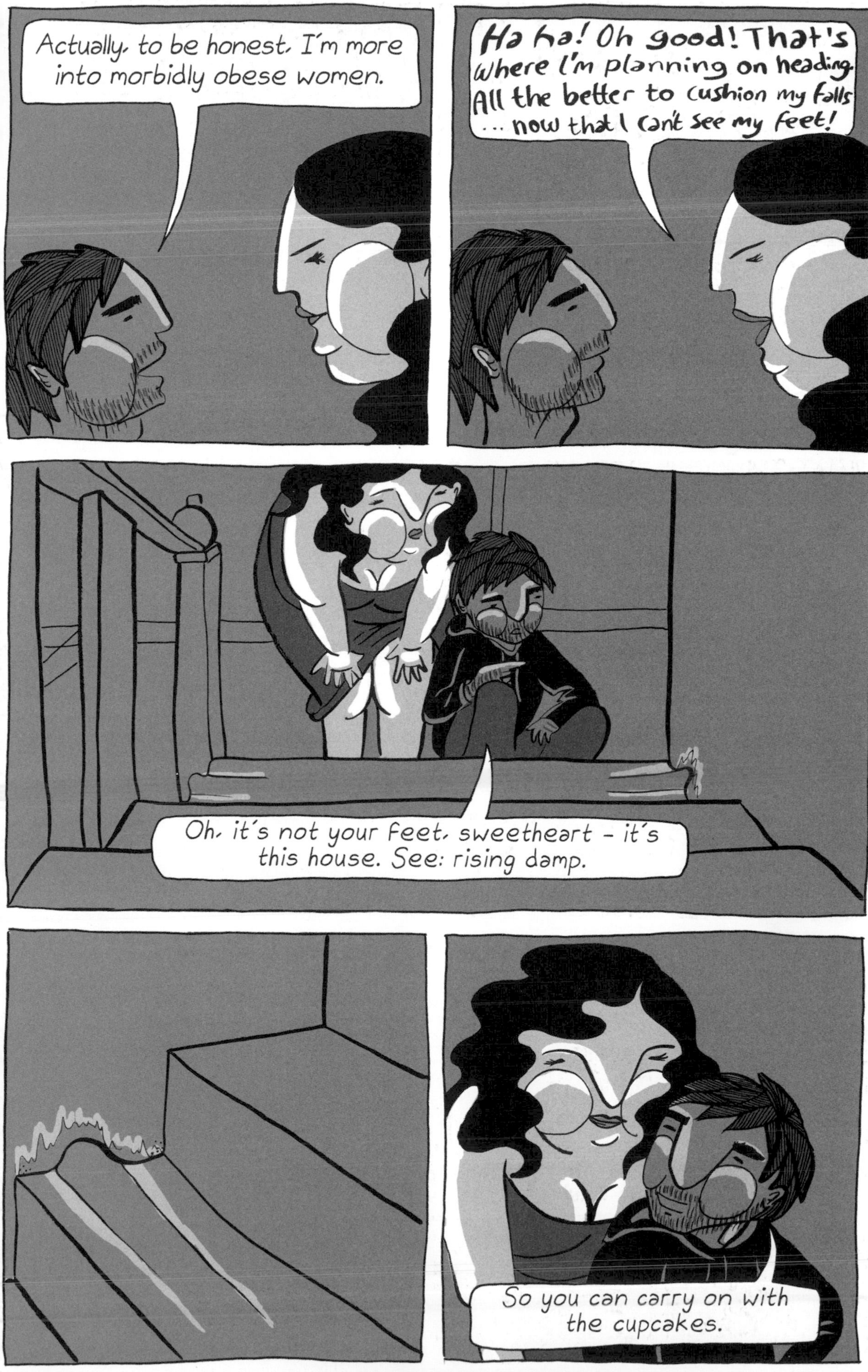
Actually, to be honest, I'm more into morbidly obese women.
Ha ha! Oh good! That's where I'm planning on heading. All the better to cushion my falls ... now that I can't see my feet!
Oh, it's not your feet, sweetheart - it's this house. See: rising damp.
So you can carry on with the cupcakes.

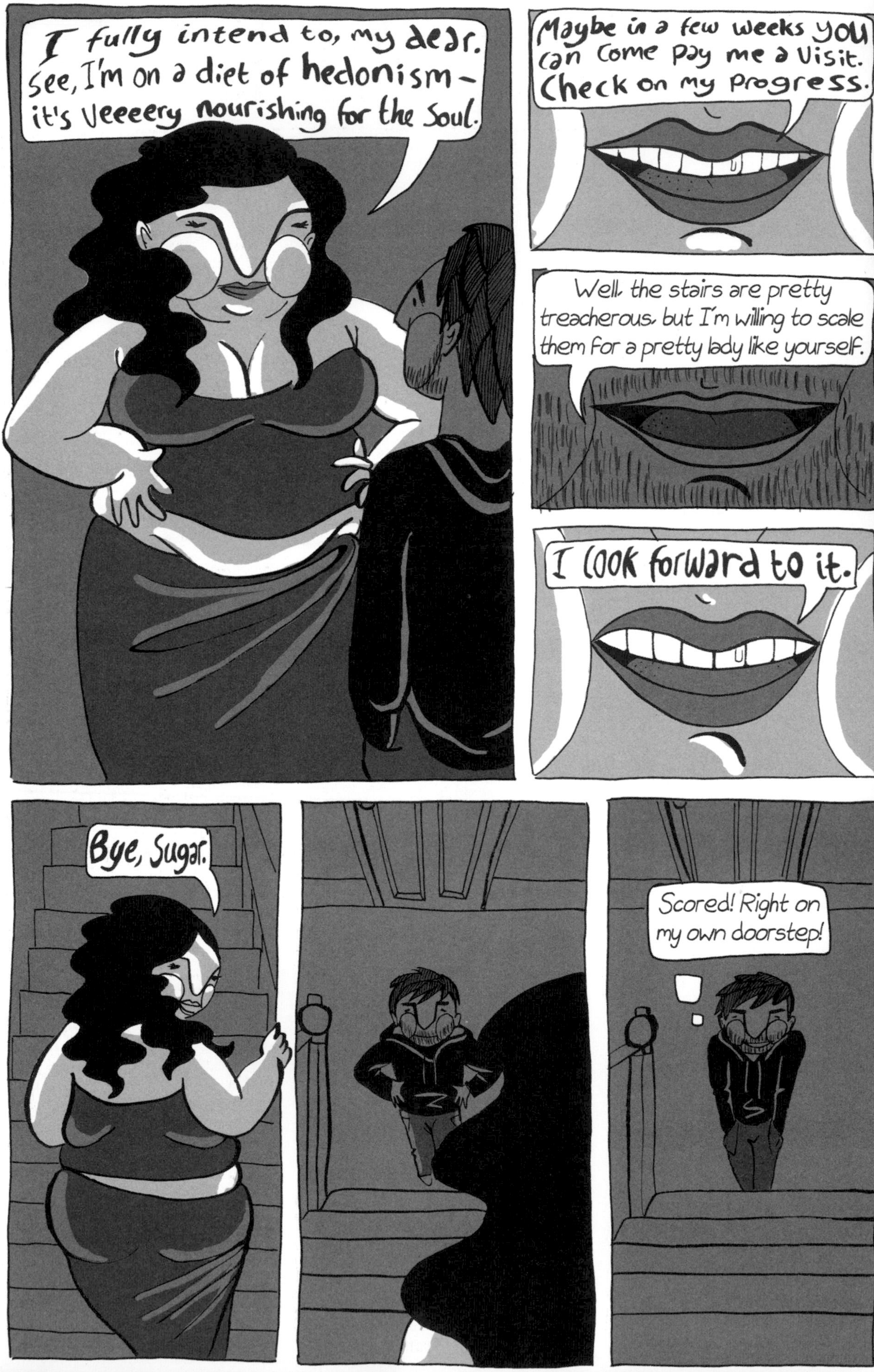
I fully intend to, my dear. See, I'm on a diet of hedonism – it's Veeeery nourishing for the Soul.
Maybe in a few weeks you can come pay me a Visit. Check on my progress.
Well, the stairs are pretty treacherous, but I'm willing to scale them for a pretty lady like yourself.
I look forward to it.
Bye, Sugar.
Scored! Right on my own doorstep!

Chapter Five

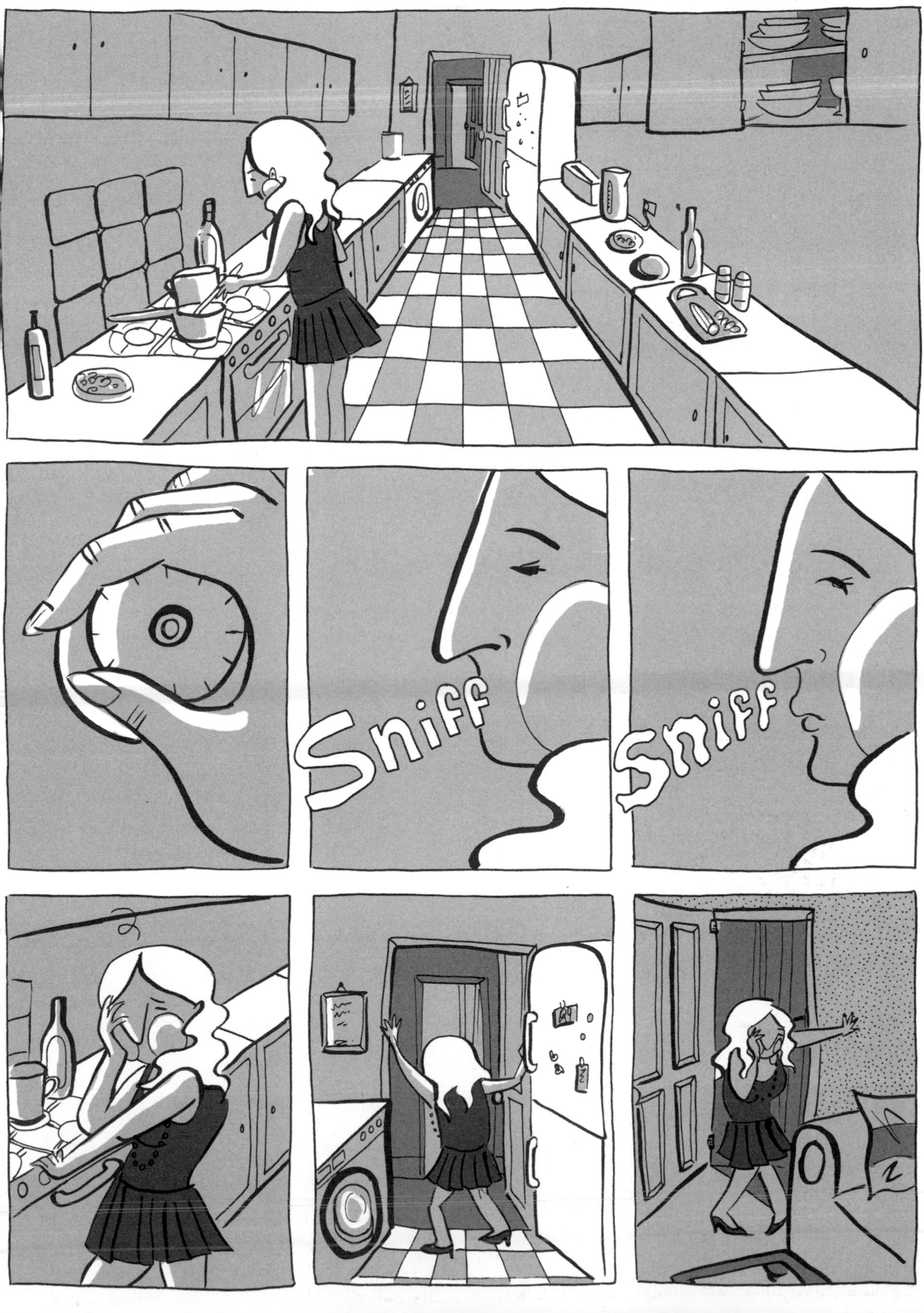
Sniff
Sniff

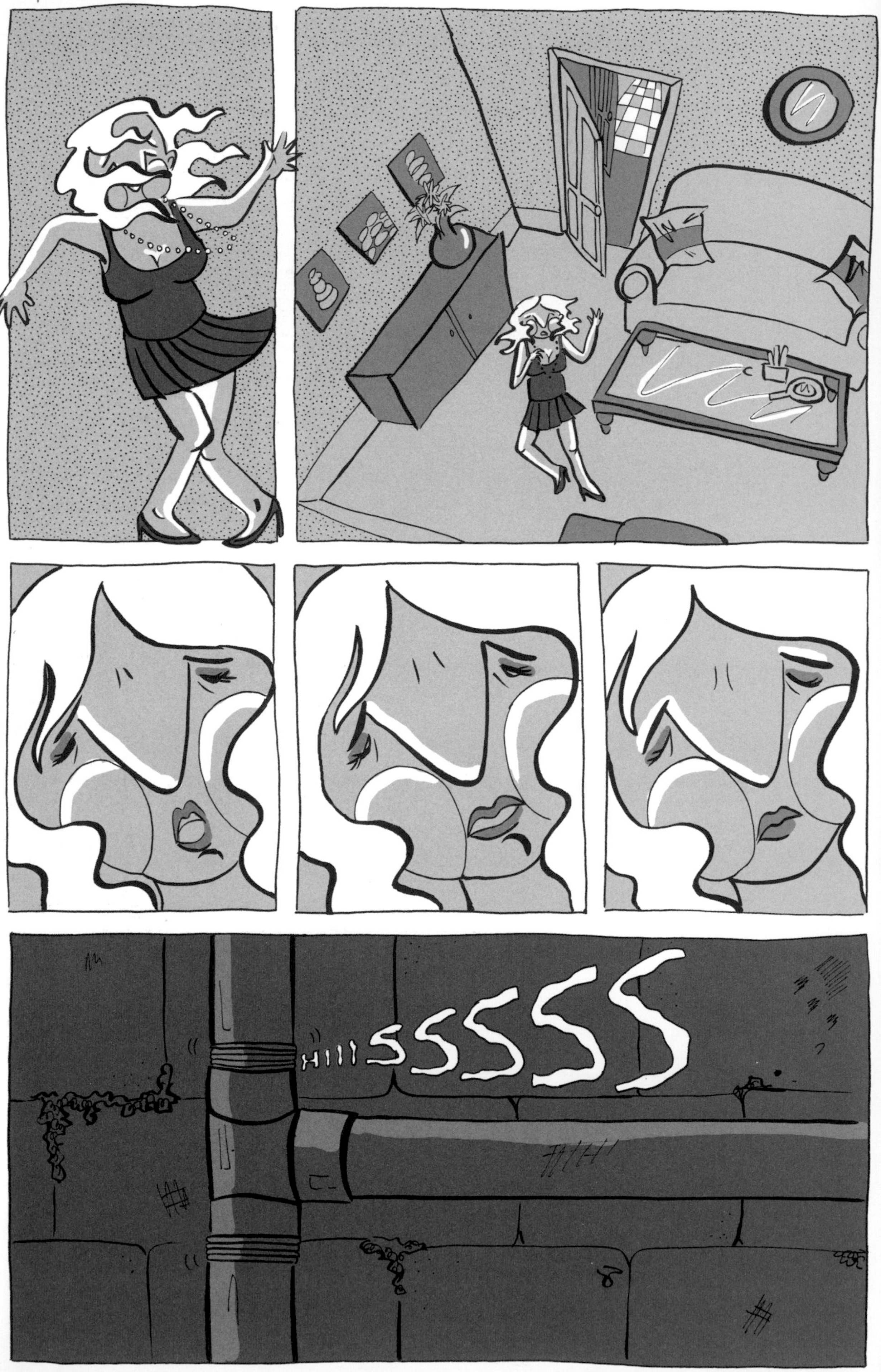
HIIISSSSSS

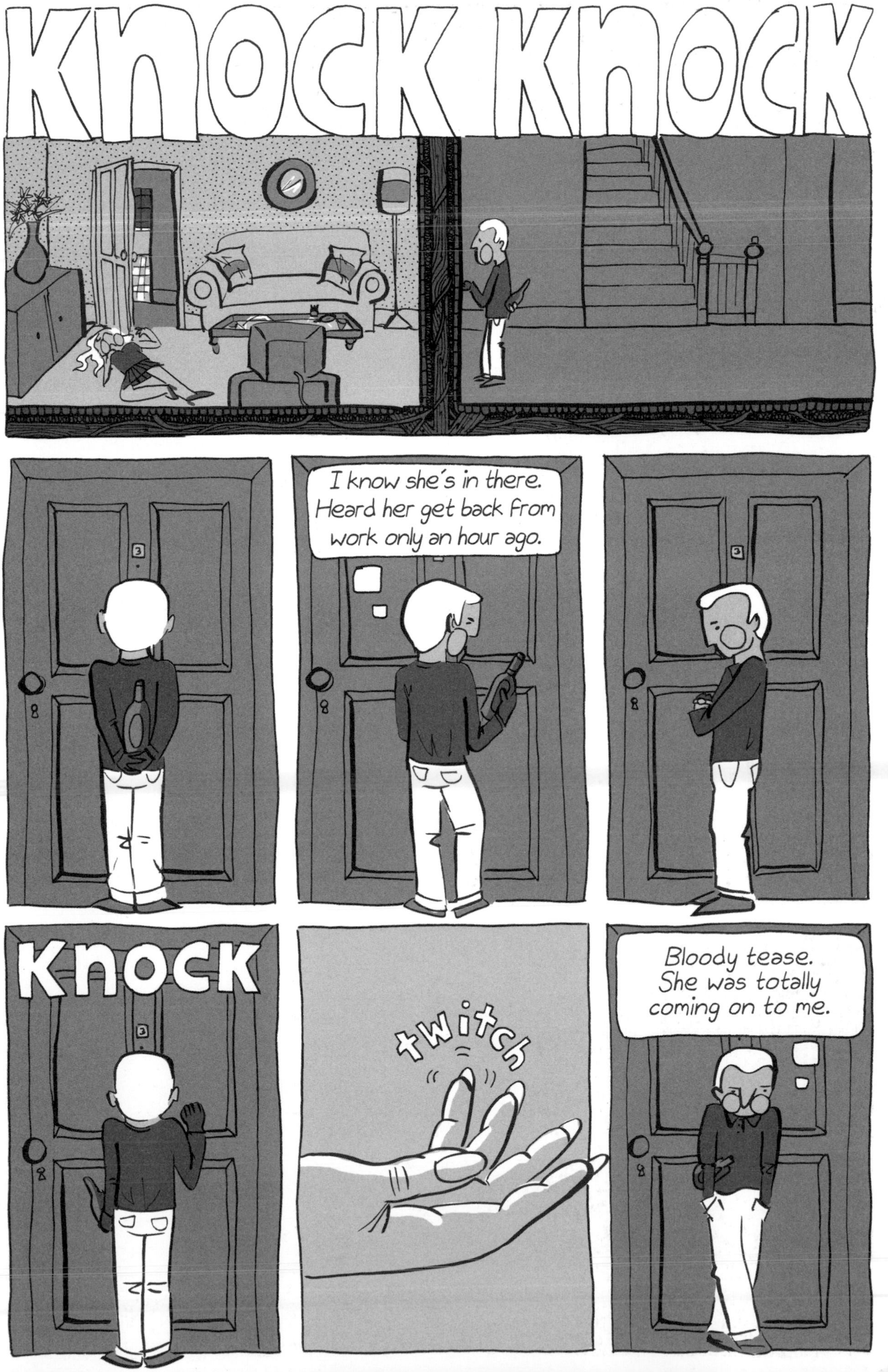
KNOCK KNOCK
I know she's in there. Heard her get back from work only an hour ago.
3
Knock
twitch
Bloody tease. She was totally coming on to me.

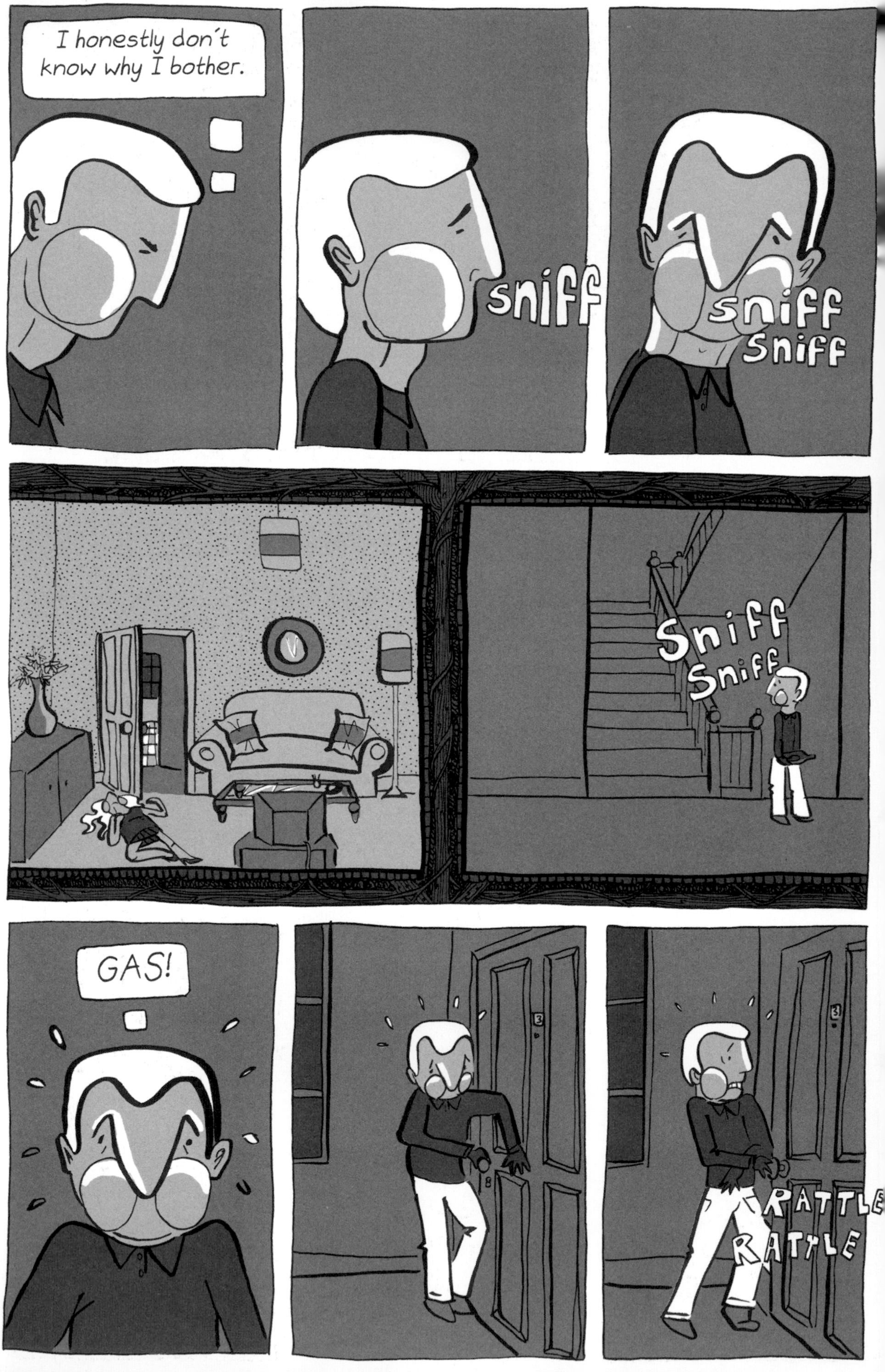

I honestly don't know why I bother.
sniff
sniff
Sniff
Sniff
Sniff
GAS!
RATTLE
RATTLE

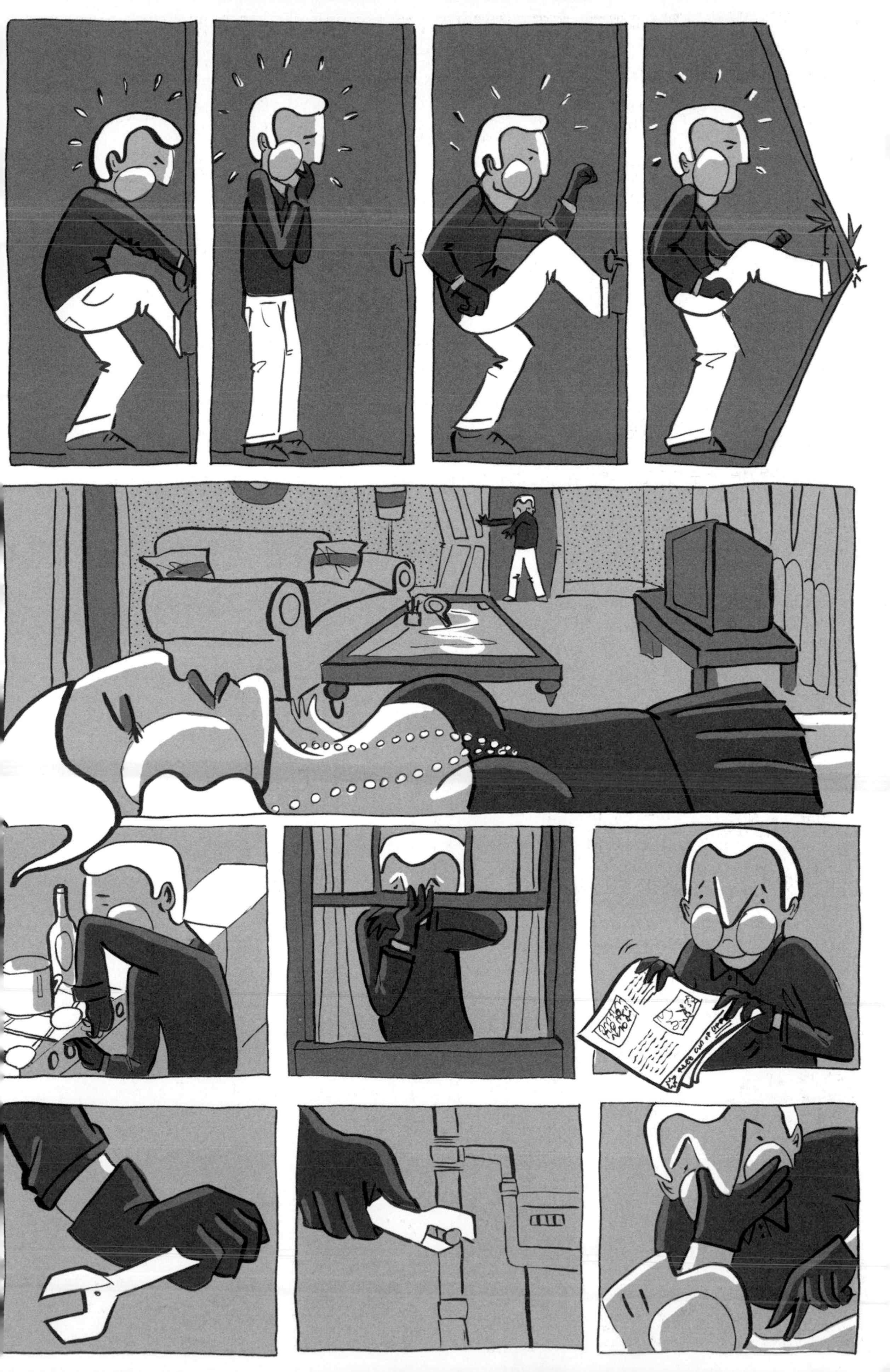

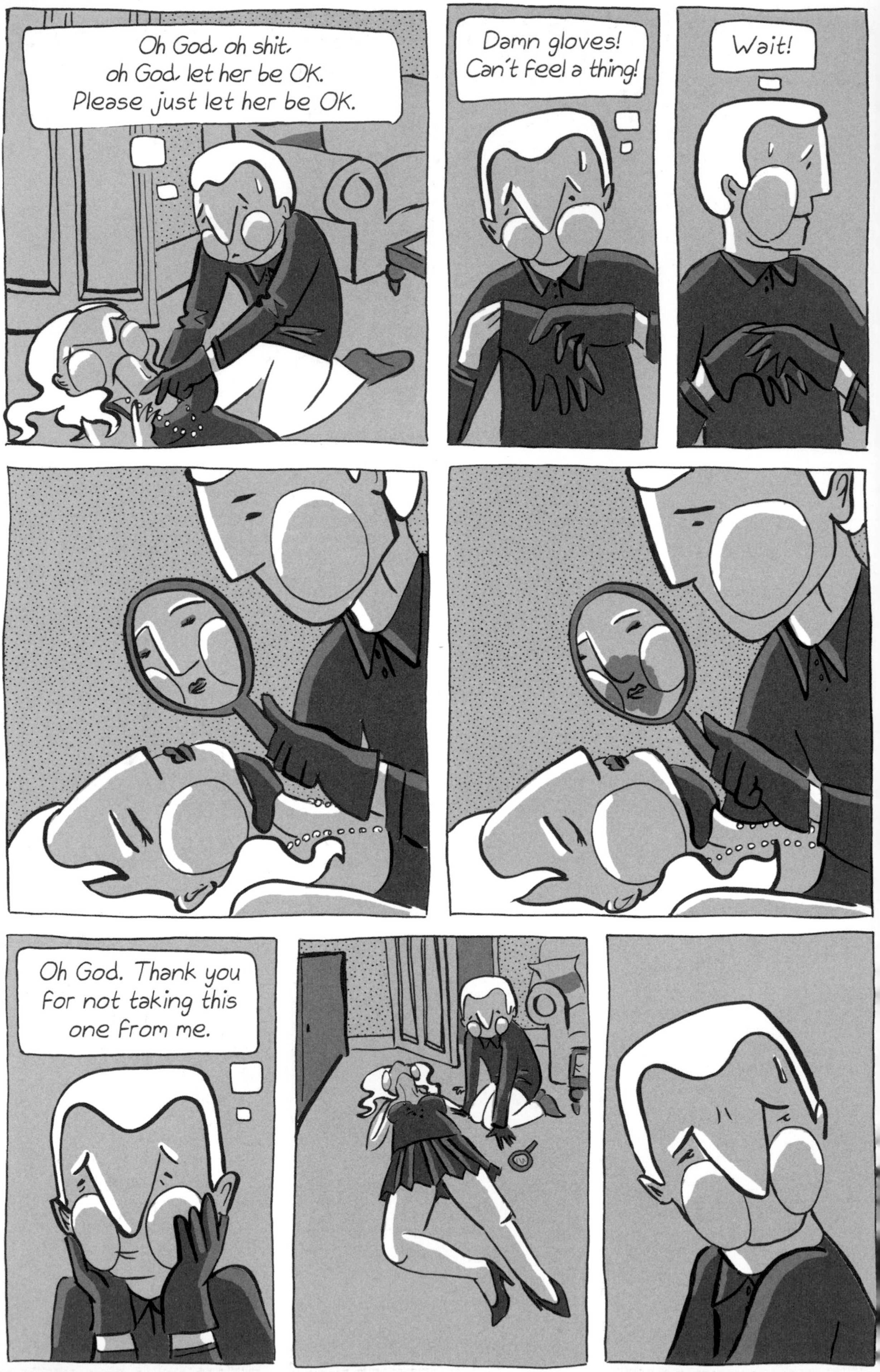
Oh God, oh shit,
oh God, let her be OK.
Please just let her be OK.
Damn gloves!
Can't feel a thing!
Wait!
Oh God. Thank you
for not taking this
one from me.

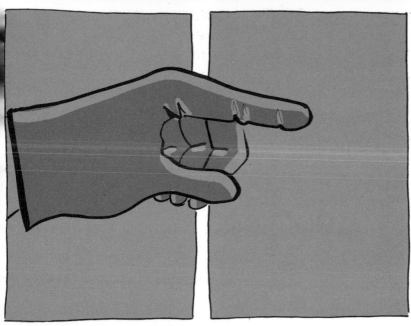

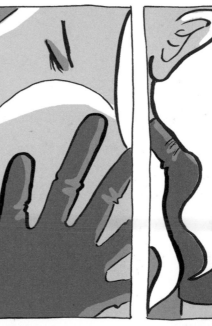

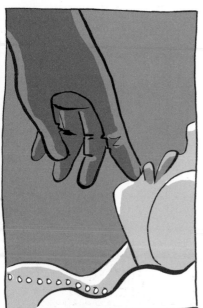

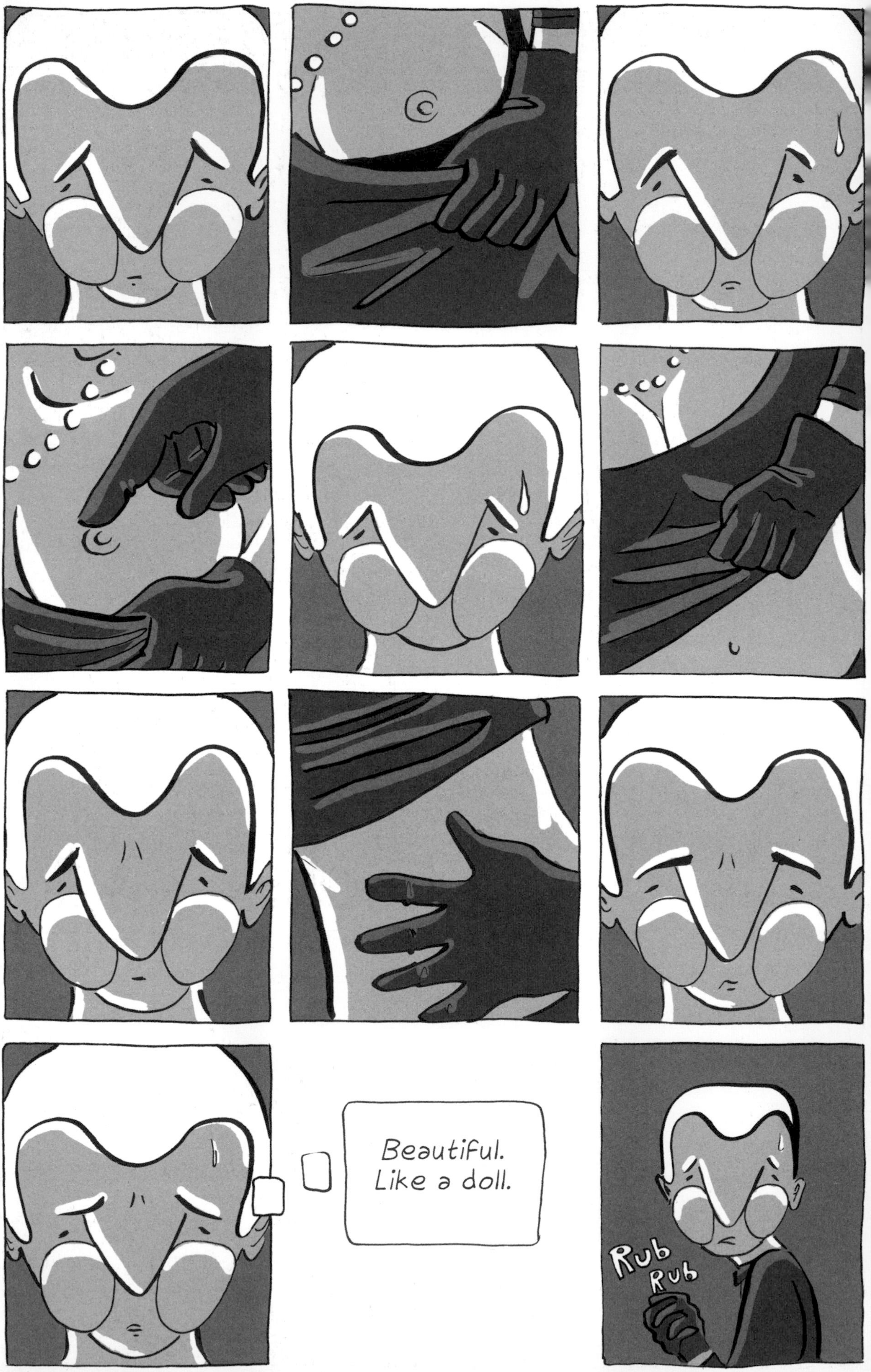
Beautiful.
Like a doll.
Rub
Rub

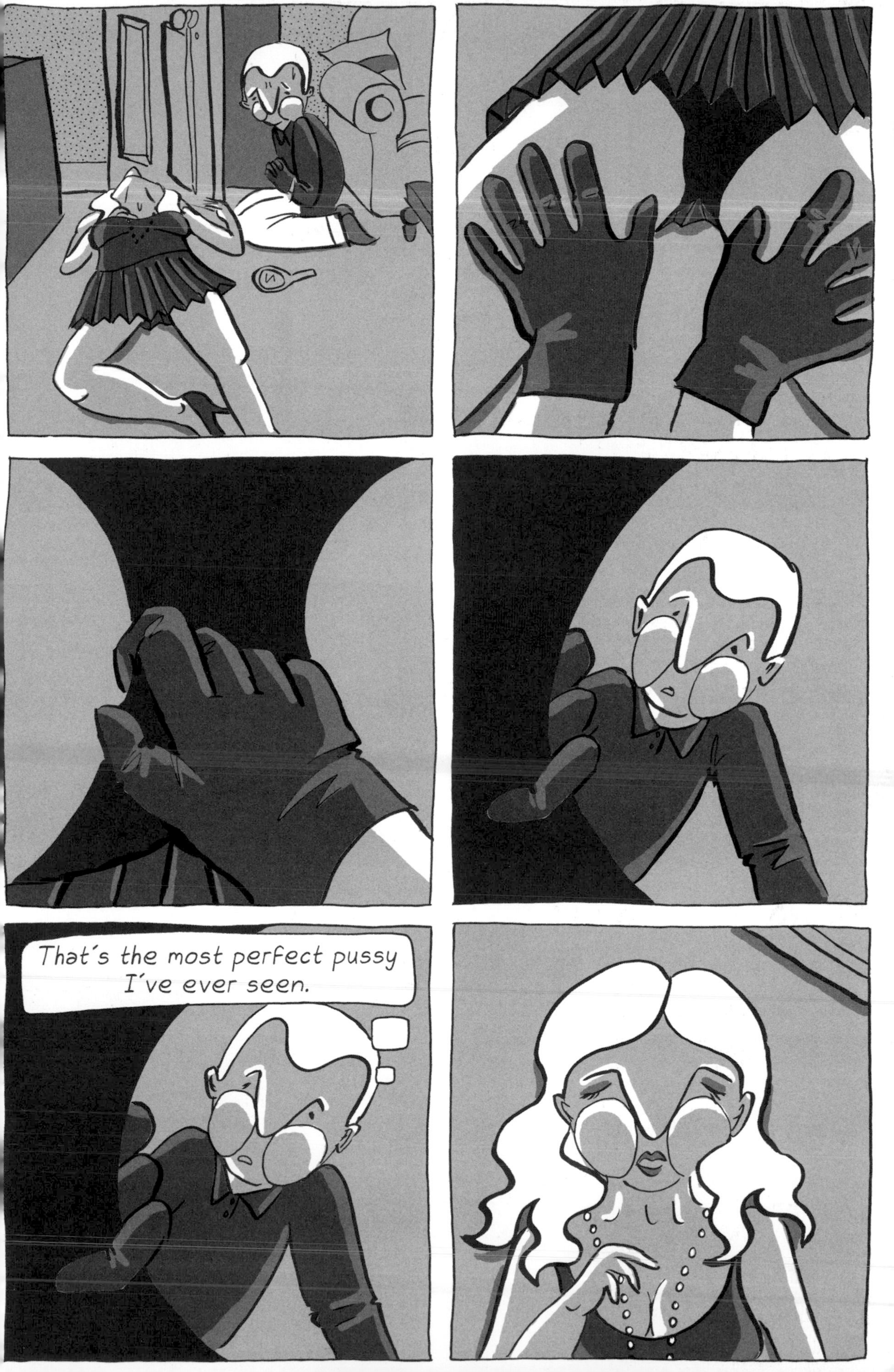
That's the most perfect pussy I've ever seen.

The Building of Rottin Road, 1865.

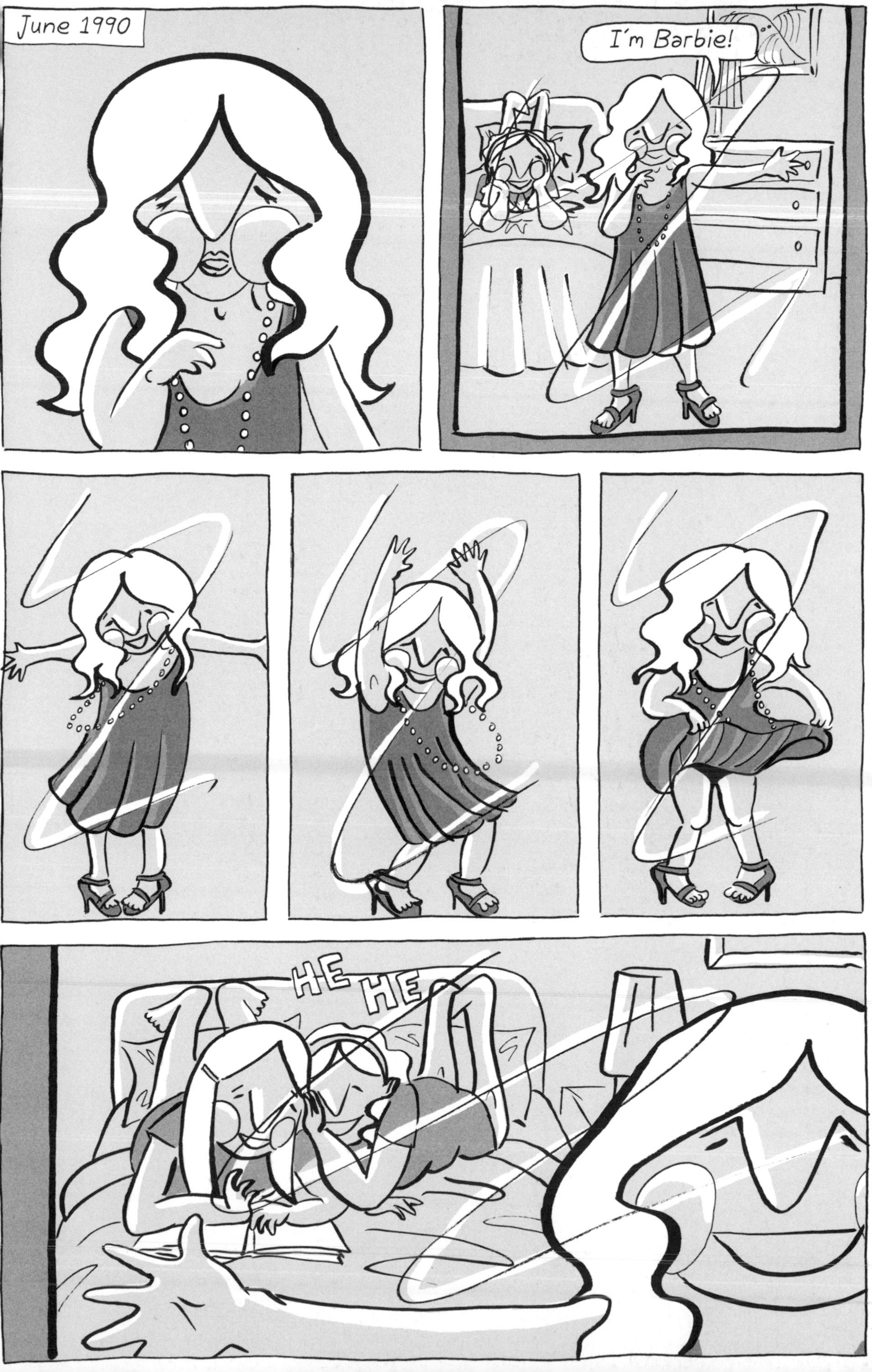
June 1990
I'm Barbie!
HE HE

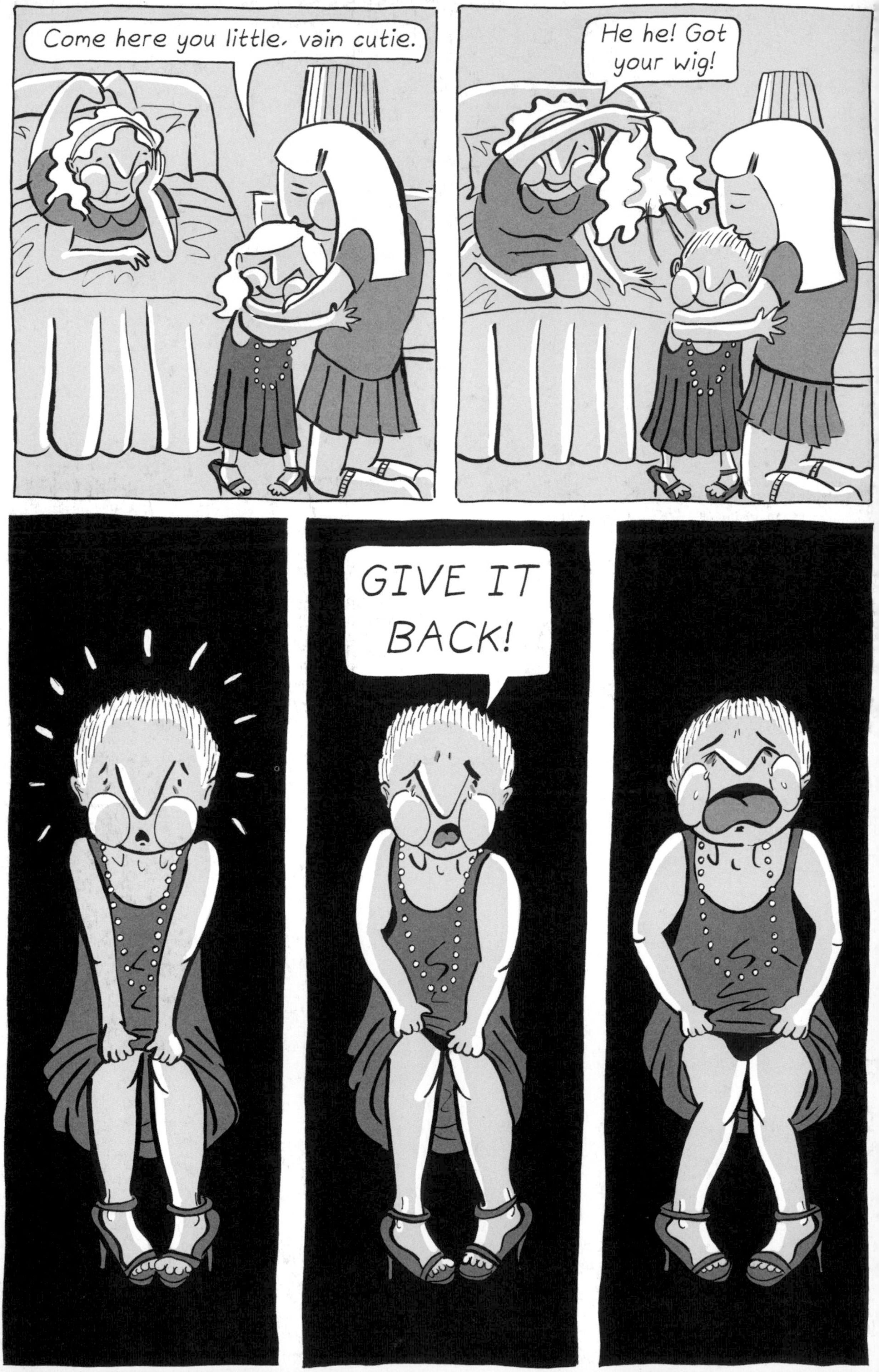
Come here you little, vain cutie.
He he! Got your wig!
GIVE IT BACK!

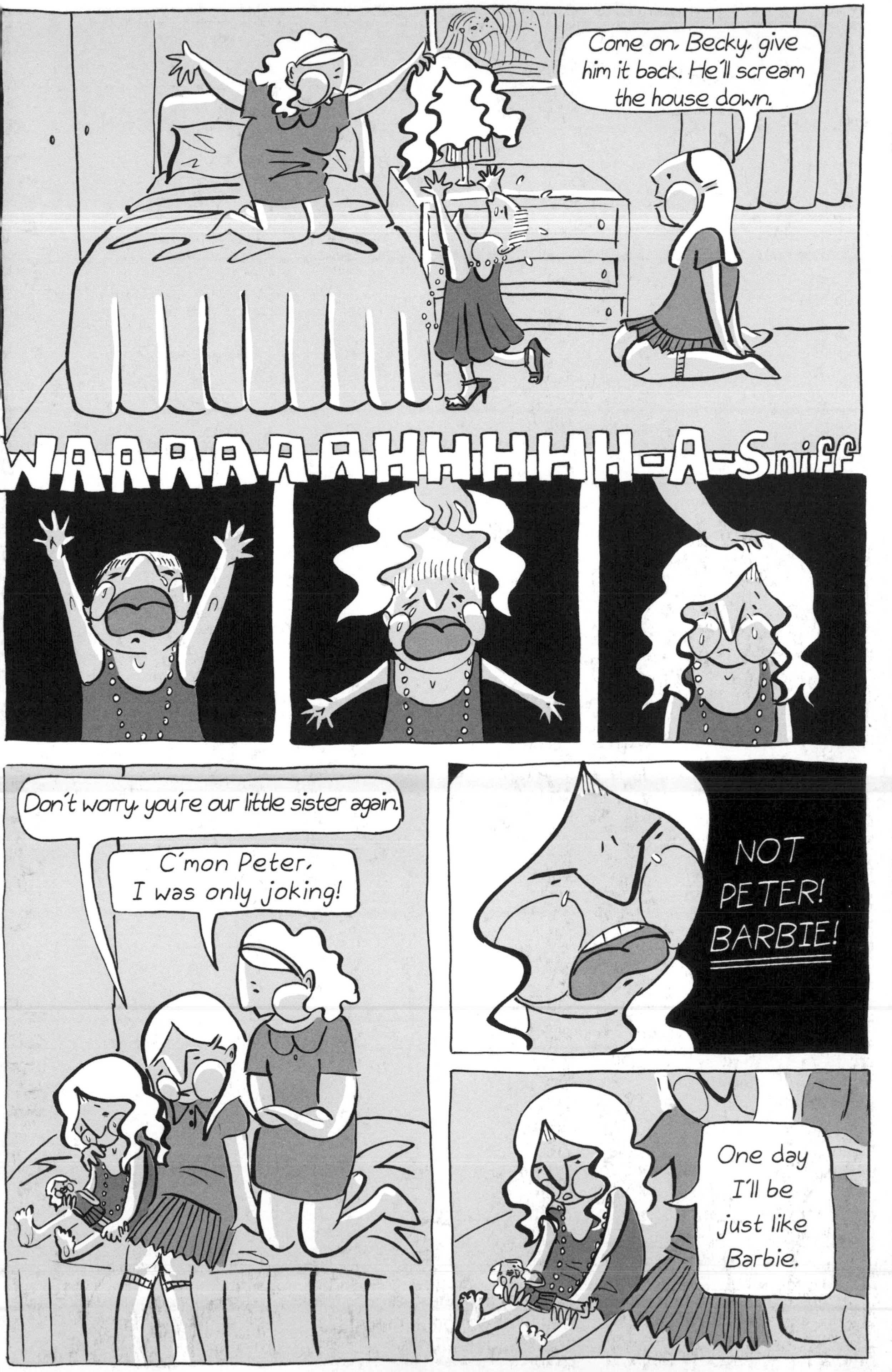
Come on, Becky, give him it back. He'll scream the house down.
WAAAAAAHHHHHH-A-Sniff
Don't worry, you're our little sister again.
C'mon Peter, I was only joking!
NOT PETER! BARBIE!
One day I'll be just like Barbie.

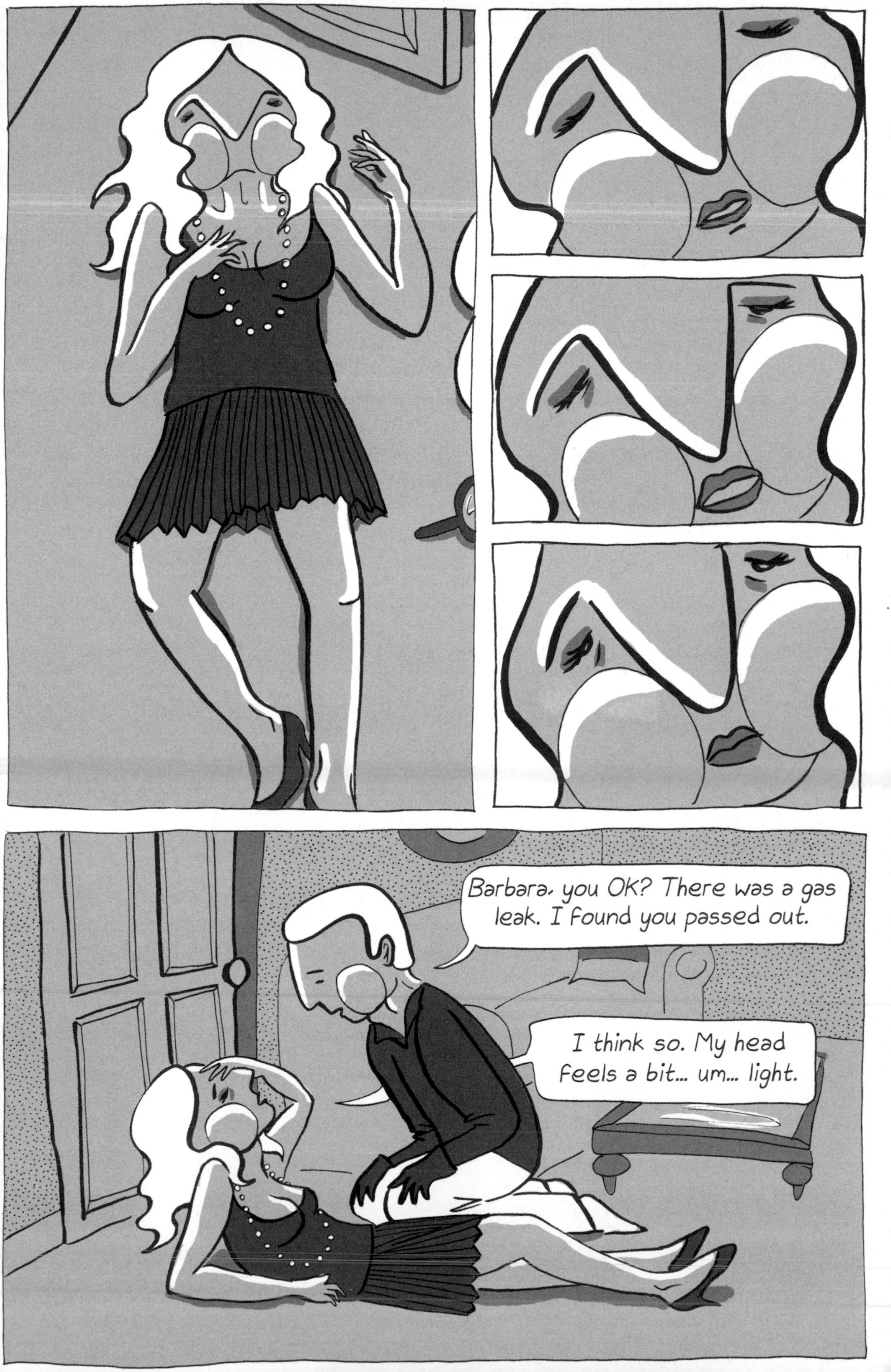
Barbara, you OK? There was a gas leak. I found you passed out.
I think so. My head feels a bit... um... light.

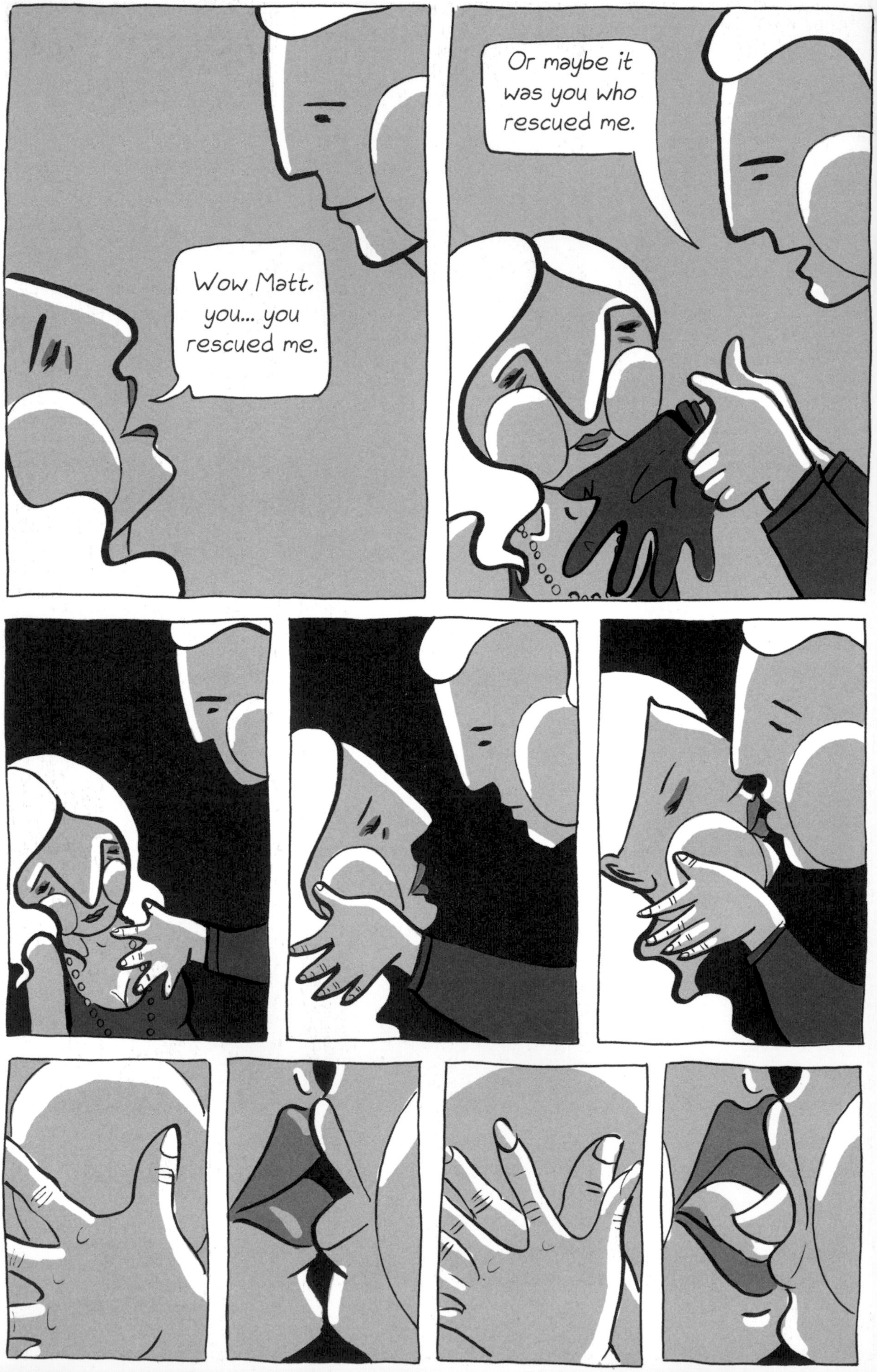
Wow Matt, you... you rescued me.
Or maybe it was you who rescued me.

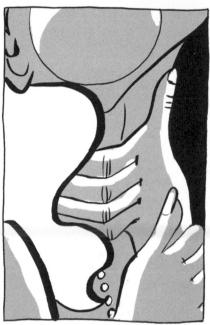
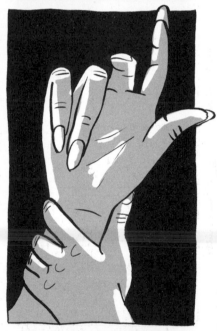

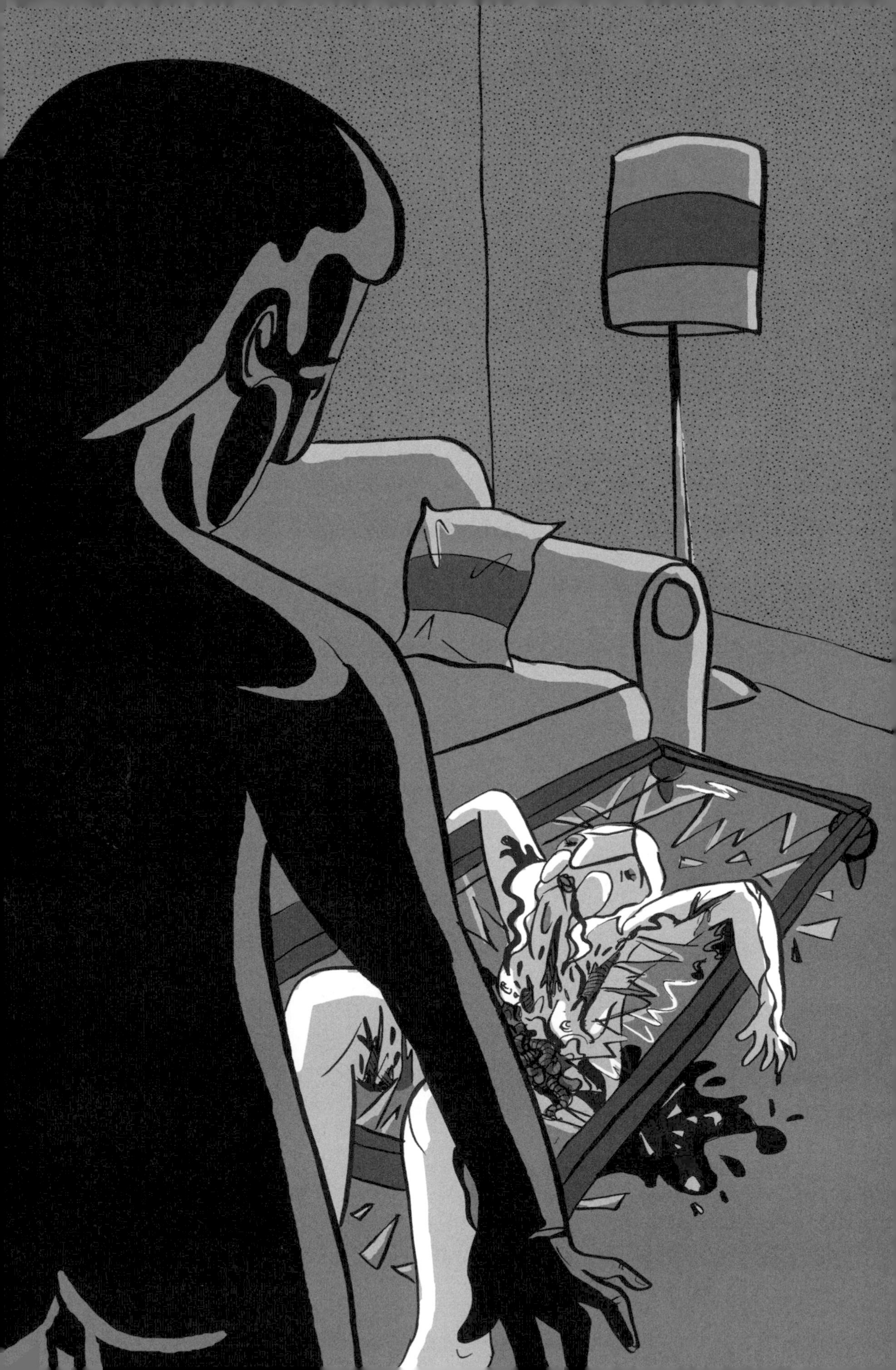

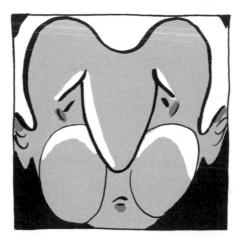

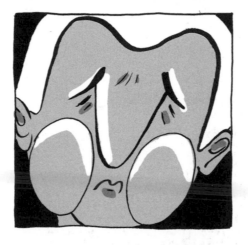

The Building of Rottin Road, 1865.

July 1981

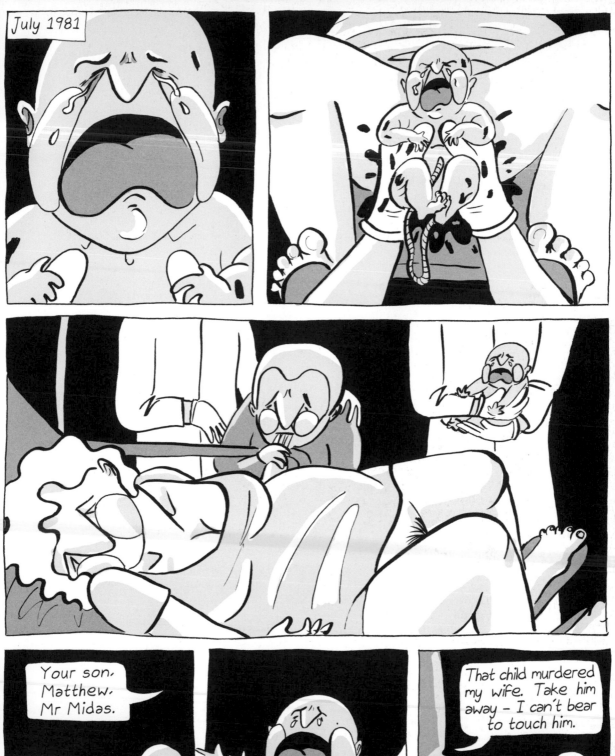

Your son, Matthew. Mr Midas.

That child murdered my wife. Take him away — I can't bear to touch him.

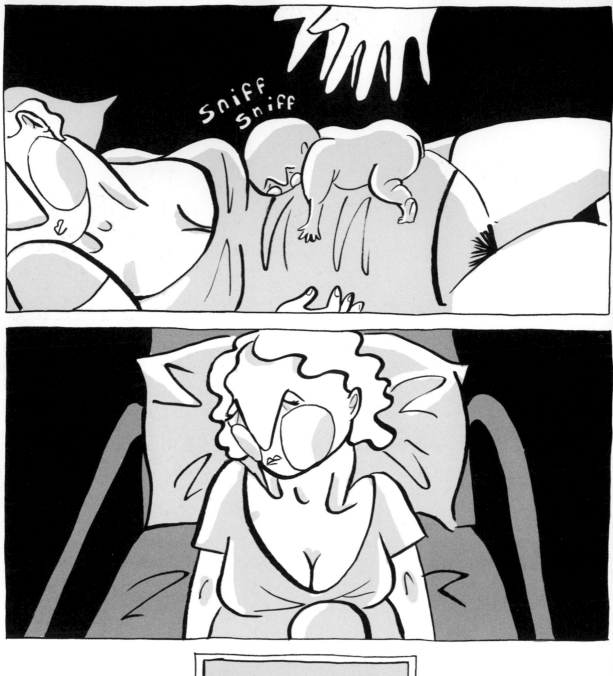

Sniff
Sniff

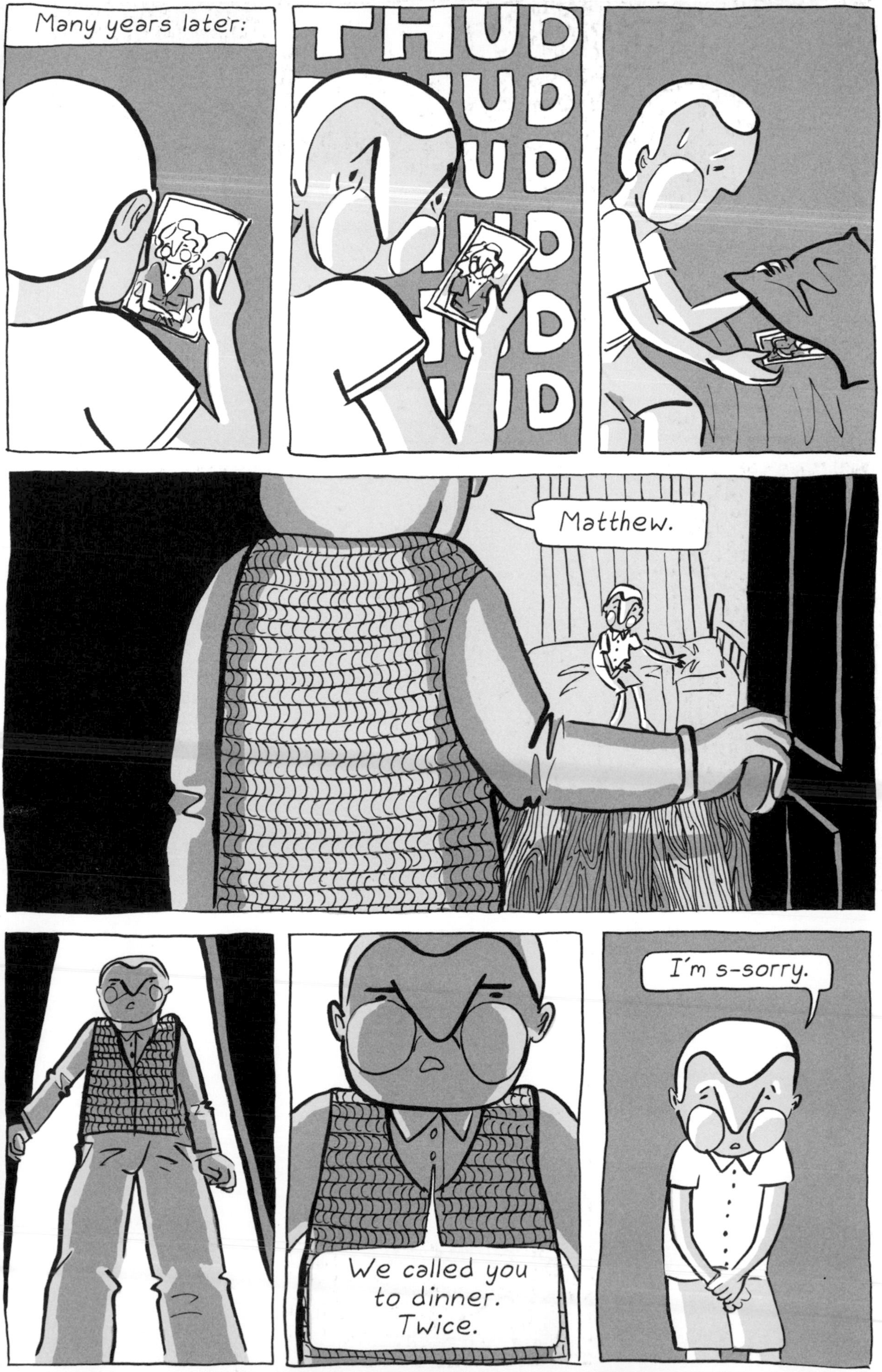
Many years later:
THUD
THUD
THUD
THUD
THUD
THUD
Matthew.
I'm s-sorry.
We called you to dinner. Twice.

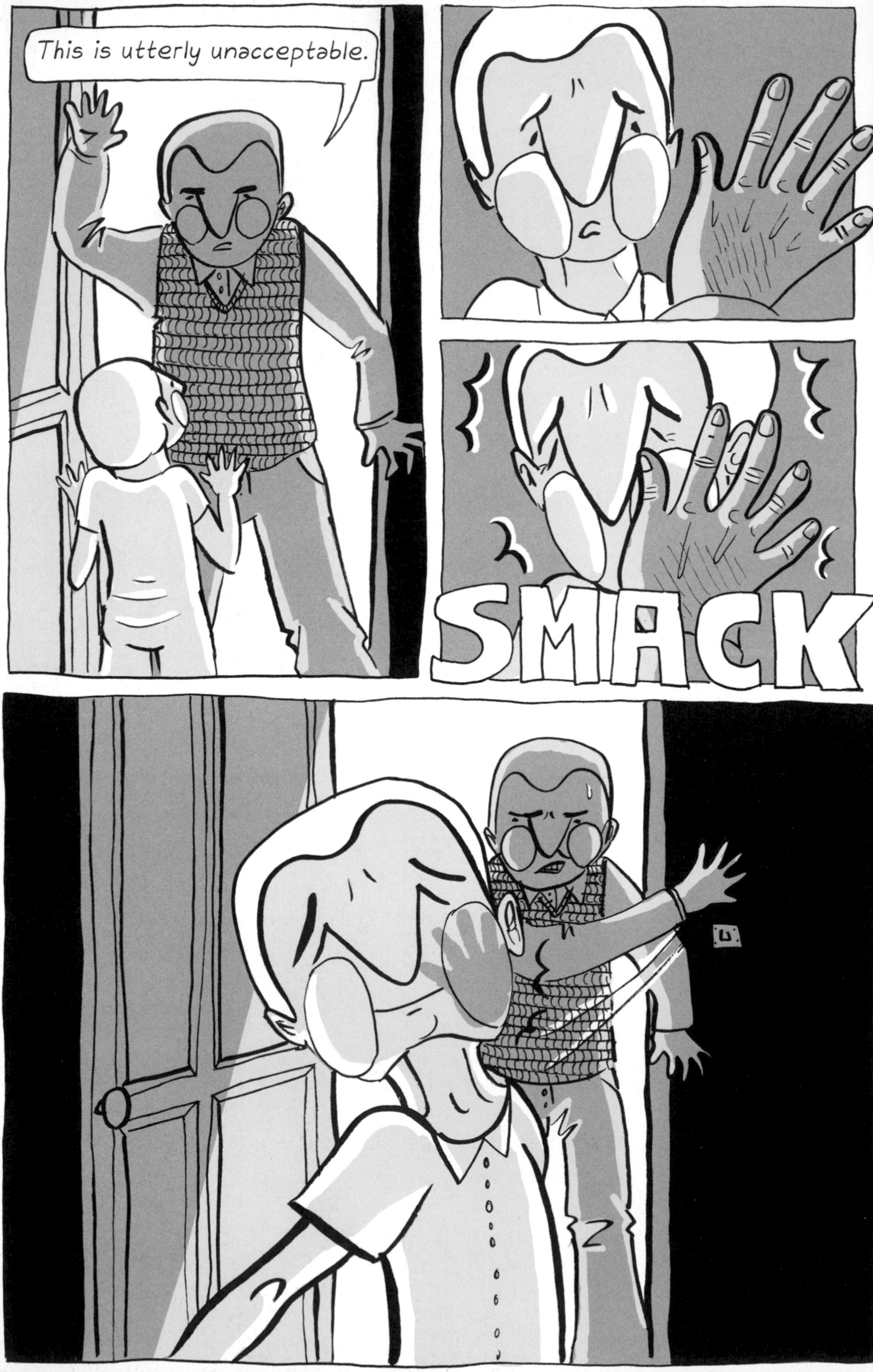
This is utterly unacceptable.
SMACK

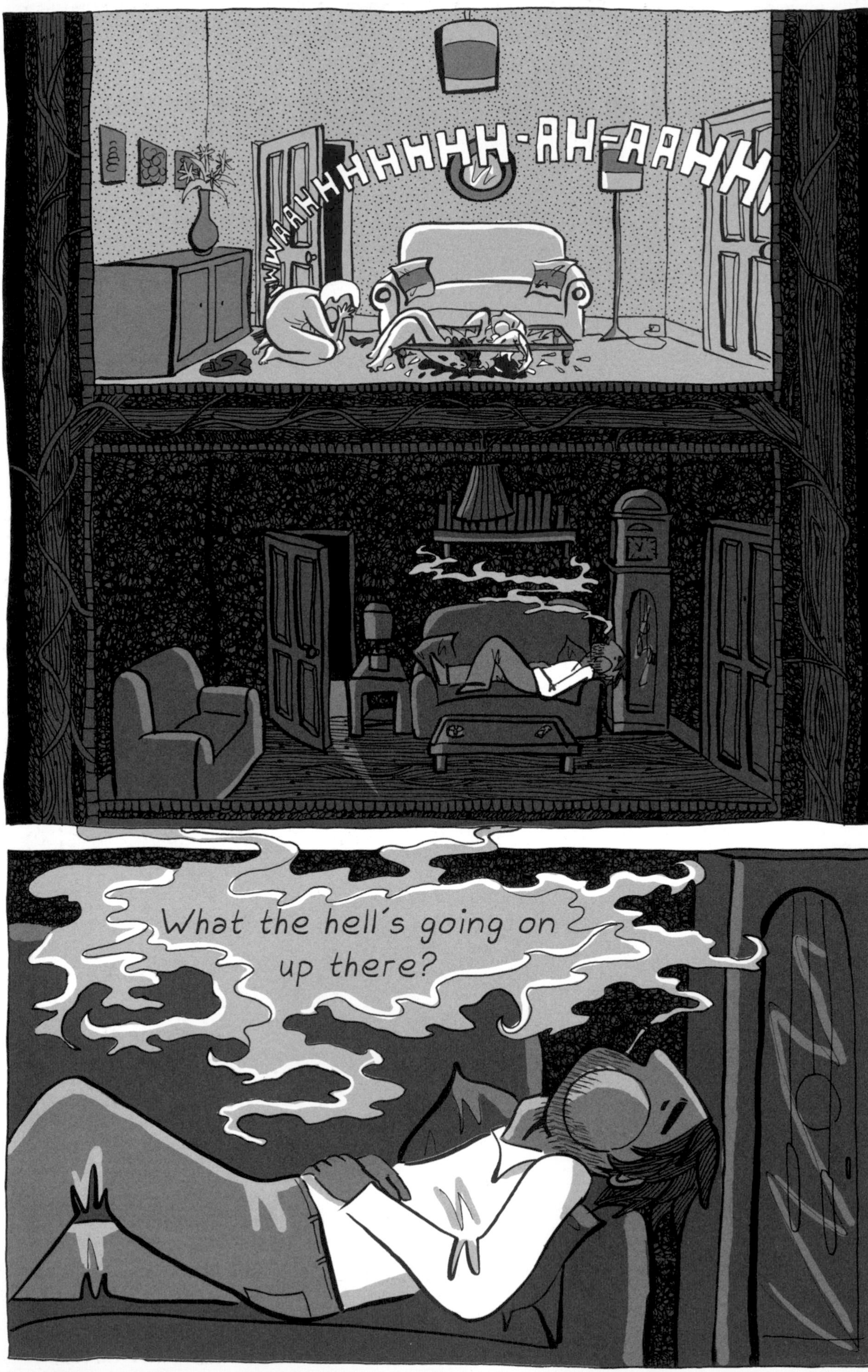
WWAAHHHHHHHHHH-AH-AAHH
What the hell's going on up there?

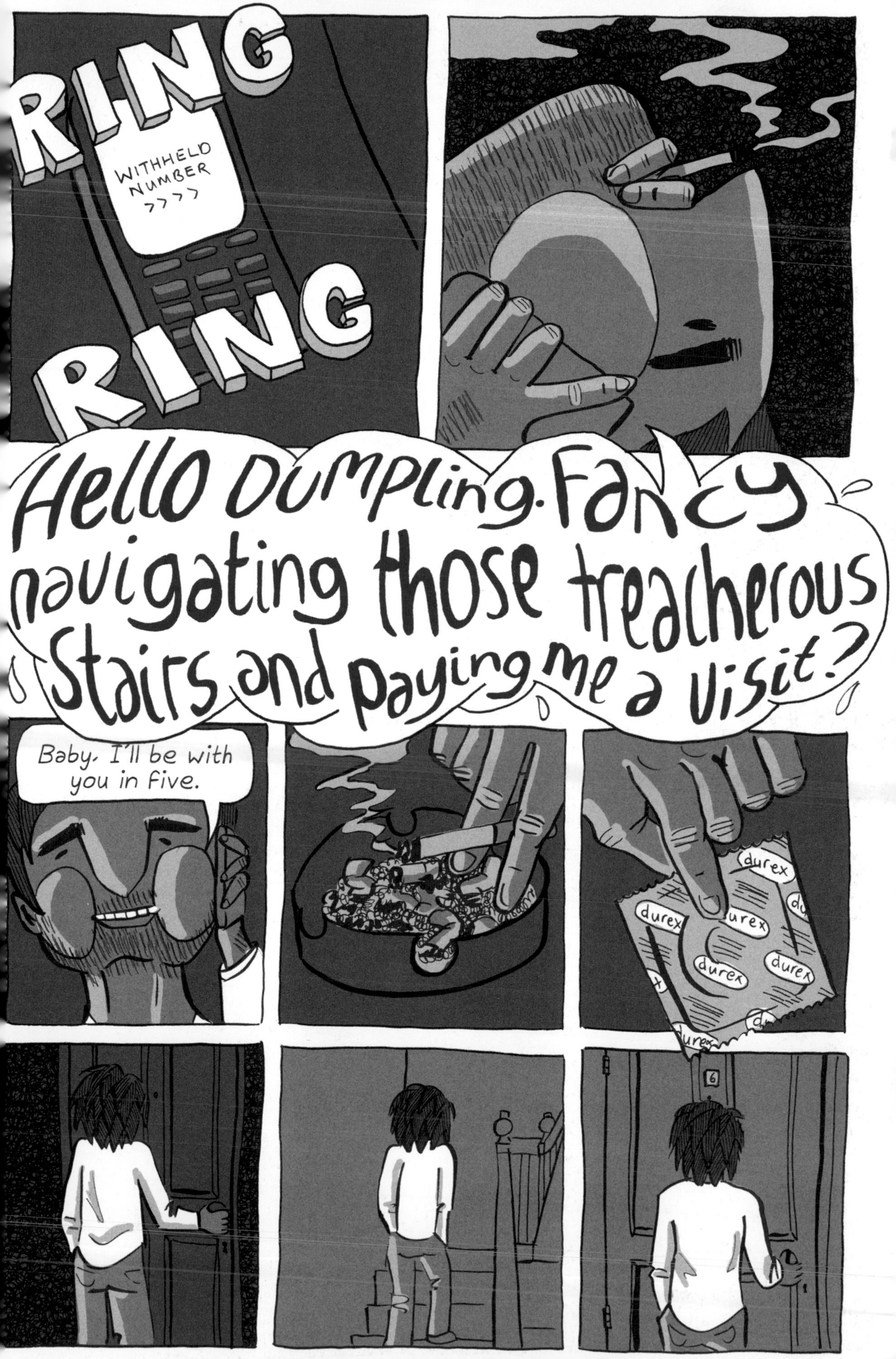
RING
WITHHELD NUMBER ????
RING
Hello Dumpling. Fancy navigating those treacherous stairs and paying me a visit?
Baby, I'll be with you in five.
durex
6

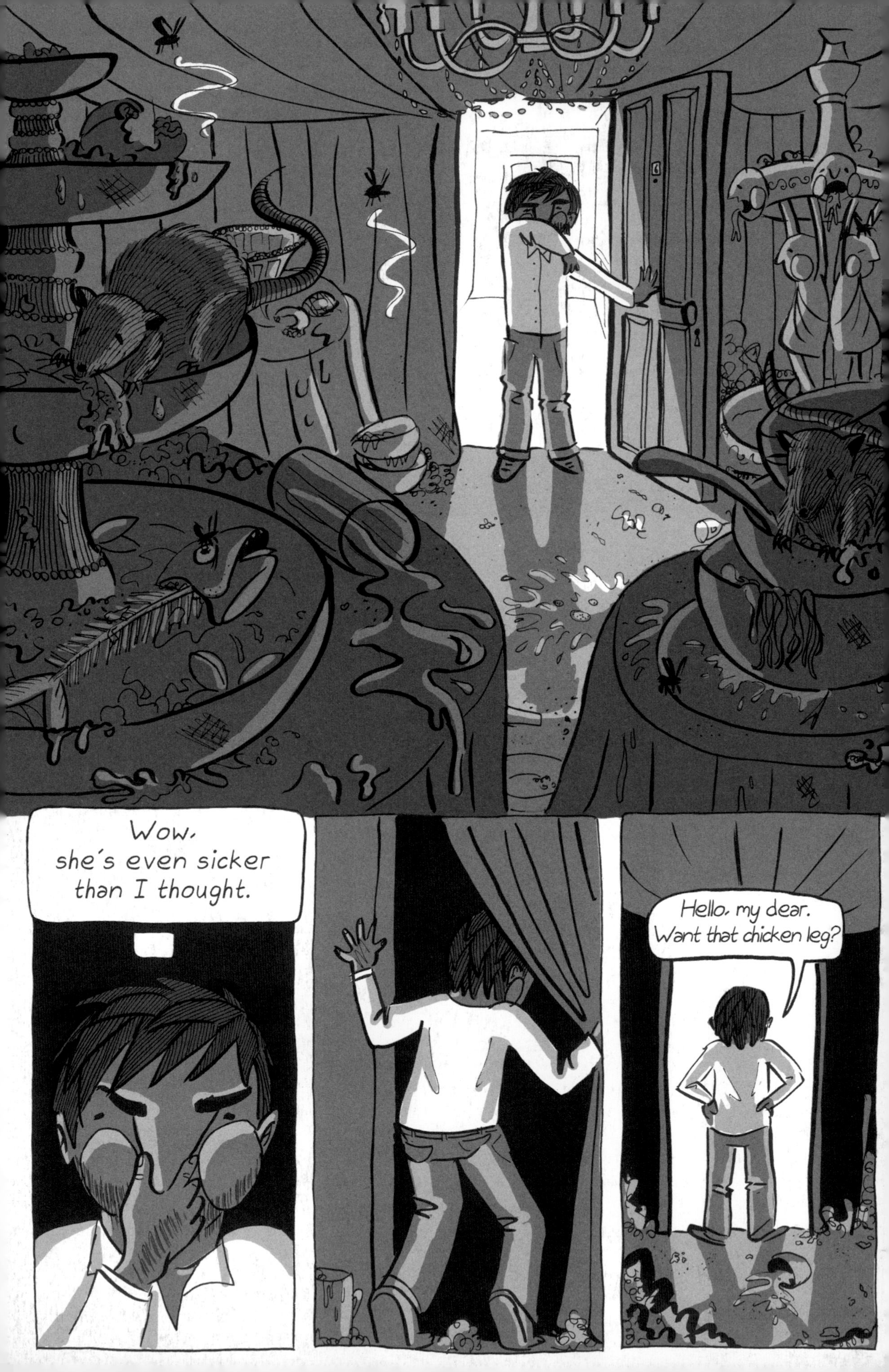
Wow,
she's even sicker
than I thought.
Hello, my dear.
Want that chicken leg?

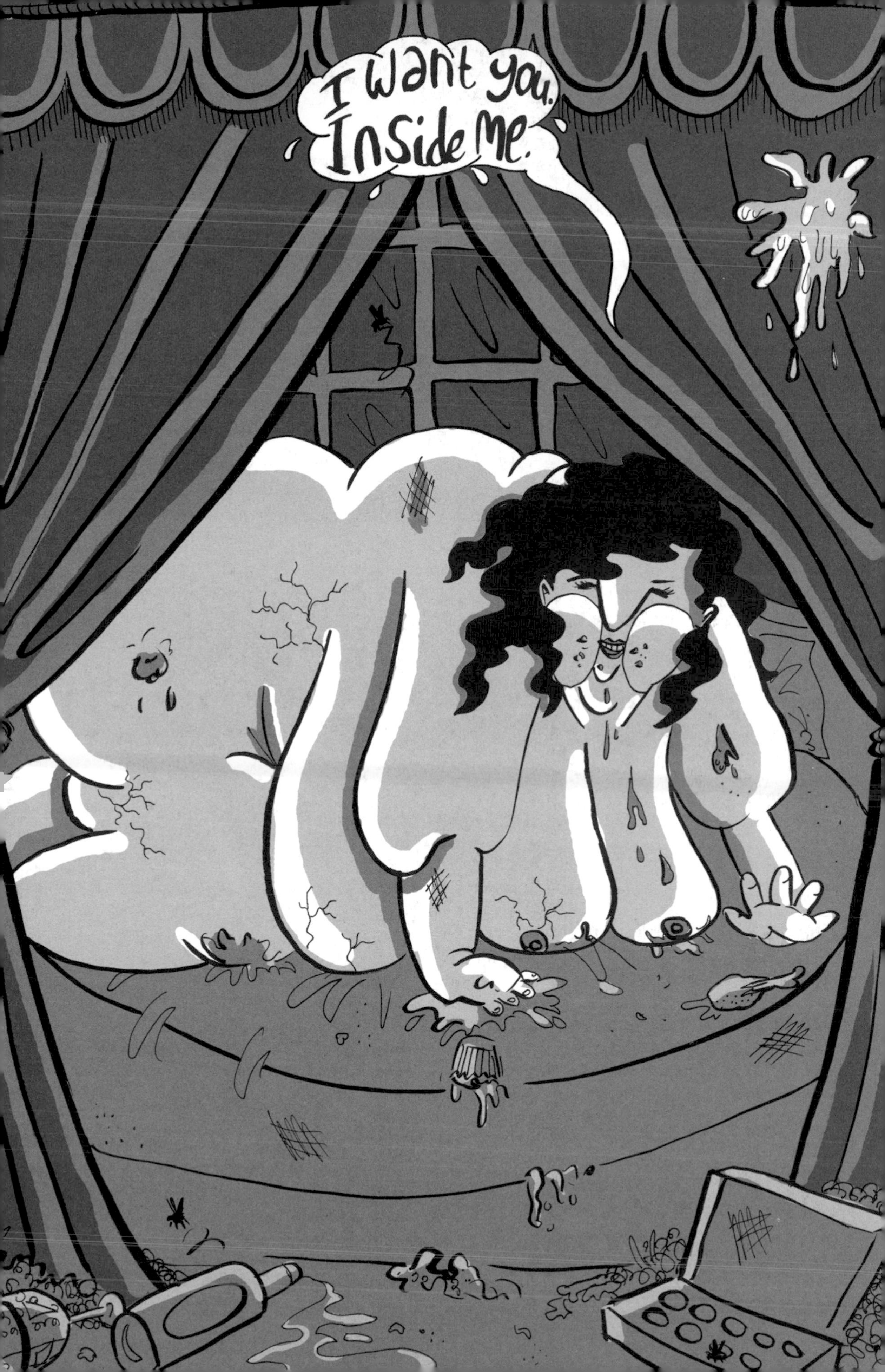
I want you.
Inside me.

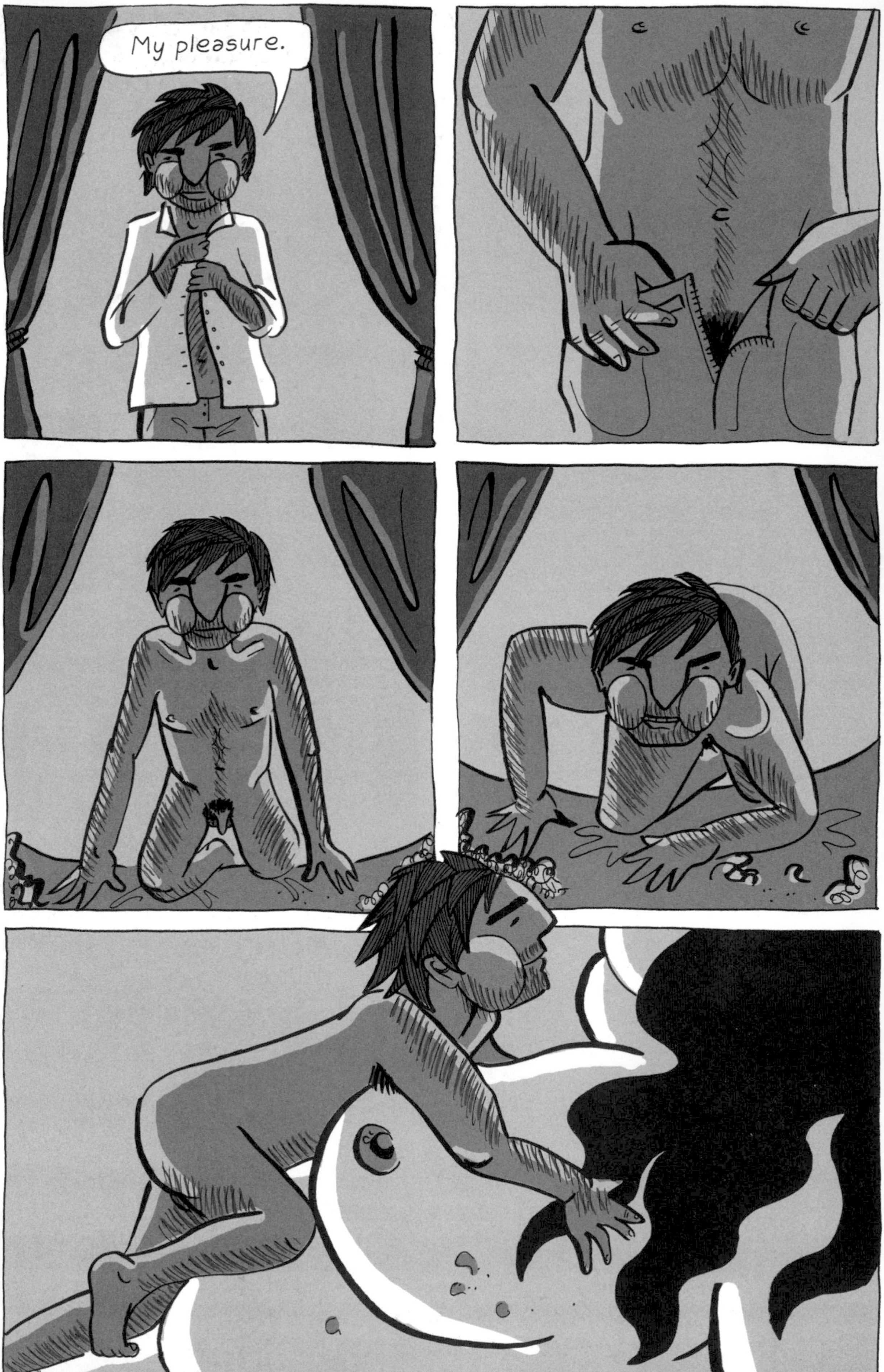
My pleasure.

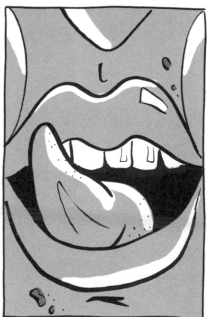

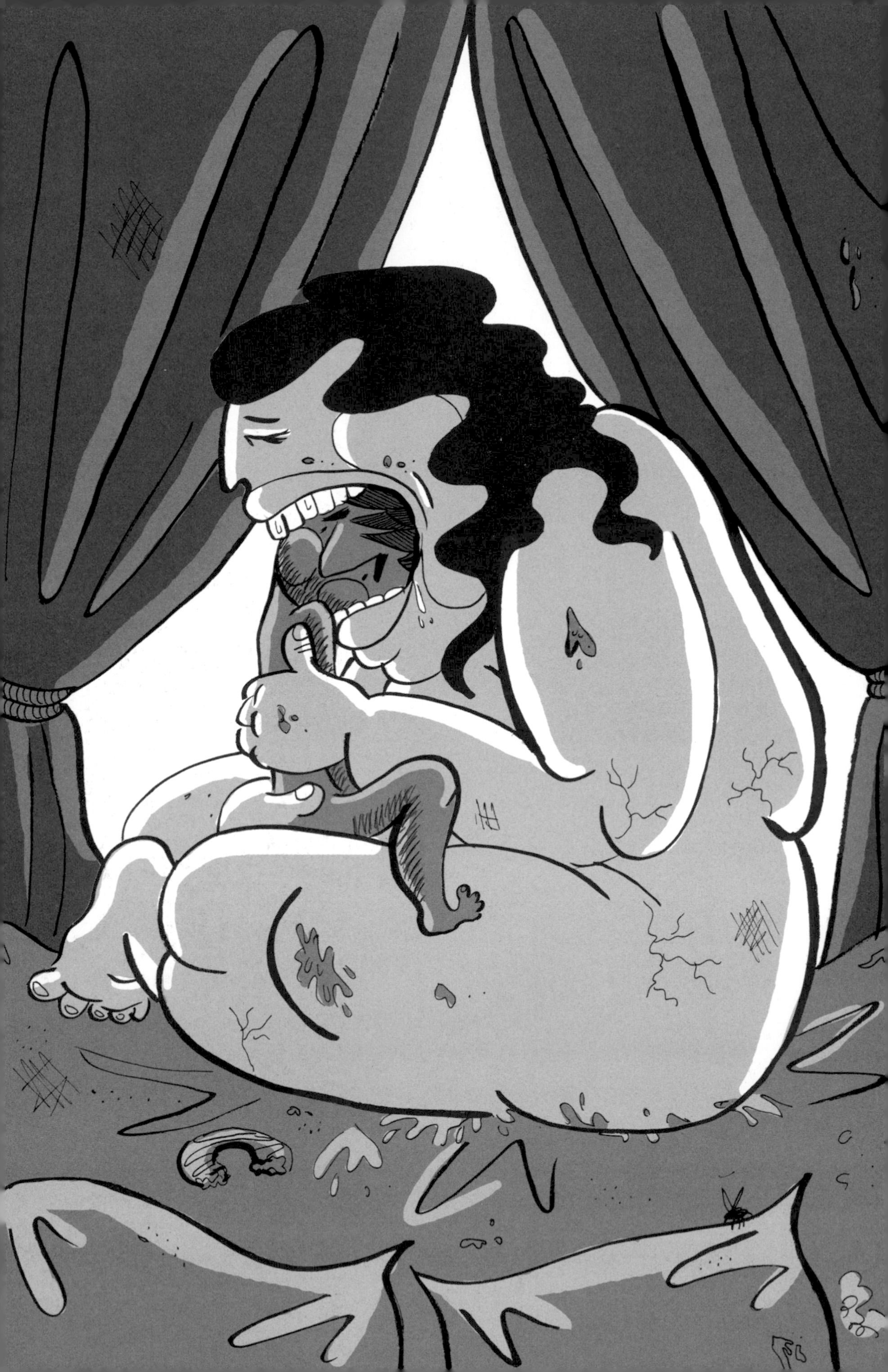

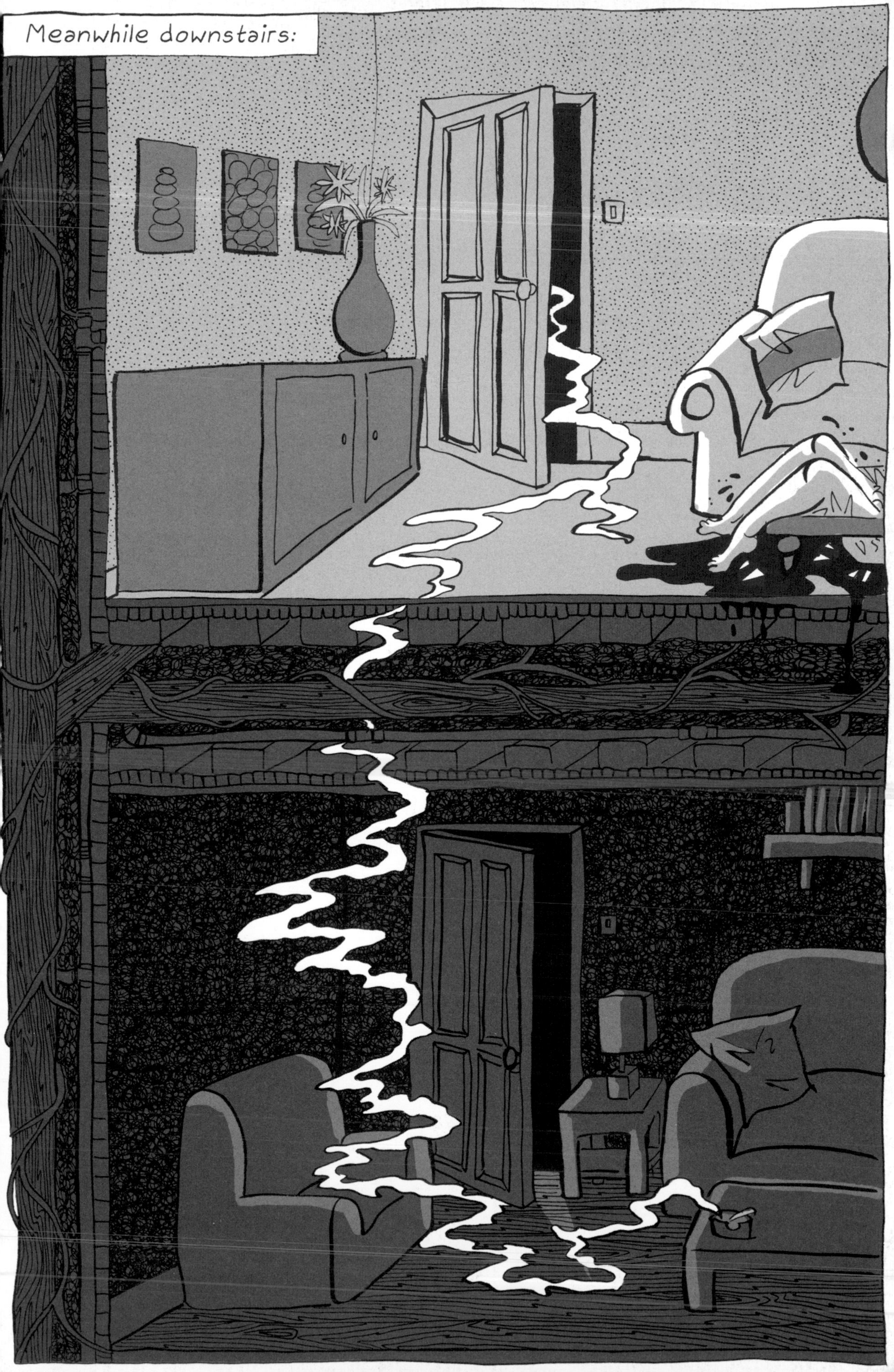
Meanwhile downstairs:

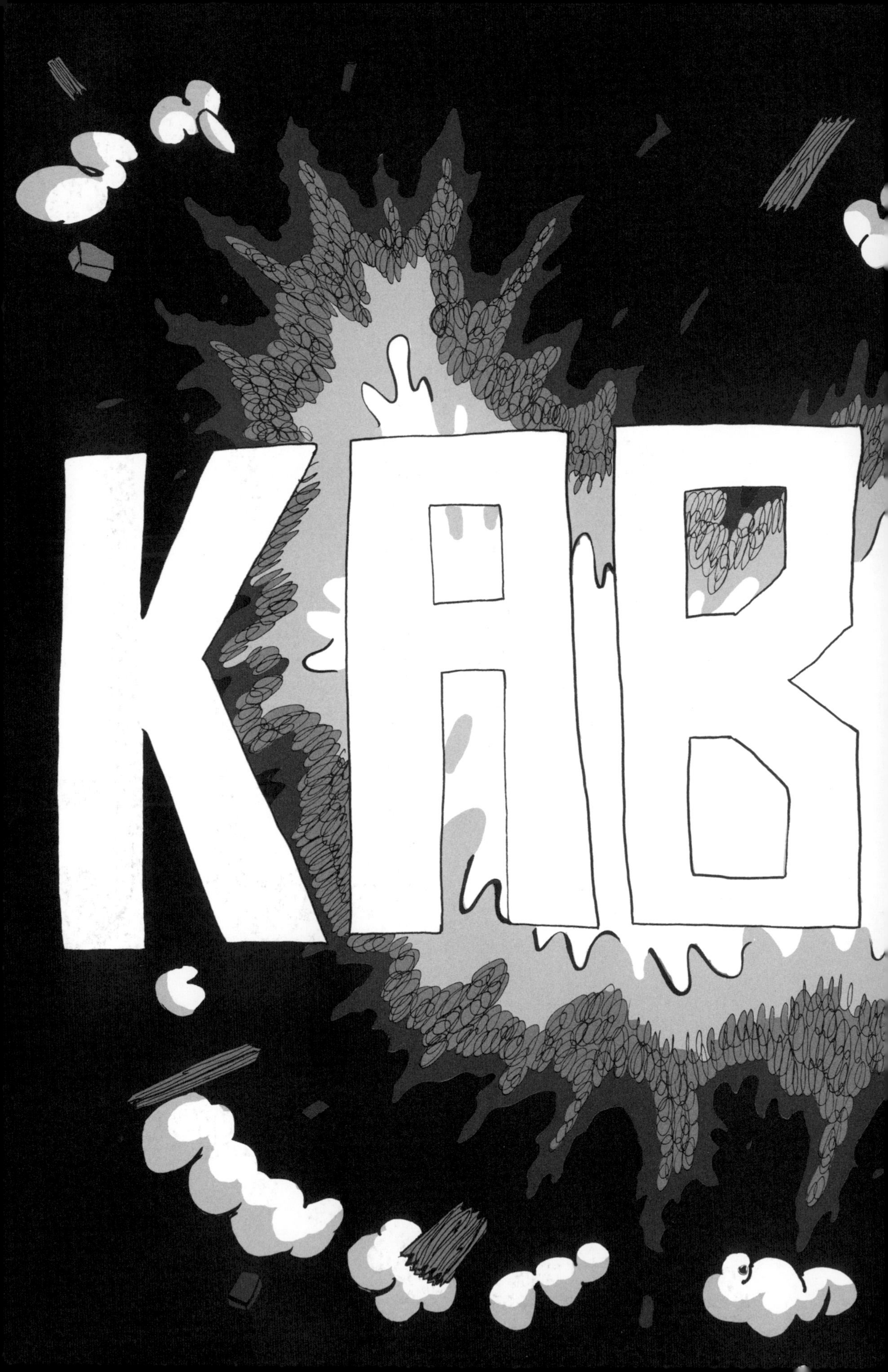
KAB

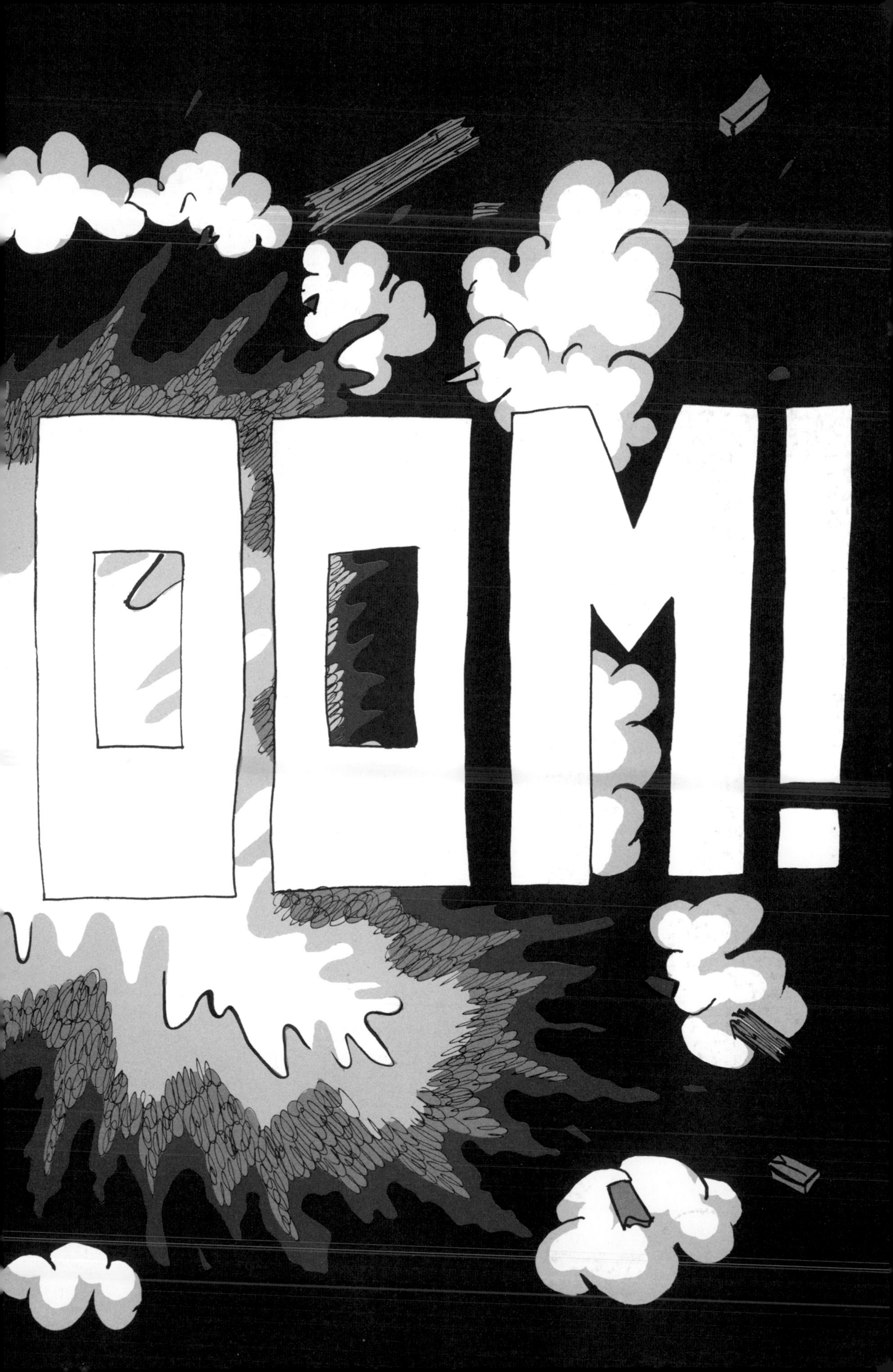
OOM!

Chapter Six

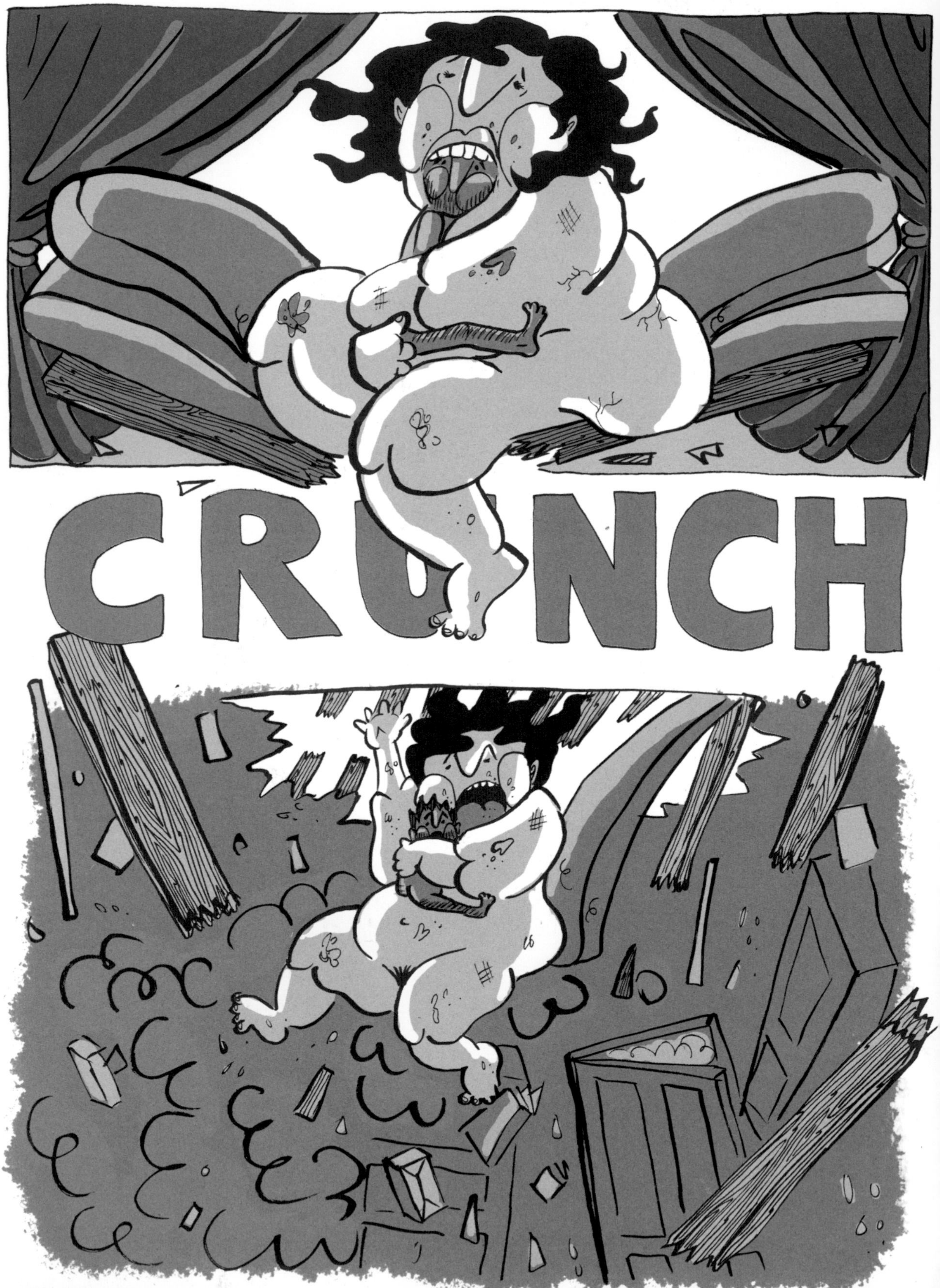
CRUNCH

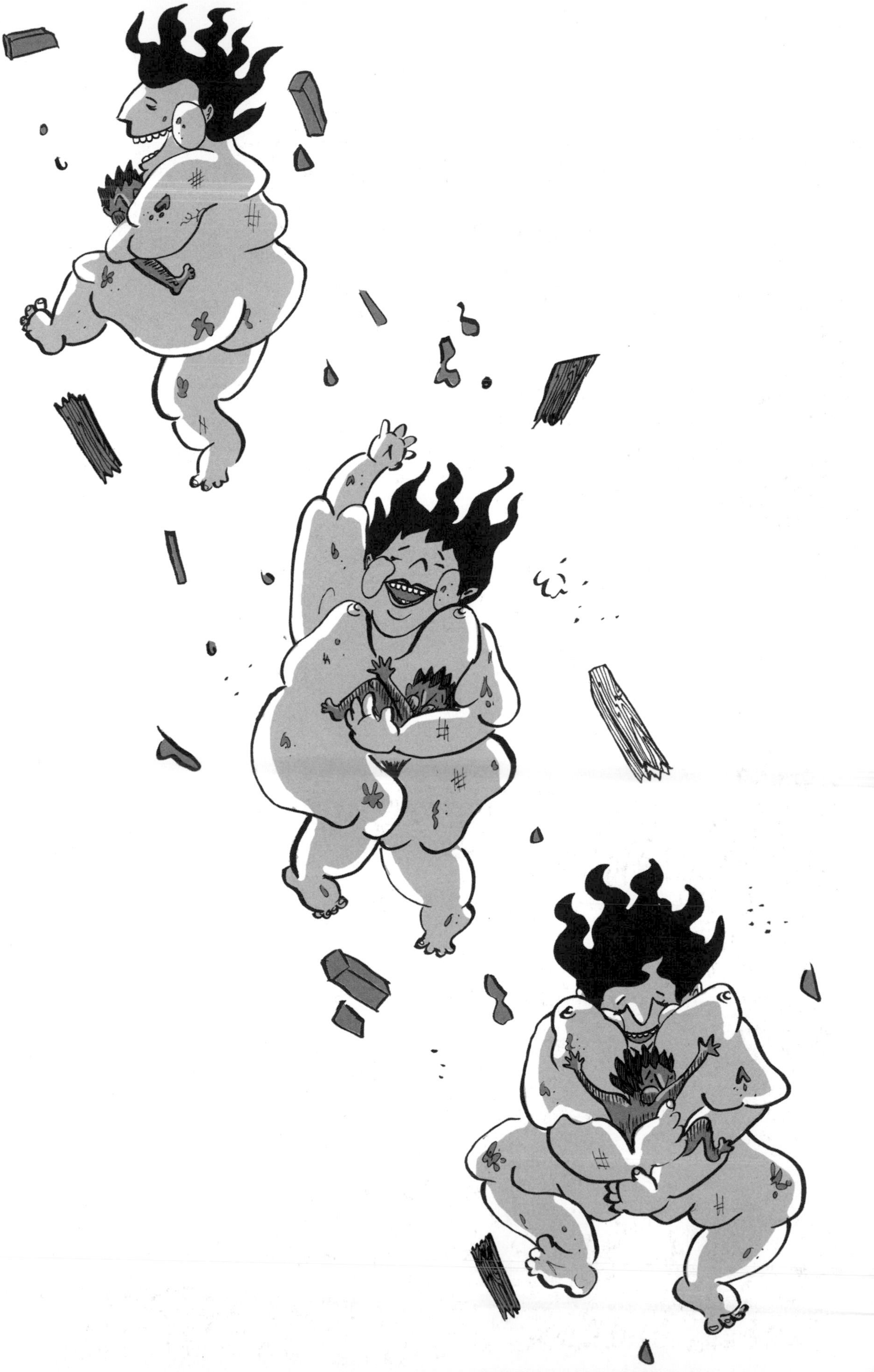

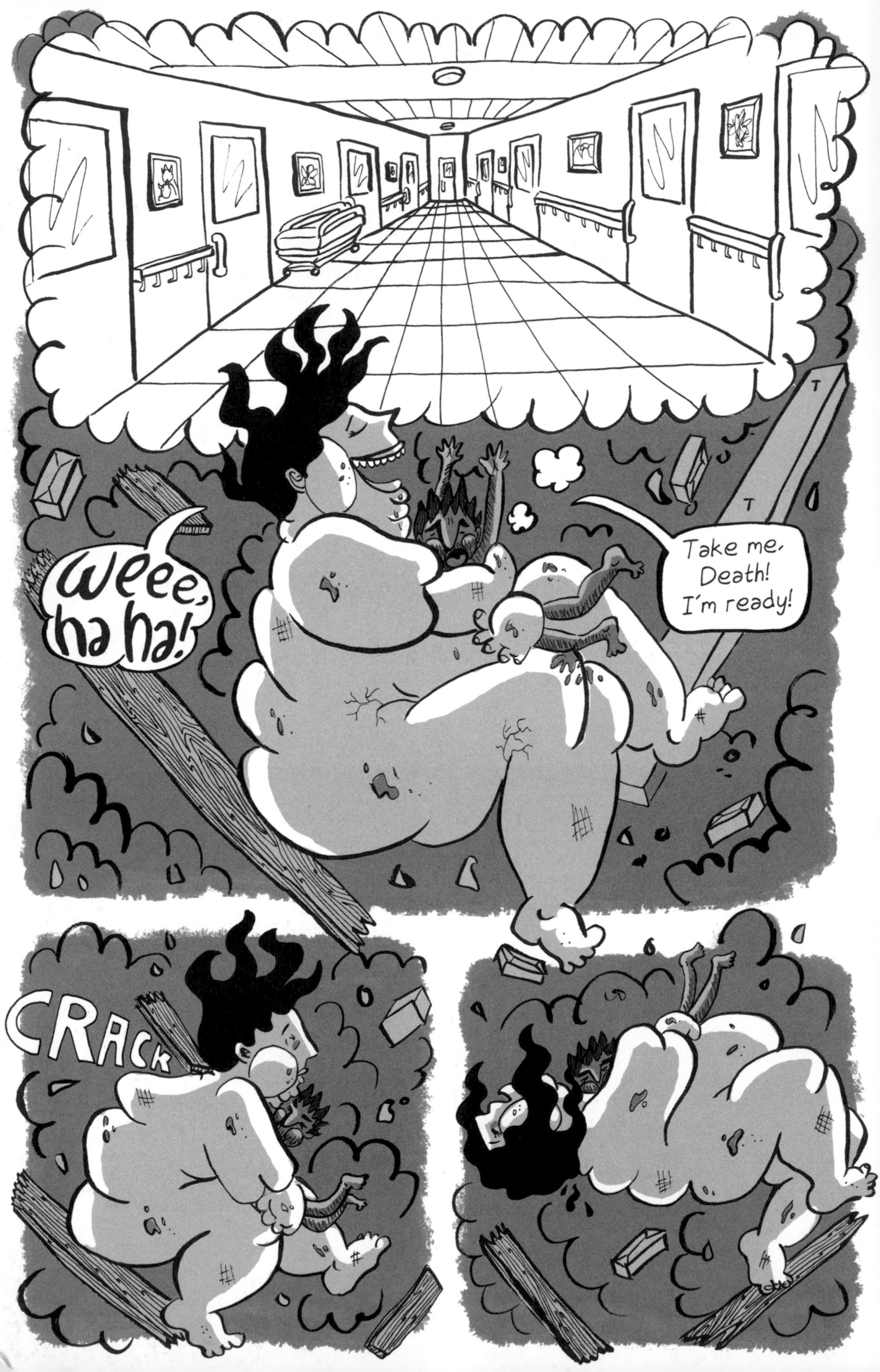
Weee, ha ha!
Take me, Death! I'm ready!
CRACK

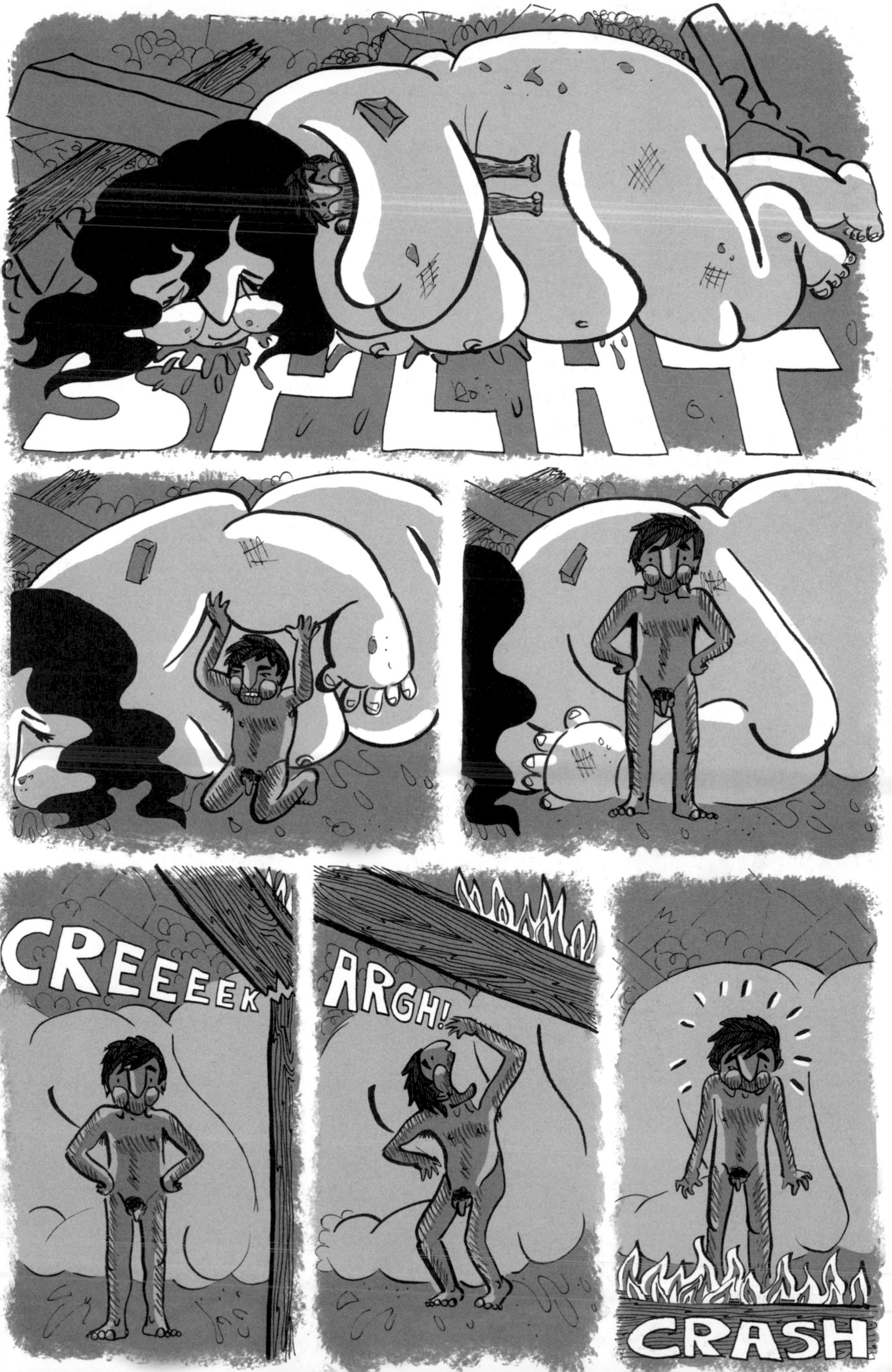
SPLAT
CREEEEEK
ARGH!
CRASH

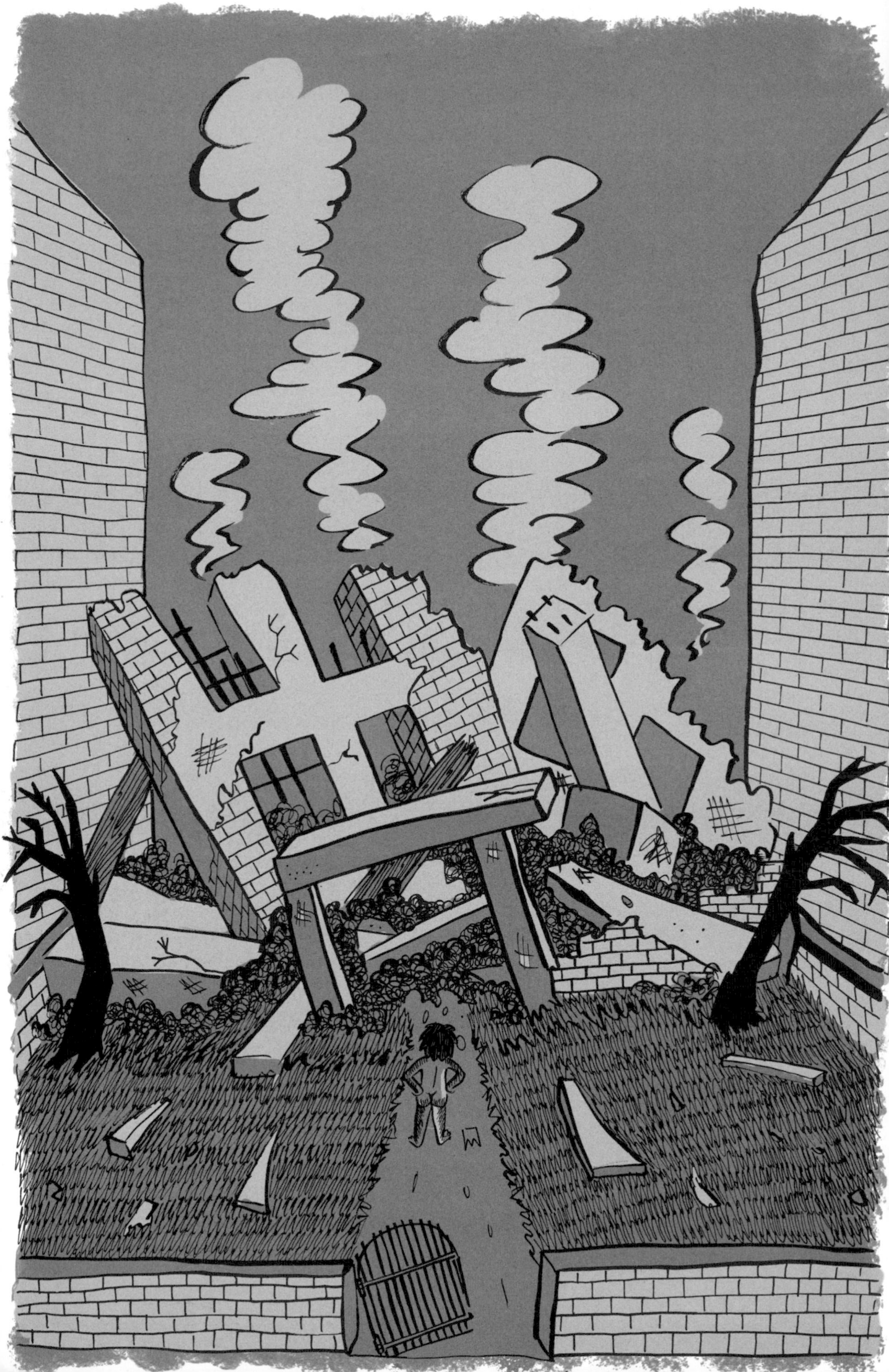

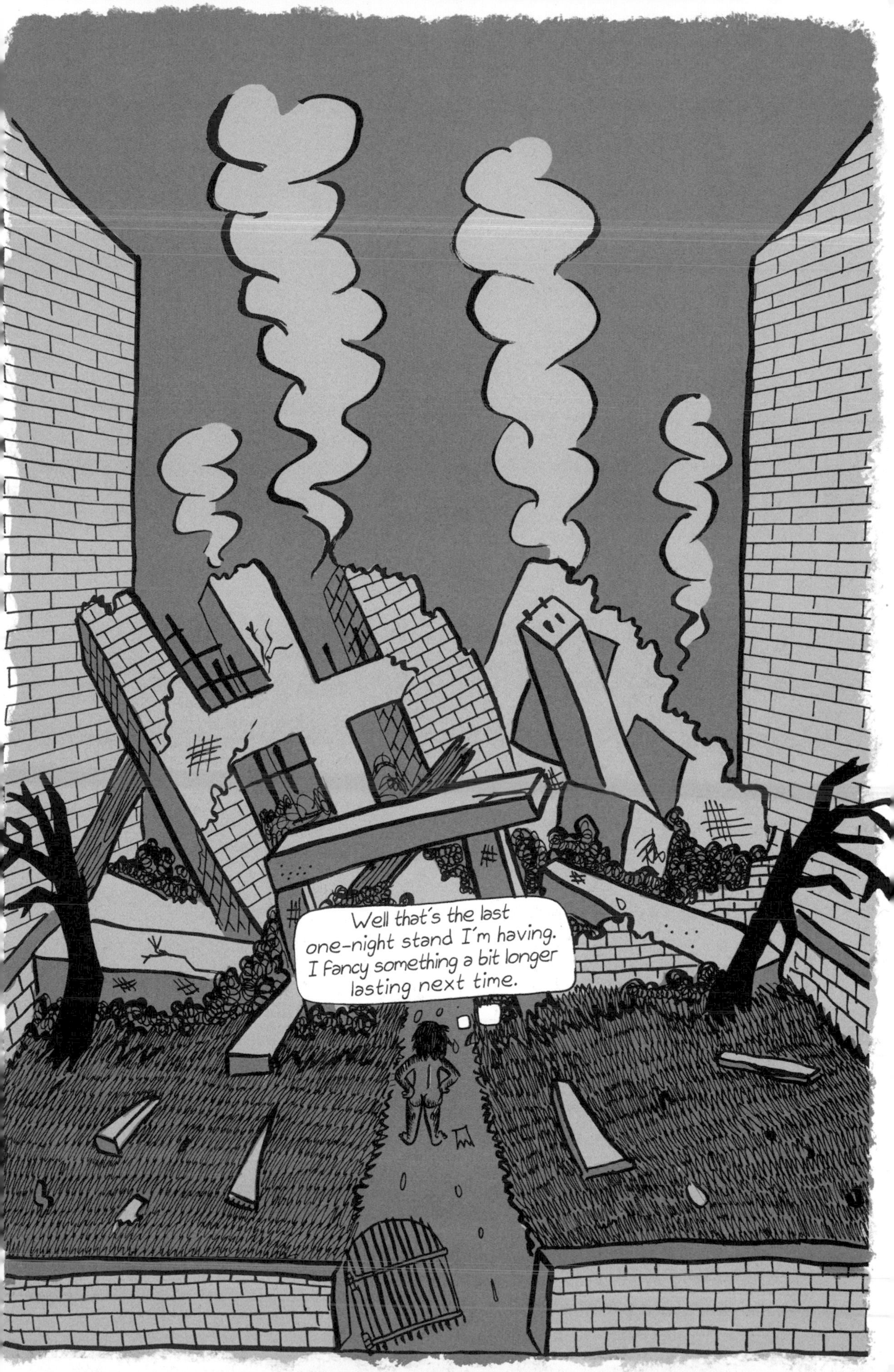
Well that's the last one-night stand I'm having. I fancy something a bit longer lasting next time.

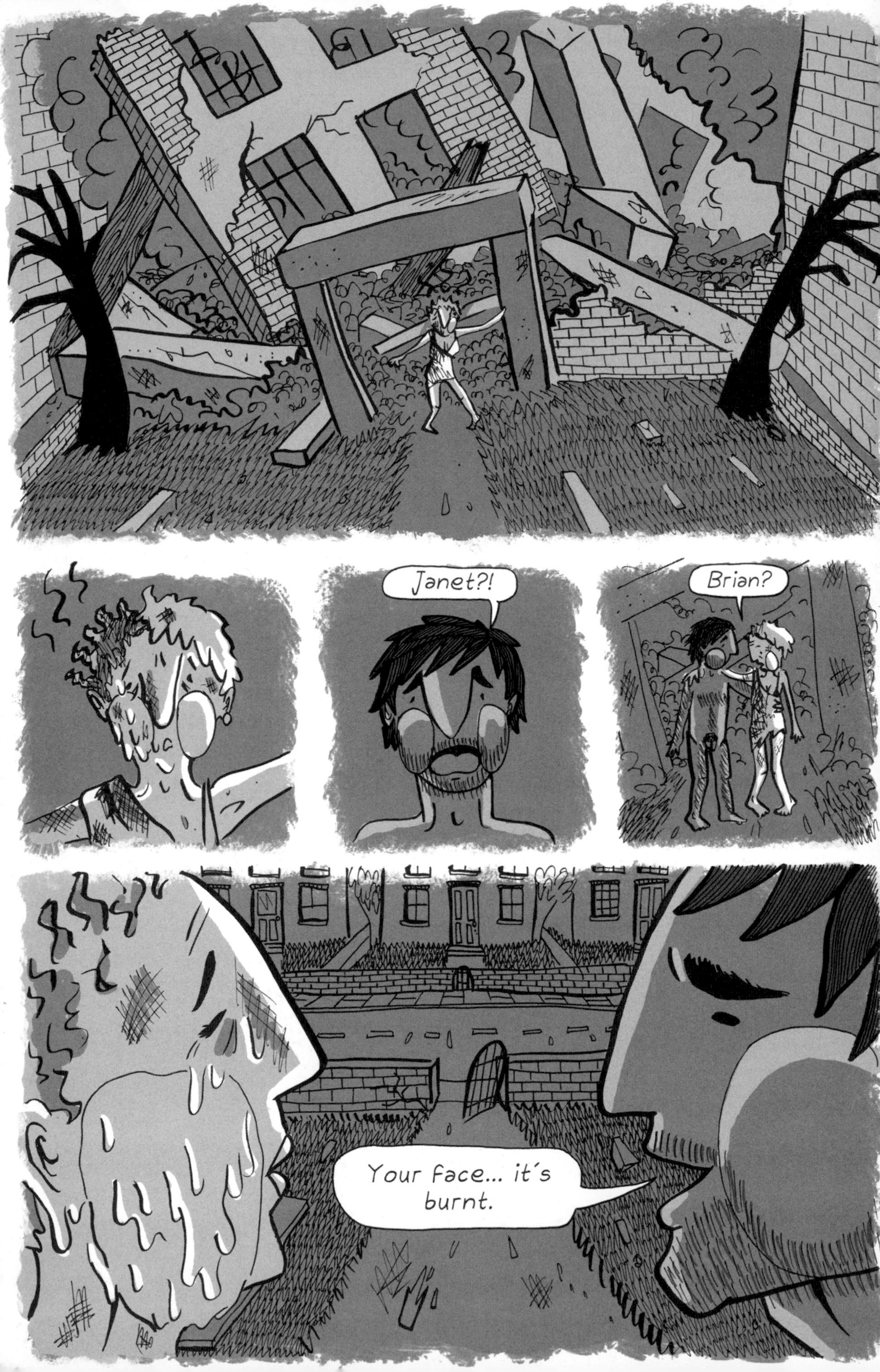
Janet?!
Brian?
Your face... it's burnt.

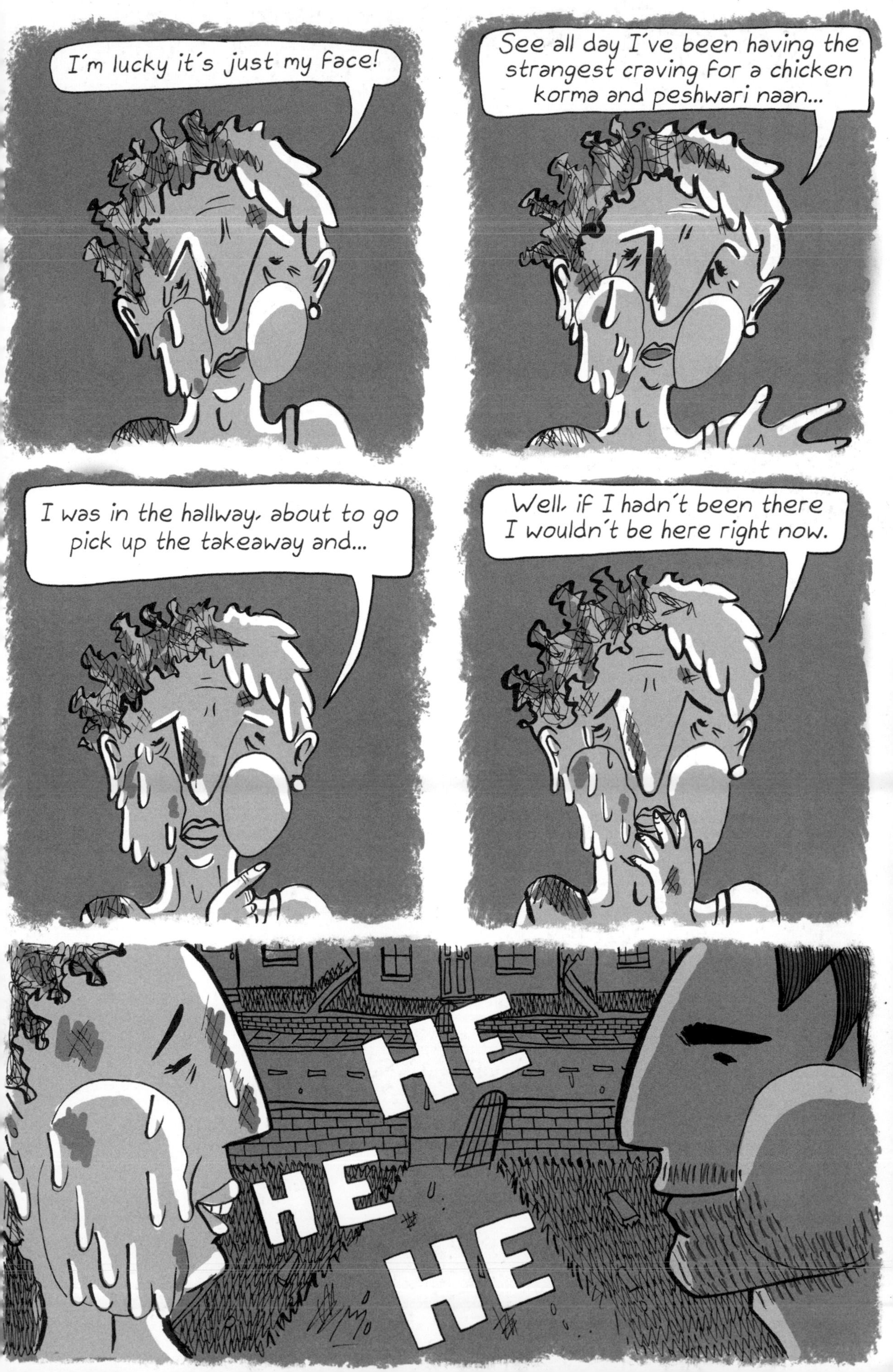
I'm lucky it's just my face!
See all day I've been having the strangest craving for a chicken korma and peshwari naan...
I was in the hallway, about to go pick up the takeaway and...
Well, if I hadn't been there I wouldn't be here right now.
HE
HE
HE

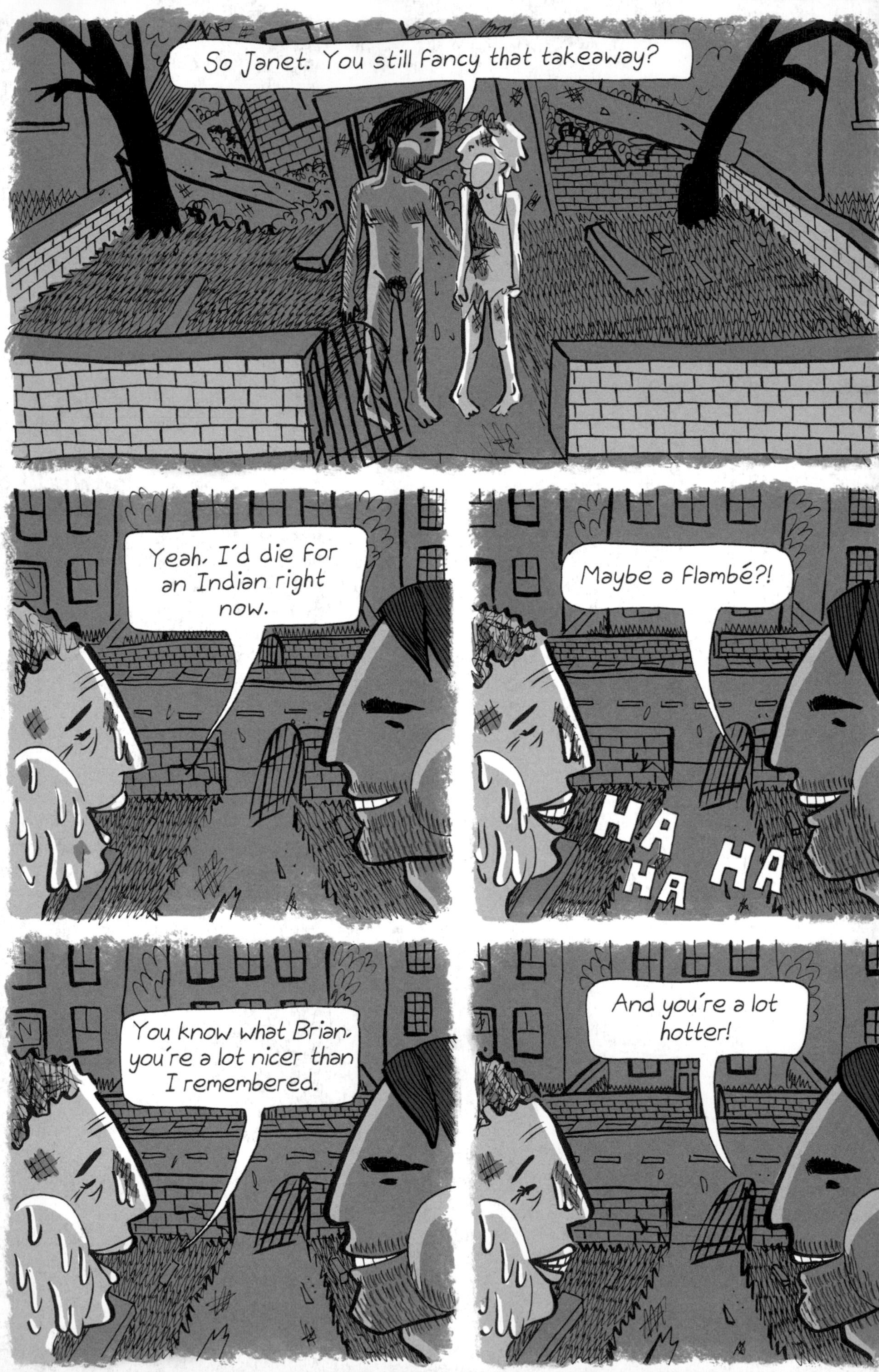
So Janet. You still fancy that takeaway?
Yeah, I'd die for an Indian right now.
Maybe a flambé?!
HA HA HA HA
You know what Brian, you're a lot nicer than I remembered.
And you're a lot hotter!

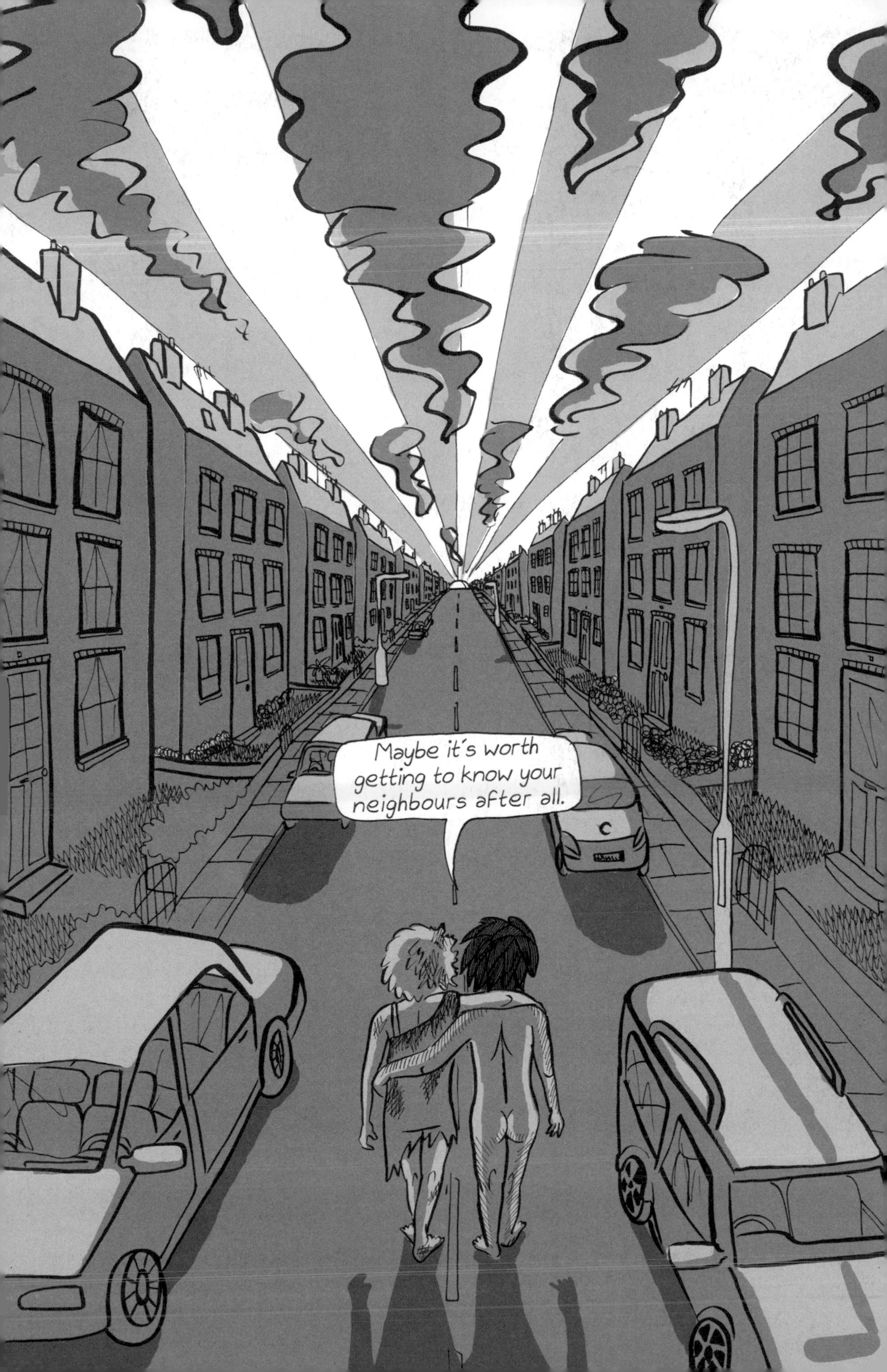
Maybe it's worth getting to know your neighbours after all.

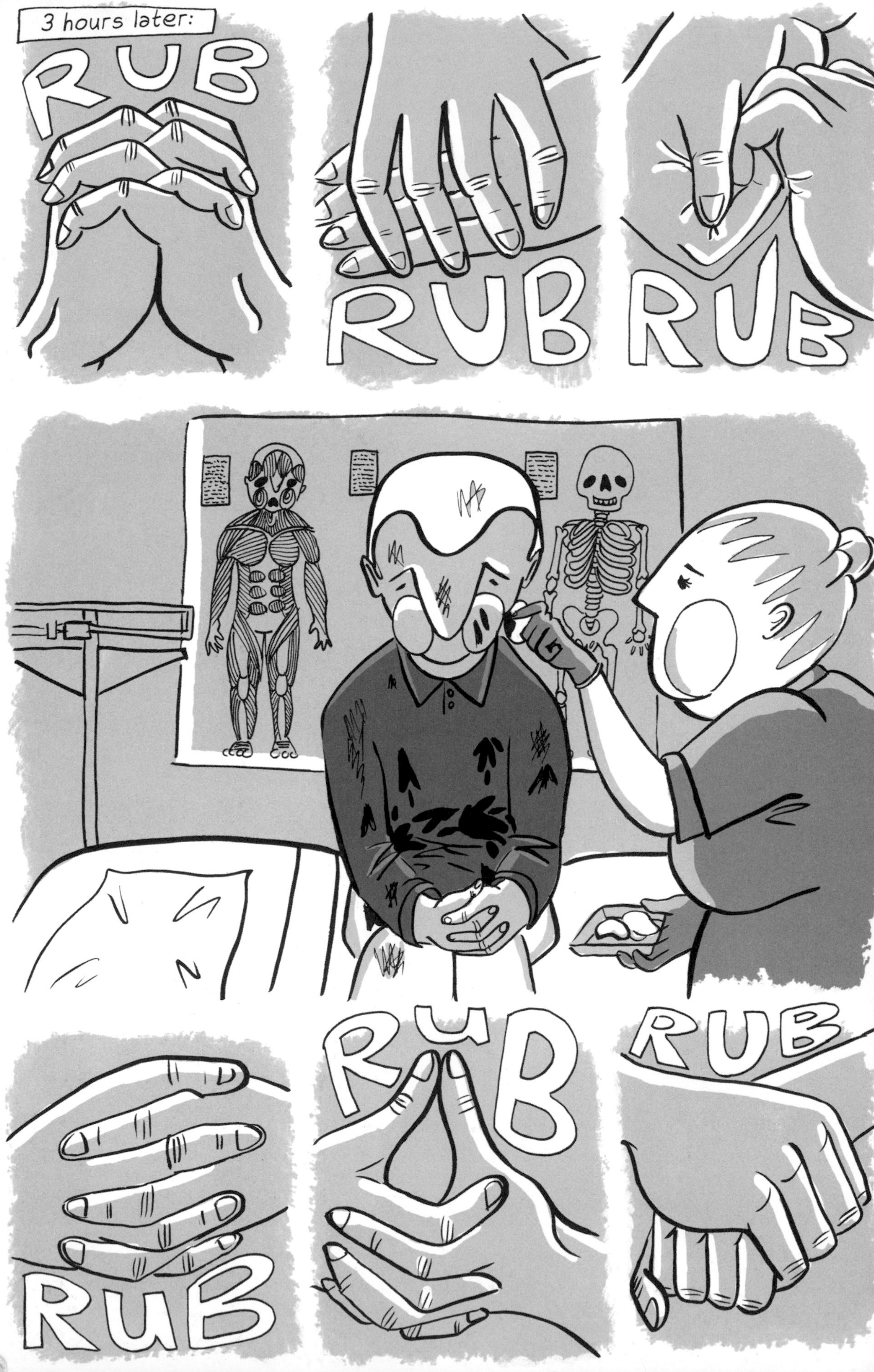
3 hours later:
RUB
RUB
RUB
RUB
RUB
RUB

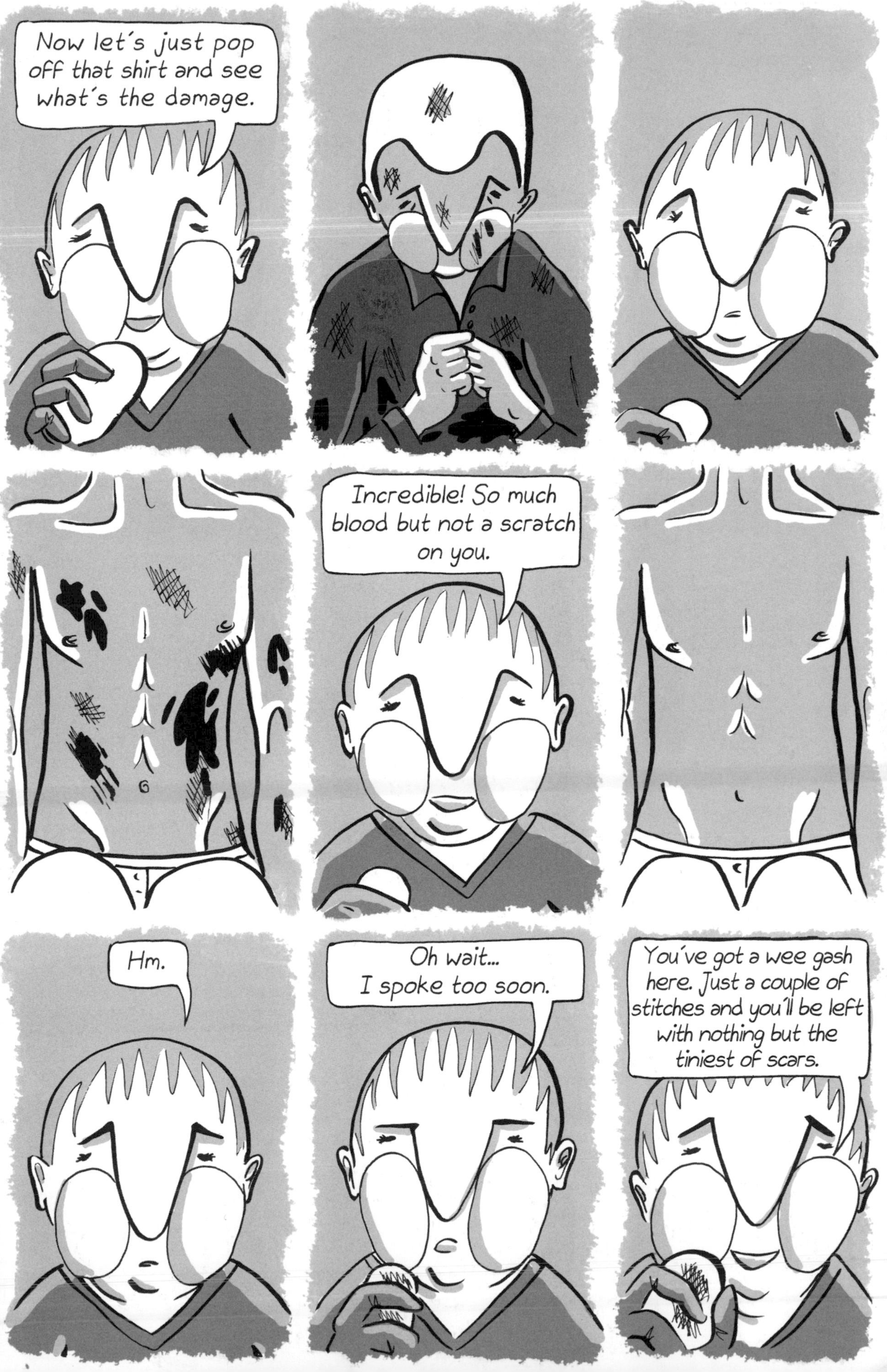
Now let's just pop off that shirt and see what's the damage.
Incredible! So much blood but not a scratch on you.
Hm.
Oh wait... I spoke too soon.
You've got a wee gash here. Just a couple of stitches and you'll be left with nothing but the tiniest of scars.

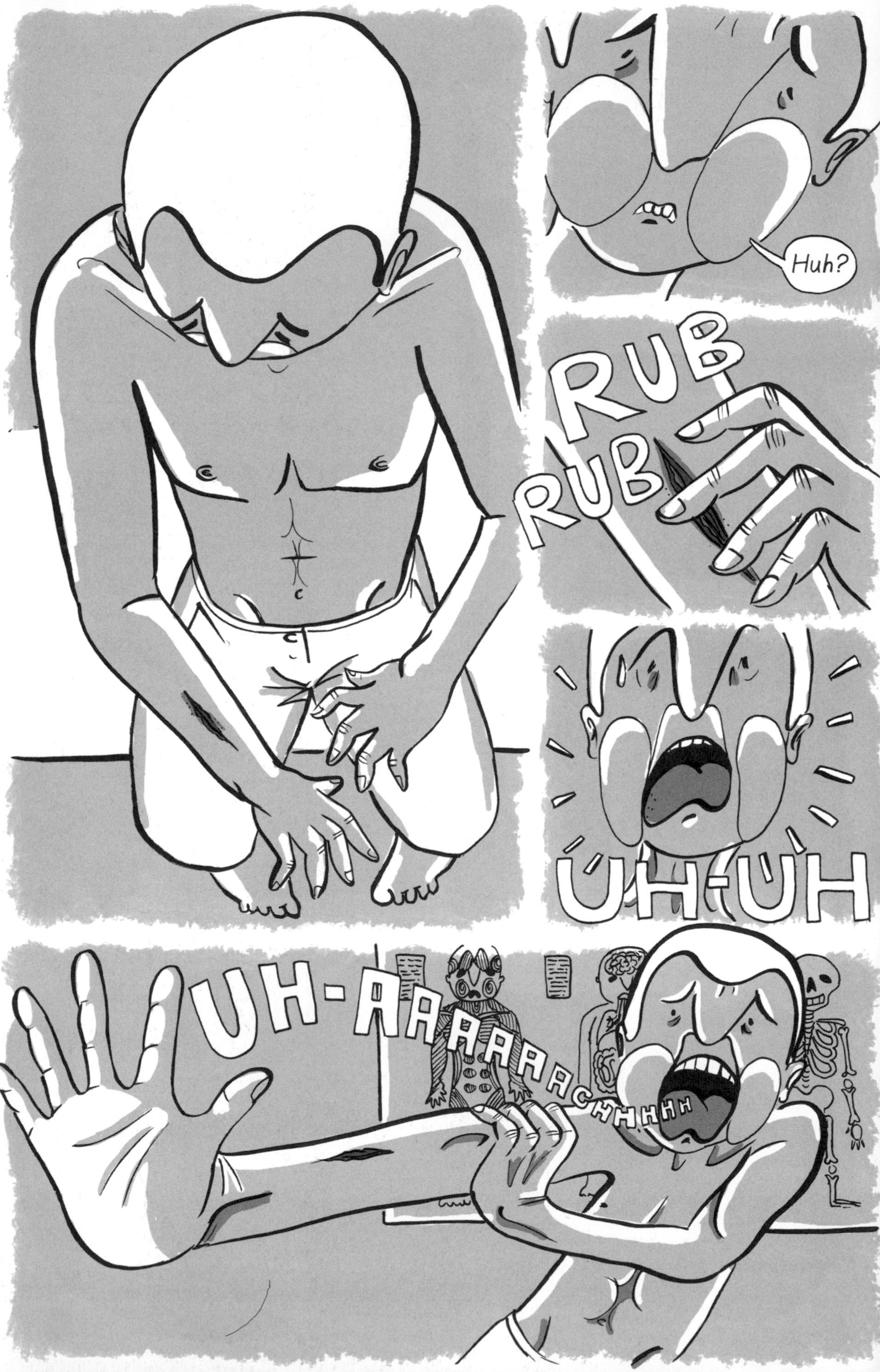
Huh?
RUB
RUB
UH-UH
UH-AAAAAAAACHHHHH

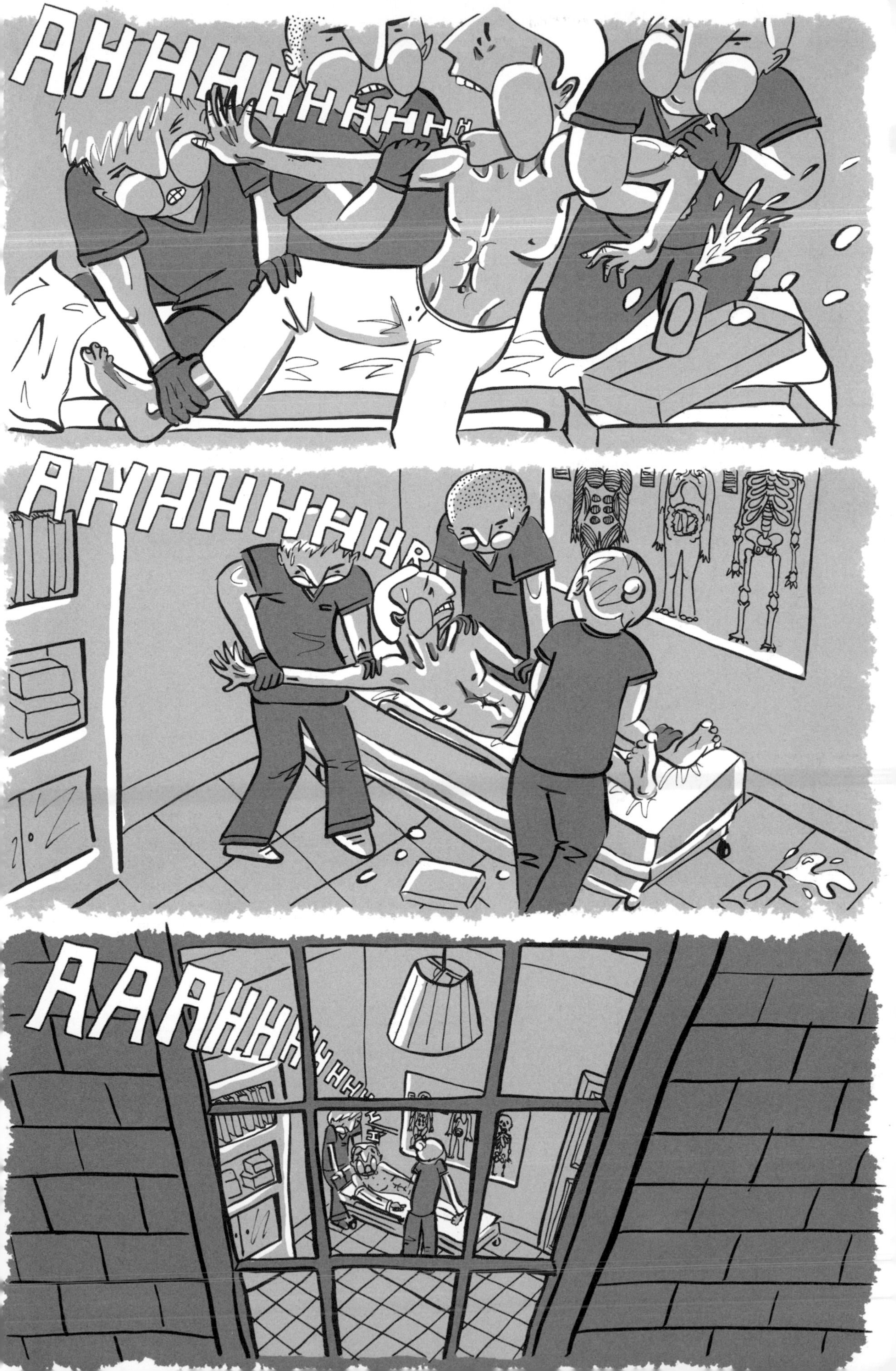
AHHHHHHHHH
AHHHHHHR
AAAHHHHHHH

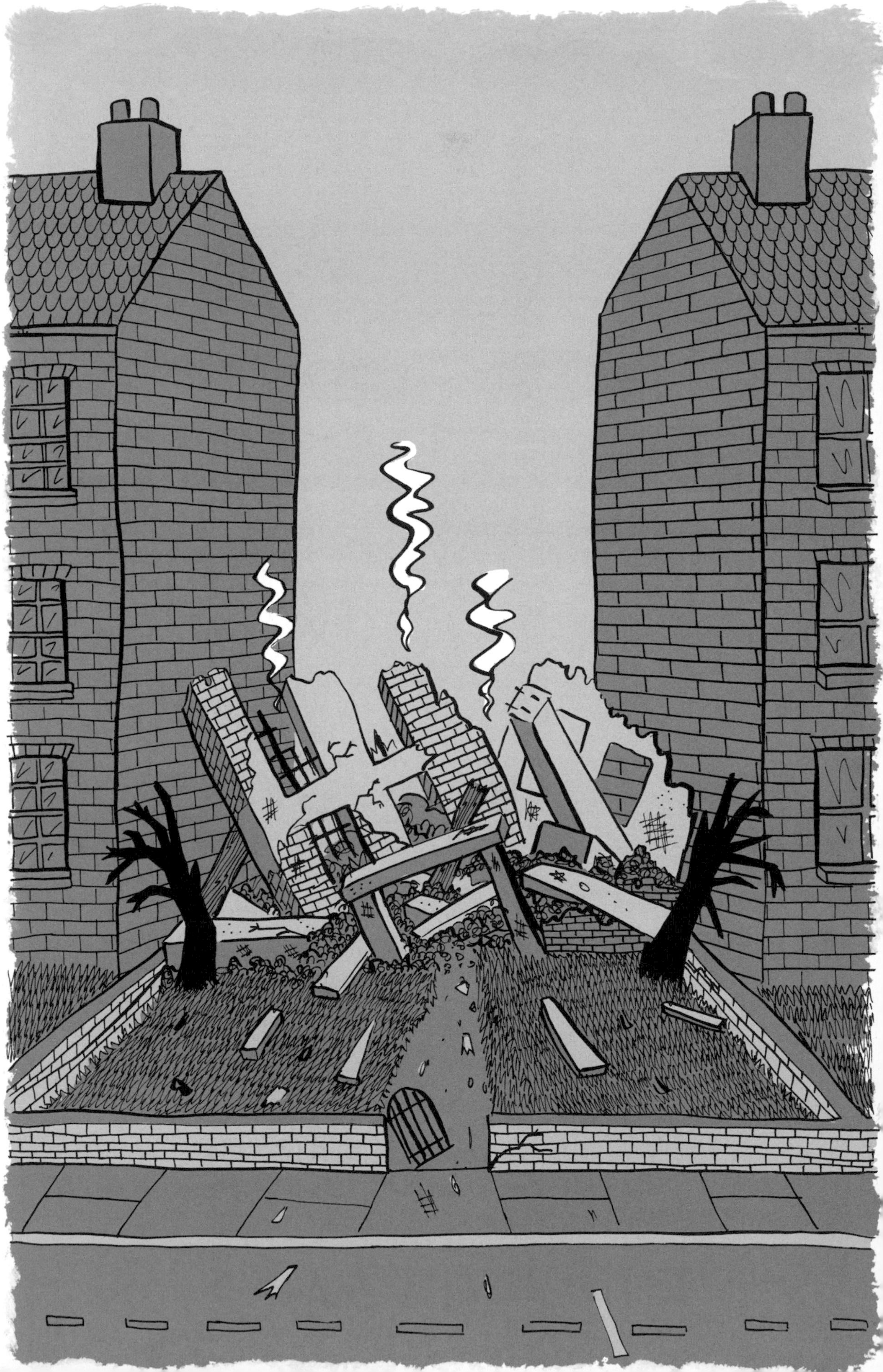

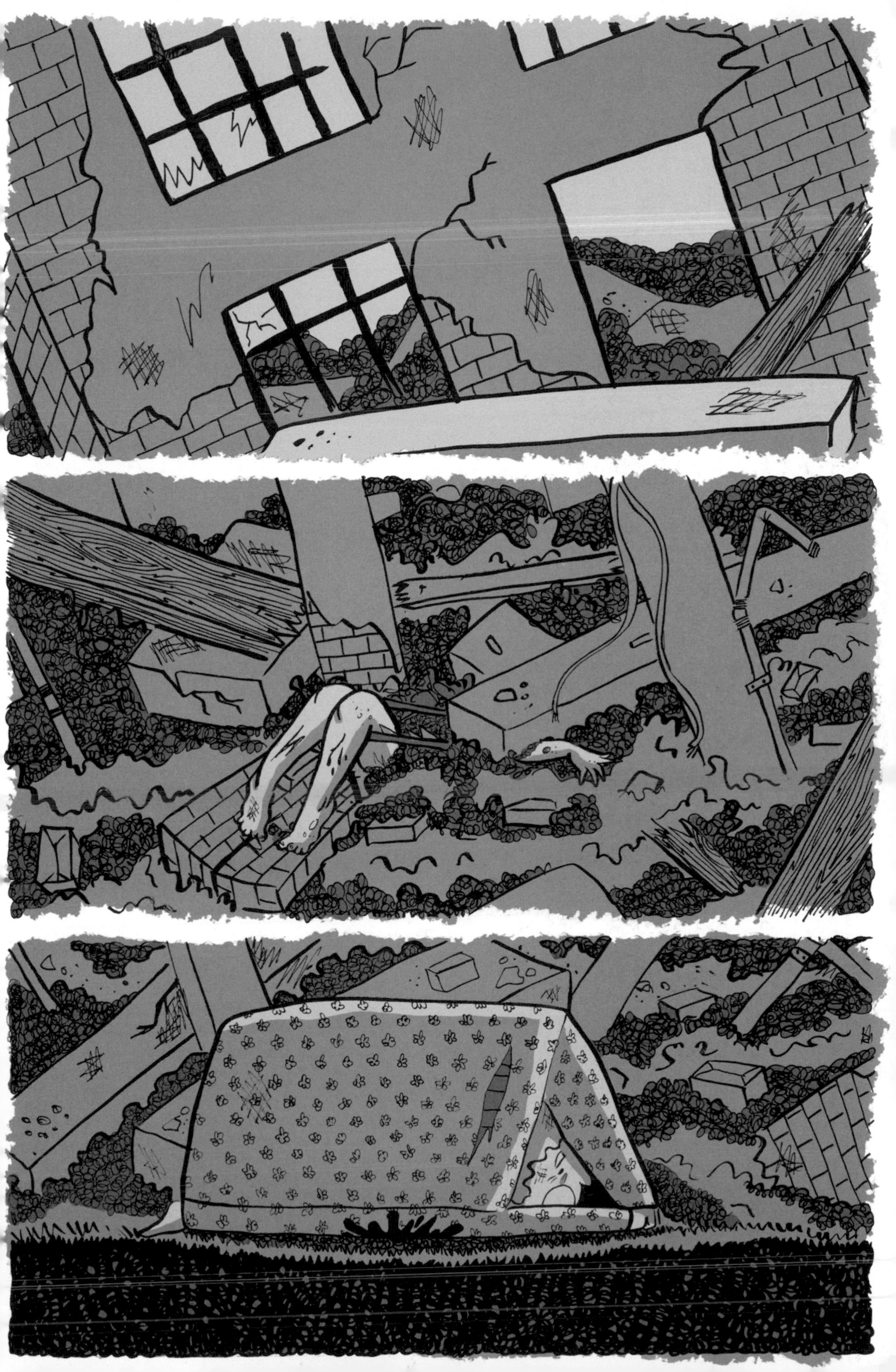

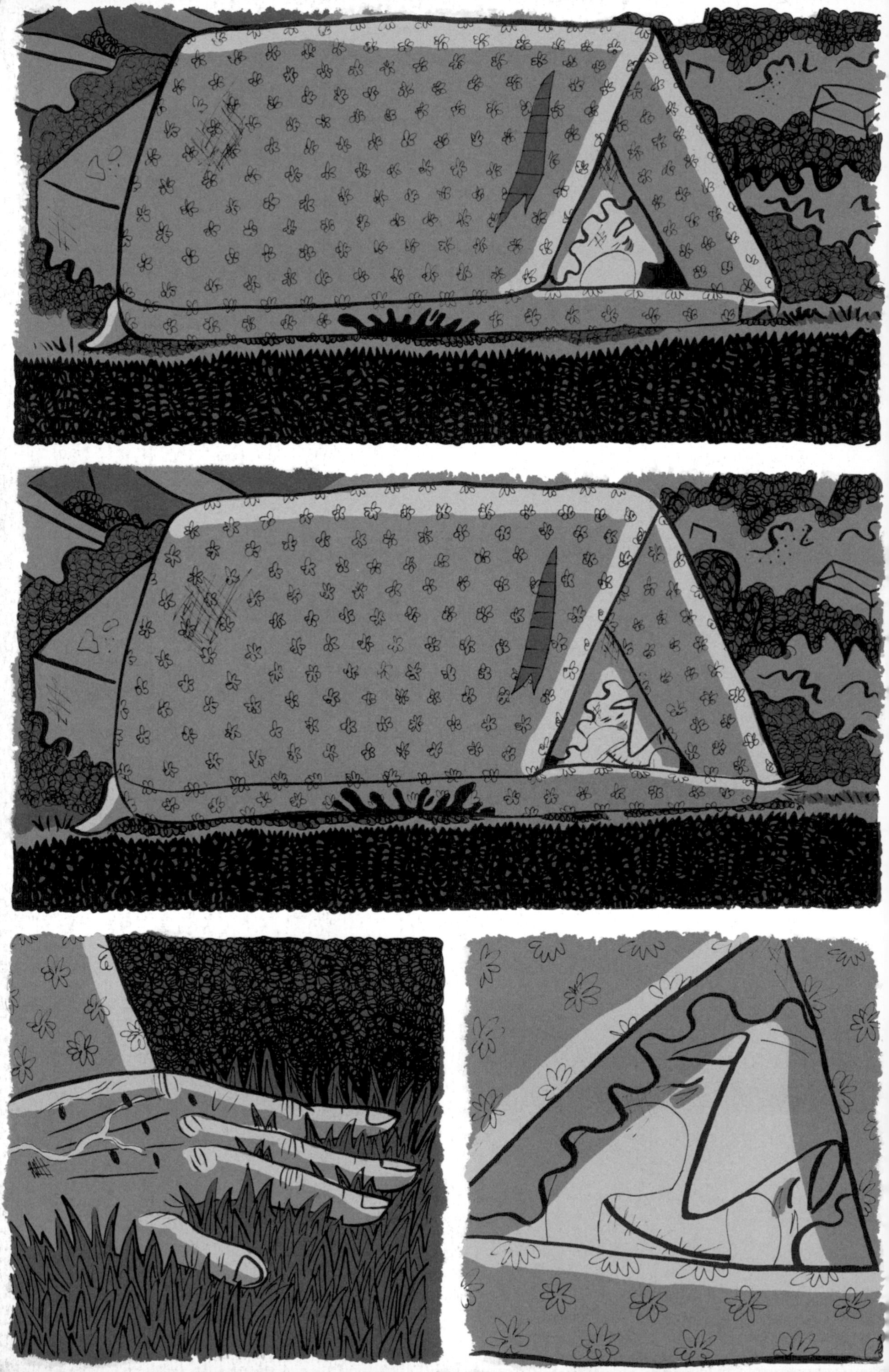

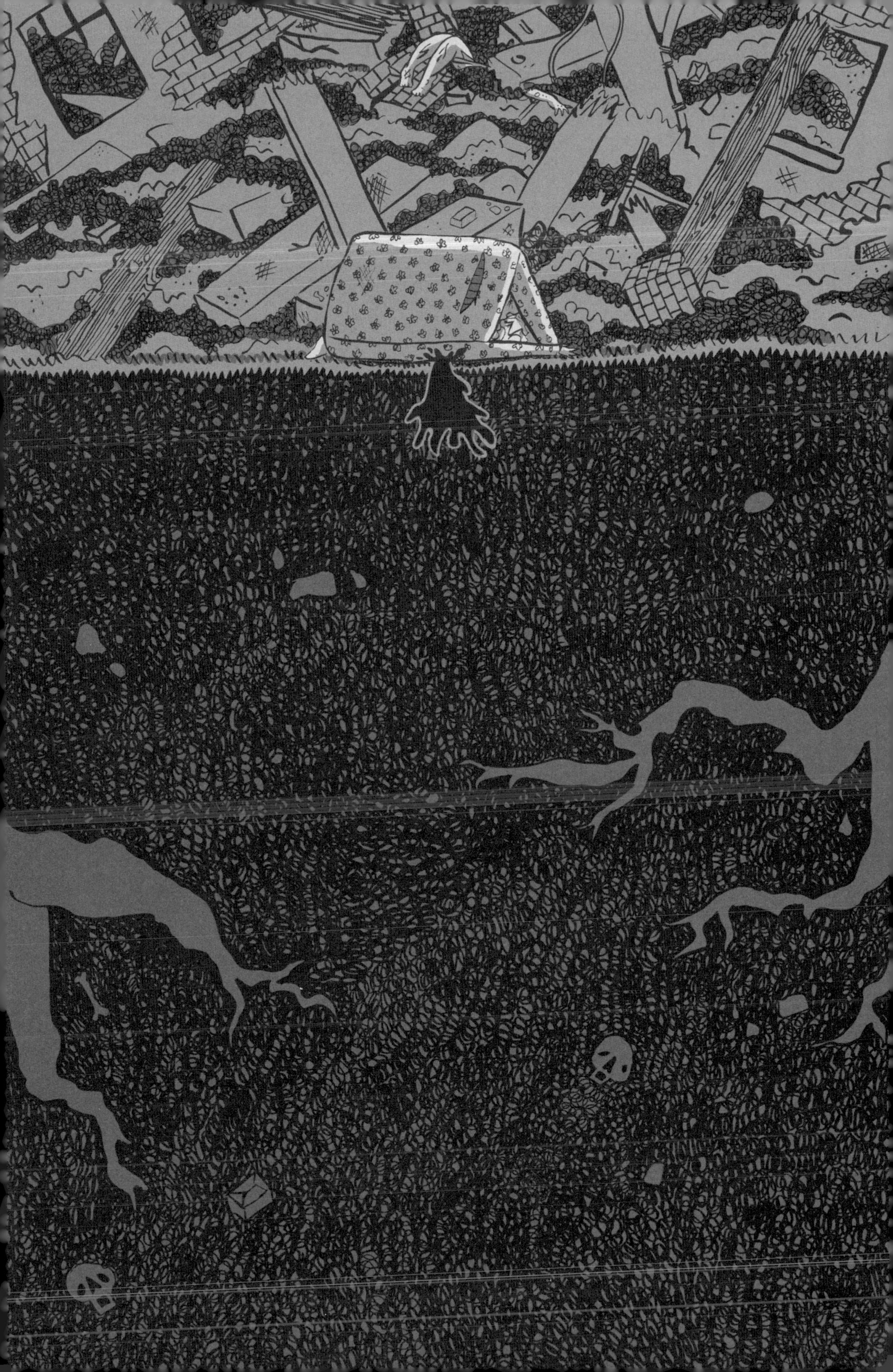

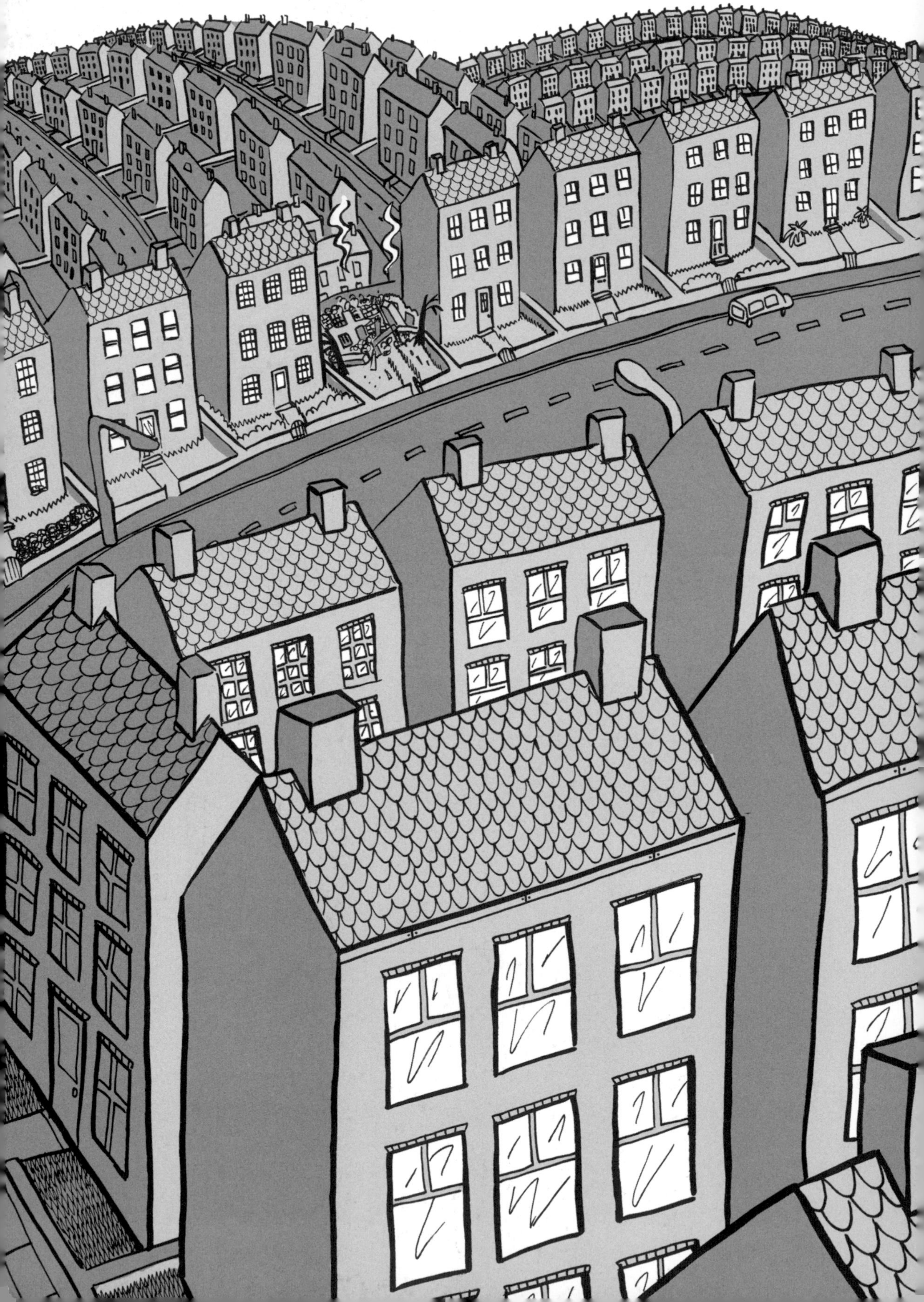

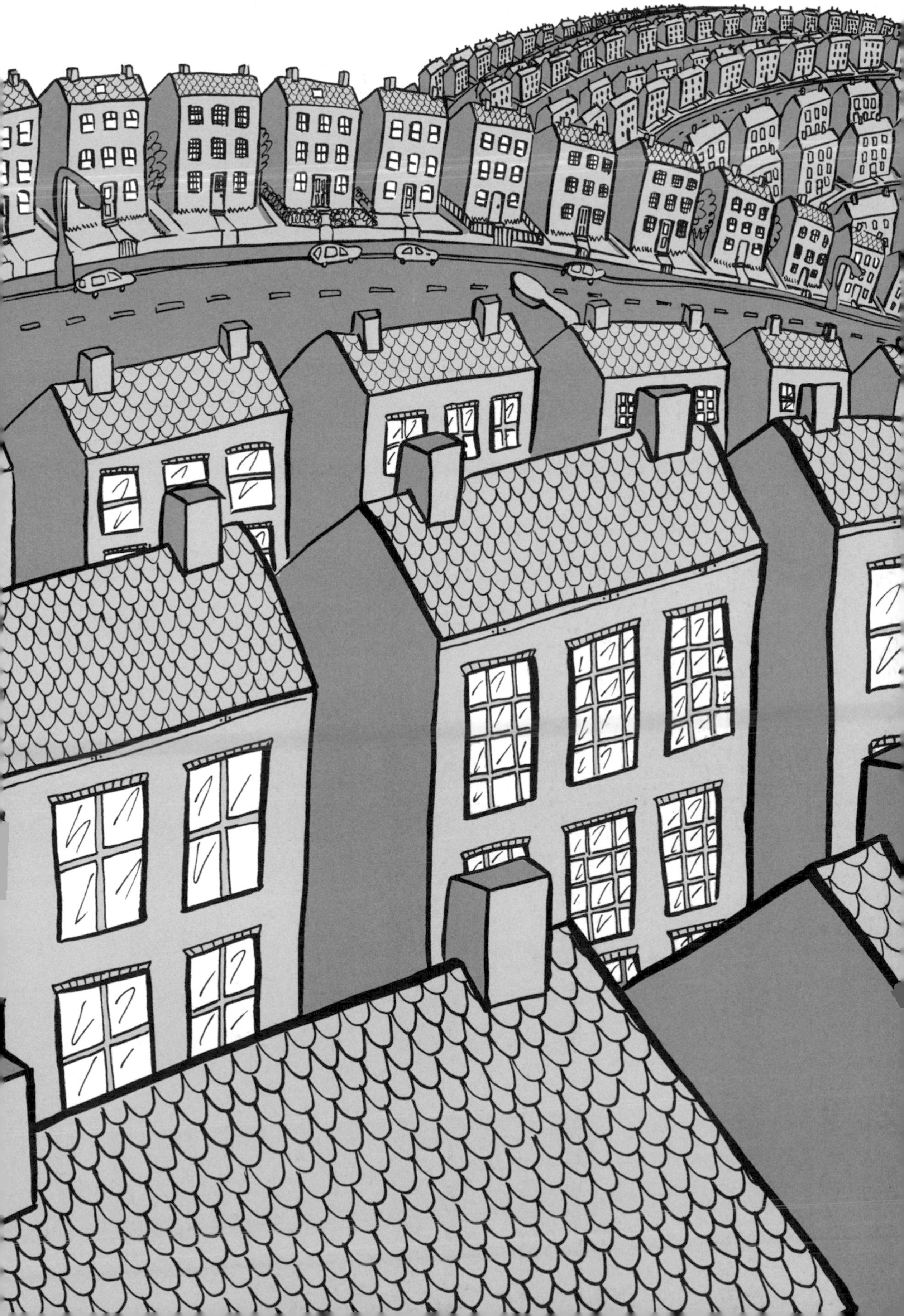

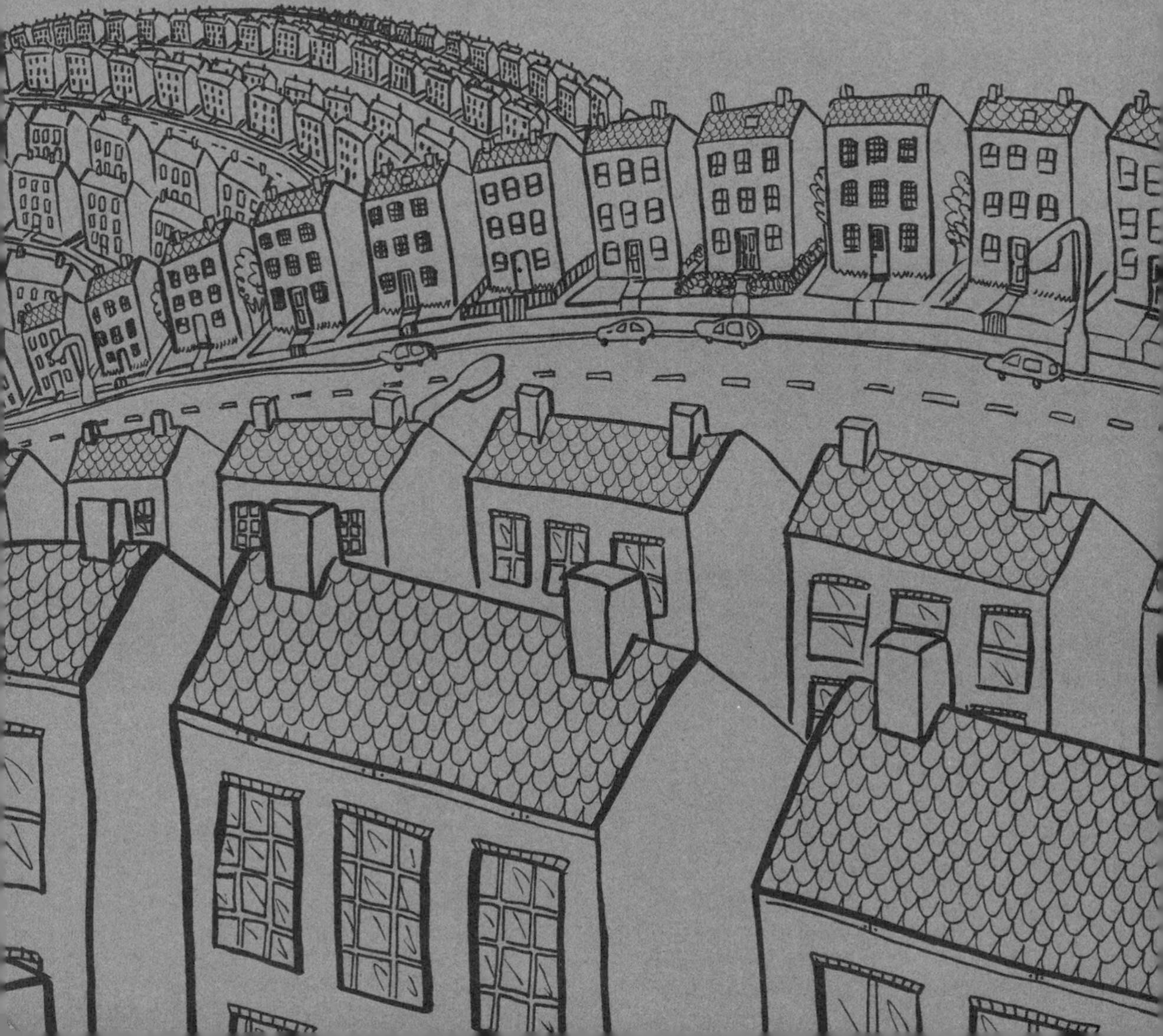

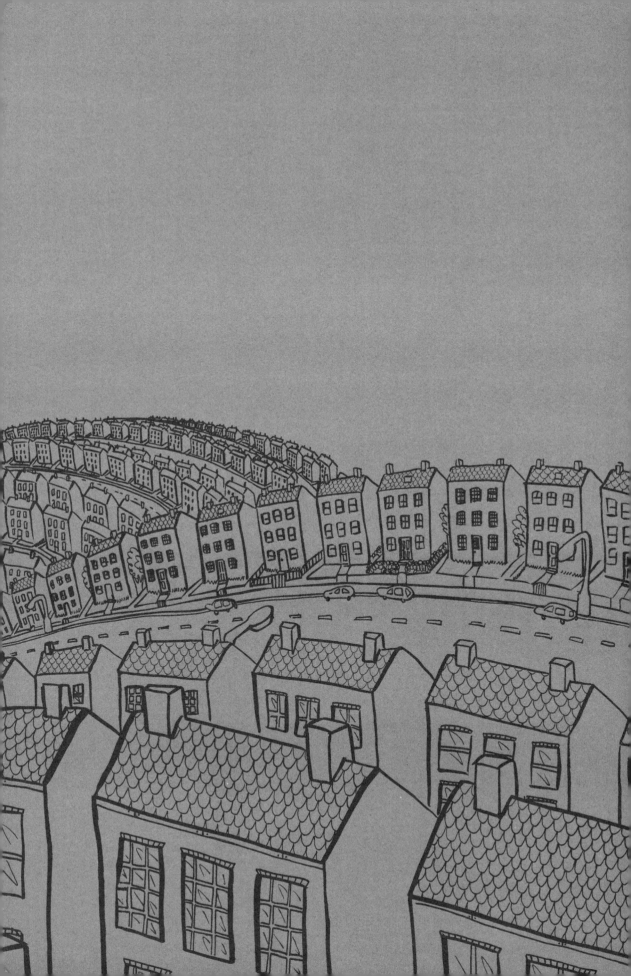

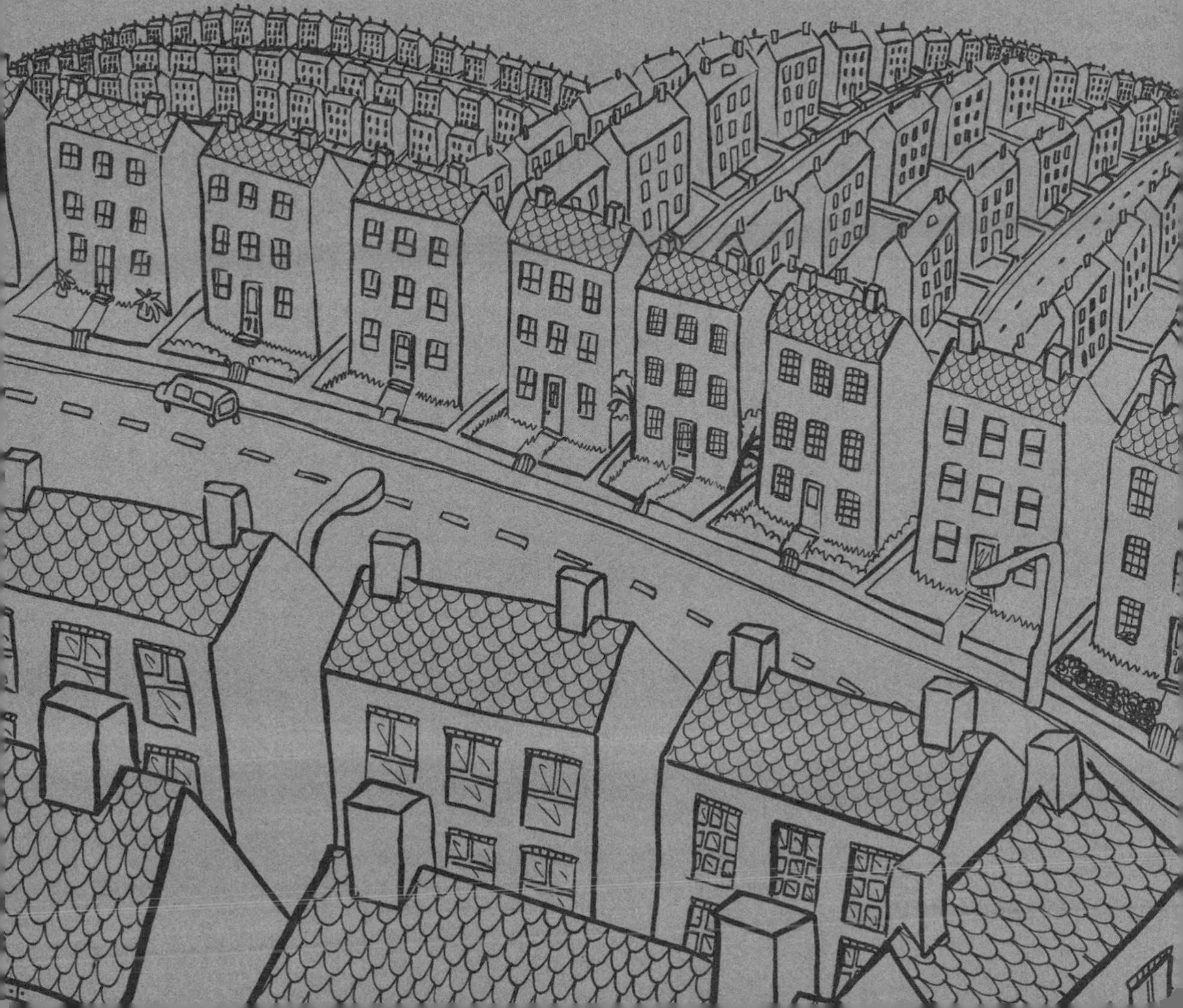

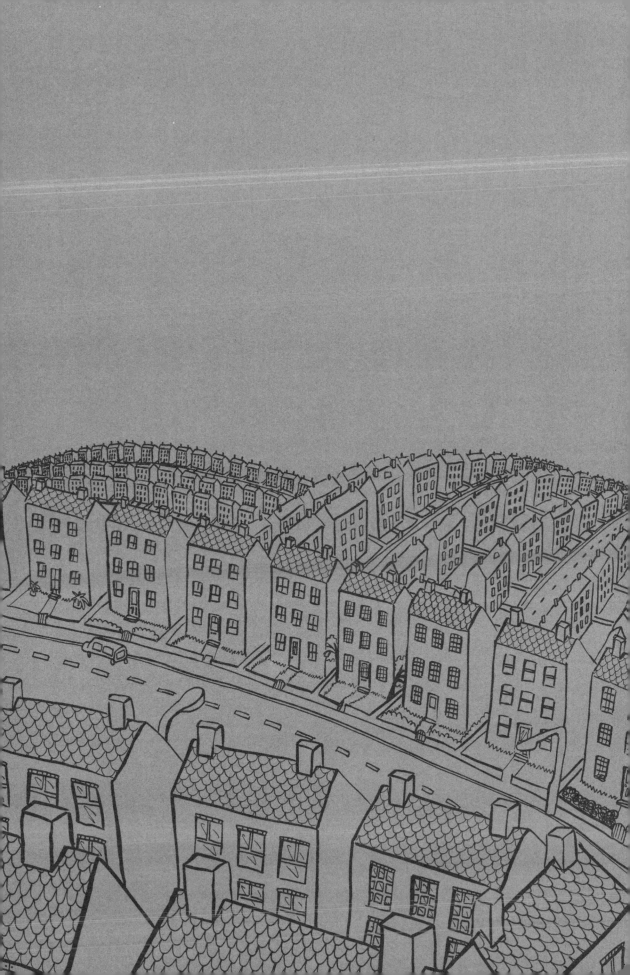

Thank You Everybody.

Many millions of thank-yous to everyone who helped get this weird little book out into the big, wide world: to Rose Davidson for supporting the darker side of my brain; to Tracy Bohan for taking a chance on a comic artist; to Nicholas Roeg for all your support and kindness; to Simon Rhodes for enduring 1001 annoying emails; to Alex Bowler and Steven Messer for proofreading and everyone at Square Peg and Random House.

First and foremost, a big puff-face of thanks to Jon for keeping me calm, sane and silly through it all. Love and thanks to my feisty family for your support; to Jude for counting all those symbolic Gladys Siegelmen; to Jonny for spilling milk on that computer; to Mum and Dad for self belief, a work ethic and that gnawing sense of guilt every time I stepped away from the drawing board; to Olly for being my best sounding board over the last six years (and hopefully many more!); to Den Pen for your belief and for being my Fairy G; to Meg and Rich for the medical suggestions and Granny Dee for helping me prepare for that zombie invasion. Thank you to the rest of the Fransmen, Ludwins and Placketts for your loveliness from near and far across the sea; to Sean Azzopardi for the rubbing out; to Jeff for keeping my support supported; to Monica for suggestions; to Suzie for the chats; to Mimi, Liz and Alexa for the advice; to Shiv's mother, dog, sister and second cousin once removed (oh OK, and Shiv!) and to Emily for fanning the flames of my early passion for comics. Thank you to all my friends for keeping me fun; to Ruth Holiday for first making me realise bodies are so much more than biology; to Ian Rakoff, Paul Gravett, Posy Simmonds and Pat Mills for helping to forge my vague ideas into a book and for your advice and support.

Published by Square Peg 2012
1 2 3 4 5 6 7 8 9

First published in Great Britain in 2012 by
Square Peg
Random House, 20 Vauxhall Bridge Road,
London SW1V 2SA
www.randomhouse.co.uk

Addresses for companies within The Random House Group Limited can be found at: www.randomhouse.co.uk/offices.htm

The Random House Group Limited Reg. No. 954009

A CIP catalogue record for this bookis available from the British Library

ISBN 9780224086813

The Random House Group Limited supports The Forest Stewardship Council® (FSC®), the leading international forest certification organisation. Our books carrying the FSC label are printed on FSC® certified paper. FSC is the only forest certification scheme endorsed by the leading environmental organisations, including Greenpeace. Our paper procurement policy can be found at www.randomhouse.co.uk/environment

FSC www.fsc.org MIX Paper from responsible sources FSC® C008047

Printed and bound in China by
C&C Offset Printing Co Ltd.

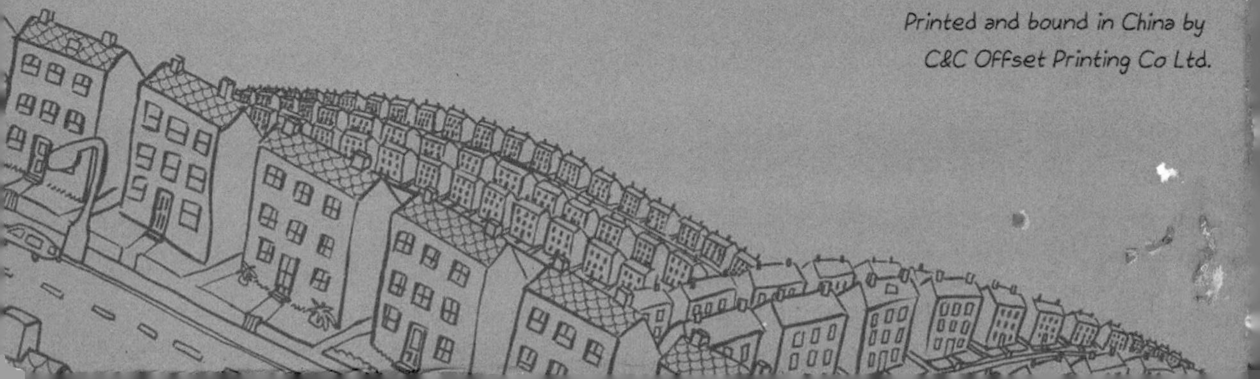